GED® TEST

Mathematical
Reasoning Prep 2015

KAPLAN)

PUBLISHING

New York

ACKNOWLEDGEMENTS

Special thanks to the team that made this book possible:
Arthur Ahn, Mikhail Alexeeff, Gina Allison, Kim Bowers, Erik Bowman, Julie Choi, Margaret Crane, Alisha Crowley, Lola Dart, Boris Dvorkin, Paula Fleming, Tom Flesher, Joanna Graham, Allison Harm, Gar Hong, Kevin Jacobson, Wyatt Kent, Jennifer Land, Heather Maigur, Terrence McGovern, Eli Meyer, Kathy Osmus, Anthony Parr, Rachel Pearsall, Neha Rao, Rachel Reina, Teresa Rupp, Scott Safir, Glen Stohr, Alexandra Strelka, Lee Weiss, and many others who have shaped this book over the years.

Published by Kaplan Publishing, a division of Kaplan, Inc.
395 Hudson Street
New York, NY 10014

Printed in the United States of America

10 9 8 7 6 5 4 3 2 1

ISBN: 978-1-62523-236-6

Kaplan Publishing books are available at special quantity discounts to use for sales promotions, employee premiums, or educational purposes. For more information or to purchase books, please call the Simon & Schuster special sales department at 866-506-1949.

CONTENTS

KAPLAN'S GED® TEST BOOK AND ONLINE CENTER

Congratulations on your decision to pursue high school equivalency, and thank you for choosing Kaplan for your GED® test preparation.

You've made the right choice in acquiring this book—you're now armed with a GED® Mathematical Reasoning test preparation program that is the result of years of researching the GED® tests and teaching thousands of students the skills they need to succeed. You have what you need to pass the GED® Mathematical Reasoning test and score higher; the next step is to make the commitment to your study plan.

The next section will tell you everything you need to know to take advantage of your book and your Online Center.

YOUR BOOK

This book contains a complete study program, including the following:

- Detailed instruction covering the essential concepts for Mathematical Reasoning
- Time-tested and effective methods and strategies for every question type
- A Pretest designed to help you diagnose your strengths and weaknesses
- Hundreds of practice questions, followed by answer explanations
- A timed, full-length Mathematical Reasoning Practice Test

YOUR ONLINE CENTER

Your Kaplan Online Center gives you access to additional instruction and practice materials to reinforce key concepts and sharpen your GED® test skills. The following list summarizes the resources available to you:

- An additional full-length Mathematical Reasoning Practice Test, so that you can practice the computer-based question formats used on the actual test
- Analysis of your performance on your Practice Test, including detailed answer explanations for the computer-based practice test
- Video lessons featuring Kaplan's top instructors

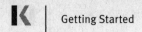

GETTING STARTED

Studying for the GED® test can be daunting, and with so many resources available to you, it may not be clear where to begin. Don't worry; we'll break it down one step at a time, just as we will with the GED® test questions that you will soon be on your way to mastering.

GETTING STARTED

1. Take the diagnostic Pretest.
2. Create a study plan.
3. Register your Online Center.
4. Learn and practice using both this book and your Online Center.
5. Work through the Practice Tests to gauge your progress.

STEP 1: TAKE THE DIAGNOSTIC PRETEST

It's essential to take the diagnostic Pretest before you begin to study. Doing so will give you the initial feedback and diagnostic information that you will need to achieve your maximum score. Place enough importance on completing the Pretest—turn off your cell phone, give the tests your full attention, and learn from your performance.

Once you have finished your Pretest, check your answers starting on page 13. Mark the questions that you got correct and **carefully read the answer explanations** of those that you got wrong.

When you have finished the Pretest, make a list of the questions that you got correct and use that list to fill out the Kaplan GED® Test Study Planner on page 16. Use the results to target your weak areas.

Another option is for you to go online and enter your answers so that the Kaplan Online Center can generate your results. Note which sections and which question types you need to target.

Review the detailed answer explanations in the book to better understand your performance. Look for patterns in the questions you answered correctly and incorrectly. Were you stronger in some areas than in others? This analysis will help you target your study time to specific concepts.

STEP 2: CREATE A STUDY PLAN

Use what you've learned from your initial Pretest to identify areas for closer study and practice. Take time to familiarize yourself with the key components of your book and Online Center. Think about how many hours you can consistently devote to GED® test study.

Schedule time for study, practice, and review. It works best for many people to block out short, frequent periods of study time throughout the week. Check in with yourself frequently to make sure you're not falling behind your plan or forgetting about any of your resources.

STEP 3: REGISTER YOUR ONLINE CENTER

Register your Online Center using these simple steps:

1. Go to **kaptest.com/booksonline**.
2. Follow the on-screen instructions for GED®. Please have your book available.

Access to the Online Center is limited to the original owner of this book and is nontransferable. Kaplan is not responsible for providing access to the Online Center to customers who purchase or borrow used copies of this book. Access to the Online Center expires one year after you register.

STEP 4: LEARN AND PRACTICE

Your book and Online Center come with many opportunities to develop and practice the skills you'll need on Test Day. Depending on how much time you have to study, you can do this work methodically, covering every lesson, or you can focus your study on those content areas that are most challenging to you. You will inevitably need more work in some areas than in others, but the more thoroughly you prepare, the better your score will be.

Initially, your practice should focus on mastering the needed skills and not on timing. Add timing to your practice as you become familiar with skills and methods.

STEP 5: WORK THROUGH THE PRACTICE TESTS

As you move through your GED® studies, take advantage of both the full-length Mathematical Reasoning Practice Test available in this book and also the one in your Online Center.

Review your Practice Test results thoroughly to make sure you are addressing the areas that are most important to your score. Allot time to review the detailed explanations so that you can learn from your mistakes and review the relevant chapters in the book for additional study.

If you find that you would like access to more of Kaplan's instructional content or practice material, look into our other subject books, our comprehensive GED® preparation books, or our On Demand course option available at **kaptest.com/GED**.

Thanks for choosing Kaplan. We wish you the best of luck on your journey to completing your high school equivalency and taking a vital step toward college and career readiness.

GED® TEST OVERVIEW

The GED® test is a widely used examination that demonstrates high school equivalency as well as college and career readiness. It includes the reading, writing, thinking, and problem-solving skills needed for postsecondary educational programs and for the world of work. This means that your high school equivalency diploma is not an end in itself—it is the springboard to more education, to better-paying jobs, and to more rewarding career paths.

TAKE FOUR SUBTESTS IN FOUR CONTENT AREAS

Reasoning through Language Arts—2.5 hours (one 10-minute break)
- Roughly 50–55 questions
- Includes 1 extended written response to reading passages—up to 45 minutes

Mathematical Reasoning—1 hour, 55 minutes
- Roughly 40–45 questions
- First section—5 questions, no calculator allowed
- Second section—calculator allowed (Texas Instruments TI-30XS MultiView™ calculator)

Social Studies—1.5 hours
- Roughly 30–35 questions
- Includes 1 extended written response to passages and/or graphics—up to 25 minutes

Science—1.5 hours
- Roughly 30–35 questions
- Includes 2 short-answer written responses to passages and/or graphics—up to 10 minutes each

You can read detailed information about the test in the *About the Test* section.

RESPOND TO SEVEN COMPUTER-BASED QUESTION FORMATS

To test a range of skills, the GED® test uses a variety of computer-based question formats. You will see examples of each type of question in *GED® Computer-Based Testing* and in the *About the Test* section. When you take the test, you will use these question formats:

- **Multiple-choice**—click to choose from four choices (A through D).
- **Fill-in-the-blank**—type a word, a phrase, or numbers in a box.
- **Drag-and-drop**—move words, numbers, or objects across the computer screen.
- **Drop-down**—select from menus embedded in text on the computer screen.
- **Hot spot**—click on graphics on the computer.
- **Short-answer**—write a paragraph or two of explanation in response to passages or graphics or a combination of the two.
- **Extended response**—compose a well-developed and supported response to passages or graphics or a combination of the two.

READ AND WRITE THROUGHOUT THE TEST

You will read and interpret passages and word problems on all four tests. In addition, three out of four subtests (*Reasoning through Language Arts, Social Studies,* and *Science*) require that you read a passage or two and compose a response about what you have read.

The type of writing that you will use is called *evidence-based writing*, which means that you need to cite specific evidence from the readings in your response. This is a key characteristic of the type of writing that is required in workplaces and in educational programs. This book contains special lessons and practice activities to help you write effectively on all three of the subtests.

PERFORM MATH SKILLS THROUGHOUT THE TEST

In addition to the questions on the *Mathematical Reasoning Test*, math items also appear on the *Science Test* and the *Social Studies Test*.

On all three of these tests, you may use either a hand-held or an on-screen version of the Texas Instruments TI-30XS MultiView™ calculator to use with math items. If you wish to use a hand-held version of the calculator, you may need to take one with you on test day. **You are strongly encouraged to purchase a hand-held version of this calculator to use with this study guide.** You can buy this calculator at stores that carry office and school supplies and through online vendors.

USE THE GED TESTING SERVICE® MYGED™ INTERNET PORTAL

MyGED™ is a personalized online program that will be your entry point to all test activities, including scheduling testing and retesting (if necessary), viewing score reports, ordering transcripts and your diploma, and investigating your next steps in making the transition to college or to a career.

TAKE THE TEST: UNDERSTAND YOUR SCORE

Each GED® Test is scored on a scale from 100 to 200. There are three possible scores that you can receive on the GED® Test:

- **Not Passing**—lower than 150 on any of the four tests. You can reschedule up to two times a year to retake any or all of the tests.
- **GED® Passing Score**—at or higher than the minimum score (150 per test) needed to demonstrate high school equivalency–level skills and knowledge. Points on one test do not carry over to the others; that is, if you score 200 on one and 100 on another, that is not equivalent to scoring 150 on both. You need to score 150 on each of the four tests.
- **GED® Score with Honors**—at or higher than the minimum needed (170 per test) to demonstrate career and college readiness

Your score is determined by the number of points you earn on each test, but questions vary in point value. Therefore, there is no fixed number of questions you need to get correct on each test in order to pass or pass with honors.

GED® COMPUTER-BASED TESTING

The GED® Test is delivered on a computer. That means that you will need to familiarize yourself with basic computer skills and computer-based question formats in order to succeed on the test.

NOTE: *The GED® Test on computer is only offered at official Pearson Vue Testing Centers. Any Internet-based test that claims to be the GED® Test is* not *the actual test. At the MyGED™ portal, you can access study resources, take a practice test, or schedule your test. You cannot take the real GED® test online.*

To become familiar with the computer-based functions, you should review the GED® Test Tutorial available through the GED® Testing Services website. Before you take the actual test, you can practice computer-based testing functions with the Practice Test available in Kaplan's Online Center and with the GED® Testing Service's GED Ready™ Test.

COMPUTER-BASED TESTING FUNCTIONS AND TOOLS

The GED® Test uses many computer **functions**, some of which you may already know. It also offers specific **tools** that you will utilize in different test areas.

 Use the **mouse** to

Tab through the pages of a reading passage

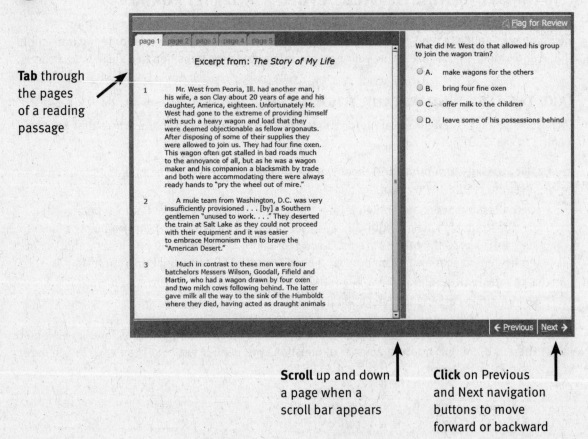

Scroll up and down a page when a scroll bar appears

Click on Previous and Next navigation buttons to move forward or backward

Use the **mouse** to (continued)

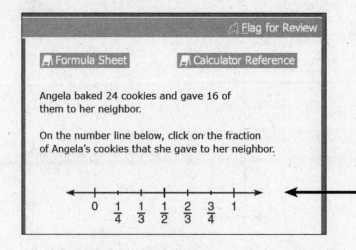

Click on an answer choice, a "Select" menu, or a point on a graphic

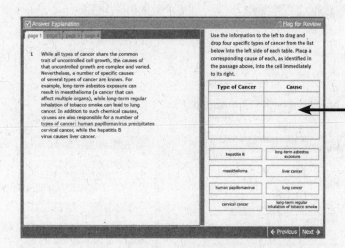

Drag and drop text, numbers, or images into a shape on the computer screen

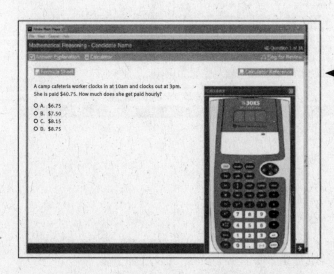

Click to open, move, and close information windows and math resources—such as the calculator, formula sheet, or symbol toolbar

Use **word processing skills** to

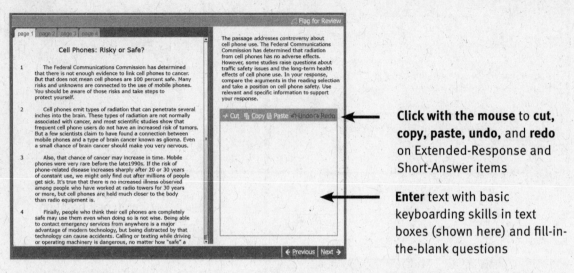

Click with the mouse to **cut, copy, paste, undo,** and **redo** on Extended-Response and Short-Answer items

Enter text with basic keyboarding skills in text boxes (shown here) and fill-in-the-blank questions

Use **the online highlighter,** operated with your mouse, to

Highlight specific information that you will use as evidence in writing your Extended Responses and Short Answers.

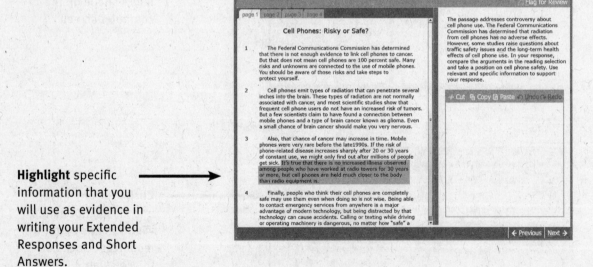

Use the offline, **erasable wipe-off board,** which will be provided at the testing center, to

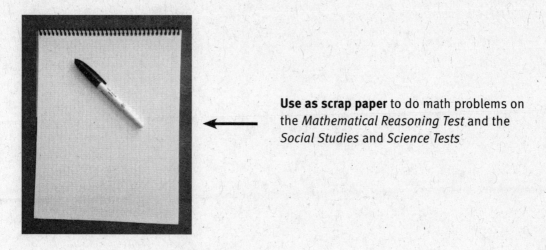

Use as scrap paper to do math problems on the *Mathematical Reasoning Test* and the *Social Studies* and *Science Tests*

Use three **onscreen test-tracking tools** at the top of the computer screen to

Test - Your Name

🕐 Time Remaining 01:04:32
⎚ Question 32 of 50

◁ Flag for Review

- **See how much time you have left**: *Time Remaining* shows how much time is left to complete each test.
- **Monitor your progress** through each test by viewing the *Question Line*. You can check how far you have progressed and how many more questions you need to answer. Budget your time carefully to allow for these writing tasks:
  - ◦ 45 minutes for the Extended Response at the end of the first section of the *Reasoning through Language Arts Test*
  - ◦ 25 minutes for the Extended Response at the end of the *Social Studies Test*
  - ◦ 10 minutes for <u>each</u> of the Short Answer questions that are interspersed with other questions in the *Science Test*
- **Click** on the *Flag for Review* if you are unsure of an answer. (You should never skip a question.) If you click on it, the flag will display in yellow and will be marked on the Review Screen.

At the end of each test, if you have time left, you can use the **Review Screen** to go back and review questions that you marked.

Pretest

The purpose of this pretest is to help you decide what you need to study to pass the actual GED® *Mathematical Reasoning Test*. You will use the pretest along with the explanations and the study planner that follows to determine what course of study works best for you.

This pretest is specially designed to make your study as efficient as possible. If you want to see what the actual GED® *Mathematical Reasoning Test* looks like, look at the *Practice Test* beginning on page 231.

1. **Take** the pretest:

    • **Mathematical Reasoning, pages 2–11**
      ○ Part I: Quantitative Reasoning—18 Questions
      ○ Part II: Algebraic Reasoning and Geometry—22 Questions

    You may fill in the circles next to the correct answers in this book, or you can write your answers on a separate piece of paper.

2. **Check** your answers with the *Pretest Answers and Explanations* that begin on page 13.

3. **Fill in** the *Pretest Study Planner* on page 16. These charts will allow you to target your problem areas so that you can study in the most efficient manner.

4. **Use the study planner** on page 16 to map out your work. Once you have completed your study, take the *Practice Test* on pages 231-244.

PART I: QUANTITATIVE REASONING—18 QUESTIONS

Directions: You may fill in the circles next to the correct answers or write your answers on a separate piece of paper. You MAY use a calculator.

<u>Questions 1 and 2</u> refer to the following information and graph.

Video Warehouse has divided the surrounding community into four advertising zones. The graph shows the total number of customers from each zone for a three-week period.

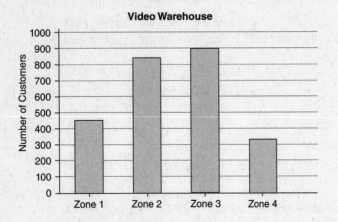

1. During the three weeks, how many customers came from Zones 3 and 4?

    ○ A. between 900 and 1,000
    ○ B. between 1,000 and 1,100
    ○ C. between 1,100 and 1,200
    ○ D. between 1,200 and 1,300

2. Approximately what is the ratio of customers from Zone 1 to customers from Zone 3?

    ○ A. 3:5
    ○ B. 3:2
    ○ C. 2:1
    ○ D. 1:2

3. A potter uses $\frac{3}{5}$ of a pound of clay to make a bowl. How many bowls could the potter make from 10 pounds of clay?

    ○ A. 6
    ○ B. 8
    ○ C. 16
    ○ D. 17

4. Janelle has recently been hired for the job of library assistant. The following graph shows what percent of her time will be spent on each of five tasks each day.

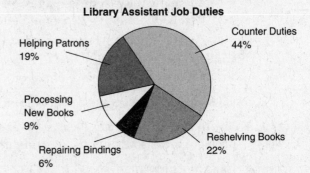

The number of hours that Janelle will spend working at the counter is about how many times the number of hours that she will spend processing new books and repairing bindings?

    ○ A. 2
    ○ B. 3
    ○ C. 4
    ○ D. 6

5. Fifteen percent of the workers at Nationwide Industries earn minimum wage. If 24 workers earn minimum wage, how many total workers are there at Nationwide Industries?

   ○ A. 4
   ○ B. 36
   ○ C. 160
   ○ D. 360

6. An accountant is going to pay the following four bills:

Bill	Amount
W	$27.10
X	$261.00
Y	$2.80
Z	$27.20

   The accountant will pay the bills in order from smallest to largest. In what order will he pay them?

   ○ A. W, X, Z, Y
   ○ B. X, W, Z, Y
   ○ C. Y, X, W, Z
   ○ D. Y, W, Z, X

7. A jar holds 16 ounces of honey. A cook is going to make two recipes. One of the recipes calls for 2.5 ounces of honey, and the other calls for 4.25 ounces of honey. After the cook has made those two recipes, how many ounces of honey will be left in the jar?

   ○ A. 6.75
   ○ B. 9.25
   ○ C. 10.00
   ○ D. 11.75

8. All numbers that are evenly divisible by both 6 and 14 are also divisible by which of the following numbers?

   ○ A. 8
   ○ B. 12
   ○ C. 21
   ○ D. 28

9. Alice, Kathy, and Sheila work as medical assistants at Valley Clinic. Alice has worked 8 years longer than Kathy. Kathy has worked half as long as Sheila. If Sheila has worked at the company for 10 years, how many years has Alice worked there?

   ○ A. 5
   ○ B. 8
   ○ C. 10
   ○ D. 13

Question 10 is based on the spinner below.

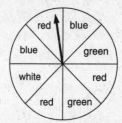

10. The spinner shown in the drawing is divided into eight equal sections. If you spin the spinner one time, what is the probability of NOT getting blue?

   ○ A. $\frac{1}{8}$
   ○ B. $\frac{1}{4}$
   ○ C. $\frac{3}{4}$
   ○ D. $\frac{7}{8}$

11. A computer monitor is regularly priced at $320. During a two-day sale, the price was decreased to $240. Which of the following is the percentage decrease of the monitor's price during the sale?

○ A. 25%
○ B. 33%
○ C. 75%
○ D. 80%

12. For a 10-day period, a bank kept track of the number of new accounts opened each day. The results are shown in the table below. What is the median number of accounts opened per day during this 10-day period?

Day	Accounts	Day	Accounts
May 7	6	May 14	4
May 8	2	May 15	8
May 9	7	May 16	6
May 10	5	May 17	4
May 11	4	May 18	7

○ A. 5
○ B. 5.3
○ C. 5.5
○ D. 6

13. Jim is a salesperson, and his employers expect him to sell at least $12,000 in merchandise per month. In April, Jim sold $2,500 in the first week of the month and twice that much in the second week. How much must he sell in the rest of April combined in order to sell the minimum expected of him?

○ A. $4,500
○ B. $5,500
○ C. $9,500
○ D. $12,000

14. Angela likes to use two walking sticks when she goes hiking, but the two walking sticks she has been given recently are different lengths. One is $3\frac{4}{5}$ feet long, and the other is $3\frac{1}{2}$ feet long.

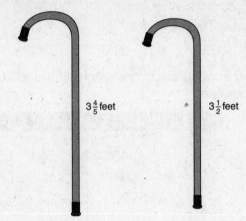

$3\frac{4}{5}$ feet $3\frac{1}{2}$ feet

Angela wants to cut the longer stick to match the shorter one. How much should she cut from the longer stick so that the two walking sticks will be the same length?

○ A. $\frac{3}{4}$ feet
○ B. $\frac{3}{5}$ feet
○ C. $\frac{3}{10}$ feet
○ D. $\frac{1}{4}$ feet

Question 15 is based on the following number line.

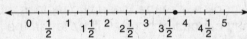

15. Which of the following is the decimal point value of the dot on the line above?

○ A. 3.25
○ B. 3.50
○ C. 3.75
○ D. 4.00

Question 16 is based on the following information and graph.

Marjorie has a class of 35 students, and she tracked their performance on a recent math exam. The graph below represents how their scores were distributed along the range of possible scores, from F to A.

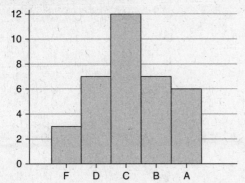

Based on the graph, which of the following is a true statement?

    A. None of Marjorie's students received an F on the exam.

    B. Most of Marjorie's students received either an A or a B on the exam.

    C. If Marjorie gave the same exam again to another group of students, most of those students would receive a C.

    D. More students received either an A or a B than received either a D or an F.

17. Jason deposits $5,000 in a bank account that will pay him 4% simple interest annually. If Jason deposits no more than the initial $5,000, how much money will be in the account at the end of five years? (The formula for simple interest is $I = prt$ or $interest = principal \times rate \times time$. Use a decimal to express the interest when using that formula.)

    A. $200
    B. $1,000
    C. $5,000
    D. $6,000

18. A local library shows movies on Thursday evenings. The library administrator has chosen the next six movies he will show, but he has not decided in which order to show them. How many possible orderings of the six movies are there?

    A.   21
    B.   36
    C.   720
    D. 1,012

Answers and explanations start on page 13.

MATHEMATICAL REASONING FORMULA SHEET

Below is a formula sheet that appears on the actual GED® test. You can refer to this page on Part II of this Pretest.

Area of a:

square	$A = s^2$
rectangle	$A = lw$
parallelogram	$A = bh$
triangle	$A = \frac{1}{2}bh$
trapezoid	$A = \frac{1}{2}h(b_1 + b_2)$
circle	$A = \pi r^2$

Perimeter of a:

square	$P = 4s$
rectangle	$P = 2l + 2w$
triangle	$P = s_1 + s_2 + s_3$
Circumference of a circle	$C = 2\pi r$ OR $C = \pi d$; $\pi \approx 3.14$

Surface area and volume of a:

rectangular/right prism	$SA = ph + 2B$	$V = Bh$
cylinder	$SA = 2\pi rh + 2\pi r^2$	$V = \pi r^2 h$
pyramid	$SA = \frac{1}{2}ps + B$	$V = \frac{1}{3}Bh$
cone	$SA = \pi rs + \pi r^2$	$V = \frac{1}{3}\pi r^2 h$
sphere	$SA = 4\pi r^2$	$V = \frac{4}{3}\pi r^3$

(p = perimeter of base with area B; $\pi \approx 3.14$)

Data

mean	mean is equal to the total of the values of a data set, divided by the number of elements in the data set
median	median is the middle value in an odd number of ordered values of a data set, or the mean of the two middle values in an even number of ordered values in a data set

Algebra

slope of a line	$m = \dfrac{y_2 - y_1}{x_2 - x_1}$
slope-intercept form of the equation of a line	$y = mx + b$
point-slope form of the equation of a line	$y - y_1 = m(x - x_1)$
standard form of a quadratic equation	$y = ax^2 + bx + c$
quadratic formula	$x = \dfrac{-b \pm \sqrt{b^2 - 4ac}}{2a}$
Pythagorean theorem	$a^2 + b^2 = c^2$
simple interest	$I = Prt$ (I = interest, P = principal, r = rate, t = time)
distance formula	$d = rt$
total cost	total cost = (number of units) × (price per unit)

Provided by GED® Testing Service.

Directions: You may fill in the circles next to the correct answers or write your answers on a separate piece of paper. Refer to the formula sheet on page 6 as needed. You MAY use your calculator.

1. Which point on the number line below represents the value $-\frac{16}{6}$?

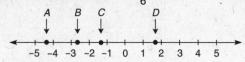

   ○ A. Point A
   ○ B. Point B
   ○ C. Point C
   ○ D. Point D

2. Evaluate the expression $2x - (4y - 3) + 5xz$, when $x = -3$, $y = 2$, and $z = -1$.

   ○ A.   45
   ○ B.   16
   ○ C.   4
   ○ D. −10

3. On April 1 of this year, the high temperature in Northville was 46 degrees Fahrenheit. Then a sudden snowstorm arose, and the temperature dropped sharply to a low of −8 degrees Fahrenheit. What was the magnitude of the change in temperature on that day?

   ○ A.   54
   ○ B.   46
   ○ C.   36
   ○ D. −36

Question 4 refers to the following drawing.

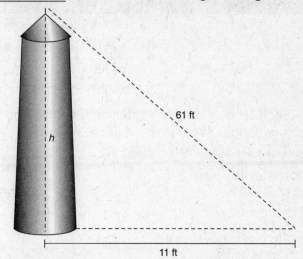

4. A tower casts a shadow 11 feet long. The distance from the top of the tower to the end of the shadow is 61 feet. How many feet tall is the tower?

   ○ A. 50
   ○ B. 60
   ○ C. 61
   ○ D. 72

Question 5 is based on the following information.

Designer Furnishings sells premade cabinets and cupboards, as shown below.

Model	Dimensions (in inches)
411R	32 by 22 by 10
412R	28 by 36 by 15
413S	24 by 72 by 18
414S	25 by 24 by 6

5. Each face of cabinet 413S is in the shape of a rectangle. What is the volume of Model 413S in cubic feet?

  A. 18
  B. 31
  C. 36
  D. 108

6. Together, Levy and Matthew earn $4,680 per month. Levy earns $520 more per month than Matthew earns. How much does Levy earn per month?

  A. $2,080
  B. $2,340
  C. $2,600
  D. $4,160

7. The design for a new cone-shaped closed container is shown below. What is the surface area of this container, in square inches? You can select the correct formula from the formula sheet on page 6.

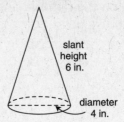

slant height 6 in.

diameter 4 in.

  A. 4π
  B. 12π
  C. 16π
  D. 28π

8. Simplify this polynomial:
$3x^3 + x + 2x^3 - 4x^2 + 14y - 2(y + x)$.

  A. $3x^3 - 3x^2 + 14(-2y + 2x)$
  B. $5x^3 - 3x^2 + 14y - 2y - 2x$
  C. $3x^3 - x + 4x^2 + 12y$
  D. $5x^3 - 4x^2 - x + 12y$

9. A rectangle is drawn on a coordinate grid. Three of its four vertices are located at points $(-1, -2)$, $(-1, 4)$ and $(2, -2)$ What is the location of the fourth vertex? Mark your answer on the coordinate grid below.

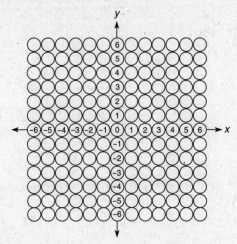

10. Which of the following expressions is equal to the expression $4x - 2(3x - 9)$?

   ○ A. $18 - 2x$
   ○ B. $-10x - 18$
   ○ C. $-2x - 18$
   ○ D. $10x - 18$

11. In the equation $3x^2 - 10x = 8$, which of the following values for x will make the equation true?

   ○ A. -4
   ○ B. -3
   ○ C. 3
   ○ D. 4

12. Solve for x: $12(x - 2) < 24$

   ○ A. $x < 0$
   ○ B. $x > 0$
   ○ C. $x < 12$
   ○ D. $x < 4$

13. Scientists estimate that Earth is 4,540,000,000 years old. What is that number expressed in scientific notation?

   ○ A. 4.54×10^7
   ○ B. 4.54×10^9
   ○ C. 454×10^{10}
   ○ D. $2(127 \times 10^7)$

14. Joe just purchased an oddly shaped piece of property, depicted in the figure below.

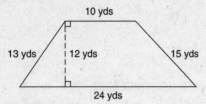

What is the area, in square yards, of Joe's new property?

○ A. 120
○ B. 134
○ C. 140
○ D. 204

15. The XYZ Company sells hats and will monogram them if customers choose. The price for each monogram varies depending on how many hats a customer would like to have monogrammed. The monogram prices for several order sizes are shown below:

Number of hats to be monogrammed (n)	Price per monogram (p)
1	$5
2	$4.50
3	$4.00
4	$3.50
5	$3.00
6	$2.50

Which of the following best expresses the relationship of price per monogram (for all nonnegative values of p) to number of hats monogrammed shown in the table above?

○ A. $p = \$5.00 - (n - 1)\$0.50$
○ B. $p = \$5.00 - n(\$0.50)$
○ C. $p = (n - 1)\$5.00$
○ D. $p = \$0.50(10n)$

16. A parallelogram has two obtuse angles and two acute angles. If the measure of one of the obtuse angles is 110°, what is the measure, in degrees, of one of the acute angles?

○ A. 10°
○ B. 70°
○ C. 110°
○ D. 240°

Question 17 refers to the following graph.

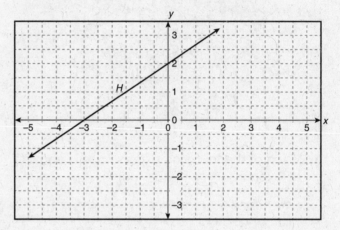

17. Line H is the graph of which of the following equations?

○ A. $y = \frac{1}{3}x + 2$
○ B. $y + 2 = \frac{2}{3}x$
○ C. $y = \frac{2}{3}x + 2$
○ D. $y = 3(x - 2) + 2$

18. A fountain's pool is enclosed by a circular plastic tank. The distance from the center of the pool to the wall of the tank is 10 feet. How long is the wall of the tank in feet?

○ A. 20π
○ B. $\frac{20}{\pi}$
○ C. 25π
○ D. 100π

19. Line *W* passes through the following points on the coordinate grid: (0, – 9) and (4, –1). What is the slope of line *W*?

- A. −2
- B. −$\frac{1}{2}$
- C. $\frac{1}{2}$
- D. 2

20. Beansey's Baked Beans, Inc., has developed a new can for its baked beans, shown below:

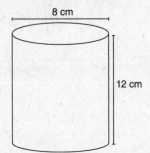

What is the volume of the new can, in cubic centimeters?

- A. 48π
- B. 96π
- C. 192π
- D. 768π

21. Tina is considering renting a commercial space for her business. The space is shown below.

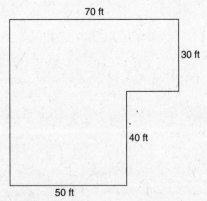

What is the area of the commercial space, in square feet?

- A. 290
- B. 2,100
- C. 2,800
- D. 4,100

22. In the system of equations $3x - 3y = -9$ and $2x + y = 9$, solve for both *x* and *y*. You may use the coordinate grid below to help your work.

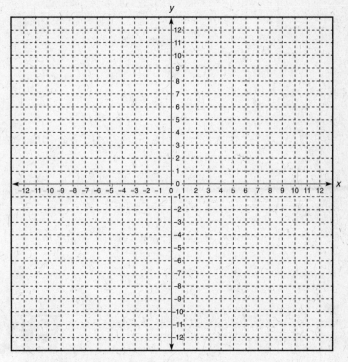

What is the solution set for *x* and *y*?

- A. (2, −5)
- B. (0, 3)
- C. (0, 9)
- D. (2, 5)

Answers and explanations start on page 13.

STOP

Congratulations! You have completed the GED® Mathematical Reasoning Pretest.

Reminder: your next step is to check your answers with the
Pretest Answers and Explanations and fill in the study
planner that follows those explanations.

PRETEST ANSWERS AND EXPLANATIONS

Part I: Quantitative Reasoning, page 2

1. **D. between 1,200 and 1,300** The graph shows that roughly 900 customers came from Zone 3 during this period, and that somewhere between 300 and 400 customers came from Zone 4 during the same period. Thus, adding them together will result in a number between 1,200 and 1,300.

2. **D. 1:2** The bar for Zone 1 is a little less than halfway between 400 and 500, so round up to 450. The best estimate for the bar for Zone 3 is 900. Make sure you write the ratio in the order stated in the problem. Zone 1: Zone 3 = 450:900, which simplifies to 1:2.

3. **C. 16** Divide 10 by $\frac{3}{5}$. The answer is 16 with a remainder. Since the question asks for how many bowls the potter can complete, ignore the remainder.

4. **B. 3** The graph doesn't give the actual number of hours Janelle will work, but it does show how her time spent at one activity compares to another. If she works 100 hours, she will spend 44 hours working at the counter, 9 hours processing new books, and 6 hours repairing bindings. Compare 44 to 15. The number 44 is about 3 times as great as 15.

5. **C. 160** To solve, set up a ratio. 15 percent $= \frac{15}{100}$. Set that equal to the ratio of employees who make minimum wage to the total number of employees, and use a variable to represent the total number of employees. $\frac{15}{100} = \frac{24}{x}$. Cross multiply: $24 \times 100 = 2400$. Divide: $2400 \div 15 = 160$.

6. **D. Y, W, Z, X** Compare the numbers and list in order from smallest to largest: $2.80, $27.10, $27.20, $261.00.

7. **B. 9.25** Add together the amounts of honey the cook will use in the two recipes: $2.5 + 4.25 = 6.75$. Subtract that amount from the total amount of honey in the jar. $16 - 6.75 = 9.25$.

8. **C. 21** One way to solve the problem is to find a number that is evenly divisible by 6 and 14, and then try dividing that number by each of the answer choices. Go through the multiples of 14 until you find one that is divisible by 6: 14, 28, 42. The number 42 is divisible by both 14 and 6. Then review the answer choices. 42 cannot be evenly divided by 8, 12, 28, or 35. It can be evenly divided by 21.

9. **D. 13** Work backward through the facts. Sheila has worked 10 years. Kathy has worked half as long as Sheila, which equals 5 years. Alice has worked 8 years longer than Kathy. $5 + 8 = 13$ years.

10. **C. $\frac{3}{4}$** Two sections, which equal $\frac{2}{8}$ or $\frac{1}{4}$, are marked "blue." Thus, the chance of not getting blue is $1 - \frac{1}{4} = \frac{3}{4}$.

11. **A. 25%** To find percent of change, divide the amount of change by the original price. Then multiply by 100 to change the result from a decimal to a percent: $\frac{\$320 - \$240}{\$320} \times 100 = \frac{\$80}{\$320} \times 100 = 0.25 \times 100 = 25\%$.

12. **C. 5.5** The median is the middle number of a group of numbers. Arrange the numbers of accounts in order: 2, 4, 4, 4, 5, 6, 6, 7, 7, 8. The middle numbers are 5 and 6. When there are two numbers in the middle, find the mean of those two numbers: $\frac{5+6}{2} = 5.5$.

13. **A. $4,500** Add together the amounts that Jim has sold so far in April: $2,500 + $5,000 = $7,500. Then subtract that amount from the minimum his employers expect him to sell: $12,000 - $7,500 = $4,500.

14. **C. $\frac{3}{10}$ feet** Subtract the length of the shorter stick from the length of the longer one: $3\frac{4}{5} - 3\frac{1}{2}$. To solve, find a common denominator: $3\frac{8}{10} - 3\frac{5}{10} = \frac{3}{10}$.

15. **C. 3.75** The number line is divided into increments, each of which equals one-fourth, or .25. The dot is three increments to the right of the number 3, so its value is 3.75.

16. **D. More students received either an A or a B than received either a D or an F.** Based on the graph, 6 students received an A and 7 students a B. $7 + 6 = 13$. Also, 7 students received a D, and 3 received an F. $7 + 3 = 10$. Since 13 is greater than 10, the A-and-B group is larger than the D-and-F group. Choice (A) is not supported because some students did fail the exam. Choice (B) suggests that most—more than half—of Marjorie's students received an A or B. However, the A-and-B group (13 students) is smaller than the total number of students who got a C (12 students), a D (around 7 students), or an F (3 students, for a total of 22 students). Choice (C) is unsupported because the graph has no information about how any other group of students would perform.

17. **D. $6,000** Use the formula provided to find the interest Jason's deposit would earn over the five years. As directed, express the percent interest as a decimal, 0.04. 5000×5 (years) $\times 0.04 = \$1000$. Then, to find out how much is in the account at the end of the five years, add that interest to Jason's original deposit: $5,000 + $1,000 = $6,000.

18. **C. 720** To find out how many possible orderings, or sequences, of six items are possible, multiply. There are six possibilities for the first movie. Then after the first movie has been chosen, there are five possibilities for the second movie, then four for the third movie, and so on: $6 \times 5 \times 4 \times 3 \times 2 \times 1 = 720$.

Part II: Algebraic Reasoning and Geometry, page 7

1. **B. Point B** Convert the improper fraction to a mixed fraction: $-\frac{16}{6} = -2\frac{4}{6} = -2\frac{2}{3}$, which is the value of Point B.

2. **C. 4** Substitute and simplify:
$$= 2x - (4y - 3) + 5xz$$
$$= 2(-3) - (4[2] - 3) + 5(-3)(-1)$$
$$= -6 - (8 - 3) + 15$$
$$= -6 - 5 + 15$$
$$= -11 + 15$$
$$= 4$$

3. **A. 54** To find the magnitude of the change in temperature, subtract the lowest temperature from the highest temperature: $46 - (-8) = 46 + 8 = 54$.

4. **B. 60** The tower, its shadow, and the distance between them form a right triangle. Use the Pythagorean relationship to find the missing distance:

$$61^2 = 11^2 + h^2$$
$$3721 = 121 + h^2$$
$$3600 = h^2$$
$$60 = h$$

5. **A. 18** To find the volume of a rectangular prism, multiply *base × width × height*. Here, however, the question asks for the volume in feet, while the measurements are given in inches. Therefore, start by converting the inches of model 413S to feet: 24 in × 72 in × 18 in = 2 ft × 6 ft × 1.5 ft = 18 ft^3.

6. **C. $2,600** The question stem gives us two equations. First, we know that $M + L = 4,680$. Also, since Levy earns $520 more than Matthew earns, that can be expressed as $L = M + 520$, or, put another way, $M = L - 520$. Since the question asks for a solution for Levy, substitute the value of M from the second equation in the first equation:

$$(L - 520) + L = 4,680$$
$$2L - 520 = 4,680$$
$$2L = 5,200$$
$$L = 2,600$$

7. **C. 16π** The formula for the surface area of a cone is: $SA = \pi rs + \pi r^2$. In that formula, *SA* means *surface area*, *r* represents the *radius*, and *s* is the *slant height*, or the distance from the bottom of one side of the cone to the point. The diagram indicates that the diameter of the base is 4, so its radius is 2. The slant height is 6. Substitute and simplify:

$$SA = \pi(2)(6) + \pi(2)^2$$
$$SA = 12\pi + 4\pi = 16\pi$$

8. **D. $5x^3 - 4x^2 - x + 12y$** Start by removing the parentheses:
$3x^3 + x + 2x^2 - 4x^2 + 14y - 2(y + x) = 3x^3 + x + 2x^3 - 4x^2 + 14y - 2y - 2x$.
Then, identify like terms that can be combined:
$3x^3$ and $2x^3$, which add to $5x^3$.
$- 4x^2$ cannot be combined with any other term.
x and $-2x$ add to $- x$.
$14y$ and $-2y$ add to $12y$.
Combine into a new expression: $5x^3 - 4x^2 - x + 12y$.

9. **(2, 4)** On scratch paper, draw the three points given in the question stem:

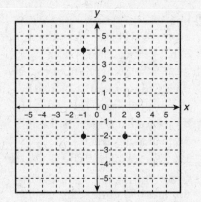

The fourth corner of the rectangle will be at (2, 4). Mark that point on the answer sheet.

10. **A. $18 - 2x$** Simplify: $4x - 2(3x - 9) = 4x - 6x + 18 = -2x + 18$. That can also be expressed as $18 - 2x$.

11. **D. 4** The simplest way to solve this problem is to try the values of x given in the answer choices in the equation. Starting with choice (A), where x equals -4: $3(-4)^2 - 10(-4) = 3(16) + 40 = 88$. That's a great deal more than 8. That result suggests that choice (B), where x equals -3, would also be likely to yield a result that's far too large. Try choices (C) or (D) to see what result a positive number yields. In choice (C), x equals 3: $3(3)^2 - 10(3) = 3(9) - 30 = -3$. That's a little too small, so the answer must be choice (D), x equals 4. Try it to confirm: $3(4)^2 - 10(4) = 3(16) - 40 = 8$. Choice (D) is correct.

12. **D. $x < 4$** Simplify the expression:

$$12(x - 2) < 24$$
$$12x - 24 < 24$$
$$12x < 48$$
$$x < 4$$

13. **B. 4.54×10^9** Writing a number in scientific notation involves expressing it as the product of two terms: one term is a number and the other is 10 raised to some power. To find how large the power of ten should be, imagine counting spaces to the left of the decimal point. Choice (B) reflects the correct number and the correct power of 10, or places to the left of the decimal point.

14. **D. 204** The shape of Joe's new property is a trapezoid, and the formula for the area of a trapezoid is $A = \frac{1}{2}h(b_1 + b_2)$. In that formula, A is area, and h means the height, which is 12 yards here. The variables b_1 and b_2 are the two bases, which here are 10 yards and 24 yards. Plug those values into the formula: $A = \frac{1}{2}(12)(10 + 24) = (6)(34) = 204$. (You can tell that Joe's property is a trapezoid because the two bases are parallel; the right angles indicated at the two ends of the *height* line indicate this.)

15. **A. $p = \$5.00 - (n - 1)\ \$0.50$** If a customer requests only one monogram, the fee is $5.00. However, if a customer requests 2, the price per monogram drops by $0.50 (which you can think of as 1 × $0.50). If a customer requests 3 monograms, the price per monogram drops another $0.50, or 2 × $0.50 in total. Thus, the price per monogram is $5.00 minus a multiple of $0.50. The multiple is one less than the number of hats ordered.

16. **B. 70°** In any four-sided figure, all four interior angles add up to 360°. In a parallelogram, the two obtuse angles are equal to one another, and the two acute angles are equal to one another. Here, you know that the two obtuse angles add up to 220°. 360° − 220° = 140°. Since there are two acute angles, divide that number by two.

17. C. $y = \frac{2}{3}x + 2$ The answer choices are in slope-intercept form, so begin by finding the y-intercept, which is 2. Then find the slope, which represents $\frac{rise}{run}$. Find two points on line H, and count the difference between the y-coordinates for those two points in order to find the *rise*. Then count the difference between the x-coordinates for those two points to find the *run*. For each vertical increase of two (*rise*), the line moves three numbers on the horizontal axis (*run*). Thus, the slope is $\frac{2}{3}$, and the equation is $y = \frac{2}{3}x + 2$.

18. A. 20π The question asks for the circumference of the pool. The question stem gives the distance from the middle of the pool to the edge—that's the radius of the circle, which is half the diameter. Thus, the diameter of the circle is 20 feet. Plug that into the formula for the circumference of a circle: $C = d\pi$. $C = 20\pi$.

19. D. 2 The slope of a line can be expressed as $\frac{rise}{run}$. To find the slope using two points, subtract one y-coordinate from another to find the *rise*, and subtract one x-coordinate from another to find the *run*. It does not matter which point you subtract from the other, as long as you are consistent about which point you are subtracting when finding both rise and run. $\frac{-1-(-9)}{4-0} = \frac{8}{4} = 2$.

20. C. 192π The formula for the volume of a cylinder is $V = \pi r^2 h$. In that formula, V is volume, r is the radius of the base, and h is height. In this case, you know that the diameter of the base of the can is 8, so the radius is 4. Plug in the values: $V = \pi \times (4 \text{ cm})^2 \times (12 \text{ cm}) = \pi \times 16 \text{ cm}^2 \times 12 \text{ cm} = 192\pi \text{ cm}^3$

21. D. 4,100 To find the area of a compound figure like this one, split it up into simpler shapes. Here, the space can be split into two rectangles:

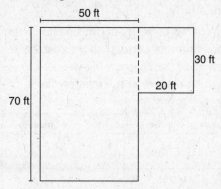

Find the area of the two rectangles and add those two areas together: $(70 \times 50) + (30 \times 20) = 3,500 + 600 = 4,100$.

22. D. (2, 5) There are two ways to solve this problem. First, you could graph both lines. After doing so, your scratchwork should have looked like this:

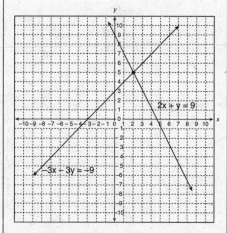

Based on that sketch, the two lines intersect at (2, 5), which means that those coordinates are the solution to the system of equations.

Alternatively, you could also have plugged each answer choice into both equations in order to find the answer choice that works in both equations. For example, to test choice (A) in this way:

Plug (2, −5) into the first equation: $3x - 3y = -9$

$3(2) - 3(-5) \stackrel{?}{=} -9$

$6 + 15 \neq -9$

Answer choice (A) does *not* work in the first equation. Therefore, it is incorrect, and there is no need to try choice (A) in the second equation. Try the other answer choices in a similar way. Only choice (D) will work in both equations.

KAPLAN GED® MATHEMATICAL REASONING TEST STUDY PLANNER

Take the Pretest, starting on page 1. Check your answers in the Pretest Answers and Explanations starting on page 13. Use the results to fill in the charts below so that you can target the areas that need the most work.

Part I: Quantitative Reasoning, 18 Questions

Circle the *Question Numbers* that you answered correctly in the second column. Write the *Number Correct* in the third column. Compare your "number correct" to the "mastery" number in the fourth column. If you do not have time to review all of the *Quantitative Reasoning* sections, target your study to the *Content Areas* in which you did not score at the mastery level.

Content Area	Question Numbers	Number Correct	Mastery/Total
Number Sense and Problem Solving Pages 22–41	6, 8, 9, 13		**3 out of 4**
Decimals and Fractions Pages 42–63	3, 7, 14, 15		**3 out of 4**
Ratio, Proportion, and Percent Pages 64–83	2, 5, 11, 17		**3 out of 4**
Data, Statistics, and Probability Pages 84–115	1, 4, 10, 12, 16, 18		**4 out of 6**

Part II: Algebraic Reasoning and Geometric Measurement, 22 Questions

Circle the *Question Numbers* that you answered correctly in the second column. Write the *Number Correct* in the third column. Compare your "number correct" to the "mastery" number in the fourth column. If you do not have time to review all of the *Algebraic Reasoning and Geometric Measurement* sections, target your study to the *Content Areas* in which you did not score at the mastery level.

Content Area	Question Numbers	Number Correct	Mastery/Total
Algebra Basics, Expressions, and Polynomials Pages 116–149	1, 2, 3, 8, 10, 13		**5 out of 6**
Equations, Inequalities, and Functions Pages 150–179	6, 9, 11, 12, 15, 17, 19, 22		**6 out of 8**
Geometry Pages 180–204	4, 5, 7, 14, 16, 18, 20, 21		**6 out of 8**

About the Mathematical Reasoning Test

The GED® *Mathematical Reasoning Test* evaluates your ability to solve mathematical problems and apply mathematics to a variety of contexts. You will have one hour and 55 minutes to answer 40-50 questions based on the following:

- **Quantitative Reasoning (45%)**, which includes problems with positive and negative whole numbers, decimals, and fractions; ratios, proportions, and percents; data and statistics; and geometric measurement
- **Algebraic Reasoning (55%)**, which includes expressions, polynomials, equations, inequalities, linear equations, quadratic equations, and patterns and functions. A variety of formats will assess evaluating, solving, and graphing skills in algebra.

You will need a minimum score of 150 to pass the *Mathematical Reasoning Test*, which is one of the four tests you will need to pass in order to earn a high school equivalency diploma.

Tools

Calculator For most of the test, you will be able to use either a hand-held or an online version of the **Texas Instruments TI-30XS MultiView™ scientific calculator**. You can access the online calculator by clicking on this icon. You can also take your own hand-held TI-30XS MultiView™ calculator to use on test day.

For the first five questions on the test, <u>you will not be able to use the calculator.</u> <u>Check all of your work carefully before you leave this section of the test.</u> You will <u>not</u> be able to return to these problems once the online calculator is enabled.

If you forget how to use a specific calculator function, you will be able to access a *Calculator Reference Sheet* from the computer screen by clicking on this icon.

Formula Sheet A copy of this formula sheet appears on page 205 of this book. You will be able to access these formulas by clicking on this icon. Other formulas that appear in this book should be memorized.

Symbol Selector On some fill-in-the-blank problems, you will need to use a symbol from the symbol selector toolbar. You can enable it when the icon to the right shows up on the light blue toolbar at the top of your screen.

At the testing center, you will be given a dry erase marker and a **wipe-off board** that you can use as scratch paper.

Computer-Based Mathematics Test Formats

Many of the questions will be *multiple-choice* with four options (A through D). You will **click** on the best answer.

> A painter needs to cover the walls of four rooms in two coats of paint. Each room measures 4 ft by 8 ft, and the ceiling is 10 feet high in each. Each gallon of paint covers 32 square feet. How many gallons of paint does he need?
>
> ○ A. 2
> ○ B. 64
> ○ C. 128
> ○ D. 256

GED® TEST TIP

Follow all directions carefully. For example, in this fill-in-the-blank problem, you are asked to type the answer, simplify the expression, and use the symbol selector to complete the result.

Fill-in-the-blank questions will require you to **type** a numerical answer to a problem or to enter an equation by **clicking** to open the symbol selector and then **inserting** the symbol in the box. You may also be asked to **type** a word or phrase in the box to answer a question about your thought process.

> Type your answer in the box. You may use numbers, symbols, and/or text in your answer.
>
> Simplify the expression completely. Leave your answer in radical form.
>
> $$\sqrt{60} \div \sqrt{5}$$
>
> (**NOTE:** Click the symbol selector when you need to insert the radical sign.)
>
> [ ]

Drop-down questions give you the opportunity to **click** the word "Select" and choose the option that correctly completes the statement.

> Sarah runs an open babysitting service on Saturday nights so that parents in the neighborhood can enjoy a night out. The chart below shows the number of children in attendance each hour.

Hour	# of children
5 pm	2
6 pm	4
7 pm	5
8 pm	6
9 pm	5
10 pm	2
11 pm	2

> The number of children in attendance ranged from [Select...] to [Select...].

Drag-and-drop items require you to **click** on an image, number, or symbol and to **drag** and **drop** it to a specified location on the computer screen to create an expression, equation, or inequality.

A clown creates an equation that relates his data of each child's head size to the length of the balloon he needs to make them a proper balloon-animal hat. For each child, he needs a balloon five times as long as the child's head size, plus $\frac{4}{5}$ of an inch extra. Complete a linear equation for child A, where x is the size of the child's head in inches and y is the length of the balloon in inches.

Click on the variables and numbers you want to select and drag them into the boxes.

Equation for Child A

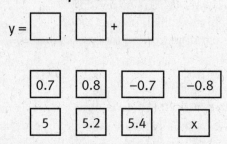

Hot-spot questions are based on a graphic such as a number line, coordinate grid, or geometric figure. You will need to **click** on a specific place or places on the figure.

Jessica has 20 hours a week to spend making scarves. Each week, she spends 2 hours purchasing the materials. Each scarf takes 3 hours to complete. The inequality $2 + 3s \leq 20$ represents the number of scarves, *s*, Jessica can make in one week.

Using the number line below, click each number to plot each possible value for *s*.

(**NOTE:** If you need to remove a point, hold the cursor over the point and left-click the mouse.)

Using the Texas Instruments TI-30XS MultiView™ Calculator

Throughout this book, you will practice using the **TI-30XS MultiView™** calculator. Remember: You <u>do not have to</u> use the calculator to solve problems; only use it if it is relevant to the problem or if you believe it will be helpful.

Below is a picture of the hand-held version and some issues to keep in mind.

- The <u>hand-held version</u> has an On/Off button at the lower-left hand side.

- To use the <u>online version</u> of the calculator, **click** the calculator icon (see page 17) to open the calculator in a new window. Use your mouse to **drag** the calculator to the side of the computer screen so that it does not cover the problem. When you are finished with a calculation, **click** on the "X" at the top of the window to close the calculator.

TI-30XS MultiView™ Calculator

- When you are finished with a calculation, use the *enter* button. (There is no "equal sign" button on this calculator.)

- Use the *white numeric keypad* to enter numbers, the decimal point, and the negative sign (–) for a negative number such as –13 .

- The *operation keys*, on the right, allow you to add, subtract, multiply, and divide. (Use the minus sign here for subtraction; use the negative sign (–) on the keypad to indicate a negative number.)

- Use the bright green *2nd button* at the left of the calculator to activate the *2nd functions* (in bright green) above the keys. Some of the main ones are square root, exponent, percent, and mixed number functions.

- The *four arrows* at the top right of the calculator allow you to move the *onscreen cursor* up, down, left, or right as needed. The *delete* key to the left of the arrows allows you to correct mistakes as you work.

- Every time you begin a calculation, press the *clear* button above the *operation keys* to clear the calculator's memory.

Accessing the Symbol Selector Toolbar

Some questions will instruct you to use a particular symbol from the "symbol selector." This is not available for all problems, but this icon shows up when you need the toolbar: Æ Symbol

When you **click** on this icon, a new window will open up with these symbols:

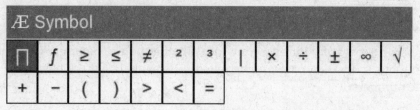

Click on a symbol to insert it in the correct place in an expression, equation, or inequality. When you are finished with the toolbar, **click** on the "X" at the top of the window to close the window.

Using the Wipe-Off Board

Even with all of the computer-based tools, you may still feel the need for some scratch paper to do the following:

- Write down the relevant numbers that you need to answer a specific question.
- Solve the problem by hand and use the calculator to check your work.
- Make a drawing or a diagram to help you picture a situation that is described in a word problem. This is an important strategy when working with measurement and geometry problems that do not contain a graphic.

At the testing center, you will be provided with a wipe-off board and dry erase marker, similar to the material shown at the right. Make use of the board throughout the *Mathematical Reasoning Test* and ask for a new one if you feel that you need it.

NUMBER SENSE AND PROBLEM SOLVING

Compare and Order Numbers

Place Value

Numbers are part of your everyday life. Whether you're paying with cash, reading bus schedules, or changing television channels, you're using whole numbers.

The value of a number depends on the **place value** of its digits. On the place-value chart below, note that the value of a digit increases as you move to the left.

Key Ideas

- When ordering numbers, compare the same place values between numbers.
- Round numbers to estimate answers or eliminate answer choices in multiple-choice questions.

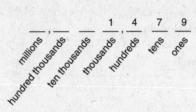

In the whole number shown on the chart, 1 has the greatest value. The number would be read as "one thousand four hundred seventy-nine."

Comparing and Ordering Values

To **order** numbers, you need to compare the value of their digits. Align the place values of the numbers you are comparing. Start at the left and compare the value of the first digit of each number.

Example 1: Place the numbers 342, 98, and 317 in order from least to greatest.

1. Compare the first digit in each number. Since 98 is a two-digit number, and the other numbers are three-digit numbers, 98 has the smallest value.

   hundreds tens ones
   342
   98
   317

2. Next, compare the first digit of the remaining numbers. Since both numbers have the same digit (3) in the hundreds place, compare the digits in the tens place. Since 1 is less than 4, 317 is less than 342.

   From least to greatest:
   98, 317, 342

Rounding Numbers

Place value is also essential to **rounding** numbers.

Example 2: Round 2451 to the nearest hundred.

24⬚51

1. Locate the place value that you want to round to. Then look at the place value to the right. If the digit to the right is 5 or greater, round up. If the digit to the right is less than 5, don't change the number in the hundreds place.

   The value to the right of the hundreds place is a 5. Round up.

2. Round up the digit in the hundreds place. Then change the digits to the right of the hundreds place to zeros.

   2451 rounds up to **2500**

PRACTICE 1

A. Write the digit from the number below that corresponds to the listed place value. The first one is done for you.

1,436,879

__4__ 1. hundred thousands   ____ 5. thousands

____ 2. hundreds   ____ 6. tens

____ 3. ones   ____ 7. ten thousands

____ 4. millions

B. Round these numbers as directed.

8. Round 544 to the nearest hundred.

9. Round 76 to the nearest ten.

10. Round 1058 to the nearest hundred.

11. Round 11,632 to the nearest thousand.

12. Round 1525 to the nearest thousand.

13. Round 84 to the nearest hundred.

C. In each of the following pairs, which number is greater?

14. 100 or 89

15. 339 or 341

16. 1099 or 1145

17. 125,391 or 119,450

D. Write these numbers in order from least to greatest.

18. 23   18   45   39

19. 111   89   109   91

20. 1087   932   909   1139

21. 1429   1420   1432   1425

22. 12,071   11,098   12,131

23. 15,356   15,309   15,298

E. Choose the one best answer to each question.

24. When stacking items, the heaviest items should be placed at the bottom. Starting at the bottom, in what order should items weighing 45 pounds, 40 pounds, 50 pounds, and 48 pounds be stacked?

     A. 40, 45, 48, 50
     B. 45, 50, 40, 48
     C. 50, 48, 45, 40
     D. 50, 40, 45, 48

25. Which of the following correctly shows 1,543,976 rounded to the nearest hundred thousand?

     A. 2,000,000
     B. 1,600,000
     C. 1,500,000
     D. 1,540,000

Answers and explanations begin on page 206.

NUMBER SENSE AND PROBLEM SOLVING

Whole Number Operations

Addition and Subtraction

You use **addition** when you need to combine amounts. The answer in an addition problem is called the **sum**, or **total**. When you are adding, it's helpful to stack the numbers in a column. Be sure to line up the place-value columns and then work from right to left, starting with the ones column.

Key Ideas

- Add when combining amounts and subtract when finding the difference.
- Align place-value columns when adding or subtracting.
- Always look to the next place-value column to regroup.

Sometimes the digits in a place-value column add up to 10 or more. When this happens, you will need to **regroup** to the next place value.

Example 1: Add 40 + 129 + 24.

1. Align the numbers you want to add on the ones column. Working from right to left, add the ones column first. Since the ones column totals 13, write the 3 in the ones column and regroup, or **carry**, the 1 ten to the tens column.

$$\begin{array}{r} 1 \\ 40 \\ 129 \\ + 24 \\ \hline 3 \end{array}$$

2. Add the tens column, including the regrouped 1.

$$\begin{array}{r} 1 \\ 40 \\ 129 \\ + 24 \\ \hline 93 \end{array}$$

GED® TEST TIP

Another way to check answers is to round the numbers in a problem and find an approximate answer.

3. Then add the hundreds column. Since there is only one value, write the 1 hundred in the answer.

$$\begin{array}{r} 1 \\ 40 \\ 129 \\ + 24 \\ \hline 193 \end{array}$$

You **subtract** when you want to find the **difference** between amounts. Write the greater number on top, and align the amounts on the ones column. You may also need to regroup as you subtract.

Example 2: If Sue is 57 and Kathy is 38, how many years older is Sue?

1. Find the difference in their ages. Start with the ones column. Since 7 is less than the number being subtracted (8), regroup, or **borrow**, 1 ten from the tens column. Add the regrouped amount to the ones column. Now subtract 17 − 8 in the ones column.

$$\begin{array}{r} {}^{4}\cancel{5}{}^{17}\cancel{7} \\ - 38 \\ \hline 9 \end{array}$$

2. Regrouping 1 ten from the tens column left 4 tens. Subtract 4 − 3 and write the result in the tens column of your answer. Check: 19 + 38 = 57.

$$\begin{array}{r} {}^{4}\cancel{5}{}^{17}\cancel{7} \\ - 38 \\ \hline 19 \end{array}$$

Sue is **19 years older** than Kathy.

Example 3: Find the difference between 205 and 67.

1. Subtract. Start with the ones column. Since 5 is less than the number being subtracted (7), regroup. Since there are 0 tens in the tens column, regroup 1 hundred from the hundreds column. From 10 tens, regroup 1 ten to the ones column. Now subtract $15 - 7$ in the ones column.

$$\begin{array}{r} \overset{9}{} \\ 1 \; \overset{}{\cancel{10}} \; 15 \\ 2 \; \cancel{0} \; \cancel{5} \\ - \; 6 \; 7 \\ \hline 8 \end{array}$$

2. Regrouping 1 ten from the tens column left 9 tens. Subtract $9 - 6$, and write the result in the tens column of your answer.

$$\begin{array}{r} \overset{9}{} \\ 1 \; \overset{}{\cancel{10}} \; 15 \\ 2 \; \cancel{0} \; \cancel{5} \\ - \; 6 \; 7 \\ \hline 3 \; 8 \end{array}$$

3. Regrouping 1 hundred from the hundreds column left 1 hundred. Subtract the hundreds column: $1 - 0$. Check: $138 + 67 = 205$.

$$\begin{array}{r} \overset{9}{} \\ 1 \; \overset{}{\cancel{10}} \; 15 \\ 2 \; \cancel{0} \; \cancel{5} \\ - \; 6 \; 7. \\ \hline 1 \; 3 \; 8 \end{array}$$

PRACTICE 2.1

A. Solve.

1. $\begin{array}{r} 54 \\ + 23 \\ \hline \end{array}$
    3. $\begin{array}{r} 73 \\ - 21 \\ \hline \end{array}$
    5. $\begin{array}{r} 105 \\ + 85 \\ \hline \end{array}$
    7. $\begin{array}{r} 100 \\ - 57 \\ \hline \end{array}$

2. $\begin{array}{r} 46 \\ + 54 \\ \hline \end{array}$
    4. $\begin{array}{r} 55 \\ - 19 \\ \hline \end{array}$
    6. $\begin{array}{r} 2386 \\ + 1692 \\ \hline \end{array}$
    8. $\begin{array}{r} 2500 \\ - 383 \\ \hline \end{array}$

B. Rewrite the problems in columns before solving.

9. $20 + 12 + 33 =$
10. $245 - 131 =$
11. $30 + 75 + 75 =$
12. $378 - 85 =$

13. $144 + 238 + 101 =$
14. $545 - 89 =$
15. $2095 + 324 =$
16. $1250 - 350 =$

17. $10,326 + 982 =$
18. $15,890 - 705 =$
19. $108,755 + 22,442 =$
20. $44,789 - 13,890 =$

C. Choose the <u>one best answer</u> to each question.

21. What is the total weight of the boxes below?

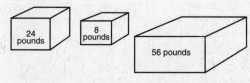

A.   78
B.   88
C.   150
D.   160

22. Celia's share for lunch is $7. If she pays with a $20 bill, how much change should she get?

A. $3
B. $7
C. $13
D. $27

Answers and explanations begin on page 206.

Multiplication and Division

You **multiply** to combine the same amount multiple times. For example, instead of adding $24 + 24 + 24$, you could multiply 24 by 3. If a problem asks you to find the **product** of two or more numbers, you should multiply.

Example 4: Find the product of 24 and 63.

1. Align place values as you rewrite the problem in a column. Multiply the ones place of the top number by the ones place of the bottom number: $4 \times 3 = 12$. Write the 2 in the ones place in the first partial product. Regroup the 1 ten.

$$\begin{array}{r} 1 \\ 24 \\ \times\, 63 \\ \hline 2 \end{array}$$

2. Multiply the tens place in the top number by 3: $2 \times 3 = 6$. Then add the regrouped amount: $6 + 1 = 7$. Write the 7 in the tens place in the partial product.

$$\begin{array}{r} 1 \\ 24 \\ \times\, 63 \\ \hline 72 \end{array}$$

3. Now multiply by the tens place of 63. Write a **placeholder** 0 in the ones place in the second partial product, since you're really multiplying by 60. Then multiply the top number by 6: $4 \times 6 = 24$. Write 4 in the partial product and regroup the 2. Multiply $2 \times 6 = 12$. Add the regrouped 2: $12 + 2 = 14$.

$$\begin{array}{r} 2 \\ 24 \\ \times\, 63 \\ \hline 72 \\ +\,1440 \\ \hline \mathbf{1512} \end{array}$$

4. Add the partial products to find the total product: $72 + 1440 = \mathbf{1512}$.

To **divide** means to find how many equal parts an amount can be divided into. The amount being divided is called the **dividend.** The number you are dividing by is the **divisor,** and the answer to a division problem is the **quotient.**

Example 5: At a garage sale, 3 children sold their old toys for a total of $54. If they share the money equally, how much money should each child receive?

1. Divide the total amount ($54) by the number of ways the money is to be split (3). Work from left to right. How many times does 3 go into 5? Write the answer 1 directly above the 5 in the dividend. Since $3 \times 1 = 3$, subtract $5 - 3 = 2$.

$$\begin{array}{r} 1 \\ 3\overline{)\$54} \\ -3 \\ \hline 2 \end{array}$$

2. Continue dividing. Bring down the 4 from the ones place in the dividend. How many times does 3 go into 24? Write the answer 8 directly above the 4 in the dividend. Since $3 \times 8 = 24$, subtract $24 - 24 = 0$.

Each child should receive $18.

$$\begin{array}{r} 18 \\ 3\overline{)\$54} \\ -3 \\ \hline 24 \\ -24 \\ \hline 0 \end{array}$$

Example 6: Divide $1006 \div 4$.

1. Divide the total amount (1006) by 4. Work from left to right. Since 4 doesn't divide into 1, use the next place value in the dividend. How many times does 4 go into 10? Write the answer 2 directly above the first 0 in the dividend. Since $4 \times 2 = 8$, subtract $10 - 8 = 2$.

$$\begin{array}{r} 2 \\ 4\overline{)1006} \\ -8 \\ \hline 2 \end{array}$$

2. Continue dividing. Bring down the 0 from the tens place in the dividend. How many times does 4 go into 20? Write the answer 5 directly above the second 0 in the dividend. Since $4 \times 5 = 20$, subtract $20 - 20 = 0$. Bring down the 6 from the ones place in the dividend. How many times does 4 go into 6? Write the answer 1 above the 6 in the dividend. Since $4 \times 1 = 4$, subtract $6 - 4 = 2$. Write the **remainder** of 2 as part of the quotient.

$$
\begin{array}{r}
251\ r2 \\
4\overline{)1006} \\
\underline{-8} \\
20 \\
\underline{-20} \\
06 \\
\underline{-4} \\
2
\end{array}
$$

By reviewing and memorizing multiplication tables, you can save yourself precious time on the GED® *Mathematical Reasoning Test*.

PRACTICE 2.2

A. Solve.

1. 121
    $\times 4$

2. 250
    $\times 4$

3. 342
    $\times 8$

4. $5\overline{)65}$

5. $7\overline{)735}$

6. $9\overline{)189}$

7. 45
    $\times 30$

8. 105
    $\times 25$

9. 211
    $\times 16$

10. $10\overline{)280}$

11. $15\overline{)225}$

12. $19\overline{)114}$

B. Solve. If multiplying more than two numbers, find the product of two numbers before multiplying by the next number, and so on.

13. $50 \times 5 =$

14. $179 \div 4 =$

15. $5 \times 6 \times 10 =$

16. $1004 \div 5 =$

17. $25 \times 3 \times 2 =$

18. $7452 \times 9 =$

19. $10{,}760 \div 20 =$

20. $12 \times 8 \times 4 =$

21. $144{,}140 \div 12 =$

C. Choose the one best answer to each question.

22. A fruit juice container holds 16 servings. If the serving size is 6 ounces, how many ounces does the container hold in all?

    A. 10
    B. 22
    C. 76
    D. 96

23. A cashier has fifteen $5 bills. How much does he have in $5 bills?

    A. $15
    B. $25
    C. $75
    D. $150

D. For question 24, write your answer on the line provided.

24. How many 2-foot lengths can be cut from the string shown below?

    _____
    12 ft
    _____

Answers and explanations begin on page 206.

GED® Test Calculator Skills

LESSON 3

Key Ideas

- For many questions, you may use either a hand-held or online version of the TI-30XS MultiView™ scientific calculator.
- Use the calculator when you think it will save you time or improve your accuracy.
- Learn the placement of the keys and how to perform specific functions before you take the test.

You will have access to an online or hand-held calculator for many questions on the *Mathematical Reasoning Test* and for some questions on the *Social Studies* and *Science Tests*. If you wish to use a hand-held calculator, you will likely need to bring your own. It must be the Texas Instruments TI-30XS MultiView™, shown here. The online version will be available when the calculator icon appears at the top of the computer screen. You will click on the icon to open the calculator and use the mouse to move it so that it does not cover the problem. See page 20 for more calculator basics.

Look at the reproduction of the calculator below and follow the examples that demonstrate how to use the calculator's **operation keys**.

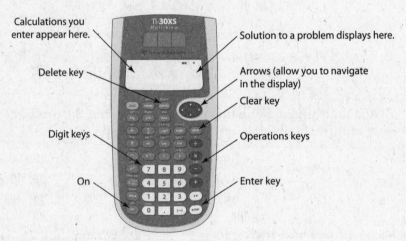

Calculations you enter appear here.

Delete key

Digit keys

On

Solution to a problem displays here.

Arrows (allow you to navigate in the display)

Clear key

Operations keys

Enter key

GED® TEST TIP

You can buy a handheld TI-30XS MultiView™ calculator for practice as you work through this study guide. It may be available online, at office supply stores, or other places where calculators are sold.

Example 1: Add $63 + 97 + 58 + 32 + 81$.

1. Always clear a calculator before starting a new computation. On the TI-30XS MultiView™, use the *clear* key.

   (clear)

2. Enter each number followed by the plus sign. As you type, the numbers and plus signs will appear on the calculator's screen. If you make a mistake, press *delete* to go back and reenter a number.

   $63 + 97 + 58 + 32 + 81$

3. Press *enter* to find the total.

   (enter)

The total, **331**, will appear on the right-hand side of the display:

   331

Example 2: Find the difference between 15,789 and 9,332.

1. Always clear a calculator before starting a new computation. [clear]
2. Enter the greater number first, followed by the minus operator. 15789 [−]
   NOTE: Use the minus key that is on the right side of the calculator with the other operation symbols. Don't use the (−) key at the bottom of the calculator; that key is used to enter a negative number.
3. Enter the number being subtracted. 9332
4. Press the *enter* key to find the answer. [enter]

The answer **6457** will appear on the right-hand side of the display. **6457**

Example 3: Find the product of 309 and 68.

1. Always clear a calculator before starting a new computation. [clear]
2. Enter the first number, followed by the multiplication operator. 309 [×]
   (The multiplication sign will appear in the display as an asterisk rather than an ×, but the *multiplication key* looks like an ×.)
3. Enter the next number. 68
4. Press the *enter* key to find the product. [enter]

The answer **21012** will appear on the right-hand side of the display. **21012**

Example 4: Divide 12,456 by 12.

1. Always clear a calculator before starting a new computation. [clear]
2. Enter the number to be divided first, followed by the division operator. 12456 [÷]
3. Enter the number you are dividing by. 12
4. Press the *enter* key to find the quotient. [enter]

The answer **1038** will appear on the right-hand side of the display. **1038**

PRACTICE 3.1

A. Practice solving the following problems on your calculator.

1. $19 + 26 + 85 + 23 =$
2. $2579 - 1392 =$
3. $4 \times 28 \times 7 =$
4. $2568 \div 107 =$
5. $12,356 + 14,728 =$
6. $107,899 - 93,457 =$
7. $209 \times 56 =$
8. $972 \div 18 =$
9. $20,540 \div 13 =$

B. Choose the one correct answer to each question.

10. Dan bought a used car with 16,741 miles on it. If the car now has 42,920 miles on it, how many miles has Dan put on the car?
    A. 16,741
    B. 26,179
    C. 42,920
    D. 59,661

11. A shipment of 20 computers arrived at a warehouse. If each computer is valued at $995, what is the total value of the shipment?
    A. $995
    B. $1015
    C. $1990
    D. $19,900

Answers and explanations begin on page 206.

Using the *2nd* Key for a Second Function

To access some of the functions on the TI-30XS MultiView™, you need to press the *2nd* key in the upper left corner of the keypad. This bright green key will activate the second function also shown in green above the corresponding key. To access the second function of a key, press the *2nd* key first—do not press it at the same time as the function key. Highlighted below are two commonly used second functions—square root and percent. Use the process shown here for all *2nd* function keys.

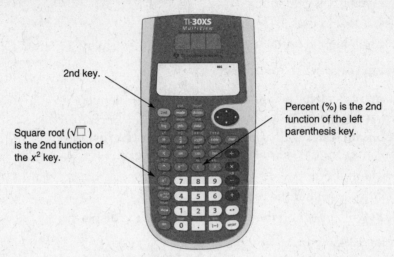

2nd key.

Square root (√☐) is the 2nd function of the x^2 key.

Percent (%) is the 2nd function of the left parenthesis key.

Example 5: Find the square root of 169.

	Keys to Press	On the Display
1. Always clear a calculator before starting a new computation.	clear	
2. Recognize that square root is a *2nd* function over the x^2 key. Press the *2nd* key. (Note that the term *2nd* now appears in the upper left corner of the display.)	2nd	2nd
3. Next, press the x^2 key to activate the square root function in green over the key. You will see a blinking cursor under the square root.	$\sqrt{x^2}$	√☐
4. Now that you have the square root function, enter the number. The number will appear under the square root symbol in the display.	169	$\sqrt{169}$▶
5. Press the *enter* key to find the square root. The answer, **13**, will appear on the right-hand side of the display.	enter	$\sqrt{169}$ 13

For more information about square roots, see page 120.

Remember: For all *2nd functions*, (1) press the *2nd* key first to activate the *2nd* function, (2) press the key, and (3) enter the numbers.

Example 6: Find the part if you are given the percent and the whole. Find 10 percent of 500.

1. Always clear a calculator before starting a new computation.   clear
2. Enter the number you want to find the percent of.   500
3. Press the multiplication sign.   ⊗
4. Enter the percent number.   10
5. Press the *2nd* key and then press the open, or left, parenthesis key to activate the percent function.   2nd %\n(
6. Press the *enter* key to find the answer.   enter

The answer, **50**, will appear on the right-hand side of the display. Ten percent of 500 is 50.   **50**

Example 7: Find the percent if you are given the whole and the part. What percent of 240 is 60?

1. Always clear a calculator before starting a new computation.   clear
2. Enter the part.   60
3. Press the division sign.   ÷
4. Enter the whole.   240
5. Press the *2nd* key and then press the close, or right, parenthesis symbol. This tells the calculator to translate the answer into a percent.   2nd ▸%\n)
6. Press the *enter* key to find the answer.   enter

The answer, **25%**, will appear on the right-hand side of the display. Sixty is 25% of 240.   **25%**

For more information about percents, see pages 68–79.

PRACTICE 3.2

A. Practice solving the following problems on your calculator.

1. $\sqrt{625}$
2. $\sqrt{324}$
3. $\sqrt{1225}$
4. Find 20% of 680.
5. Find 10% of 1250.

6. 15 is what percent of 300?
7. Find 5% of 40.
8. Find 30% of 450.
9. 20 is what percent of 400?

B. Choose the <u>one best</u> answer to each question.

10. Tanya paid 20% of $1680 as a down payment. How much was the down payment?

    A. $20
    B. $168
    C. $336
    D. $840

11. Aaron received a credit of $48 on a purchase of $960. What percent of $960 is $48?

    A. 5%
    B. 20%
    C. 48%
    D. 912%

Answers and explanations begin on page 206.

Word Problems

To pass the *Mathematical Reasoning Test*, you will need to solve word problems. These questions are easier to manage if you use a **five-step problem-solving process**. Practice this process with word problems in this book.

Step 1. What is the **question** asking me to find?

> *Read the problem carefully. State the question in your own words.*

Step 2. What **information** from the problem do I need?

> *Select only the information you need to answer the question.*

Step 3. Which **operation** do I need to perform—addition, subtraction, multiplication, or division?

> *Choose from one of the four operations above based on your understanding of the question.*

Step 4. What is my **solution**?

> *Carry out the operation with the numbers you chose in step 2.*

Step 5. Does my answer **make sense**?

> *Look back to make sure that you answered the question. Check that your answer makes sense.*

To help you decide which operation to use, keep the following ideas in mind.

Key Ideas

- Successful math problem solvers use a five-step process.
- Read carefully to understand the question and select only the information needed to answer it.
- When you have found an answer, check that it makes sense.

You...	in order to...
add	combine amounts of different sizes
subtract	find the difference between amounts
multiply	combine the same amount multiple times
divide	separate one amount into equal-sized groups

Example 1: To cover a sofa, Sophia needs 12 yards of fabric that costs $14 per yard. How many yards does Sophia need for 3 sofas?
  A. 4
  B. 36
  C. 42
  D. 168

The correct answer is **B. 36 yards** of fabric. The question asked you to find the total number of yards of fabric Sophia needs for 3 sofas. Note that the cost of a yard of fabric is not needed to answer the question.

Since you were asked to find the amount of fabric for 3 sofas, you should multiply 12 yards × 3 sofas = 36 yards. Here are two common errors to avoid:

- If you had mistakenly divided, you would have gotten the incorrect answer of 4 yards of fabric for 3 sofas.

- If you had used the $14 price per yard and multiplied by either 3 sofas or 12 yards, you would have been tempted by wrong answers 42 or 168. However, the cost per yard is not needed.

ON THE GED® TEST

Many Mathematical Reasoning Test questions include information that is not needed to answer the specific question. In multiple-choice questions, wrong answer choices may be based on mistakenly using this "extra" information, so read carefully.

PRACTICE 4.1

1. Peter wants to repaint his 700-square-foot apartment. He calculates that he has 3500 square feet of wall space to paint. (He will not paint the floor or the ceiling.) If each gallon of paint will cover 350 square feet of wall space, how many gallons will Peter need?

   A. 2
   B. 5
   C. 10
   D. 15

2. For a family get-together, Darryl wants to be sure that each child gets 2 party favors. The party favors cost $3 each, and there are 11 children coming. How many party favors will Darryl need?

   A. 9
   B. 11
   C. 18
   D. 22

3. Sarah and Kate live 18 miles apart, and they both work at the same office. If Sarah lives 25 miles from the office and Kate lives 30 miles from the office, how many miles farther from the office does Kate live than Sarah?

   A. 5
   B. 7
   C. 12
   D. 15

For question 4, <u>write your answer</u> on the line provided.

4. The Navarro family uses an average of 225 gallons of water per day, 5 gallons of which goes through the family's water filter. The Navarros' water filter can process 450 gallons before it needs to be replaced. After how many days of average water use will the family need to replace their filter?

   _____

<u>Questions 5 and 6</u> are based on the following information.

Joyce owns a beauty salon, and she has posted the following information in her salon.

Service	Minutes to complete	Price
Manicure	30	$15
Pedicure	30	$25
Manicure & Pedicure	45	$35
Facial	45	$45
Makeover	60	$60

5. How many minutes will it take Joyce to give 3 pedicures?

   A. 30
   B. 55
   C. 75
   D. 90

6. How much more does a customer pay for the makeover than for the manicure & pedicure combination?

   A. $15
   B. $20
   C. $25
   D. $35

For questions 7 and 8, <u>write your answers</u> on the lines provided.

7. Brandon is planning his part of the local community garden. He has calculated that he can plant 6 seedlings per row, and the garden allots 7 rows to each gardener. What is the maximum number of seedlings Brandon could plant?

   _____

8. Sumayyah knits gloves and hats each winter and sells them through a local shop. If Sumayyah received $189 from the sale of her hats and gloves this past winter, and she spent $27 on yarn, how much money did she earn from her knitting?

   $ _____

Answers and explanations begin on page 206.

Multi-Step Word Problems

The word problems on the previous two pages involved only one operation to solve. However, on the GED® *Mathematical Reasoning Test* and other tests, you may need to do several math processes to solve a problem. These are called **multi-step problems**.

When you are working on multi-step problems, there are two important ideas to keep in mind. *What is the question asking me to find?* and *Did I answer the question?*

Review this example of a multi-step problem and the problem-solving process below.

Example 1: To win a prize, Sarah's daughter has to sell 75 boxes of cookies in 3 days. If she sold 16 boxes on day 1 and 34 boxes on day 2, how many boxes would she need to sell on day 3 to win the prize?

        (1) 18
        (2) 25
        (3) 50

Step 1. What is the question asking me to find?

The question asks me to find how many boxes Sarah's daughter needs to sell on the third day to make her goal of 75 boxes.

Step 2. What information from the problem do I need?

I know the total number of boxes she needs to sell (75 boxes).

I know how many boxes she sold on day 1 (16 boxes) and day 2 (34 boxes).

Step 3. Do I need to do only one operation, or do I need to do more than one?

I can add to find how many boxes Sarah's daughter has sold so far: 16 + 34 = 50.

However, that doesn't tell me <u>how many boxes she needs to sell on day 3</u>. I need one more step.

Step 4. What is my solution?

75 boxes total − 50 boxes sold = 25 boxes for day 3. The correct answer is (2) 25.

Step 5. Does my answer make sense? Did I answer the question?

By taking the additional step, I answered the question of how many boxes need to be sold on day 3.

This sample multi-step problem involved only two operations: adding and subtracting. On the actual test, you may need to do three or more operations to answer a question, so read and think carefully about each problem.

As you think about the example, note the most common mistake people make with multi-step problems. Often they stop short of answering the question. Notice that choice (3) 50 is a **partial solution**, but it is not the answer to the question. Using the five-step problem-solving process will help you avoid that mistake.

PRACTICE 4.2

Questions 1–3 are based on the information below.

Farhana's produce company distributes to several restaurants. The table below shows how many cases of different produce each restaurant ordered from Farhana's company in July.

Produce Orders in July					
	Asparagus	Boston lettuce	Carrots	Romaine lettuce	Tomatoes
Restaurant A	2	3	1	4	3
Restaurant B	4	4	2	2	1
Restaurant C	0	0	3	4	3
Restaurant D	1	2	2	3	4
Restaurant E	3	0	3	2	1

1. If Boston lettuce costs $17 per case and romaine lettuce costs $23 per case, how much did Restaurant D spend on lettuce ordered from Farhana in July?

   A. $85
   B. $93
   C. $103
   D. $143

2. Delivery costs $2 per case for the first 5 cases and $1 per case for each additional case of produce. What was Restaurant B's delivery charge in July?

   A. $13
   B. $18
   C. $20
   D. $26

3. If asparagus costs $22 per case and tomatoes cost $15 per case, which of the following restaurants spent the most on asparagus and tomatoes combined?

   A. Restaurant A
   B. Restaurant B
   C. Restaurant C
   D. Restaurant D

4. At a certain store, loose-leaf paper comes only in packages of 400 sheets. If a student buys enough paper at this store to fill 3 binders with 150 sheets of paper each, how many sheets will be left over?

   A. 17
   B. 50
   C. 350
   D. 450

5. Three friends are baking cupcakes for a bake sale. Each batch of 24 cupcakes requires 2 cups of flour. The friends have a single 5-pound bag of flour that contains 19 cups of flour. How many whole batches of cupcakes can they bake?

   A. 9
   B. 38
   C. 216
   D. 228

6. A certain health insurance plan costs $3000 per year for a family of six. If each member of the family has $750 in medical expenses in a year, and the plan pays 100% of those expenses, how much will the family save by purchasing the plan?

   A. $1500
   B. $2000
   C. $2500
   D. $3000

Answers and explanations begin on page 206.

NUMBER SENSE AND PROBLEM SOLVING

Distance and Cost

Key Ideas

- The following all indicate multiplication:

  $n \times r \quad nr \quad n(r) \quad n \cdot r$

- The following indicate division:

  $c \div n \quad \dfrac{c}{n}$

- A formula can be rewritten to solve for each of its variables.

  $c = nr \quad \dfrac{c}{n} = r \quad \dfrac{c}{r} = n$

  $d = rt \quad \dfrac{d}{r} = t \quad \dfrac{d}{t} = r$

ON THE GED® TEST

Substitute all of the values for variables back into a formula to check your answer.

Distance

On the *Mathematical Reasoning Test*, you'll see questions that will require you to apply formulas. When a relationship is constant, use a formula to set up the information about how the different parts relate to each other. One of the most commonly tested formulas deals with distance, rate, and time. Distance is a product of the rate at which something travels and the amount of travel time:

$$\text{distance} = \text{rate} \times \text{time, or} \quad d = rt$$

Notice that letters, or variables, can be used to represent the different parts of a formula. A formula allows you to substitute known values for certain variables and solve for the unknown variable.

Example 1: How many miles can you travel if you drive at an average speed of 55 miles per hour for 3 hours?

1. You know the rate (55 miles per hour) and the time (3 hours). Substitute the values in the distance formula.

   $\text{distance} = 55 \times 3$

2. Multiply to find the distance.

   $55 \times 3 = \textbf{165 miles}$

Cost

Another helpful formula is the cost formula. It expresses the relationship between cost, the number of units, and rate (price per unit). **NOTE:** The word *per* means for every one unit. The cost formula can be written as follows:

$$\text{total cost} = (\text{number of units}) \times (\text{price per unit}), \quad \text{or} \quad c = nr$$

Example 2: At a bakery, a package of frosted cookies is priced at $3 per package. If a teacher treats her class by buying 4 packages, how much would the cookies cost before tax?

1. You know the number of units (4 packages) and the price per unit ($3 per package). Substitute the values in the cost formula.

   $c = nr$
   $\text{total cost} = 4 \times \$3$

2. Multiply to find the total cost.

   $4 \times \$3 = \textbf{\$12}$

If you know any two of the three variables in a formula, you can solve for the third variable.

Example 3: Max bought a set of 4 floor mats for $44. How much was the price per floor mat?

1. You know the total cost ($44) and the number of units (4 floor mats). Rewrite the formula to solve for the price per unit (r).

   $c = nr$
   $r = \dfrac{c}{n}$

2. Substitute the known values in the cost formula. Divide to find the price per unit.

   $\dfrac{\$44}{4} = \textbf{\$11}$

PRACTICE 5

A. Each problem below includes two of the three variables from either the distance formula or the cost formula. Write the missing variable you need to solve for. Then decide which of the following formula variations you would use in each situation. The first one is done for you.

$$d = rt \qquad \frac{d}{r} = t \qquad \frac{d}{t} = r \qquad c = nr \qquad \frac{c}{n} = r \qquad \frac{c}{r} = n$$

1. Given: distance and time
   Solve for: rate
   Formula: $\frac{d}{t} = r$

2. Given: rate and time
   Solve for: _____
   Formula: _____

3. Given: distance and rate
   Solve for: _____
   Formula: _____

4. Given: cost and number of units
   Solve for: _____
   Formula: _____

5. Given: number of units and price per unit
   Solve for: _____
   Formula: _____

6. Given: cost and price per unit
   Solve for: _____
   Formula: _____

B. Use the formulas provided in part A above to help you set up the problems. Solve for the unknown variable.

7. Find the total cost of 4 flats of plants at $12 each.

8. Find the total cost of 12 boxes of cookies if each box costs $3.

9. If 4 tires cost $320, how much does a single tire cost?

10. How many tickets would you get for $25 if raffle tickets cost $5 apiece?

11. If you paid $20 for 10 bus transfer tickets, how much did you pay per ticket?

12. Find the distance traveled by a car averaging 60 miles per hour for 3 hours.

13. Find the distance traveled by a train averaging 50 miles per hour for 4 hours.

14. How long does it take for a bus to travel 25 miles at an average rate of 25 miles per hour?

15. If a train travels 270 miles in 3 hours, what is the train's average speed?

16. How long does it take to complete a delivery route of 75 miles at a rate of 25 miles per hour?

C. Choose the <u>one best answer</u> to each question.

17. A company sold a total of $640 in gift boxes. If the gift boxes cost $20 apiece, how many gift boxes did the company sell?
    A. 32
    B. 320
    C. 660
    D. 1280

18. A truck driver traveled 275 miles in 5 hours. What was his average speed in miles per hour?
    A. 1375
    B. 280
    C. 270
    D. 55

Answers and explanations begin on page 206.

NUMBER SENSE AND PROBLEM SOLVING PRACTICE QUESTIONS

Directions: You MAY use your calculator.

1. A beverage container holds 12 servings. If the serving size is 8 ounces, how many ounces does the container hold in all?

   A. 20
   B. 32
   C. 48
   D. 96

2. Sales at 3 concession stands are $839, $527, and $726. What is the total amount in sales?

   A. $1581
   B. $2092
   C. $2178
   D. $2517

3. If you want to cut 24 two-foot braces, how many boards of the length shown below would you need?

   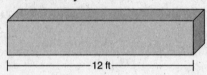
   └─ 12 ft ─┘

   A. 4
   B. 6
   C. 12
   D. 24

4. Using your calculator, find the value of $\sqrt{441}$.

   A. 11
   B. 21
   C. 221
   D. 441

5. Angelo bought a used car with 39,451 miles on it. If the car now has 70,040 miles on it, how many miles has Angelo driven the car?

   A. 30,589
   B. 39,459
   C. 70,040
   D. 109,491

6. Use your calculator to solve this problem. If Emory paid 20% of $3280 as a down payment, how much was the down payment?

   A. $164
   B. $328
   C. $656
   D. $6560

7. Inventory shows that a warehouse has 45 printers in stock. If each printer is valued at $125, what is the total value of the printer inventory?

   A. $5625
   B. $170
   C. $80
   D. $45

8. Lydia can drive 180 miles in 3 hours. On Tuesday, she drove for 7 hours at that rate. How many miles did she drive on Tuesday?

   A. 60
   B. 420
   C. 600
   D. 1260

9. Janelle wants to drive from Danville to Brownsville. If she averages 60 miles per hour, how many hours will it take her to drive the distance?

480 miles

Danville   Brownsville

A.   6
B.   8
C.   60
D. 540

10. A company sold a total of $1440 in gift bears for Valentine's Day. If the gift bears cost $15 apiece, how many gift bears did it sell?

A.   15
B.   96
C.   144
D. 1440

11. In addition to interest charges, Richard's credit card company charges a $25 late fee for payments made after the payment due date. If he was charged a late fee for 8 different monthly bills, how much could he have saved by paying the bills on time?

A. $200
B. $80
C. $33
D. $25

12. A waiter has seven $5 bills and eighteen $1 bills from tips. In all, how much does he have in tips?

A. $18
B. $25
C. $35
D. $53

13. April has taken her car in for the recommended oil and filter change every 3,500 miles. If April bought her car brand-new, and the odometer now shows just over 17,500 miles, how many oil changes has her car received?

A.   5
B.   14
C.   123
D. 1236

14. A clinic treated 536 children over a 4-month period. At this rate, how many children did the clinic treat in 1 month?

A.   134
B.   536
C.   540
D. 2144

15. Attendance at a local play was 438 Friday night, 820 Saturday night, and 636 Sunday afternoon. How many more people attended the play on Sunday than on Friday?

Write your answer on the line below.

_____

16. Raquel has 4 payments left on her car. If each payment is $268, how much does she still owe on her car?

Write your answer on the line below.

_____

17. In what order should items weighing 51 pounds, 40 pounds, 48 pounds, and 44 pounds be stacked if you want them in order from <u>heaviest to lightest</u>?

A. 51, 44, 40, 48
B. 40, 44, 48, 51
C. 51, 48, 44, 40
D. 51, 40, 44, 48

18. Which of the following correctly shows 2,354,769 rounded to the nearest ten thousand?

A. 2,400,000
B. 2,355,000
C. 2,350,000
D. 2,000,000

19. What is the total weight in pounds of the packages below?

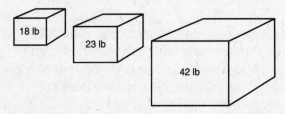

18 lb   23 lb   42 lb

A. 83
B. 65
C. 60
D. 42

20. Jason paid a $14 dinner bill with a $20 bill. How much change should he receive?

A. $6
B. $7
C. $14
D. $34

21. Maria spent 8 minutes installing a new showerhead, 33 minutes rodding out a drain, and 18 minutes fixing a leaking faucet. <u>About</u> how many minutes did it take Maria to complete all three tasks?

A. 90
B. 60
C. 30
D. 20

22. Carla drove 248 miles in 4 hours. What was her average rate of speed, in miles per hour?

Write your answer on the line below.

_____

23. A bulk bag of nuts contains 144 ounces of nuts. If the nuts are packaged in smaller 8-ounce bags, how many bags will there be?

A.   8
B.   12
C.   18
D. 136

24. If you drove 299 miles on 9 gallons of gasoline, <u>about</u> how many miles per gallon did the car get?

A.   10
B.   30
C. 270
D. 300

25. A shipment of 33 crates like the one shown below is delivered. <u>Approximately</u> how many pounds did workers unload?

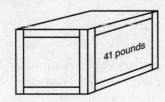

41 pounds

A. 40
B. 120
C. 1200
D. 2000

26. Four friends bought a birthday cake for $21 and balloons for $15. If they divided the cost equally, how much did each friend pay toward the birthday party?

A. $4
B. $5
C. $9
D. $36

27. David paid $20 toward a dinner bill of $128. If the remainder of the bill is divided equally among the remaining 9 people in the group, how much should each person other than David pay?

A. $12
B. $18
D. $20
E. $108

28. A driver traveled 4 hours at an average rate of 65 miles per hour. How many miles did the person drive?

A. 61
B. 69
C. 240
D. 260

29. Using the following information, how much would a large pizza with 3 toppings cost?

| Large 1-Topping Pizza for $14 |
| $2 for Each Additional Topping |

A. $20
B. $18
C. $16
D. $14

30. Bagels are 2 for $1. What is the maximum number of bagels you could buy for $7?

A. 7
B. 10
C. 14
D. 15

31. How many months would it take to save $1800 at $75 per month?

Write your answer on the line below.

_____

32. How many 45-page documents would a binder hold if its maximum capacity is 630 sheets of paper?

Write your answer on the line below.

_____

Answers and explanations begin on page 207.

Decimal Basics

The Decimal System

Decimals are numbers that use place value to show amounts less than 1. You already use decimals when working with money. For example, in the amount $10.25, you know that the digits to the right of the **decimal point** represent cents, or hundredths of a dollar.

The first four decimal place values are labeled on the chart below.

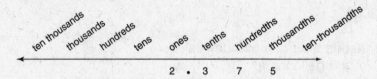

The number 2.375 is shown on the chart. Read *and* in place of the decimal point. After reading the decimal part, say the place value of the last decimal digit. This number would be read "two *and* three hundred seventy-five *thousandths*."

Rounding

Round decimals the same way you round whole numbers.

Example 1: A calculator display reads 3.62835. Round to the hundredths place.

1. Look at the digit to the right of the hundredths place.

    3.62⬚35

2. If the digit to the right is 5 or greater, round up. If the digit is less than 5, don't change the number. Then drop all digits to the right of the place you are rounding to.

    Since 8 is greater than 5, round up. 3.62835 rounds to **3.63.**

Comparing and Ordering

Comparing decimals is similar to comparing whole numbers.

Example 2: Matt ran the 400-meter race in 45.8 seconds. Alonzo ran the same race in 45.66 seconds. Which runner had the faster time?

1. Line up the decimal points. Add a zero at the **end** of 45.8 so that both times have the same number of digits after the decimal.

    45.**8**0
    45.66

2. Compare the decimal parts of the numbers as though they were whole numbers. **Alonzo's time was faster.**

    80 is greater than 66, so 45.8 is greater than 45.66.

Key Ideas

- The decimal point separates the whole number from the decimal part.
- To round decimals, use the same rules as with rounding whole numbers.
- Adding zeros to the right of the last digit after the decimal does not change the number's value.

ON THE GED® TEST

The Mathematical Reasoning Test *may show a zero written before the decimal point. The zero does not change the value of the number. Example: 0.75 = .75*

When you compare more than two numbers, it is helpful to compare one place-value column at a time, working from left to right.

Example 3: Arrange the numbers 0.85, 1.8, 0.8, and 0.819 in order from greatest to least.

1. Write the numbers in a column, lining up the decimal points. Add zeros so that the numbers have the same number of decimal places.

0.850
1.800
0.800
0.819

2. Compare the digits, working from left to right. Only 1.8 has a whole number part, so it is greatest. The remaining numbers each have 8 in the tenths column. Looking at the hundredths column, 0.85 is next, followed by 0.819. The least number is 0.8.

In order: **1.8**
0.85
0.819
0.8

PRACTICE 1

A. Round these numbers as directed.

1. Round 3.75 to the tenths place.
2. Round 5.908 to the ones place.
3. A calculator display reads 0.4285714. Round to the nearest hundredth.
4. Round 0.66667 to the nearest thousandth.
5. Round 8.125 to the nearest tenth.
6. A calculator display reads 2.7142857. Round to the nearest thousandth.

B. In each of the following pairs, which number is greater?

7. 0.45 or 0.449
8. 0.008 or 0.08
9. 4.68 or 4.086
10. 0.75 or 1.85
11. 1.0275 or 1.029
12. 0.14 or 0.104

C. Write these numbers in order from <u>least to greatest</u>.

13. 5.6   5.08   5.8   5.802
14. 0.1136   0.12   0.2   0.115
15. 14.005   4.52   4.8   4.667
16. 0.8023   0.8   0.803   0.823

D. Choose the <u>one best answer</u> to each question.

17. In a circuit board assembly, the weights of three parts are 0.572 grams, 0.0785 grams, and 0.6 grams. Which of the following lists the weights in order from <u>greatest to least</u>?

    A. 0.0785 g, 0.572 g, 0.6 g
    B. 0.6 g, 0.0785 g, 0.572 g
    C. 0.6 g, 0.572 g, 0.0785 g
    D. 0.572 g, 0.6 g, 0.0785 g

18. Which of the following correctly shows 1.3815 rounded to the nearest hundredth?

    A. 1.4
    B. 1.382
    C. 1.381
    D. 1.38

Answers and explanations begin on page 207.

Decimal Operations

Addition and Subtraction

Adding decimals is much like adding whole numbers. The trick is to make sure you have lined up the place-value columns correctly. You can do this by writing the numbers in a column and carefully lining up the decimal points.

Example 1: Add $0.37 + 13.5 + 2.638$.

1. Write the numbers in a column, lining up the decimal points.

2. You may add placeholder zeros so that the decimals have the same number of decimal places.

$$\begin{array}{r} 0.370 \\ 13.500 \\ + \ 2.638 \\ \hline \end{array}$$

3. Add. Start on the right and add each column. Regroup, or carry, as you would with whole numbers.

4. Place the decimal point in the answer directly below the decimal points in the problem.

$$\begin{array}{r} {\scriptstyle 1 \ 1} \\ 0.370 \\ 13.500 \\ + \ 2.638 \\ \hline 16.508 \end{array}$$

To find the difference between decimals, write the numbers in a column with the greater number on top. Make sure the decimal points are in a line.

Example 2: Find the difference between 14.512 and 8.7.

1. Write the numbers in a column, lining up the decimal points. Add placeholder zeros so that the numbers have the same number of decimal places.

$$\begin{array}{r} 14.512 \\ - \ 8.700 \\ \hline \end{array}$$

2. Subtract. Regroup, or borrow, as needed. Place the decimal point in the answer directly in line with the decimal points in the problem.

$$\begin{array}{r} {\scriptstyle 13 \ 15} \\ 1\!\!\!/4.\!\!\!/5 12 \\ - \ 8.700 \\ \hline 5.812 \end{array}$$

The greater number may have fewer or no decimal places. In the next example, a decimal is subtracted from a whole number.

Example 3: What does 9 minus 3.604 equal?

1. Line up the place-value columns. Put a decimal point after the whole number 9 and add placeholder zeros.

$$\begin{array}{r} 9.000 \\ -3.604 \\ \hline \end{array}$$

2. Subtract, regrouping as needed. Place the decimal point in the answer.

$$\begin{array}{r} {\scriptstyle 8 \ 9 \ 9 \ 10} \\ 9.\!\!\!/0\!\!\!/0\!\!\!/0 \\ -3.6\ 0\ 4 \\ \hline 5.3\ 9\ 6 \end{array}$$

Key Ideas

- Always add and subtract like place-value columns.
- Always line up the decimal points when you write a problem in columns.
- When adding or subtracting, place the decimal point in the answer directly below the decimal point in the problem.

GED® TEST TIP

To make sure that your answer makes sense, mentally round the numbers to the nearest whole number and then add or subtract. The result should be close to your answer.

PRACTICE 2.1

A. Solve. You MAY NOT use a calculator.

1. $\begin{array}{r} 4.025 \\ + 3.971 \\ \hline \end{array}$

4. $\begin{array}{r} 8.04 \\ - 2.19 \\ \hline \end{array}$

7. $\begin{array}{r} 17.294 \\ + 0.8 \\ \hline \end{array}$

10. $\begin{array}{r} 3.8 \\ - 2.905 \\ \hline \end{array}$

2. $\begin{array}{r} 6.5 \\ + 4.008 \\ \hline \end{array}$

5. $\begin{array}{r} 8.5 \\ - 1.074 \\ \hline \end{array}$

8. $\begin{array}{r} 4.07 \\ + 1.047 \\ \hline \end{array}$

11. $\begin{array}{r} 14.64 \\ - 10.8 \\ \hline \end{array}$

3. $\begin{array}{r} 2.8 \\ + 9.46 \\ \hline \end{array}$

6. $\begin{array}{r} 10 \\ - 7.89 \\ \hline \end{array}$

9. $\begin{array}{r} 17.52 \\ + 3.8 \\ \hline \end{array}$

12. $\begin{array}{r} 100.5 \\ - 98.15 \\ \hline \end{array}$

13. $0.236 + 2.4 + 2.87 =$

14. $38.06 - 16.9 =$

15. $0.006 + 0.09 + 0.549 =$

16. $8.5 - 6.074 =$

17. $1.02 - 0.87 =$

18. $0.45 + 1.8 + 0.07 + 2.56 =$

19. $12.5 - 0.7 =$

20. $25 - 10.984 =$

21. $0.01 + 2.052 + 0.96 + 1.5 =$

22. $12.9 - 10.54 =$

23. $0.68 + 12.3 + 4.9 =$

24. $32.9 - 15.675 =$

B. Choose the <u>one best answer</u> to each question.

25. James ran 3 miles. His times for the individual miles were 7.2 minutes, 6.8 minutes, and 8.25 minutes. How long did it take him, in minutes, to run the 3-mile distance?

    A. 22.25
    B. 22.7
    C. 23.35
    D. 96.5

26. Claudia earns overtime pay when she works more than 40 hours in one week. How many hours of overtime pay did she work for the week of March 4?

    Work Record for March 4–10

March 4	8.5
March 5	Off
March 6	9.25
March 7	8.75
March 8	10
March 9	Off
March 10	7.75

    A. 44.25
    B. 40.0
    C. 4.25
    D. 2.25

27. A plumber cut two lengths of pipe measuring 2.8 and 1.4 meters from a 6-meter length.

    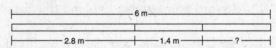

    Assuming there was no waste when the cuts were made, what is the length in meters of the remaining piece?

    A. 1.8
    B. 3.2
    C. 4.2
    D. 7.4

28. Mona purchased the following art supplies: a storage box for $16.98, a set of art markers for $31.78, and a pad of paper for $6.50. What was the cost of the three items?

    A. $48.76
    B. $53.26
    C. $55.26
    D. $61.76

Answers and explanations begin on page 207.

Multiplication and Division

The rules you used to multiply whole numbers can be used to multiply decimals. You don't have to line up the decimal points. You will wait until you are finished multiplying before you place the decimal point in the answer. The number of decimal places in the answer equals the total number of decimal places in the numbers you are multiplying.

Example 4: Find the product of 2.6 and 0.45.

$$\begin{array}{r} 2.6 \\ \times\,.45 \\ \hline \end{array}$$

1. Set up the problem as though you were multiplying the whole numbers 26 and 45.

2. Ignore the decimal points while you multiply.

$$\begin{array}{r} 2.6 \\ \times\,.45 \\ \hline 130 \\ 1\,040 \\ \hline 1.170 \\ \end{array}$$

3. Now count the decimal places in the numbers you multiplied. The number 2.6 has one decimal place, and 0.45 has two decimal places, for a total of three.

4. Starting from the right, count three places to the left and insert the decimal point. Thus, the answer is **1.17**.

When you divide decimals, you must figure out where the decimal point will go in the answer before you divide.

Example 5: Divide 14.4 by 6.

$$\begin{array}{r} 2.4 \\ 6\overline{)14.4} \\ -12 \\ \hline 24 \\ -24 \\ \hline 0 \end{array}$$

1. Set up the problem. Since the divisor (the number you are dividing by) is a whole number, place the decimal point in the answer directly above the decimal point in the dividend (the number you are dividing).

2. Divide. Use the rules you learned for dividing whole numbers. The answer is **2.4**.

If the divisor is a decimal, you must move the decimal points in both the divisor and the dividend before you divide.

Example 6: Divide 4.9 by 0.35.

$$.35\overline{)4.90}$$

1. Set up the problem. There are two decimal places in the divisor. Move the decimal point in *both* the divisor and the dividend two places to the right. Note that you need to add a zero in the dividend in order to move the decimal two places.

$$\begin{array}{r} 14. \\ 35\overline{)490.} \\ -35 \\ \hline 140 \\ -140 \\ \hline 0 \end{array}$$

2. Place the decimal point in the quotient directly above the decimal point in the dividend.

3. Divide. The correct answer is **14**.

Note: You may not need to finish dividing in order to choose the correct answer. You may be able to eliminate all but one of the answer choices after only one or two division steps.

PRACTICE 2.2

A. Solve. You **MAY NOT** use a calculator.

1. 5.3
    $\times 0.5$

2. 64
    $\times 0.2$

3. 12.4
    $\times 0.04$

4. $6\overline{)3.12}$

5. $8\overline{)28.8}$

6. $5\overline{)20.45}$

7. 6.25
    $\times 1.4$

8. 13.5
    $\times 0.25$

9. 9.62
    $\times 1.005$

10. $1.25\overline{)30}$

11. $2.8\overline{)39.76}$

12. $0.003\overline{)47.4}$

13. $15.5 \times 2.2 =$

14. $0.944 \div 0.4 =$

15. $2.05 \times 0.32 =$

16. $1.32 \div 0.5 =$

17. $2.75 \times 0.6 =$

18. $12.825 \div 3 =$

19. $3.36 \times 1.1 =$

20. $15.03 \div 15 =$

21. $0.12 \times 0.06 =$

B. Choose the one best answer to each question.

22. One container of floor cleaner holds 3.79 liters. If Zachary bought 4 containers, how many liters of cleaner did he buy?
    A. 0.9475
    B. 7.79
    C. 12.83
    D. 15.16

23. Ribbon costs $0.45 per foot. A sewing project calls for 20.5 feet of ribbon. To the nearest cent, what will be the cost of the ribbon for the project?
    A. $0.92
    B. $9.23
    C. $9.90
    D. $45.56

24. Armando drove 278.7 miles over a 3-day period. On average, how many miles did he drive each day?
    A. 9.3
    B. 90.3
    C. 92.9
    D. 836.1

Questions 25 and 26 are based on the following information.

Cereal	Net Weight	Servings per Box
Toasted Oats	22.8 oz	19
Crisp Rice	16.9 oz	13
Honey Mix	12.5 oz	10

25. A box of Toasted Oats cereal is priced at $4.94. What is the cost per serving? (*Hint:* Divide the price by the number of servings.)
    A. $0.49
    B. $0.29
    C. $0.26
    D. $0.22

26. Lee bought 4 boxes of Honey Mix cereal. How many ounces of cereal did she buy?
    A. 31.25
    B. 50.0
    C. 67.6
    D. 91.2

Answers and explanations begin on page 207.

DECIMALS AND FRACTIONS

Fraction Basics

A **fraction** uses two numbers to represent part of a whole. The bottom number, called the **denominator**, tells how many equal parts are in the whole group or item. The top number, called the **numerator**, tells how many parts you are working with.

Key Ideas

- The bottom number of a fraction tells how many parts the group or object has.
- The top number tells how many parts you are working with.
- When the top number is greater than the bottom number, the fraction is greater than 1.

There are 4 equal parts in this rectangle. Since 3 are shaded, we say that $\frac{3}{4}$ of the rectangle is shaded.

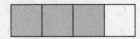

In a proper fraction, the numerator is less than the denominator. A **proper fraction** represents a quantity less than 1. An **improper fraction** is equal to or greater than 1.

There are 6 equal parts in the figure, and 6 are shaded; therefore, $\frac{6}{6}$ of the figure is shaded. $\frac{6}{6} = 1$

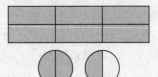

In this grouping, each figure is divided into 2 equal parts. A total of 3 parts are shaded, so $\frac{3}{2}$ are shaded.

A **mixed number** is another way to show an amount greater than 1. It consists of a whole number and a proper fraction. Another name for the shaded portion in the last figure is $1\frac{1}{2}$. The improper fraction $\frac{3}{2}$ equals $1\frac{1}{2}$.

You can also change an improper fraction to a whole or mixed number.

Example 1: Change $\frac{16}{5}$ to a mixed number.

1. Divide the numerator (16) by the denominator (5). Since 16 is not evenly divisible by 5, there is a remainder of 1.

   $16 \div 5 = 3\,r\,1.$

2. The answer becomes the whole number, and the remainder becomes the numerator of the proper fraction. The denominator is the same as the original fraction.

   $\frac{16}{5} = 3\frac{1}{5}$

> **GED® TEST TIP**
>
> *If you have trouble visualizing the fractions in a problem, draw a quick sketch of the information presented in the problem similar to the ones on this page.*

You can also change a mixed number to an improper fraction.

Example 2: Change $7\frac{2}{3}$ to an improper fraction.

1. Multiply the whole number (7) by the denominator of the fraction (3), and add the numerator (2).

   $7 \times 3 = 21$
   $21 + 2 = 23$

2. Write the sum over the denominator of the original fraction.

   $7\frac{2}{3} = \frac{23}{3}$

To perform operations with fractions, you need to be able to write equal fractions in higher or lower terms. The **terms** are the numerator and the denominator. A fraction is **reduced to lowest terms** when the two terms do not have any common factor except 1.

To **raise** a fraction, multiply both terms by the same number: $\frac{3}{4} = \frac{3 \times 3}{4 \times 3} = \frac{9}{12}$.

To **reduce** a fraction, divide both terms by the same number: $\frac{10}{15} = \frac{10 \div 5}{15 \div 5} = \frac{2}{3}$.

PRACTICE 3

A. Write a proper fraction for the shaded portion of each figure.

1. 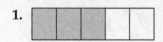   **2.**   **3.**

B. Write an improper fraction and a mixed number for the shaded portion of each figure.

4.   **5.**   **6.**

C. Write improper fractions as mixed numbers and mixed numbers as improper fractions.

7. $\frac{17}{3} =$ **9.** $\frac{24}{6} =$ **11.** $\frac{19}{4} =$ **13.** $\frac{43}{9} =$ **15.** $\frac{33}{4} =$

8. $3\frac{3}{5} =$ **10.** $5\frac{2}{9} =$ **12.** $2\frac{5}{12} =$ **14.** $1\frac{3}{4} =$ **16.** $5\frac{7}{10} =$

D. Write an equal fraction with the given denominator.

17. $\frac{3}{4} = \frac{}{16}$ **18.** $\frac{1}{3} = \frac{}{21}$ **19.** $\frac{4}{5} = \frac{}{60}$ **20.** $\frac{3}{8} = \frac{}{40}$ **21.** $\frac{6}{25} = \frac{}{100}$

(*Hint for question 17:* $4 \times ? = 16$)

E. Reduce each fraction to lowest terms.

22. $\frac{21}{28} =$ **23.** $\frac{4}{24} =$ **24.** $\frac{12}{20} =$ **25.** $\frac{26}{30} =$ **26.** $\frac{60}{90} =$

F. Choose the <u>one best answer</u> to each question.

27. Eighteen out of every 24 people surveyed say they went to at least one movie in December. What fraction of the people surveyed went to a movie in December?

A. $\frac{3}{4}$

B. $\frac{2}{3}$

C. $\frac{1}{3}$

D. $\frac{1}{4}$

28. Which of the following fractions equals $\frac{2}{5}$?

A. $\frac{15}{100}$

B. $\frac{30}{100}$

C. $\frac{40}{100}$

D. $\frac{80}{100}$

Answers and explanations begin on page 208.

DECIMALS AND FRACTIONS

Fraction Operations

Addition and Subtraction

You can add or subtract **like fractions.** Like fractions have a **common denominator.** In other words, their denominators are the same.

Example 1: Add $\frac{3}{10} + \frac{5}{10}$.

1. Since the denominators are the same, add the numerators.

$$\frac{3}{10} + \frac{5}{10} = \frac{8}{10}$$

2. Reduce the answer to lowest terms.

$$\frac{8}{10} = \frac{8 \div 2}{10 \div 2} = \frac{4}{5}$$

Example 2: Subtract $\frac{2}{9}$ from $\frac{7}{9}$.

Subtract the numerators. The answer is already in lowest terms.

$$\frac{7}{9} - \frac{2}{9} = \frac{5}{9}$$

If the denominators are not the same, raise one or both fractions to higher terms so that they become like fractions.

Example 3: Add $\frac{5}{6} + \frac{1}{4}$.

1. One way to find a common denominator is to think of the multiples of both denominators. The lowest is 12.

Multiples
of 6: 6, [12], 18
of 4: 4, 8, [12], 16

2. Raise each fraction to higher terms with a denominator of 12.

$$\frac{5 \times 2}{6 \times 2} = \frac{10}{12}, \frac{1 \times 3}{4 \times 3} = \frac{3}{12}$$

3. Add the like fractions. Rewrite the sum as a mixed number.

$$\frac{10}{12} + \frac{3}{12} = \frac{13}{12} = 1\frac{1}{12}$$

Use the same process to add or subtract mixed numbers. Example 4 shows how to regroup when subtracting mixed numbers.

Example 4: Subtract $4\frac{1}{16} - 1\frac{3}{8}$.

1. Raise the second fraction so that it also has a denominator of 16.

$$\frac{3 \times 2}{8 \times 2} = \frac{6}{16}$$

2. Set up the problem. To subtract the fractions, you need to regroup 1 from the whole number column and add it to the top fraction.

$$4\frac{1}{16} = 3\frac{16}{16} + \frac{1}{16} = 3\frac{17}{16}$$

3. Subtract the fractions and then the whole numbers.

$$3\frac{17}{16} - 1\frac{6}{16} = 2\frac{11}{16}$$

Key Ideas

- You can add or subtract fractions, but they must have the same denominator.
- If denominators are not the same, find a common denominator and raise one or both fractions.
- Always reduce answers to lowest terms and change improper fractions to mixed numbers.

GED® TEST TIP

If your solution to a fraction problem is not one of the given answer choices, make sure that you reduced your answer to lowest terms. On the Mathematical Reasoning Test, *answer choices are always written in lowest terms.*

PRACTICE 4.1

A. Solve. Reduce answers to lowest terms. Simplify improper fractions as mixed numbers.

1. $\begin{array}{r} \frac{3}{8} \\ +\frac{1}{8} \\ \hline \end{array}$

3. $\begin{array}{r} \frac{8}{9} \\ -\frac{5}{9} \\ \hline \end{array}$

5. $\begin{array}{r} \frac{1}{4} \\ +\frac{2}{3} \\ \hline \end{array}$

7. $\begin{array}{r} \frac{9}{10} \\ -\frac{3}{5} \\ \hline \end{array}$

9. $\begin{array}{r} 2\frac{1}{5} \\ +1\frac{2}{3} \\ \hline \end{array}$

2. $\begin{array}{r} \frac{1}{6} \\ +\frac{5}{6} \\ \hline \end{array}$

4. $\begin{array}{r} \frac{7}{12} \\ -\frac{5}{12} \\ \hline \end{array}$

6. $\begin{array}{r} \frac{1}{2} \\ +\frac{5}{8} \\ \hline \end{array}$

8. $\begin{array}{r} \frac{7}{9} \\ -\frac{1}{2} \\ \hline \end{array}$

10. $\begin{array}{r} 4\frac{1}{2} \\ -2\frac{3}{4} \\ \hline \end{array}$

11. $5\frac{5}{6} + 2\frac{2}{3} =$ 16. $\frac{3}{8} + \frac{7}{12} + 1\frac{2}{3} =$ 21. $14\frac{1}{4} - 10\frac{3}{7} =$

12. $6\frac{7}{8} + 4\frac{3}{4} =$ 17. $16\frac{2}{3} + 25\frac{3}{4} =$ 22. $9\frac{11}{12} - 8\frac{5}{8} =$

13. $12\frac{1}{10} + 9\frac{3}{5} =$ 18. $10\frac{1}{2} + 8\frac{4}{5} + 3\frac{1}{4} =$ 23. $6 - 3\frac{4}{7} =$

14. $2\frac{2}{9} + \frac{2}{3} + 4\frac{5}{6} =$ 19. $8\frac{1}{2} - 3\frac{4}{9} =$ 24. $13\frac{1}{3} - 4\frac{4}{9} =$

15. $3\frac{1}{3} + 5\frac{2}{3} + 3\frac{5}{6} =$ 20. $15 - 3\frac{7}{8} =$ 25. $5\frac{5}{7} - 4\frac{4}{5} =$

B. Choose the one best answer to each question.

26. To make the top of a dining room table, Craig glues a piece of oak that is $\frac{5}{16}$ inch thick to a piece of pine that is $\frac{7}{8}$ inch thick. What is the total thickness, in inches, of the tabletop?

   A. $\frac{9}{16}$

   B. $1\frac{3}{16}$

   C. $1\frac{1}{4}$

   D. $1\frac{9}{16}$

27. Carol will use the two bolts shown below to assemble a book cart. How much longer, in inches, is bolt A than bolt B?

A $2\frac{7}{8}$ in

B $1\frac{1}{4}$ in

   A. $\frac{5}{8}$

   B. $1\frac{3}{8}$

   C. $1\frac{5}{8}$

   D. $1\frac{3}{4}$

28. At a fabric store, Melissa sold $8\frac{7}{8}$ yards of cloth to a customer. If the material was cut from a bolt of fabric containing $23\frac{1}{4}$ yards, how many yards are left on the bolt?

   A. $14\frac{3}{8}$

   B. $15\frac{3}{8}$

   C. $15\frac{3}{4}$

   D. $31\frac{7}{8}$

29. A batch of salad dressing requires $1\frac{2}{3}$ cups of olive oil, $\frac{1}{2}$ cup of vinegar, and $\frac{3}{4}$ cup of water. How many cups of salad dressing will this recipe produce?

   A. $1\frac{2}{3}$

   B. $2\frac{5}{6}$

   C. $2\frac{11}{12}$

   D. $3\frac{7}{12}$

Answers and explanations begin on page 208.

Multiplication and Division

It isn't necessary to find a common denominator to multiply and divide fractions. To multiply fractions, simply multiply the numerators and then the denominators. Reduce the answer, if necessary.

Example 5: What is the product of $\frac{7}{8}$ and $\frac{1}{2}$?

Multiply the numerators together and then the denominators. The answer is in lowest terms.

$$\frac{7}{8} \times \frac{1}{2} = \frac{7 \times 1}{8 \times 2} = \frac{7}{16}$$

Before multiplying a mixed number, change it to an improper fraction.

Example 6: What is $\frac{1}{3}$ of $3\frac{3}{4}$?

1. Change $3\frac{3}{4}$ to an improper fraction.

$$3\frac{3}{4} = \frac{15}{4}$$

2. Multiply the numerators and the denominators.

$$\frac{15}{4} \times \frac{1}{3} = \frac{15 \times 1}{4 \times 3} = \frac{15}{12}$$

3. Change to a mixed number and reduce to lowest terms.

$$\frac{15}{12} = 1\frac{3}{12} = \mathbf{1\frac{1}{4}}$$

You can use a shortcut called **canceling** to reduce the fractions as you work the problem. To cancel, divide both a numerator and a denominator by the same number. The numerator and the denominator can be in different fractions.

Example 7: Multiply $1\frac{1}{2}$ by $1\frac{1}{5}$.

1. Change to improper fractions.

$$1\frac{1}{2} = \frac{3}{2} \text{ and } 1\frac{1}{5} = \frac{6}{5}$$

2. Set up the multiplication problem. Both 6 (a numerator) and 2 (a denominator) are evenly divisible by 2. Divide them by 2. Then multiply using the new numerator and denominator. Finally, change the improper fraction to a mixed number.

$$\frac{3}{2} \times \frac{6}{5} = \frac{3}{\cancel{2}} \times \frac{\cancel{6}^{3}}{5} = \frac{9}{5} = \mathbf{1\frac{4}{5}}$$

The slash marks show that the numbers have been divided.

You will need two additional steps to divide fractions. Before dividing, **invert** the divisor (the fraction you are dividing by). To invert the fraction, switch the numerator and the denominator. Finally, change the division symbol to a multiplication symbol and multiply.

Example 8: Jim has an 8-pound bag of nuts. He wants to fill smaller $\frac{1}{2}$-pound bags using the nuts. How many small bags can he make?

1. Divide 8 by $\frac{1}{2}$. Set up the division problem. Always write whole or mixed numbers as improper fractions.

$$8 \div \frac{1}{2} = \frac{8}{1} \div \frac{1}{2} =$$

2. Invert the fraction you are dividing by. Then change the operation sign to multiplication. Multiply, following the rules for multiplying fractions. Jim can make **16 small bags.**

$$\frac{8}{1} \times \frac{2}{1} = \frac{16}{1} = \mathbf{16}$$

NOTE: When you multiply by a fraction less than 1, the answer is smaller than the number you started with because you are finding a "part of." When you divide by a fraction less than 1, the answer is greater than the number.

PRACTICE 4.2

A. Solve. Reduce answers to lowest terms. Simplify improper fractions as mixed numbers.

1. $\frac{2}{3} \times \frac{1}{4} =$

2. $1\frac{5}{6} \times \frac{1}{2} =$

3. $\frac{2}{3} \times 21 =$

4. $50 \times \frac{3}{8} =$

5. $3\frac{1}{2} \times \frac{1}{4} =$

6. $\frac{3}{4} \times \frac{7}{8} =$

7. $2\frac{1}{3} \times 3\frac{2}{5} =$

8. $15 \times 2\frac{3}{4} =$

9. $\frac{5}{8} \times 3\frac{1}{4} =$

10. $\frac{7}{8} \div \frac{1}{16} =$

11. $\frac{4}{5} \div \frac{2}{5} =$

12. $12 \div \frac{1}{4} =$

13. $6 \div 2\frac{1}{2} =$

14. $3\frac{3}{4} \div 1\frac{2}{3} =$

15. $9 \div \frac{1}{3} =$

16. $26\frac{2}{3} \div 3\frac{1}{3} =$

17. $40\frac{3}{8} \div 4\frac{1}{4} =$

18. $3\frac{7}{8} \div 5\frac{1}{6} =$

B. Choose the _one best answer_ to each question.

19. A city is considering raising taxes to build a football stadium. A survey of registered voters yielded the following results:

Position	Fraction of Those Surveyed
Against Tax Hike	$\frac{7}{16}$
For Tax Hike	$\frac{3}{16}$
Undecided	$\frac{3}{8}$

If 400 people were surveyed, how many support the tax hike?

A. 48
B. 75
C. 150
D. 175

20. A tailor has 20 yards of shirt fabric. How many shirts can she <u>complete</u> if each shirt requires $2\frac{3}{4}$ yards of fabric?

A. 6
B. 7
C. 8
D. 10

21. An insurance agent estimates that it takes $\frac{2}{3}$ hour to process a customer's claim. If the agent spends 22 hours per week processing claims, about how many claims does he process in a week?

A. $14\frac{2}{3}$
B. 33
C. 44
D. 66

22. A fluorescent lighting panel is $12\frac{5}{8}$ inches wide. If three of the panels are installed as shown below, what will be the width in inches of the combined panels?

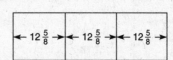

A. $13\frac{7}{8}$
B. $36\frac{5}{8}$
C. $37\frac{7}{8}$
D. $42\frac{7}{8}$

Answers and explanations begin on page 208.

DECIMALS AND FRACTIONS

Fraction and Decimal Equivalencies

Key Ideas

- To change a fraction to a decimal, divide the numerator by the denominator.
- To change a decimal to a fraction, write the number without the decimal point over the place value of the last decimal digit. Reduce.
- Avoid time-consuming calculations by using fraction-decimal equivalents.

Fractions and decimals are two ways to show part of a whole. You can change fractions to decimals by dividing.

Example 1: Change $\frac{3}{8}$ to a decimal.

The fraction $\frac{3}{8}$ means $3 \div 8$. Use a calculator to divide. $3 \div 8 = \mathbf{0.375}$

You can also change a decimal to a fraction.

Example 2: Change 0.35 to a fraction.

Write the decimal number over the place value name of the last decimal digit on the right. The last digit, 5, is in the hundredths column. Reduce to lowest terms. $\dfrac{35}{100} = \dfrac{35 \div 5}{100 \div 5} = \dfrac{7}{20}$

You will find it useful to memorize the most common fraction and decimal equivalents. These equivalents will also help you solve percent problems.

Decimal	Fraction	Decimal	Fraction	Decimal	Fraction
0.1	$\frac{1}{10}$	0.375	$\frac{3}{8}$	0.7	$\frac{7}{10}$
0.125	$\frac{1}{8}$	0.4	$\frac{2}{5}$	0.75	$\frac{3}{4}$
0.2	$\frac{1}{5}$	0.5	$\frac{1}{2}$	0.8	$\frac{4}{5}$
0.25	$\frac{1}{4}$	0.6	$\frac{3}{5}$	0.875	$\frac{7}{8}$
0.3	$\frac{3}{10}$	0.625	$\frac{5}{8}$	0.9	$\frac{9}{10}$
$0.33\overline{3}$	$\frac{1}{3}$	$0.66\overline{6}$	$\frac{2}{3}$		

GED® TEST TIP

Look at the answer choices before you begin working a multiple-choice problem. Knowing whether you need an answer in fraction or decimal form may affect how you approach the problem.

The decimal equivalents for $\frac{1}{3}$ and $\frac{2}{3}$ are marked with a bar. The bar shows that the decimal repeats indefinitely.

You can use fraction and decimal equivalents to save time when solving math problems.

Example 3: Each dose of cough medicine contains 0.25 ounce of medication. How many ounces of medication are in 48 doses?

To solve the problem, you need to multiply 48 by 0.25, a time-consuming calculation. However, since $0.25 = \frac{1}{4}$, you can find $\frac{1}{4}$ of 48 to solve the problem. The answer is **12 ounces**. $48 \times \frac{1}{4} = \frac{48}{4} = \mathbf{12}$

Knowing fraction-decimal equivalents can also help you interpret remainders when using a calculator.

Example 4: Ray inspects machine assemblies. He must inspect 12 assemblies during his 40-hour workweek. On average, how many hours can he spend on each inspection?

Using a calculator, divide 40 by 12: 40 $\div$ 12 enter. The right side of the display reads 3.333333333.

Since you know that $0.33\overline{3} = \frac{1}{3}$, the answer is $3\frac{1}{3}$ **hours.**

PRACTICE 5

Solve. When possible, use fraction and decimal equivalents to make the work easier. You MAY use a calculator on questions 5 and 6.

1. During a 25%-off sale, store clerks find the amount of the discounts by multiplying the regular price by 0.25. What is the discount on an item with a regular price of $80?
   A. $32.00
   B. $20.00
   C. $16.40
   D. $2.00

2. At Linton Products, $\frac{3}{10}$ of the workers are in the company's ride-share program. If there are 480 workers, which of the following expressions could be used to find the number in the ride-share program?
   A. 480×0.7
   B. $480 \div 0.7$
   C. 480×0.3
   D. $480 \div 0.3$

3. Sharon is using a calculator to find out how many hours she has spent on a certain job. She divides, and her display reads:

   [4.666666666]

   Assuming her calculations are correct, how many hours did she spend on the job?
   A. $4\frac{1}{6}$
   B. $4\frac{2}{3}$
   C. $4\frac{6}{7}$
   D. 46

4. A gourmet candy company charges the following prices per pound.

Jelly Beans	$9.60
Peanut Brittle	$12.00
Almond Toffee	$28.50

   How much would a customer pay for 1.5 pounds of peanut brittle?
   A. $6.00
   B. $14.40
   C. $18.00
   D. $42.75

5. At 1 p.m., the amount of rain in a rain gauge is 1.125 inches. At 3 p.m., the gauge holds 1.875 inches. What fraction of an inch of rain fell between 1 p.m. and 3 p.m.?
   A. $\frac{7}{8}$
   B. $\frac{3}{4}$
   C. $\frac{7}{10}$
   D. $\frac{1}{8}$

6. A steel rod, 3 meters in length, is cut into 8 equal pieces. What is the length in meters of each piece?
   A. 0.125
   B. 0.333
   C. 0.375
   D. 2.333

Answers and explanations begin on page 208.

DECIMALS AND FRACTIONS

Decimals and Fractions on the Number Line

Key Ideas

- A number line is a picture that helps you compare the sizes of numbers. Numbers on the left are smaller than numbers on the right.
- Number lines can also be used to represent and compare decimals.
- Fractions and mixed fractions can also be represented on a number line.

On the GED® *Mathematical Reasoning Test* you may need to recognize or locate fractions, mixed fractions, or decimals on a **number line**. A number line represents numbers in order from least to greatest. As you move to the left along a number line, numbers decrease in value. As you move to the right, numbers increase in value.

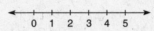

The arrows on the ends indicate that numbers continue forever in both directions. If you imagine zooming in on a portion of that number line, it might look like this:

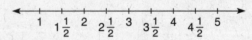

Thus, a number line can include decimals and whole numbers. For example, the point represents 0.75, which is greater than 0.5 and less than 1.

A number line can also represent fractions and mixed fractions in order from least to greatest:

$$\xleftarrow{\quad} 0 \quad \frac{1}{4} \quad \frac{1}{2} \quad \frac{3}{4} \quad 1 \quad 1\frac{1}{4} \quad 1\frac{1}{2} \xrightarrow{\quad}$$

Use this question to practice working with number lines:

Example 1: John works five shifts per week. His boss asks him to spend exactly half of his time this week working on a specific project. How many work shifts will John devote to that project? Circle the answer on the number line below.

$$\xleftarrow{\quad} 1 \quad 1\frac{1}{2} \quad 2 \quad 2\frac{1}{2} \quad 3 \quad 3\frac{1}{2} \quad 4 \quad 4\frac{1}{2} \quad 5 \xrightarrow{\quad}$$

If you circled $2\frac{1}{2}$, you are correct. Multiply 5 by $\frac{1}{2}$ to determine that John will spend $2\frac{1}{2}$ shifts on the project.

PRACTICE 6

A. Choose the <u>one best answer</u> to each question.

1. What is the value of the point on the number line below?

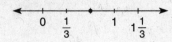

   A. 0
   B. $\frac{1}{2}$
   C. $\frac{2}{3}$
   D. $1\frac{1}{3}$

2. What is the value of the point on the number line below?

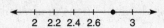

   A. 2
   B. 2.5
   C. 2.7
   D. 2.8

3. In the number line below, what is the value of *A* minus *B*?

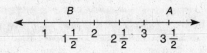

   A. 1
   B. $1\frac{1}{2}$
   C. 2
   D. $3\frac{1}{2}$

4. Angela baked 24 cookies and gave 16 of them to her neighbor. On the number line below, circle the fraction of Angela's cookies that she gave to her neighbor.

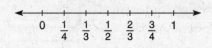

B. Write the decimal values of the points on the number lines.

For each of the number lines below, fill in the value of the point using decimals.

5.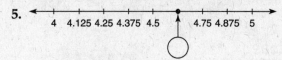

6.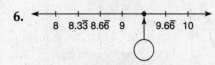

C. Write the fraction values of the points on the number lines.

For each of the number lines below, fill in the value of the point using mixed fractions.

7.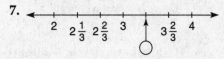

8.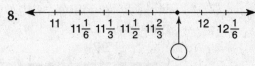

Answers and explanations begin on page 208.

DECIMALS AND FRACTIONS

Decimal and Fraction Calculator Skills

Several important calculator keys are used to work with decimals and fractions.

Cursor keys move the cursor on the screen up, down, left, and right.

The **fraction key** is used to enter fractions; the **mixed number 2nd function** is in green above it.

The **toggle key** changes between equivalent fraction and decimal forms of a number.

The **decimal point** key enters a decimal point.

Key Ideas

- Fraction and decimal operations are entered in the same order as whole-number operations.
- On the TI-30XS MultiView™ calculator, use the decimal point key (.) for decimals and the fraction key, $\frac{n}{d}$, for fractions.
- To work with mixed fractions, use the 2nd function, $U\frac{n}{d}$, which is in green over the fraction key.

Calculator **decimal operations** are performed in the same way that you use operations with whole numbers. You need to use the **decimal point key** ⊙ under the 2 in the white **numeric keypad**. Practice with these examples:

To solve this problem...	Press these keys...	The right-hand side of the display reads...
3.89 + 2.5	3.89 (+) 2.5 (enter)	6.39
5.2 − 0.78	5.2 (−) .78 (enter)	4.42
0.9 × 15	.9 (×) 15 (enter)	13.5
1.7 ÷ 2	1.7 (÷) 2 (enter)	0.85

You will use several calculator functions to work with **fractions** and **mixed fraction operations**. First practice entering fractions and converting to decimals.

Example 1: Reduce $\frac{56}{448}$ to lowest terms and then convert to a decimal.

1. Clear the calculator.
2. Press the $\frac{n}{d}$ button to enter a fraction. Enter 56 at the blinking cursor, in the numerator.
3. Use the down cursor key ▼ to enter 448 in the denominator.
4. Press (enter) to reduce the fraction to lowest terms, which appears on the right of your screen: $\frac{1}{8}$
5. To express the fraction as a decimal, press the *toggle* button: (◄►). The decimal **0.125** appears on the right display.

On the Display

Now practice operations with **mixed fractions** using the *2nd function* key.

Example 2: A plastic pipe is to be cut into pieces measuring $1\frac{7}{8}$ feet. The original pipe was $20\frac{5}{8}$ feet long. How many pieces can be cut from the pipe?

	Keys to Press	**On the Display**
1. Clear the calculator	(clear)	
2. Recognize that a mixed fraction is a green *2nd* function: $\boxed{\cup\frac{n}{d}}$ over the $\boxed{\frac{n}{d}}$ key. Press the (2nd) key and the $\boxed{\frac{n}{d}}$ key. Note both a whole number and a blinking fraction cursor on the display.	(2nd) $\boxed{\frac{n}{d}}$	$\boxed{\blacksquare \vdots}$
3. Enter the number being divided first–the whole pipe: $20\frac{5}{8}$. Enter 20, then follow the direction of the onscreen arrow and press the right arrow button to move to the fraction cursors. Enter 5 and then use the down arrow to enter the 8. Exit the fraction by pressing the right arrow again.	20 ▶ 5 ▼ 8 ▶	$20\frac{5}{8}$
4. Press the division key. Then follow the same process with the second number: $1\frac{7}{8}$, starting with the 2nd function: $\boxed{\cup\frac{n}{d}}$	÷ (2nd) $\boxed{\frac{n}{d}}$ 1 ▶ 7 ▼ 8 ▶	$20\frac{5}{8} \div 1\frac{7}{8}$
5. Press the (enter) button for the solution. The answer 11 for **11 pieces** appears on the right side of the screen.	(enter)	$20\frac{5}{8} \div 1\frac{7}{8}$ 11

PRACTICE 7

A. Solve the following problems using your calculator.

1. $3.5 + 1.87 + 2.009$ 2. $3\frac{2}{3} - 1\frac{5}{12}$ 3. $\$25.35 \times 15$ 4. $10\frac{1}{2} \div \frac{1}{4}$

5. Linda earns $95 per day. If she works $\frac{8}{9}$ of a day, how much will she earn?

6. Aaron bought a refrigerator for $956.88. The price includes tax and interest charges. If he makes 12 equal monthly payments, how much will he pay each month?

7. An insurance agent estimates the annual cost of insurance on a home by multiplying the sale price of the home by 0.0125. What will be the yearly cost of insurance on a home priced at $118,000?

8. In a recipe, the total liquid added to a mixture is $1\frac{1}{2}$ cups of water and $2\frac{3}{4}$ cups of chicken broth. How many cups of liquid are used in the recipe?

9. A quilt costs $84.99 and weighs 5.56 pounds. The shipping charge is $1.20 per pound. To the nearest cent, what would be the shipping charge on the quilt?

   A. $5.56
   B. $6.67
   C. $8.26
   D. $10.20

10. A state park contains 64 acres. A wildlife preserve makes up $\frac{3}{8}$ of the park. How many acres are in the preserve?

    A. 8
    B. 21
    C. 24
    D. 27

Answers and explanations begin on page 209.

DECIMALS AND FRACTIONS PRACTICE QUESTIONS

Directions: You MAY use your calculator.

1. A wooden flooring strip is $20\frac{1}{2}$ inches long. If you cut off $4\frac{3}{4}$ inches from one end, what will be the new length of the strip in inches?

   A. $16\frac{3}{4}$

   B. $16\frac{1}{4}$

   C. $15\frac{3}{4}$

   D. $15\frac{1}{4}$

2. A box of cereal costs $4.69. The package label says that the box contains 19 servings. What is the cost of 1 serving to the nearest cent?

   A. $0.02
   B. $0.25
   C. $0.47
   D. $2.46

3. How much would a computer system cost if it is priced as shown below?

Pay $200 down and make 12 monthly payments of only $98.85.

   A. $3586.20
   B. $2400.00
   C. $1386.20
   D. $1186.20

4. Unleaded gasoline sells for $2.869 per gallon. How much would $10\frac{1}{2}$ gallons cost? Round your answer to the nearest cent.

   A. $13.40
   B. $28.69
   C. $30.12
   D. $301.20

5. Three packages weigh $1\frac{1}{2}$ pounds, $4\frac{3}{4}$ pounds, and $2\frac{3}{10}$ pounds. What is the average weight, in pounds, of the packages? (*Hint:* Add the weights, then divide by the number of packages.)

   A. 2.14
   B. 2.85
   C. 4.75
   D. 8.55

6. Gina is paid $8 an hour. If she earned $258 in 1 week, how many hours did she work?

   A. $34\frac{1}{2}$

   B. $32\frac{1}{3}$

   C. $32\frac{1}{4}$

   D. $32\frac{1}{5}$

7. A developer plans to build homes on $20\frac{1}{2}$ acres. She estimates that $6\frac{1}{4}$ acres will be used for roads. The remaining land will be divided into $\frac{1}{4}$-acre lots. How many lots can the subdivision include?

   A. 7
   B. 57
   C. 81
   D. 107

8. A school buys 1000 white-board markers. Below is the price per marker for two brands. How much did the school save by buying Brand A instead of Brand B?

   Brand A: $0.27 each
   Brand B: $0.36 each

   A. $0.09
   B. $0.90
   C. $9.00
   D. $90.00

Madison Small Animal Clinic Scheduling Guidelines	
New-Patient Appointment	$\frac{3}{4}$ hr
Immunizations	$\frac{1}{4}$ hr
Routine Physical	$\frac{1}{3}$ hr
Dental Scaling	$\frac{3}{4}$ hr
Sick Animal Visit	$\frac{1}{2}$ hr
Serious-Injury Visit (includes X-rays)	$1\frac{1}{4}$ hr

9. Ray is a veterinarian at the small-animal clinic. He has four appointments scheduled for Monday morning: two new-patient appointments, a serious-injury visit, and a dental scaling. In hours, how much time should these appointments take?

    A. $2\frac{3}{4}$
    B. $3\frac{1}{2}$
    C. $3\frac{3}{4}$
    D. 4

10. Jennifer works $3\frac{1}{2}$ hours each morning at the clinic. How many routine physicals could she complete in one morning?

    A. 4
    B. 9
    C. 10
    D. 11

11. A minor-league baseball stadium has 6000 seats. On Beach Towel Night, the stadium sold 5500 of its available seats. What fraction of the seats were sold?

    A. $\frac{5}{6}$
    B. $\frac{8}{9}$
    C. $\frac{9}{10}$
    D. $\frac{11}{12}$

12. The City Center parking garage charges $3.50 for the first hour and $1.25 for each additional $\frac{1}{2}$ hour. How much would it cost to park at the garage for $2\frac{1}{2}$ hours?

    A. $4.75
    B. $6.25
    C. $7.25
    D. $9.75

13. Susan scheduled 84 appointments for patients at a hospital outreach clinic. Only 56 patients kept their appointments. What fraction of the scheduled appointments were kept?

    Write your answer on the line below.

    _____

14. This portion of a gas bill compares a household's natural gas usage for December of this year and last year.

Gas Bill Comparison Average Daily Usage			
This Year		Last Year	
Dec	3.13 therms	Dec	3.97 therms

How many more therms of natural gas did the household use in December of last year than December of this year? Express your answer as a decimal.

Write your answer on the line below.

_____

15. Jim and Carl have until 1 p.m. to load 250 boxes. By 12:30 p.m., 175 of the boxes are loaded. What fraction of the boxes has <u>not</u> been loaded?

    A. $\frac{1}{5}$

    B. $\frac{3}{10}$

    C. $\frac{3}{5}$

    D. $\frac{7}{10}$

16. On the number line below, what is the value of *A* minus *B*?

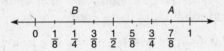

    A. $\frac{1}{4}$

    B. $\frac{5}{8}$

    C. $\frac{7}{8}$

    D. $1\frac{1}{8}$

17. Scott is driving about 380 miles from Los Angeles to San Francisco. He plans to cover $\frac{3}{4}$ of the distance before noon. How many miles does he plan to drive before noon?

    A. 285
    B. 254
    C. 126
    D. 95

18. A cookie recipe calls for $1\frac{2}{3}$ cups of sugar. If you wanted to make half the quantity shown in the recipe, how many cups of sugar would you use?

    A. $\frac{2}{5}$

    B. $\frac{2}{3}$

    C. $\frac{5}{6}$

    D. $1\frac{1}{6}$

Question 19 is based on the following information.

Carbide Steel Drill Bits		
Description	**Size (inches)**	**Price**
Cutter	$\frac{9}{16}$	$6.19
Core Box	$\frac{5}{32}$	$16.40
Classic	$\frac{3}{8}$	$17.85
Bevel	$\frac{1}{2}$	$10.50

19. Which of the following shows the drill bits arranged in order from least to greatest in size?

    A. cutter, bevel, classic, core box
    B. core box, bevel, classic, cutter
    C. bevel, classic, cutter, core box
    D. core box, classic, bevel, cutter

20. Joe is going to order a pizza. He will eat at least $\frac{1}{2}$ of it. If he's very hungry, he might eat as much as $\frac{7}{8}$ of it. Place two points on the number line below to represent the minimum fraction of the pizza Joe might have left over and the maximum fraction of the pizza Joe might have left over.

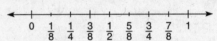

21. A project should take no more than 60 hours. If John can spare 7.5 hours per day to work on the project, what is the maximum number of days it will take him to finish?

    A. 6
    B. 7
    C. 8
    D. 9

22. How many miles would a map distance of $\frac{5}{8}$ inch represent if 1in. = 240 mi?

    A.   40
    B. 130
    C. 150
    D. 200

23. A survey shows that $\frac{2}{3}$ of all homeowners have a pet. Of those, $\frac{3}{4}$ have either a dog or cat. Of the homeowners surveyed, what fraction has either a dog or a cat?

   A. $\frac{1}{2}$

   B. $\frac{3}{4}$

   C. $\frac{5}{7}$

   D. $\frac{6}{7}$

24. At Wyman Shipping, 140 employees work during the day shift. At night, the crew is $\frac{2}{5}$ the size of the day shift. How many workers are scheduled to work the night shift?

   A. 28
   B. 56
   C. 70
   D. 94

Question 25 refers to the following map.

The map below shows the distance, in miles, between four stores.

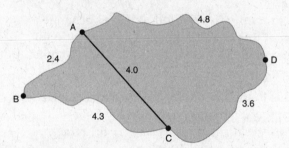

25. Maya drives a van that delivers supplies to each of the stores. On Friday, she traveled the following route.

   Store A to Store B
   Store B to Store C
   Store C to Store D
   Store D to Store C
   Store C to Store A

   How many miles did she drive in all?

   A. 13.9
   B. 15.1
   C. 17.9
   D. 19.1

26. From a wooden dowel $12\frac{1}{2}$ feet long, Jamie cut two pieces, each $3\frac{3}{4}$ feet long. How long, in feet, is the remaining piece?

   A. $8\frac{3}{4}$

   B. $7\frac{1}{2}$

   C. $6\frac{1}{2}$

   D. 5

27. Luis bought 20 shares of stock, priced at $26.38 per share. He also paid an $8 transaction fee. How much did he pay?

   A. $687.60
   B. $535.60
   C. $527.60
   D. $519.60

28. A mat board is 60 inches wide. How many strips measuring 0.75 inches wide can be cut from the board? (Assume no waste from the cuts.)

   Write your answer on the line below.

   _____

29. Of his take-home pay each month, Jerry spends $\frac{1}{6}$ on a car payment and $\frac{1}{4}$ on food. What fraction of his take-home pay is left after paying for these two items?

   Write your answer on the line below.

   _____

Answers and explanations begin on page 209.

Ratio and Proportion

Ratio

A **ratio** compares two numbers. You can write a ratio using the word *to*, using a colon (:), or using fraction form.

Example 1: A softball pitcher strikes out four batters for every one batter that she walks. What is the ratio of strikeouts to walks?

Always write the numbers in the ratio in the same order in which they appear in the question.

$$\text{4 to 1} \qquad \text{4:1} \qquad \frac{4}{1}$$

Ratios are similar to fractions. They have two terms, and they can be simplified by reducing to lowest terms.

Example 2: Frank manages a small drugstore. During a two-hour period, he counts 25 cash sales and 15 credit card sales. What is the ratio of credit card to cash sales?

1. Write the ratio as a fraction with the terms in the correct order: credit card to cash sales.

$$\frac{\text{credit card sales}}{\text{cash sales}} = \frac{15}{25}$$

2. Reduce to lowest terms. The ratio of credit card to cash sales is **3 to 5.**

$$\frac{15 \div 5}{25 \div 5} = \frac{3}{5}$$

There are some fraction rules that ratios do not follow. Do not change a ratio that is an improper fraction to a mixed number. Also, if a ratio in fraction form has a denominator of 1, <u>do not</u> write it as a whole number. Leave it in fraction form.

Another important difference is in the use of labels. The terms in a fraction have the same unit labels: $\frac{5}{6}$ *of a pie means 5 slices out of 6 slices.* Ratios <u>may</u> have different labels: *The sale advertised 6 cans for $1, a 6:1 ratio.*

To write a ratio, you may need to perform one or more basic operations to find one of the terms.

Example 3: A football team won 12 games and lost 8. There were no tied games. What is the ratio of games won to games played?

1. The problem does not tell you the number of games played. Add the games won to the games lost to find the games played.

$$12 \text{ won} + 8 \text{ lost} = 20 \text{ played}$$

2. Write the ratio in the correct order and simplify. **The team won 3 games for every 5 games it played, a 3:5 ratio.**

$$\frac{\text{games won}}{\text{games played}} = \frac{12}{20} = \frac{12 \div 4}{20 \div 4} = \frac{3}{5}$$

PRACTICE 1.1

A. Write each ratio as a fraction in lowest terms.

1. Stan made 24 sales in 6 hours. What is the ratio of sales to hours?

2. Carol's monthly take-home pay is $1500. She spends $250 a month on food. What is the ratio of food costs to take-home dollars?

3. A toy rocket travels 180 ft in 15 sec. What is the ratio of feet to seconds?

4. At Phil's work, there are 12 part-time workers and 18 full-time workers. What is the ratio of part-time workers to total workers?

5. Juanita drove 336 miles on 14 gallons of gasoline. What is the ratio of miles to gallons?

6. Lynn estimates that a roofing job will cost $1500. Bo estimates that the same job will cost $2400. What is the ratio of Lynn's estimate to Bo's estimate?

7. A basketball player attempted 32 free throws and made 20. What is the ratio of free throws made to free throws missed?

8. There are 10 men and 14 women in Kathleen's math class. What is the ratio of women to the total number of students in the class?

9. To paint his apartment, Alex bought 6 gallons of paint to cover 1440 square feet. What is the ratio of square feet to gallons of paint?

B. Choose the one best answer to each question.

Questions 10 through 12 refer to the following information.

Three candidates are running for mayor. Below are the results of a survey of 600 registered voters.

Candidate	Number of Supporters
Stothard	220
Mesa	180
Newmark	50
Undecided	150

10. What is the ratio of Mesa's supporters to Stothard's supporters?

   A. 9:11
   B. 11:9
   C. 11:20
   D. 20:11

11. What is the ratio of voters who prefer Mesa to the total number surveyed?

   A. 3 to 7
   B. 3 to 10
   C. 3 to 13
   D. 11 to 30

12. What is the ratio of undecided voters to voters who have made a decision?

   A. $\frac{1}{4}$
   B. $\frac{1}{3}$
   C. $\frac{3}{1}$
   D. $\frac{4}{1}$

13. Soan made a $400 down payment on a washer and dryer that cost a total of $1200. What is the ratio of the amount Soan has paid to the amount he still owes?

   A. 1 to 4
   B. 1 to 3
   C. 1 to 2
   D. 2 to 3

14. A team played 77 games and won 56 of them. There were no tied games. What is the ratio of wins to losses?

   A. 3:8
   B. 8:11
   C. 11:8
   D. 8:3

Answers and explanations begin on page 209.

Proportion

A **proportion** is an equation that shows that two ratios are equal. The **cross products** in a true proportion are equal. In other words, when you multiply diagonally across the equals sign, the products are equal.

Example 4: The directions on a can of powdered drink mix say to add 3 cups of water to every 2 scoops of drink mix. Matt adds 12 cups of water to 8 scoops of drink mix. Did he make the drink correctly?

1. Write a proportion, making sure the terms of the ratios are in the same order.

$$\dfrac{\text{Cups}}{\text{scoops}} \quad \dfrac{3}{2} \times \dfrac{12}{8}$$

2. Cross multiply and compare the products. Since the products are the same, the ratios are equal. **Matt made the drink correctly.**

$$3 \times 8 = 24$$
$$2 \times 12 = 24$$

In most proportion problems, you are asked to solve for a missing term.

Example 5: A map scale says that 2 inches = 150 miles. What actual distance would a map distance of 5 inches represent?

1. Write a proportion with both ratios in the same form: inches to miles. The variable x represents the unknown distance.

$$\dfrac{\text{inches}}{\text{miles}} \quad \dfrac{2}{150} = \dfrac{5}{x}$$

2. Locate the term in the first ratio that is diagonal from the known term in the second ratio. Cross multiply.

$$\dfrac{2}{150} \times \dfrac{5}{x}$$
$$150 \times 5 = 750$$

3. Divide the result by the remaining known term to find the value of x.

$$750 \div 2 = \textbf{375 miles}$$

Some proportion problems ask you to find a **rate.** A rate compares a quantity to 1. When a rate is written in fraction form, its denominator is always 1. In word form, rates are often expressed using the word *per.*

Example 6: Connie drove 276 miles on 12 gallons of gasoline. How many miles per gallon did she get on the trip?

1. Gas mileage is one kind of rate. You need to find how many miles Connie drove on one gallon of gasoline.

$$\dfrac{\text{miles}}{\text{gallons}} \quad \dfrac{276}{12} = \dfrac{x}{1}$$

2. Solve.

$$276 \times 1 = 276$$
$$276 \div 12 = \textbf{23 miles per gallon}$$

Using your calculator, you can solve proportion problems in one series of calculations.

Example 7: Find the value of x in the proportion $\dfrac{6}{16} = \dfrac{21}{x}$.

You need to multiply 16 and 21, then divide by 6. On the TI-30XS MultiView™ calculator:

1. Press 16 ⨯ 21 ÷ 6.

2. Then press enter. The right side of the display will read 56.

The missing term is **56.**

NOTE: When working a problem, ask yourself if it can be solved using proportion. This may be possible when two quantities are compared or when three values are given and you are asked to find a fourth.

PRACTICE 1.2

A. Solve for the missing term in each proportion problem. You MAY use your calculator for questions 9 through 16. NOTE: Answers will not always be whole numbers.

1. $\frac{2}{3} = \frac{x}{18}$

2. $\frac{3}{5} = \frac{27}{x}$

3. $\frac{6}{5} = \frac{3}{x}$

4. $\frac{15}{2} = \frac{x}{8}$

5. $\frac{4}{\$212} = \frac{7}{x}$

6. $\frac{25}{6} = \frac{400}{x}$

7. $\frac{7}{30} = \frac{x}{9}$

8. $\frac{0.5}{12} = \frac{3}{x}$

9. $\frac{20}{2.5} = \frac{100}{x}$

10. $\frac{\$5.96}{2} = \frac{x}{3}$

11. $\frac{12}{5} = \frac{3}{x}$

12. $\frac{4}{60} = \frac{2.5}{x}$

13. $\frac{3}{19} = \frac{x}{114}$

14. $\frac{9}{\$80.10} = \frac{x}{\$284.80}$

15. $\frac{\$26.00}{4} = \frac{x}{7}$

16. $\frac{24}{96} = \frac{7}{x}$

B. Choose the <u>one best answer</u> to each question. You MAY use your calculator for questions 20 through 22.

17. A store is advertising the following sale:

> Tomato Soup
> 4 cans for $0.98

To the nearest cent, how much would five cans of tomato soup cost?

A. $0.25
B. $1.23
C. $2.45
D. $4.90

18. The Bay City Cardinals have won 5 out of 8 games. At the same rate, how many games will they have to play to win 60 games?

A. 180
B. 120
C. 96
D. 12

19. Carla drove her truck 414 miles on 18 gallons of gasoline. How many miles did she drive per gallon?

A. 18
B. 23
C. 74
D. 95

20. The scale on a map reads, "2 cm = 150 km." How many kilometers would be represented by a distance of 4.6 centimeters?

A. 300
B. 345
C. 690
D. 1380

21. Two ingredients in a recipe are $2\frac{1}{2}$ cups of flour and $1\frac{1}{2}$ cups of sugar. If June keeps the proportion the same, how many cups of flour should she add to 4 cups of sugar?

A. $6\frac{2}{3}$
B. 6
C. 5
D. $3\frac{3}{4}$

22. Claudia drove 155 miles in 2.5 hours. Which of the following expressions could be used to find how many miles she can drive in 7 hours?

A. $155 \times 7 \div 2.5$
B. $2.5 \times 7 \div 155$
C. $155 \times 2.5 \div 4\,7$
D. $7 \times 2.5 \times 155$

Answers and explanations begin on page 210.

Percents

Percent means "per hundred" or "out of one hundred." For example, if you have $100 and you spend $25, you spent $25 out of $100, or 25% of your money.

Since percent is a way of showing part of a whole, it has much in common with fractions and decimals. To convert a percent to a fraction, write the percent over 100 and reduce. To convert percents to decimals, drop the percent symbol and move the decimal point two places to the left.

Percent to Fraction
$$25\% = \frac{25}{100} = \frac{1}{4}$$

Percent to Decimal
$$25\% = .25 = 0.25$$

In any percent problem, there are three elements: the base, the part, and the rate. The **base** is the whole quantity, or amount, that the problem is about. The **part** (also called a **percentage**) is a portion of the base. The **rate** is a number followed by the percent symbol (%).

Example 1: At a restaurant, Janice's bill is $20. She gives the waiter a tip of $3, which is 15% of her bill. Identify the base, part, and rate in this situation.

The entire bill of $20 is the base. The $3 tip is part of the base, and the rate is 15%.

One way to think of a percent problem is as a proportion. In Example 1, there are two ratios. The $3 tip is part of the $20 total bill, and 15% is the same as $\frac{15}{100}$. Since the two ratios are equal, they can be written as a proportion.

$$\frac{part}{base} \quad \frac{3}{20} = \frac{15}{100}$$

Cross multiply to prove the ratios are equal.

$$20 \times 15 = 300$$
$$3 \times 100 = 300$$

You can solve percent problems by setting up a proportion and solving for the missing elements. Just remember to express the percent as a number over 100.

Example 2: At a plant that manufactures lighting fixtures, it is expected that about 2% of the fixtures assembled each day will have some type of defect. If 900 fixtures are completed in one day, how many are expected to be defective?

1. Write a proportion. Remember that 2% means 2 out of 100. Use the variable x to stand for the number of defective fixtures.

$$\frac{part}{base} = \frac{rate}{100}$$
$$\frac{x}{900} = \frac{2}{100}$$

2. Solve for x. Cross multiply and divide by the remaining number. **The company can expect about 18 defective fixtures.**

$$900 \times 2 = 1800$$
$$1800 \div 100 = \mathbf{18}$$

PRACTICE 2

A. For each situation, identify and label the base, part, and rate.

1. Victor owes his uncle $1000. Recently, he gave his uncle $200. The payment was 20% of the money he owes.

2. On a test with 80 problems, Sophie got 72 problems right. In other words, she answered 90% of the problems correctly.

3. The Kang family made a down payment of $2,740 on a new car. The down payment was 20% of the purchase price of $13,700.

4. Zoe's take-home pay each month is $2000. She spends $500 on rent each month, which is 25% of her take-home pay.

5. This year, Rafael has 60 regular customers, which is 150% of the 40 regular customers he had last year.

6. Kayla bought a dress for $38. She paid $3.23 in sales tax. The sales tax rate in her state is 8.5%.

7. Misako's employer withholds 15% of her salary each paycheck for taxes. Misako earns $900 each week, and her tax withholding is $135.

8. Harrison got a 10% raise. Before the raise, his hourly wage was $10.70. Now he earns an additional $1.07 per hour.

9. Kim Industries has 800 employees. Of those, 200 workers, or 25%, work part-time.

10. In an election, 5,000 of the 12,500 registered voters actually voted. Only 40% of the registered voters actually voted.

B. Choose the one best answer to each question. Use the proportion $\dfrac{\text{part}}{\text{base}} = \dfrac{\text{rate}}{100}$ to solve each problem.

Questions 11 and 12 refer to the following information.

A local newspaper printed the following high school basketball standings:

Team	Wins	Losses
Fairfax	9	3
Hamilton	8	4
Bravo	6	6
Mountain View	4	8
Lincoln	3	9

11. Which of the following expressions could be used to find what percent of its total games Fairfax has won?

   A. $\dfrac{9 \times 100}{12}$

   B. $\dfrac{3 \times 100}{12}$

   C. $\dfrac{12 \times 100}{9}$

   D. $\dfrac{6 \times 100}{12}$

12. What percent of its games did Bravo win?

   A. 100%
   B. 75%
   C. 60%
   D. 50%

13. A jacket with a price tag of $128 is on a rack with the following sign:

   > All Items:
   > 25% off marked price
   > Discount taken at register

   By how much will the price be reduced when the jacket is taken to the register?

   A. $4
   B. $25
   C. $32
   D. $96

Answers and explanations begin on page 210.

Using the Percent Formula

Solving for Part

You have seen how to use proportion to solve percent problems. You can also solve percent problems using the formula **Base × Rate = Part**.

Study the diagram at the right to learn how to use the formula. To use the diagram, cover the element you need to solve for: B = Base, R = Rate (percent), and P = Part. Then perform the operation that connects the remaining elements.

Example 1: A company offers its employees two health plans. In a recent newsletter, the personnel department stated that 70% of the employees chose Plan A. If the company has 320 workers, how many chose Plan A?

1. The rate is 70%, and the base is 320, the total number of workers. You need to solve for the part. Using the diagram, cover P for part. You can see that you need to multiply to solve the problem.

2. Change the percent to a decimal and multiply.
   Out of 320 workers, 224 chose Plan A.

   70% = 0.7

   $320 \times 0.7 = 224$

Solving for Rate

Rewrite the percent formula to solve for rate. Use the formula **Part ÷ Base = Rate**. You can use the diagram to help you remember the formula.

Example 2: A computer system is regularly priced at $1600. On Friday, the manager reduced the price by $640. By what percent did the manager discount the computer system?

1. The base is $1600, the regular price. The part is $640, the amount the price was reduced. You are asked to find the rate of the discount. Cover R for rate (percent). You need to divide the part by the base to solve the problem.

2. Divide 640 by 1600.

3. Convert the decimal answer to a percent by moving the decimal point two places to the right and adding the percent sign. The price reduction was a **40% discount.**

$$1600\overline{)640.0}$$
$$\underline{640.0}$$
$$0.4 = 40 = 40\%$$

Always ask yourself whether your answer seems reasonable. For example, you know that 40% is a little less than $\frac{1}{2}$, and $\frac{1}{2}$ of $1600 is $800. Since $640 is a little less than $800, it is a reasonable answer.

Key Ideas

- You can use a formula to solve percent problems: *Base × Rate = Part*.
- To change a percent to a decimal, drop the % sign and move the decimal point two places to the left.
- To change a decimal to a percent, move the decimal point two places to the right and add the % sign.

GED® TEST TIP

When you take the Mathematical Reasoning Test, *make a quick sketch of the percent diagram on the wipe-off board to help you analyze percent problems.*

PRACTICE 3.1

A. Solve. You MAY use a calculator for questions 9 through 16.

1. What is 20% of $25?

2. Find 90% of 200.

3. What is 35% of 400?

4. What percent is 19 out of 20?

5. 42 is what percent of 168?

6. What percent is $18 out of $600?

7. Find $33\frac{1}{3}$% of 51. (*Hint:* $33\frac{1}{3}\% = \frac{1}{3}$)

8. What is 125% of $48?

9. 240 is what percent of 120?

10. What percent is 3 out of 60?

11. $52 is what percent of $650?

12. Find $8\frac{1}{2}$% of $46.

13. $0.65 is what percent of $10.00?

14. Find 28% of $1300.

15. What percent is 2.5 out of 4?

16. Find $66\frac{2}{3}$% of 108. (*Hint:* $66\frac{2}{3}\% = \frac{2}{3}$)

B. Choose the one best answer to each question. You MAY use your calculator.

17. Pat called 120 customers to offer a software upgrade. Of those he called, 72 purchased the upgrade. What percent agreed to the purchase?

    A. 40%
    B. 48%
    C. 60%
    D. $66\frac{2}{3}$%

18. Douglas received a 6% raise. If his old monthly salary was $2,250, what is his monthly salary now? (*Hint:* Find the amount of the raise. Then add the raise to the previous monthly salary.)

    A. $2,256
    B. $2,385
    C. $3,600
    D. $13,500

19. At a restaurant, Levy's total bill is $46. If he wants to tip 15%, how much should he leave as a tip?

    A. $690.00
    B. $31.00
    C. $15.00
    D. $6.90

20. The following advertisement for sporting goods appeared in the newspaper. What percent of the original price is the sale price?

    > Little League Package
    > Magnum bat, tote bag, and youth cleats
    > Only $45.50
    > Originally $65

    A. 20%
    B. 31%
    C. 44%
    D. 70%

21. Lydia pays $3 sales tax on a $50 purchase. Which of the following expressions could be used to find the sales tax rate in her state?

    A. $\dfrac{\$3 \times 100}{\$50}$

    B. $\dfrac{\$3 \times \$50}{100}$

    C. $\$3 \times \$50 \times 100$

    D. $\$3 \div \$50$

Answers and explanations begin on page 210.

Solving for Base

Some problems on the *Mathematical Reasoning Test* may require you to solve for the base in a percent situation. Remember, the base represents the whole item or group. Read each situation carefully to figure out which element is missing. Then choose the correct method for solving the problem.

Example 3: In a math class, 75% of the students got at least a B grade on the final exam. If 18 students got at least a B, how many students are in the class?

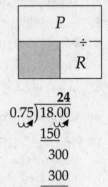

1. Analyze the situation. The 18 students are part of the larger class. You know that the 18 students are 75% of the whole group, so 75% is the rate and the base is unknown.

   Use the diagram. Cover *B* for base. You need to divide the part by the rate to solve the problem.

2. Convert the rate to a decimal (75% = 0.75) and divide. There are **24 students** in the class.

$$\begin{array}{r} 24 \\ 0.75\overline{)18.00} \\ \underline{150} \\ 300 \\ \underline{300} \end{array}$$

Most of the time, we work with percents that are less than 100%. When a percent is less than 100%, the part is less than the base. However, it is possible to have a situation in which the part is greater than the base. When this occurs, the percent will be greater than 100%.

Example 4: The workforce at Eastland Inc. is growing rapidly. The number of employees this year is 225% of the number last year. If there are 135 employees this year, how many employees did the company have last year?

1. The base is the number of employees the company had last year. This year's number is a percent of last year's number. Therefore, the rate is 225%, the part is 135, and the base is unknown.

2. Convert 225% to a decimal. Drop the % sign and move the decimal point two places to the left.

   $225\% = 2.25 = 2.25$

3. Divide the part (135) by the rate (2.25). Last year, there were only **60 employees**.

$$\begin{array}{r} 60 \\ 2.25\overline{)135.00} \\ \underline{135.0} \end{array}$$

There is often more than one way to approach the solution to a problem. Both the percent formula presented in this lesson and the proportion method from Lesson 1 can be used to solve Example 4.

Formula method: $\dfrac{135}{2.25}$ Proportion method: $\dfrac{135 \times 100}{225}$

If you evaluate both methods using a calculator, both expressions equal 60, the correct solution.

NOTE: Don't begin calculations before you completely analyze a situation. Every percent problem has three elements. Make sure you know which one is missing before you multiply or divide.

PRACTICE 3.2

A. Find the missing element in each set. You MAY NOT use a calculator.

1. $35 is 20% of what amount?
2. 5% of what number is 14?
3. 3.2 is 50% of what number?
4. $170 is 85% of what amount?
5. 24 is 80% of what number?
6. $105 is 125% of what amount?
7. 190 is 95% of what number?
8. What number is 15% of 60?
9. 90% of $15 is what number?

10. $42 is what percent of $168?
11. $150 is 200% of what amount?
12. 15% of $62 is what amount?
13. 9 is 1% of what number?
14. What percent is 126 of 140?
15. 65% of $1200 is what amount?
16. 5% of an amount is $156. What is the amount?
17. $2\frac{1}{2}$% of a number is 100. What is the number?
18. What percent is $15.60 of $156.00?

B. Choose the one best answer to each question. You MAY use your calculator.

19. Kevin's total payroll deductions are 30% of his earnings. If his deductions add up to $369 for a two-week period, how much were his earnings for the period?

    A. $110.70
    B. $123.00
    C. $1,230.00
    D. $11,070.00

20. A city council established the following budget to improve public transportation.

	Project Budget
Salaries	50%
Office lease	35%
Equipment	6%
Supplies	2%
Miscellaneous	7%

    If $72,000 is allotted for equipment, what is the total budget for the project?

    A. $432,000
    B. $940,000
    C. $1,200,000
    D. $120,000,000

21. Jack earns a 5% commission on each sale. If he is paid a $160 commission, which of the following expressions could be used to find the amount of the sale?

    A. $\dfrac{5 \times 100}{160}$

    B. $\dfrac{160 \times 100}{5}$

    C. $\dfrac{5 \times 160}{100}$

    D. $5 \times 100 \times 1.60$

22. American Loan Company mailed 3600 customers an application for a new credit card. Only 20% of the customers returned the application. How many customers returned the application?

    A.   72
    B.   180
    C.   720
    D.   180,000

Answers and explanations begin on page 210.

RATIO, PROPORTION, AND PERCENT

Percent Calculator Skills

By changing a percent to either a fraction or decimal, you can use a calculator to solve percent problems.

Example 1: What is 25% of 120? Try both decimals and fractions.

On the Display

Key Ideas

- One way to solve percent problems on the calculator is to change the percent to a decimal or a fraction.
- On the TI-30XS MultiView™ calculator, you can use the percent 2nd function to find the part and the base.
- To create a percent, use the 2nd function, %, which is in green over the left parenthesis (key.

Change 25% to the decimal (.25), multiply times 120, and press (enter). **30** is on the right of the display.

Change 25% to the fraction $\frac{25}{100}$ using the $\frac{n}{d}$ key, multiply times 120, and press (enter). **30** is on the right of the display.

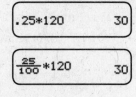

Using either decimals or fractions, you can find that **30** is 25% of 120.

When you use the *percent 2nd* function, you don't have to convert the percent to a fraction or decimal. Practice this function below to multiply to find the **part** when you are given the rate (percent).

Example 2: What is 65% of $360?	**Keys to Press**	**On the Display**
1. Type the base, 360, and press the multiplication sign.	360 ⊗	360*
2. Type the rate (65). Press the 2nd function key and engage the percent 2nd function—over the (key. Then press (enter).	65	360*65% 234

The amount **$234** is 65% of $360.

You can use the percent function to divide to find the **base** when given the rate.

Example 3: Ned paid $150 for a stereo. The amount Ned paid was 20% of the original cost. What was the original cost of the stereo?	**Keys to Press**	**On the Display**
1. Enter the base, 150, and press the division sign.	150 ÷	150÷
2. Enter 20 and press the 2nd function key and the (key. Then press *enter*.	20 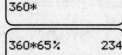	150÷20% 750

The original cost of the stereo appears on the right of the display: **$750**.

GED® TEST TIP

Practice using the Delete *key when you make a mistake in a problem. That will erase your latest entry. The* Clear *key will erase the entire entry.*

PRACTICE 4

A. Solve. You MAY use your calculator.

1. Find 46% of $130.

2. 14% of what amount is $13.44?

3. What is 12% of $126?

4. What number is $62\frac{1}{2}$% of 64?

5. 12 is what percent of 400?

6. A number is 32% of 6500. What is the number?

7. 36 is what percent of 144?

8. 90% of what number is 63?

9. Find 7% of 360.

10. What number is $33\frac{1}{3}$% of 237?

11. 25 is what percent of 1000?

12. What is $12\frac{1}{2}$% of 384?

13. 390 is what percent of 500?

14. Find 2% of $800.

15. 32% of what number is 80?

16. What number is $87\frac{1}{2}$% of 16?

17. $112 is what percent of $1600?

18. A number is $66\frac{2}{3}$% of 414. What is the number?

B. Choose the one best answer to each question. You MAY use your calculator.

Questions 19 and 20 refer to the following chart.

Shipping and Handling Information	
For items costing:	**% of order + handling:**
$20 or less	3% + $1.50
$20.01 to $50	4% + $2.50
$50.01 to $100	5% + $4.00
$100.01 or more	8%

19. Chanel placed an $84 order. How much shipping and handling will she be charged on her order?
    - A. $4.20
    - B. $4.40
    - C. $8.20
    - D. $8.36

20. Jason placed an order totaling $110. Zola placed a $90 order. How much more did Jason pay in shipping and handling than Zola?
    - A. $0.30
    - B. $4.30
    - C. $4.50
    - D. $20.00

21. In an election, 3190 out of 3625 registered voters voted against a tax increase. What percent of the registered voters voted against the increase?
    - A. 43%
    - B. 83%
    - C. 88%
    - D. 98%

22. A baseball player has the following statistics. To the nearest percent, what percent of the player's at bats were strikeouts?

At Bats	Hits	Home Runs	Walks	Strikeouts
410	108	2	70	63

   - A. 90%
   - B. 58%
   - C. 26%
   - D. 15%

Answers and explanations begin on page 210.

Simple Interest

Interest is a fee paid for the use of someone else's money. If you put money in a savings account, you receive interest from the bank. If you borrow money, you pay interest. In each case, the amount that you invest or borrow is called the **principal**.

Simple interest is a percent of the principal multiplied by the length of the loan. The formula for finding simple interest is given on the formulas sheet of the *Mathematical Reasoning Test* (see page 205). It reads:

simple interest Interest = principal × rate × time

You may find it easier to remember the formula using **variables** (letters that stand for numbers): $I = prt$, where I = interest, p = principal, r = rate, and t = time. Writing variables next to each other means that they are to be multiplied.

Example 1: Asher borrows $2500 from his uncle for three years at 6% simple interest. How much interest will he pay on the loan?

1. Write the rate as a decimal.

$$6\% = 0.06$$

2. Substitute the known values in the formula. Multiply.

$$I = prt$$
$$= \$2500 \times 0.06 \times 3$$
$$= \mathbf{\$450}$$

Asher will pay **$450** in interest.

Some problems ask you to find the **amount paid back.** This adds an additional step to an interest problem. In Example 1, Asher will owe $450 in interest at the end of three years. However, he will pay back the interest ($450) plus the principal ($2500): $2500 + $450 = $2950. When he has finished paying the loan, Asher will have paid his uncle $2950.

In a simple interest problem, the rate is an annual, or yearly, rate. Therefore, the time must also be expressed in years.

Example 2: Eva invests $3000 for 9 months. She will be paid 8% simple interest on her investment. How much interest will she earn?

1. Write the rate as a decimal.

$$8\% = 0.08$$

2. Express the time as a fraction of a year by writing the length of time in months over 12, the number of months in a year.

$$9 \text{ months} = \frac{9}{12} = \frac{3}{4} \text{ year}$$

3. Multiply.

$$I = prt$$
$$= \$3000 \times 0.08 \times \frac{3}{4}$$

Eva will earn **$180** in interest.

$$= \mathbf{\$180}$$

Key Ideas

- Simple interest is found by multiplying principal, rate, and time: $I = prt$.
- The time must be written in terms of years. Write months as a fraction of a year.
- To find the amount paid back, add the principal and the interest.

GED® TEST TIP

An onscreen formula sheet (see page 205) is provided when you take the Math-ematical Reasoning Test. *The formula for simple interest is printed close to the bottom of that sheet. Every time you see a formula in this book, check to see if it is on the formula sheet. If the formula is not there, you will need to memorize it.*

PRACTICE 5

A. Solve these problems using the formula for simple interest. You MAY use your calculator.

1. Leah borrows $1500 for 2 years at a 12% interest rate. Find the interest on the loan.

2. How much interest would you pay on a loan of $800 for 6 months at 14% interest?

3. Dominica invested $2000 for 3 years at an interest rate of 7%. How much interest did she earn on her money?

4. How much interest would you earn on an investment of $600 for 8 years at 10% interest?

5. Todd invests $6500 for $3\frac{1}{2}$ years at 5% interest. How much interest will he be paid at the end of the time period?

6. Ricardo borrows $1850 for 8 months at 12% interest. What is the amount he will pay back at the end of the loan period?

7. Yanira puts $5000 in an investment account for 4 years. If she is paid $8\frac{1}{2}$% simple interest, how much interest will she earn?

B. Choose the one best answer to each question. You MAY use your calculator.

8. Jean borrowed $1300 to buy tools for her job as an auto mechanic. The loan is for 1 year 6 months at 9% simple interest. Which of the following expressions could be used to find the amount she will pay back at the end of the loan period?

   A. $1300 \times 1.5 \times 0.09$
   B. $1300 \times 1.5 \times 9$
   C. $1300 + (\$1300 \times 9 \times 1.5)$
   D. $1300 + (\$1300 \times 0.09 \times 1.5)$

9. Noah borrows $8000 for 5 years to make improvements to his home office. If the simple interest rate is 6%, how much will he pay in interest?

   A. $2400
   B. $1040
   C. $420
   D. $400

10. Caleb borrowed $1500 from his aunt. He plans to pay his aunt back in 9 months. If he pays 4% interest on the loan, what is the total amount he will pay back in 9 months?

    A. $1455
    B. $1545
    C. $1560
    D. $2040

Questions 11 and 12 refer to the following information.

Option	Length of Loan	Simple Interest Rate
A	$2\frac{1}{2}$ years	12%
B	3 years	10%
C	4 years	9%

11. Charlotte needs to borrow $2400. She is considering the three loan options shown above. How much more interest would Charlotte pay if she takes loan option C instead of option A?

    A. $108
    B. $144
    C. $720
    D. $864

12. Charlotte chooses Option B, but she decides to borrow $2800. What is the total amount she will pay back when the loan is due?

    A. $2830
    B. $3240
    C. $3556
    D. $3640

Answers and explanations begin on page 211.

RATIO, PROPORTION, AND PERCENT

Percent of Change

Percent is often used to show change.

Example 1: Michelle recently started her own business. Last month, she earned $1000. This month, she earned $2000. How could she describe the increase in her earnings?

All of the following statements accurately describe the change.

- Michelle's earnings doubled from last month to this month.

- This month, her earnings increased by 100%.

- This month's earnings are 200% of last month's earnings.

Percent of change compares a new number, which shows an **increase** or a **decrease**, to the original number—the number before the change.

Example 2: Before her raise, Lisa earned $10.50 per hour. Now she earns $11.34 per hour. What percent raise did her boss give her?

1. Subtract to find the amount of change. $11.34 - $10.50 = $0.84

2. Divide the amount of change by $10.50, Lisa's wage before the change. Convert the decimal to a percent. Lisa's hourly wage **increased by 8%.** $\frac{\$0.84}{\$10.50} = 0.08 = \mathbf{8\%}$

Think carefully about a situation to decide which number is the original amount.

Example 3: A jacket is on sale for $90. Three days ago, the jacket was on sale for $120. By what percent was the price of the jacket reduced?

1. Subtract to find the amount of change. $120 - $90 = $30

2. The price of the jacket was $120 before it was $90, so $120 is the original price. Divide the amount of change by $120. The new price is **25% less** than the price three days ago. $\frac{\$30}{\$120} = 0.25 = \mathbf{25\%}$

Percent of increase may be greater than 100%.

Example 4: Calvin started his business with 10 employees. Now he has 60 employees. By what percent has his workforce increased?

1. Subtract to find the amount of change. $60 - 10 = 50$

2. Divide by the original number. Convert the number to a percent. Calvin's workforce has **increased by 500%.** $\frac{50}{10} = 5.0 = \mathbf{500\%}$

Key Ideas

- The amount of change is the difference between the new number and the original number.
- Find the percent of change by dividing the amount of change by the original number.
- Percent of increase may be greater than 100%.

GED® TEST TIP

You can work backward to check your answers. For example, if a price has decreased by 25%, the new price should be 75% of the original price, since 25% + 75% = 100%.

PRACTICE 6

A. Solve as directed. If necessary, round your answer to the nearest percent. You MAY use your calculator for questions 7 through 10.

1. Find the percent of increase from 2000 to 3000.

2. Find the percent of decrease from $2.00 to $1.25.

3. What is the percent of increase from 30 to 90?

4. Find the percent of decrease from 20 to 11.

5. Find the percent of increase from $25 to $30.

6. What is the percent of decrease from 500 to 340?

7. Find the percent of increase from $1.89 to $2.29.

8. What is the percent of decrease from 21 to 3?

9. Find the percent of increase from 65 to 338.

10. What is the percent of decrease from $1550 to $1025?

B. Choose the one best answer to each question. You MAY use your calculator.

11. Justin recently moved from a part-time to a full-time job. Because of the change, his weekly pay increased from $280 to $448. To the nearest percent, by what percent did his income increase?

   A. 38%
   B. 60%
   C. 168%
   D. 267%

12. David bought a computer game on sale for $36. The game was originally $48. What was the percent of decrease in the game's price?

   A. 12%
   B. 25%
   C. $33\frac{1}{3}$%
   D. 75%

13. The Utleys' rent increased from $600 to $636 per month. By what percent did the rent increase?

   A. 4%
   B. 5%
   C. 6%
   D. 7%

Questions 14 and 15 refer to the following information.

Marc sells computer equipment. He buys printers at wholesale and sells them at retail price. Customers who join his discount club pay the member's price.

Printer Pricing Chart

Model Number	Wholesale Price	Retail Price	Member's Price
L310	$63.00	$141.75	$92.15
L1430	$86.00	$150.50	$105.35

14. What is the percent of increase from wholesale to retail price of the L310 model?

   A. 56%
   B. 78%
   C. 125%
   D. 225%

15. For the L1430 model, what is the percent of decrease from retail price to member's price?

   A. 26%
   B. 30%
   C. 43%
   D. 53%

Answers and explanations begin on page 211.

RATIO, PROPORTION, AND PERCENT PRACTICE QUESTIONS

Directions: You MAY use your calculator.

1. From a total yearly budget of $360,000, the Kimball Foundation spends $30,000 on leasing office space. What is the ratio of dollars spent on office space to dollars spent on other costs?

   A. 12:1
   B. 11:1
   C. 1:11
   D. 1:12

2. A worker can assemble 5 motors in 2 hours. Which of the expressions below could be used to find how long it would take the worker to assemble 50 motors?

   A. $2 \times \dfrac{50}{5}$

   B. $\dfrac{5 \times 50}{2}$

   C. $\dfrac{5}{2 \times 50}$

   D. $2 \times 5 \times 50$

3. Frank owns a discount music store. The table below shows how much Frank pays for certain merchandise items.

Item	Wholesale Price
CDs	$7.20
Posters	$5.60

   To find his selling price, Frank increases each price by 35%. What is the selling price of a poster?

   A. $9.72
   B. $7.56
   C. $5.95
   D. $1.96

4. Neva's car is now worth $12,000. This is 60% of what she paid for it. How much did she pay for the car?

   A. $7,200
   B. $18,000
   C. $19,200
   D. $20,000

5. At a shop, the ratio of union to non-union workers is 7 to 3. If there are 18 nonunion workers at the shop, how many union workers are there?

   A. 21
   B. 25
   C. 42
   D. 126

6. Camilla earned $954 in commission on $15,900 in sales. What is her rate of commission?

   A. 6%
   B. 9%
   C. $16\frac{2}{3}$%
   D. 60%

7. John spent the following amounts of time building a workbench:

drawing the plans:	2 hours
cutting the wood:	$1\frac{1}{2}$ hours
assembling the workbench:	2 hours
sanding and sealing:	$3\frac{1}{2}$ hours

   What is the ratio of time spent cutting wood to total time spent on the project?

   A. 1:9
   B. 1:6
   C. 1:5
   D. 3:7

Questions 8 and 9 refer to the following information.

Ford County Farmland Usage Total Acreage: 40,000	
Usage	**Number of Acres**
Dairy	22,000
Nursery/greenhouse	3,600
Vegetables/fruits	5,200
Grains	9,200

8. What percent of Ford County farmland is used for the growing of grains, vegetables, or fruits?

   A. 23%
   B. 36%
   C. 57%
   D. 64%

9. One dairy farmer in Ford County is considering selling her farm to developers, who will convert it from a dairy farm to a resort. If this happens, the amount of farmland devoted to dairy in Ford County will decrease by 20%. How many acres of farmland will Ford County then have if the dairy farmer decides to sell?

   A. 35,600
   B. 32,000
   C. 17,600
   D. 4,400

10. A serving of peanut butter contains 3 grams of saturated fat and 13 grams of unsaturated fat. This amount of fat is 25% of the recommended amount of fat in a 2000-calorie diet. What is the ratio of grams of saturated fat to total fat in a serving of peanut butter?

    A. $\frac{3}{16}$
    B. $\frac{3}{13}$
    C. $\frac{13}{16}$
    D. $\frac{16}{3}$

11. A drawing of a company logo is 4 inches wide and 5 inches long. If the drawing is enlarged so that it is 12.5 inches long, and the original proportions remain unchanged, how many inches wide will the enlarged drawing be?

    A. 7.5
    B. 10
    C. 15.625
    D. 20

12. A local hospital currently has 184 male patients. If the ratio of male to female patients is 4:3, how many female patients are there in the hospital?

    Write your answer on the line below.

    _____

13. A newspaper advertisement contains the following information.

Busy Body Fitness Center Inventory Reduction Blowout! All sale prices are 20% off original price!	
Equipment	**Sale Price**
Treadmill	$1512
Upright bike	$720
Home gym	$3148

In dollars, what was the original price of the upright bike?

Write your answer on the line below.

_____

14. The Tigers' ratio of wins to losses is 5 to 4. If the team continues winning at the same rate, how many games will the Tigers win in a 72-game season?

    A. 20
    B. 40
    C. 37
    D. 52

15. A television station called 400 adults and asked the following question: "Do you approve of the governor's new education program?" The table below shows the results of the survey:

Response	Percent
Undecided	16%
Yes	32%
No	52%

    Of the people called, how many did NOT answer "no"?

    A. 64
    B. 128
    C. 192
    D. 208

16. The price of a carton of computer paper decreased from $25 to $20. What was the percent decrease in the price?

    A. 80%
    B. 50%
    C. 20%
    D. 5%

17. Six months ago, Sandra had 55 regular customers. Now, she has 220% as many regular customers as she had six months ago. How many regular customers does Sandra have now?

    A. 121
    B. 90
    C. 66
    D. 25

18. If 1 gram of fat equals 9 calories, what percent of the calories in a Munchies roast beef sandwich come from fat?

Munchies Sandwich Facts		
Sandwich	Fat (grams)	Calories
Roast Beef	6	300
Club Classic	5	335

    A. 2%
    B. 3%
    C. 6%
    D. 18%

19. For every $8 in their budget, the Parks spend $3 on food. If their weekly budget is $704, how much do they spend on food each week?

    A. $88
    B. $192
    C. $235
    D. $264

20. Suddeth Travel estimates that 80% of its employees have more than 12 days of unused sick leave. If 140 employees have more than 12 days of unused sick leave, how many employees work at the agency?

    A. 112
    B. 164
    C. 175
    D. 700

21. The Gladstone Theater has 900 seats. At a recent show, the ratio of tickets sold to tickets unsold was 11 to 1. How many tickets were sold?

    A. 75
    B. 810
    C. 818
    D. 825

22. Matthew put $2200 in a savings account for one year and six months. If he earns simple interest at an annual rate of 8%, how much will he have in the account at the end of the time period?

    A. $2212
    B. $2376
    C. $2464
    D. $2640

23. A television set that is regularly priced at $410 is on sale for 20% off. What is the sale price of the television set?

    A. $82
    B. $328
    C. $390
    D. $492

24. On a county map shown below, the map scale reads, "0.5 in. = 60 mi."

    What is the actual distance in miles between Lakeview and Riverside?

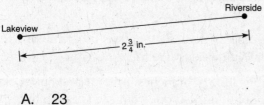

    A. 23
    B. 165
    C. 300
    D. 330

Question 25 refers to the following information.

Leo's Bookstore kept track of the number of customers who visited the store over a 3-day period. Employees also recorded the number of customers who made a purchase for each day during the same period.

Day	Number of Customers	Number of Customers Who Made a Purchase
Friday	112	83
Saturday	138	45
Sunday	140	91

25. Which of the following could be used to find what percent of Sunday's customers did NOT make a purchase?

    A. $\dfrac{91}{140}$

    B. $\dfrac{91}{140} \times 100$

    C. $\dfrac{(140 - 91)}{140} \times 100$

    D. $\dfrac{(140 - 91)}{91} \times 100$

26. A school admits 9 out of every 14 who apply. At that rate, how many students will be admitted if 420 apply?

    Write your answer on the line below.

27. In a 40-hour workweek, Marcie spends 15 hours answering telephones. What is the ratio of hours spent answering telephones to hours doing other types of work? (Record your answer as a fraction.)

    Write your answer on the line below.

Answers and explanations begin on page 211.

DATA, STATISTICS, AND PROBABILITY

Tables and Pictographs

Data are facts and information. By analyzing data, we can make predictions, draw conclusions, and solve problems. To be useful, data must be organized in some way. A **table** organizes data in columns and rows. The labels on the table will help you understand what the data mean.

Key Ideas

- Tables and graphs are often used to display data.
- Always read all labels to understand what data are presented in the table or graph.
- If symbols are used in a graph, a key will explain what each symbol represents.

Example 1: The table below shows population figures for selected counties in 2000 and 2010 and the land area in square miles for each county.

County	2000 Pop.	2010 Pop.	Land Area in sq mi
Adams	11,128	15,295	4,255
Bell	25,199	22,707	2,523
Cook	6,532	6,518	2,398
Davis	82,204	90,834	1,139
Evans	139,510	130,748	921

Which county showed the greatest percent of increase in population from 2000 to 2010?

1. **Read the labels.** The first column shows the county names. The second and third columns show population figures. The fourth column shows land area data. You don't need land area to answer this question.

2. **Analyze the data.** Only Adams and Davis counties show increases from 2000 to 2010.

3. **Use the data.** Find the percent of increase for Adams and Davis counties.

Adams: $\frac{15,295 - 11,128}{11,128} \approx 0.374 \approx 37\%$;   Davis: $\frac{90,834 - 82,204}{82,204} \approx 0.105 \approx 10\%$

Adams County shows the greatest percent of increase in population from 2000 to 2010.

A **pictograph** is another way to display data. Pictographs use symbols to compare data. A key shows what value each symbol represents.

Example 2: A city has three public library branches. A librarian kept track of the numbers of books checked out from each branch in a week. He used the data to create the pictograph below.

GED® TEST TIP

Tables provide a lot of information. When you are answering a question based on a table, use only the information that is needed to answer the question. In Example 1, the question is about population, so you do not need to use information from the last column.

From March 4 to March 10, how many books were checked out from the South and West branches combined?

1. There are $4\frac{1}{2}$ symbols for the South Branch and 9 symbols for the West branch. Add: $4\frac{1}{2} + 9 = 13\frac{1}{2}$ symbols.

2. Find the value of the symbols. The key states that each symbol equals 150 books. Multiply by 150: $13\frac{1}{2} \times 150 = $ **2025 books.**

PRACTICE 1

A. **Use the table on page 84 to answer questions 1 and 2. Use the pictograph on page 84 to answer questions 3 and 4. You MAY use a calculator.**

1. On average, how many people were there per square mile in Bell County in 2010?

2. To the nearest percent, what was the percent of decrease in Evans County's population from 2000 to 2010?

3. How many more books were checked out from North Branch than from South Branch during the week of March 4?

4. How many books were checked out from all three branches combined?

B. **Choose the one best answer to each question.**

Questions 5 and 6 refer to the following table.

Percent of 3-year-old children with school-readiness skills for the years 2004 and 2010	2004	2010
Recognizes all letters	11%	17%
Counts to 20 or higher	37%	47%
Writes own name	22%	34%
Reads or pretends to read	66%	67%

5. If 100 children were surveyed in each year, which category showed the least percent of increase from 2004 to 2010?

    A. Recognizes all letters
    B. Counts to 20 or higher
    C. Writes own name
    D. Reads or pretends to read

6. A community had 350 three-year-old children in 2010. If the chart is representative of the community, how many were able to write their own name?

    A. 34
    B. 97
    C. 119
    D. 134

Questions 7 and 8 refer to the following graph.

Mayfair Parking Garage
Daily Average of Parked Cars by Timed Period

Time of Day	Average Number of Cars
8:00 a.m. – noon	🚗🚗🚗🚗🚗🚙
12:01 – 4:30 p.m.	🚗🚗🚗🚗🚗🚗🚗🚙
4:31 – 8:00 p.m.	🚗🚗🚗🚗

Key 🚗 = 50 cars

7. How many cars are parked in the garage from 12:01 to 4:30 p.m.?

    A. 275
    B. 350
    C. 375
    D. 650

8. How many more cars are parked from 8 a.m. to noon than are parked after 4:30 p.m.?

    A. 75
    B. 100
    C. 175
    D. 200

Answers and explanations begin on page 212.

DATA, STATISTICS, AND PROBABILITY

Bar and Line Graphs

Working with Bar Graphs

A **bar graph** uses bars to represent values. Bar graphs have two axis lines. One line shows a number scale, and the other shows labels for the bars. By comparing the length of a bar to the scale, you can estimate what value the bar represents.

Example 1: A national corporation made a bar graph (shown below) to show the number of discrimination complaints made by employees during a six-year period. About how many more complaints were made in 2010 than in 2009?

Key Ideas

- A bar graph uses bars to represent numbers.
- To find the value of a bar, compare its length to the scale shown on one of the axis lines. Estimate the value.
- A double-bar graph compares groups of data. Read the key to find the meaning of the bars.

1. **Read the labels.** Each bar represents the number of complaints made within a year. The years are shown beneath the bars.

2. **Analyze the data.** Compare the bars for 2009 and 2010 to the scale. There were 20 complaints in 2009 and about 32 complaints in 2010.

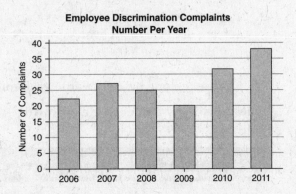

3. **Use the data.** Subtract: $32 - 20 = 12$. There were **about 12 more** complaints in 2010 than in 2009.

A **double-bar graph** compares more than one type of data.

Example 2: A studio released four films in one year. The graph below compares the cost of making each movie to its box-office receipts, or ticket sales. Film B's cost is what percent of its box-office receipts?

1. **Read the labels.** Read the key to find the meaning of the bars. Notice that the scale represents millions of dollars.

2. **Analyze the data.** Film B's cost is about $30 million. It brought in about $65 million in receipts.

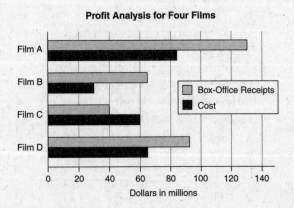

3. **Use the data.** Find what percent $30 is of $65.

$$\frac{\$30}{\$65} \approx 0.462 \approx 46\%$$

PRACTICE 2.1

A. For questions 1 through 3, use the bar graph entitled "Employee Discrimination Complaints" on page 86. For questions 4 through 6, use the bar graph entitled "Profit Analysis for Four Films" on page 86.

1. To the nearest 10, how many employee discrimination complaints were there in 2006 and 2007?

2. To the nearest 5, how many more complaints were there in 2011 than in 2006?

3. By what percent did the number of complaints decrease from 2008 to 2009?

4. About how much more did it cost to make Film A than Film D?

5. Which film made the greatest amount of profit? (*Hint:* profit = receipts − cost)

6. Film C's cost was what percent of its box-office receipts?

B. Choose the **one best answer** to each question.

<u>Questions 7 and 8 refer to the following</u> graph.

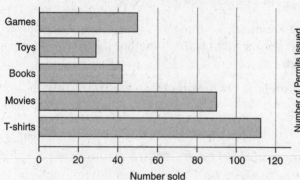

Items Sold for the Week of September 20

<u>Questions 9 and 10 refer to the following</u> graph.

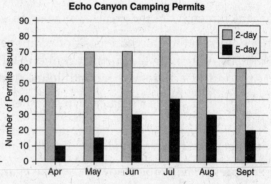

Echo Canyon Camping Permits

7. Approximately how many more T-shirts were sold than books and toys combined?

   A. 40
   B. 70
   C. 80
   D. 90

8. One-half of the games sold during the week of September 20 were on sale for $16. The rest sold for the full price of $24. Approximately how much money did the store take in for games sold during the week of September 20?

   A. $400
   B. $600
   C. $800
   D. $1000

9. In May, what was the ratio of the number of 2-day permits to the number of 5-day permits?

   A. 2:5
   B. 3:17
   C. 14:3
   D. 14:17

10. In which month was there a <u>total</u> of 80 permits issued?

    A. June
    B. July
    C. August
    D. September

Answers and explanations begin on page 212.

Working with Line Graphs

A **line graph** is useful for showing changes over time. By analyzing the rise and fall of the line, you can tell whether something is increasing, decreasing, or staying the same. Like a bar graph, a line graph has two axis lines. One is marked with a scale; the other is marked in regular time intervals.

Example 3: The graph below shows the number of patients who visited an emergency room for the treatment of scooter-related injuries.

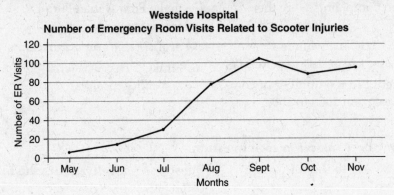

In which month did the greatest increase in scooter-related injuries occur?

The points on the graph are positioned above the months, which are arranged in calendar order. By examining the line that connects the points, you can tell whether there was an increase or decrease from one month to the next.

A steeper line shows a greater increase; therefore, the **greatest increase was from July to August**.

If a line graph has more than one line, a key will tell you what the lines represent.

Example 4: The graph below shows the changes in ticket prices for two amusement parks.

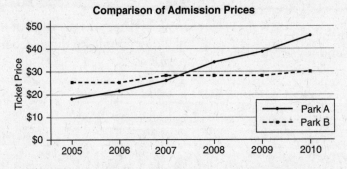

What was the last year in which the admission price to Park B was greater than the admission price to Park A?

The admission prices for Park A are represented by a solid line. Park B's prices are shown with a dotted line. The graph begins in 2005. In 2005, Park B's ticket price is greater than Park A's. Follow the two lines to the right. Between 2007 and 2008, the lines cross, and Park A's prices climb higher than Park B's. **The year 2007** was the last time that Park B charged more than Park A for a ticket.

NOTE: The steepest line shows the greatest increase or decrease, but it may not show the greatest <u>percent</u> of change. When the original value is small, a small change may result in a high percent of change.

PRACTICE 2.2

A. For questions 1 through 3, use the graph from Westside Hospital on page 88. For questions 4 through 6, use the graph "Comparison of Admission Prices" on page 88.

1. In which month did the number of scooter-related injuries decrease?

2. To the nearest 10, how many emergency room visits were due to scooter injuries in August, September, and October combined?

3. Which of the following shows the greater percent of increase: the change in injuries from June to July or the change from August to September?

4. About how much more did it cost to buy a ticket to Park A than a ticket to Park B in 2009?

5. What was the percent of increase in the ticket prices at Park B from 2005 to 2010?

6. To the nearest 10, how much more did it cost to buy a ticket to Park A in 2010 than in 2005?

B. Choose the one best answer to each question.

<u>Questions 7 and 8 refer to the graph below.</u>

Inflation Facts

If a purchase cost $100 in the year 2000, what would its cost have been in the past?

<u>Questions 9 and 10 refer to the graph below.</u>

Lamp Depot has two stores. The graph shows the sales data from the two stores for an 8-week period.

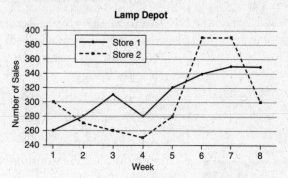

7. Over what period of time did the price of goods actually decrease?

   A. 1930 to 1940
   B. 1940 to 1950
   C. 1960 to 1970
   D. 1970 to 1980

8. Goods purchased in 1970 were about what fraction of their cost in the year 2000?

   A. $\frac{4}{5}$
   B. $\frac{1}{2}$
   C. $\frac{1}{3}$
   D. $\frac{1}{5}$

9. About how many more sales were there at Store 2 than at Store 1 in week 6?

   A. 110
   B. 50
   C. 40
   D. 25

10. During which week did Store 1 experience the greatest increase in sales from the week before?

    A. Week 2
    B. Week 3
    C. Week 4
    D. Week 5

Answers and explanations begin on page 212.

Circle Graphs

A **circle graph** is used to show how a whole amount is broken into parts. The sections of a circle graph are often labeled with percents. The size of each section corresponds to the fraction it represents. For example, a section labeled 25% is $\frac{1}{4}$ of the circle.

Example 1: A graph below shows how a children's sports camp spends its weekly budget.

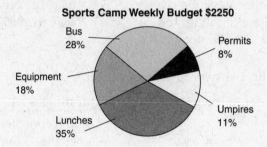

Sports Camp Weekly Budget $2250

Bus 28%
Permits 8%
Equipment 18%
Umpires 11%
Lunches 35%

How much does the sports camp spend on lunches each week?

1. **Analyze the graph.** According to the heading, the entire circle represents the camp's weekly budget of $2250. Find the section labeled "lunches." According to the section label, lunches make up 35% of the weekly budget.

2. **Use the data.** To find the amount spent on lunches, find 35% of $2250: $2250 \times 0.35 = $**$787.50**.

A circle graph may also be labeled using fractions or decimals. One common kind of circle graph labels each section in cents to show how a dollar is used.

Example 2: According to the graph, what percent of the average energy bill is spent on drying clothes, lighting, and heating water?

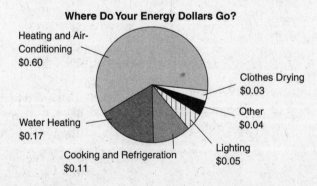

Where Do Your Energy Dollars Go?

Heating and Air-Conditioning $0.60
Clothes Drying $0.03
Other $0.04
Water Heating $0.17
Cooking and Refrigeration $0.11
Lighting $0.05

1. **Analyze the graph.** The entire circle represents $1. The amounts in the sections mentioned in the problem are $0.03, $0.05, and $0.17.

2. **Use the data.** Add the amounts: $0.03 + $0.05 + $0.17 = $0.25. Since $0.25 is 25% of a dollar, **25%** of an average bill is spent on these items.

Key Ideas

- In a circle graph, the circle represents a whole amount, and the sections represent parts of the whole.
- Sections are usually labeled with percents, but they can show amounts.
- The size of each section of a circle graph is equal to the fraction or percent it represents.

PRACTICE 3

A. For questions 1 through 3, use the **Sports Camp Weekly Budget** circle graph on page 90. For questions 4 through 6, use the **Where Do Your Energy Dollars Go** circle graph on page 90.

1. What percent of the total sports camp budget is spent on equipment and umpires?

2. What <u>fraction</u> of the sports camp budget is spent on permits?

3. What amount does the camp spend each week on busing?

4. A family's energy bill is $180. Assuming the family's energy use is typical, how much did the family spend on water heating?

5. Which section is greater than 50% of an energy dollar?

6. Which energy cost is about $\frac{1}{10}$ of the energy dollar?

B. Choose the <u>one best answer</u> to each question.

<u>Questions 7 and 8 refer to the following graph.</u>

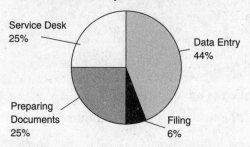

Time Spent on Tasks by Records Clerks, Woods County Recorders Office

7. During a 40-hour workweek, how many hours does a records clerk spend preparing documents?

   A. 10
   B. 15
   C. 25
   D. 30

8. What percent of a records clerk's time is spent on tasks other than data entry?

   A. 25%
   B. 31%
   C. 44%
   D. 56%

<u>Questions 9 and 10 refer to the following graph.</u>

The employees of National Bank are given the following graph to explain how their retirement fund is invested.

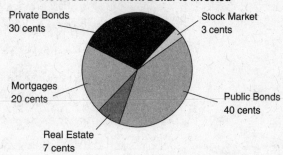

How Your Retirement Dollar Is Invested

9. What percent of each retirement dollar is invested in real estate and the stock market?

   A. 4%
   B. 10%
   C. 40%
   D. 90%

10. Steve contributes $120 of each paycheck to his National Bank retirement fund. How much of each contribution is invested in public bonds?

    A. $36
    B. $40
    C. $48
    D. $84

Answers and explanations begin on page 213.

DATA, STATISTICS, AND PROBABILITY

Measures of Central Tendency

Using a Frequency Table

A **frequency table** shows how often an item appears in a data set. The data is in the form of tally marks next to a list of items.

Example 1: The sales manager at Montana Motors asked her sales staff to keep a record of the color of the cars that were chosen for test-drives in one month. Then she combined the data to make the frequency table shown below.

Montana Motors—Car Color Preferences	
white	⊞ ⊞ ⊞ ⊞ ⊞ ⊞
black	⊞ ⊞ ⊞ ⊞ ⊞ II
red	⊞ ⊞ ⊞
green	⊞ ⊞ I
silver	⊞ IIII
other	⊞ ⊞ ⊞ I

What was the ratio of black cars driven to silver cars driven?

1. Count the tally marks. There are 27 marks for black and 9 for silver.

2. Write the ratio and reduce to lowest terms. $\frac{27}{9} = \frac{3}{1}$.

The ratio of black to silver is **3 to 1**. You can also say that the black cars are 3 times as popular as the silver cars.

Numerical data is often grouped in intervals. The table below shows data grouped in intervals of 18 to 24, 25 to 40, and so on. This way of presenting data is called a **grouped frequency table**.

Example 2: The table below shows the ages of the customers at Louise's Diner for a four-day period. What percent of the customers were from 25 to 40 years old?

Louise's Diner Customers by Age Group, February 19–22	
under 18	⊞ I
18–24	⊞ ⊞ ⊞ III
25–40	⊞ ⊞ ⊞ ⊞ ⊞ III
41–55	⊞ ⊞
over 55	⊞ III

1. Find the data you need. There are 28 marks for the 25–40 age group. Add the tally marks for all age groups to find the total number of customers for the three-day period: $6 + 18 + 28 + 10 + 8 = 70$.

2. Find the percent. The base is 70, the total number of customers. The part is 28, the number of customers in the desired age group. Solve for the rate: $\frac{28}{70} = \frac{4}{10} = 0.4 = \mathbf{40\%}$.

PRACTICE 4.1

A. For questions 1 through 3, use the frequency table from Montana Motors on page 92. For questions 4 through 6, use the frequency table from Louise's Diner on page 92.

1. What was the total number of test drives of black and white cars combined?

2. How many more drivers chose red than silver cars?

3. What was the ratio of red cars to white cars chosen for test-drives?

4. What is the ratio of customers under 18 to those over 55?

5. What was the total number of customers from 18 to 40 years of age?

6. What percent of the total customers were from 41 to 55 years of age? (Round your answer to the nearest whole percent.)

B. Choose the <u>one best answer</u> to each question.

<u>Questions 7 and 8</u> refer to the following information.

The frequency table shows the reasons customers gave for returning clothing merchandise to a store.

Reason	Number
Wrong size	⊞⊞ ⊞⊞ ⊞⊞ I
Unwanted gift	⊞⊞ ⊞⊞ ⊞⊞ ⊞⊞
Found flaw after purchase	III
Changed mind	⊞⊞

7. What is the ratio of customers saying the clothes were the wrong size to all the returns represented?

   A. $\frac{4}{15}$

   B. $\frac{4}{11}$

   C. $\frac{4}{7}$

   D. $\frac{4}{5}$

8. Approximately what percent of the customers who returned clothing said that the clothes were an unwanted gift?

   A. 20%
   B. 25%
   C. 45%
   D. 50%

<u>Questions 9 and 10</u> refer to the following information.

A personnel office gives typing tests to people applying for a job. The test shows how many words per minute (wpm) a job applicant can enter correctly. After testing 90 applicants, the manager made the following table.

Typing Speed	Number
Under 30 wpm	⊞⊞ ⊞⊞ ⊞⊞ ⊞⊞ ⊞⊞ ⊞⊞ ⊞⊞
30–45 wpm	⊞⊞ ⊞⊞ ⊞⊞ ⊞⊞ ⊞⊞
46–60 wpm	⊞⊞ ⊞⊞ ⊞⊞ III
Over 60 wpm	⊞⊞ ⊞⊞ II

9. What percent of the applicants had a speed of under 30 wpm?

   A. 14%
   B. 25%
   C. 28%
   D. 39%

10. What is the ratio of applicants who could type at a speed above 45 wpm to those who could type at a speed of 45 wpm or less?

    A. 1:3
    B. 1:2
    C. 2:3
    D. 6:5

Answers and explanations begin on page 213.

Mean, Median, and Mode

Suppose you were asked how much money you usually spend on groceries in a week. Some weeks, you may spend a great deal; other weeks, much less. You would probably choose an amount in the middle to represent what you typically spend. This middle value is called an **average**, or **measure of central tendency**.

The most common type of average is the **mean**, or the arithmetic average.

Example 3: In five football games, a team scored 14, 21, 3, 20, and 10 points. What is the mean, or average, score per game?

1. Add the values. $14 + 21 + 3 + 20 + 10 = 68$

2. Divide by the number of items in $68 \div 5 = \textbf{13.6 points per game}$
   the data set.

Although it is impossible for a football team to score 13.6 points in a game, the number represents the center of the scores from the five games.

A calculator is useful for finding the mean. Do the calculations in two steps. Enter the addition operations. Then, if you are using the TI-30XS MultiView™, press *enter* to find the sum. Then key in the division operation. Try Example 1 above with a calculator.

Another measure of average is the median. The **median** is the middle value in a set of data.

Example 4: During a 7-hour period, a bookstore recorded the following numbers of sales. Find the median number of sales.

Hour 1	Hour 2	Hour 3	Hour 4	Hour 5	Hour 6	Hour 7
43	28	24	36	32	37	48

1. Arrange the values by size.   24, 28, 32, 36, 37, 43, 48

2. Find the middle number.   24, 28, 32, 36, 37, 43, 48

If there is an even number of values, the median is the mean of the two middle values.

Example 5: Robert has the following test scores in his math class: 90, 72, 88, 94, 91, and 80. What is the median score?

1. Arrange the values by size and find the   72, 80, 88, 90, 91, 94
   middle.

2. Find the mean of the two middle values. The   Add: $88 + 90 = 178$
   median score is **89**.   Divide by 2: $178 \div 2 = \textbf{89}$

The **mode** is the value that occurs most often in a set of data. A set of data could have more than one mode if several items occur the same number of times. If each item of data occurs only once, there is no mode.

Example 6: Six weather stations recorded the following temperatures at 3:00 p.m.: 45°, 44°, 45°, 47°, 46°, and 45°. What is the mode of the data?

The temperature 45° occurs most often (3 times). The mode is **45°**.

PRACTICE 4.2

A. **For each data set, find the mean, median, and mode. Round calculations to the nearest hundredth or cent. You MAY use a calculator.**

1. Golf scores for 7 rounds:
   76, 82, 75, 87, 80, 82, and 79

2. Sales totals for 6 weeks:
   $5,624; $10,380; $8,102; $6,494; $12,008;
   and $8,315

3. Cost of lunch for 8 days:
   $4.50, $5.25, $4.50, $3.75, $4.50, $5.25,
   $6.10, and $4.25

4. Miles driven per day for 5 days:
   330, 286, 342, 300, and 287

5. Grocery bills for 4 weeks:
   $97.48, $106.13, $110.98, and $92.74

6. Scores on 7 quizzes:
   90, 72, 86, 100, 88, 78, and 88

7. High temperatures for 10 days:
   96°, 103°, 98°, 101°, 98°, 100°, 100°, 97°,
   98°, and 100°

8. Inches of rainfall over 3-day period:
   2.5, 1.8, and 1.4

9. Attendance figures at a play:
   305, 294, 328, 296, 305, 315, and 292

10. Hours worked per week for 5 weeks:
    36, 40, 38, 40, and 40

B. **Choose the <u>one best answer</u> to each question. You MAY use your calculator.**

<u>Questions 11 and 12 refer to the following</u> information.

Homes Sold in Fairfield Heights in June		
Home	**Asking Price**	**Selling Price**
#1	$124,600	$116,500
#2	$132,400	$124,800
#3	$118,900	$116,500
#4	$98,500	$103,600
#5	$105,800	$109,000
#6	$122,400	$118,400

11. What was the mean asking price of the homes sold in Fairfield Heights in June?

    A. $117,100
    B. $116,500
    C. $115,450
    D. $114,800

12. What was the median selling price of the homes sold in Fairfield Heights in June?

    A. $112,750
    B. $114,800
    C. $116,500
    D. $117,450

13. The numbers of patients enrolled at four health clinics are 790, 1150, 662, and 805. Which expression could be used to find the mean number of patients per clinic?

    A. $\dfrac{790 + 1150 + 662 + 805}{4}$
    B. $790 + 1150 + 662 + 805$
    C. $\dfrac{662 + 1150}{2}$
    D. $(790 + 1150 + 662 + 805) \div 2$

14. What is the median value of $268, $1258, $654, $1258, $900, $1558, and $852?

    A. $1258
    B. $964
    C. $900
    D. $852

15. What is the mode of the following points scored: 14, 17, 14, 12, 13, 15, 22, and 11?

    A. 13.5
    B. 14
    C. 14.75
    D. 16.5

Answers and explanations begin on page 213.

Line Plots

The same kind of information that can be expressed in a frequency table (see page 92) can also be expressed in a **line plot**. A line plot shows the frequency of data along a number line. Study the following example.

Key Ideas

- A line plot is a graph that shows the frequency of data along a number line.
- Based on frequency tables, line plots consist of a horizontal scale and points or *x*'s placed over corresponding numbers.
- Line plots help us to interpret the distribution of data.

Example 1: The student health services department at a university surveyed several students and asked them how many times per week they visited the school's gym. The following frequency table shows the results for several students.

Weekly Gym Visits	Number of Students
0	I
1	II
2	II
3	III
4	0
5	I
6	0
7	I

Next, the health services department decided to create a line plot in order to see the distribution of gym visits. Each *x* represents a student.

```
        x
    x   x
    x   x   x
x   x   x   x       x           x
←—+———+———+———+———+———+———+———+——→
  0   1   2   3   4   5   6   7
```

You can see from this line plot that there is an uneven **distribution**, or arrangement, of students across the numbers of possible gym visits. Three visits per week has the **highest frequency**, meaning that more students go to the gym three times per week than any other number of visits. You can also see that the data **range** extends from zero visits per week to seven visits per week—no student visits the gym more often than that. The data point showing the one student who visits the gym seven times per week is an **outlier**—that is, a data point that is distant from where most of the data is clustered.

ON THE GED® TEST

One type of question may ask you to analyze data on a line plot. Another type of question could ask you to use a frequency table to place an element on a line plot.

The *Mathematical Reasoning Test* may ask you to identify highest frequency, range, and outliers, or it may give you some data and ask you to place *x*'s or dots on a number line to create a line plot.

Use the following example to study these concepts further.

Example 2: Students in Ms. Jones's class took a math test. Their scores on the test are displayed on the line plot below. Each dot represents a student. Which grade displayed the highest frequency?

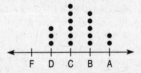

More students received a C than received any other grade. Therefore, grade **C** has the highest frequency of any grade on the line plot.

The range of grades on the math test was from D (the lowest grade received by any student) to A (the highest grade received by any student).

PRACTICE 5

For questions 1 and 2, <u>choose the line plot</u> that matches each frequency table. Use choices A–D below for both questions.

1. Zoologists have counted the number of stripes on certain zebras in a zoo. The set of data from these observations is represented by the following frequency table:

Number of stripes per side	Number of zebras with that many stripes
24	I
25	0
26	II
27	0
28	II
29	0
30	II
31	0
32	I

Which line plot below represents this data?

A.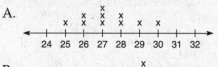

B.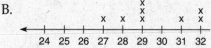

2. At a certain elementary school, classes may have different numbers of students. The following frequency table represents how many students are in the classes this year:

Number of students	Number of classes with that many students
24	0
25	0
26	0
27	I
28	I
29	III
30	0
31	I
32	II

Which line plot below represents this data?

C.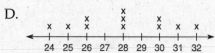

D.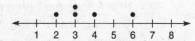

<u>Questions 3 and 4 are based on the following</u> information.

Juana runs a community garden. She is interested in how many different types of vegetables garden members are planting. She collects the following data:

Garden Member	Types of Vegetables Planted
Alberta	4
Paul	3
Eileen	6
Donato	2
Vijay	3
Janelle	2
Zara	1
Wahib	8
Bill	4
Yeo	3

3. The line plot below is based on the information in the table. Each point represents one of the members of the community garden. Place as many additional points as necessary to complete the line plot.

4. Which value (number of types of vegetables) has the highest frequency in the data?

A. 2
B. 3
C. 4
D. 8

Answers and explanations begin on page 213.

DATA, STATISTICS, AND PROBABILITY

Histograms

Like line plots, **histograms** display **frequencies**, but they do so in a very different way. Consider the following example:

Example 1: Graham is a veterinarian. Last year he decided to track client appointments for spring shots. The following table and histogram represent his results:

Key Ideas

- A histogram is another form of data display based on groups and counts within a group.
- Groups are plotted on the horizontal axis, and frequencies are plotted on the vertical axis.

Week of	Number of Appointments
March 1–7	2
March 8–14	4
March 15–21	8
March 22–28	11
March 29–April 4	14
April 5–11	17
April 12–18	13
April 19–25	7
April 26–May 2	5

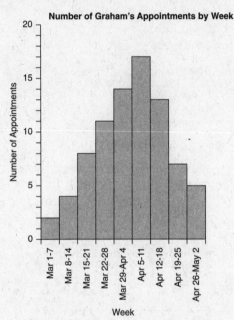

The **histogram** above on the right has two axes: a **vertical axis** (or *y*-axis) representing numbers of appointments and a **horizontal axis** (also called an *x*-axis) that has increments representing the weeks. The **area** of each bar represents the number of appointments for that week. Thus, you can see not only how many appointments were in any given week but also how the **frequency** of appointments changed over the weeks in the chart.

Finally, histograms can also be used to show percentages. If we alter the histogram about Graham's appointments so that each bar represents the *percent* of total appointments each week, it would look like the one on the right.

Because the percentages add up to 100%, the areas of all the bars add up to 100.

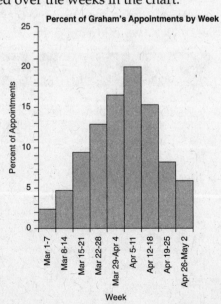

Example 2: What percent of appointments for spring shots occurred during the first two weeks of March?

You can figure this out by adding the percentages for those weeks (you can approximate based on the histogram): for March 1–7, about 2%; for March 8–14, about 5%. Approximately 7% of appointments for spring shots occurred during those two weeks.

PRACTICE 6

A. Choose the <u>histogram</u> that matches each frequency table. Use choices A–D below for <u>both</u> questions 1 and 2.

1. Josefina runs a retail business. She posted a coupon to a social media site from 9:00 a.m. to 5:00 p.m. The table shows how many people downloaded or printed the coupon.

Hour Beginning With:	Number of People Who Downloaded or Printed Coupon:
9:00 a.m.	30
10:00 a.m.	56
11:00 a.m.	80
12:00 p.m.	71
1:00 p.m.	56
2:00 p.m.	31
3:00 p.m.	22
4:00 p.m.	14

2. Mike administered a skills assessment to his employees. Possible scores on the skills assessment ranged from 200 to 1800. The following table shows how his employees performed on the assessment:

Score Range	Number of Employees
200–399	15
400–599	22
600–799	35
800–999	62
1000–1199	80
1200–1399	69
1400–1599	47
1600–1800	20

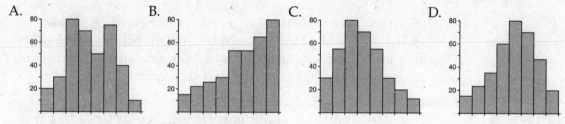

A.   B.   C.   D.

B. Choose the <u>one best answer</u> to each question.

<u>Question 3</u> refers to the following histogram and information.

Influenza, or "flu," season in the United States tends to last from fall through spring.

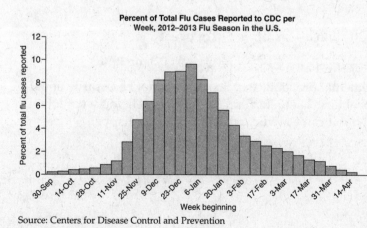

Source: Centers for Disease Control and Prevention

3. Approximately what percentage of flu cases was reported to the CDC during the 2012–2013 season during the time period of December 9 to January 5?

A. 7%
B. 15%
C. 36%
D. 50%

Answers and explanations begin on page 213.

LESSON

7

Probability

Simple Probability

Probability tells whether something is likely or unlikely to happen. The probability of any event can be expressed by a number from 0 to 1. If an event has 0 probability, the event is impossible. An event with a probability of 1 is certain to happen. Most events are somewhere in between.

To find the probability of a simple random event, we must identify favorable and possible outcomes. A **favorable outcome** is the event that we are interested in. The **possible outcomes** are all the possible events that could occur. **Theoretical probability** (sometimes called **simple probability**) is the ratio of favorable outcomes to possible outcomes.

Example 1: The spinner is divided into 8 equal sections. What is the probability of spinning a 4 on the spinner?

1. There are two sections labeled 4 on the spinner, and there are 8 sections in all.

2. Use the probability ratio: $\frac{\text{favorable outcomes}}{\text{possible outcomes}} = \frac{2}{8} = \frac{1}{4}$.

The probability of spinning a 4 on the spinner is **1 out of 4**, $\frac{1}{4}$, **0.25, or 25%**.

In Example 1, probability was based on what we knew could happen. Another type of probability, called **experimental probability**, is based on what actually happens during the trials of an experiment. The number of trials are the number of times you try the experiment.

Example 2: Ricardo and Scott used the same spinner to play a game. They kept track of the numbers that they got on each spin for 20 spins. The numbers are shown below.

2, 4, 4, 6, 4, 3, 4, 6, 4, 3, 1, 6, 2, 2, 5, 2, 4, 2, 1, 2

Based on their results, what is the experimental probability of spinning a 4?

1. Ricardo and Scott spun a 4 six times out of twenty.

2. Use this ratio: $\frac{\text{favorable outcomes}}{\text{number of trials in experiment}} = \frac{6}{20} = \frac{3}{10}$, **0.3, or 30%.**

Notice that experimental probability is close to, but not necessarily equal to, theoretical probability. Theoretical probability can tell you what will probably happen, but it can't predict what will actually happen.

Key Ideas

- Probability is a ratio. It can be expressed as a ratio, fraction, decimal, or percent.
- Theoretical probability is the ratio of favorable outcomes to possible outcomes.
- Experimental probability is the ratio of favorable outcomes to the number of trials in an experiment.

GED® TEST TIP

In a multiple-choice probability problem, skim the answer choices to see if they are in fraction, percent, or ratio form. Knowing the answer form will help you decide how to do your calculation.

PRACTICE 7.1

A. Express probability as a fraction, decimal, and percent for questions 1 through 5. Do not use a calculator.

1. A game has 50 wooden tiles. Players draw tiles to spell words. If 20 of the tiles are marked with vowels, what is the probability of drawing a vowel from the tiles?

2. A spinner has five equal sections colored either red, white, or blue. After 40 spins, a player has the following results:

Color	Frequency
red	⊞⊞
white	⊞⊞ II
blue	⊞⊞ ⊞⊞ ⊞⊞ ⊞⊞ ⊞⊞ III

What is the experimental probability of not spinning blue on the spinner?

3. There are four red, four blue, and two green marbles in a bag. If one marble is chosen at random from the bag, what is the probability that the marble will be green?

4. A movie theater sells 180 adult tickets and 60 children's tickets to a movie. As part of a special promotion, one ticket will be chosen at random, and the winner will receive a prize. What is the probability that the winner will be a child?

5. A spinner has six equal sections numbered from 1 to 6. What is the probability of spinning either a 5 or 6?

B. Choose the one best answer to each question. You MAY use your calculator.

Questions 6 and 7 refer to the following information.

A deck of 12 cards is marked with the following symbols.

6. If a card is chosen at random, what is the probability of selecting a diamond (♦)?

   A. 6%
   B. 12%
   C. 50%
   D. 60%

7. If a card is chosen at random, what is the probability of selecting something other than a club (♣)?

   A. $\frac{3}{4}$
   B. $\frac{2}{3}$
   C. $\frac{1}{3}$
   D. $\frac{9}{100}$

Questions 8 and 9 refer to the following information.

Erin flipped a coin 40 times and made this table to show how many outcomes were "heads" and how many were "tails."

heads	⊞⊞ ⊞⊞ ⊞⊞ ⊞⊞ IIII
tails	⊞⊞ ⊞⊞ ⊞⊞ I

8. Based on Erin's data, what is the experimental probability of getting tails on a coin flip?

   A. 3 out of 5
   B. 3 out of 4
   C. 2 out of 3
   D. 2 out of 5

9. Based on Erin's data, what is the experimental probability of getting heads on a coin flip?

   A. 3 out of 5
   B. 3 out of 4
   C. 2 out of 3
   D. 1 out of 2

Answers and explanations begin on page 214.

Dependent and Independent Probability

You know how to find the probability of a single event. You can use this knowledge to find the probability of two or more events.

Example 3: Brad tosses two quarters into the air. What is the probability that both will land so that the heads' sides are showing?

One way to solve the problem is to list or diagram all the possible outcomes.

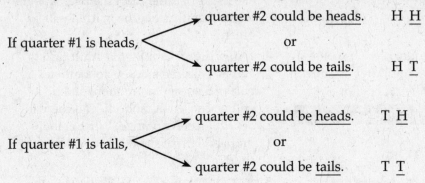

There are four possible outcomes, and only one is favorable (HH). Therefore, the probability of having both land with the heads side up is $\frac{1}{4}$, or **25%**.

You can also use multiplication to find the probability.

1. Find the probability of the individual events. The probability that one coin will be heads is $\frac{1}{2}$, and the probability that the other will be heads is $\frac{1}{2}$.

2. Multiply to find the probability of both events: $\frac{1}{2} \times \frac{1}{2} = \frac{1}{4}$.

The two coin tosses in Example 3 are **independent events**. When events are independent, one does not affect the probability of another. In Example 4 below, the events are **dependent**. Once the first event takes place, the probability of the second event is changed.

Example 4: A box contains four blue marbles and two red marbles. If you select two marbles, what is the probability that both will be blue?

(*Hint:* Even though the marbles in the box are taken out at the same time, think of one as the first marble and the other as the second marble.)

1. There are six marbles in the box, and four are blue. The probability that the first marble will be blue is $\frac{4}{6}$, which reduces to $\frac{2}{3}$.

2. Assume the first marble selected is blue. Now there are only five marbles in the box, and three are blue. The probability that the second marble will be blue is $\frac{3}{5}$.

3. Multiply to find the probability of the two events: $\frac{2}{3} \times \frac{3}{5} = \frac{6}{15}$, or $\frac{2}{5}$.

The probability that both marbles will be blue is **2 out of 5**.

NOTE: The events in Example 4 would not be dependent if the first marble were replaced before the second marble was selected. Always think carefully about the situation to decide whether two events are dependent or independent.

PRACTICE 7.2

A. Solve as directed. Express answers as fractions.

1. Kim rolls two standard six-sided dice. What is the chance that both will be 4s?

2. Ten cards are numbered from 1 to 10.. Toni draws out a card, replaces it, and then draws another card. What is the probability that both cards will be numbers greater than 5?

3. A spinner has four equal sections. Two sections are red, one is green, and one is blue. If the spinner is spun three times, what is the probability that all three spins will be red?

4. Twenty marbles are placed in a bag. Ten are red, and ten are black. One marble is drawn from the bag and set aside. Another marble is drawn from the bag. What is the chance that both marbles will be red?

5. Allison tosses a coin four times. What is the chance that the coin will be heads all four times?

6. If you roll two standard dice, what is the probability that both will be an odd number?

B. Choose the one best answer to each question. You MAY use your calculator.

Questions 7 and 8 refer to the following information.

In a game a player rolls a die, numbered from 1 to 6, and spins a spinner. The spinner is shown below.

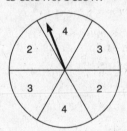

Daniel uses the ten cards below in a magic trick.

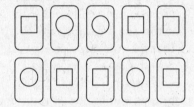

7. What is the probability of rolling a 5 and then spinning an even number?

   A. $\frac{1}{9}$

   B. $\frac{1}{6}$

   C. $\frac{2}{3}$

   D. $\frac{5}{6}$

8. What is the chance that a player will get the same number on both the die and the spinner?

   A. $\frac{5}{6}$

   B. $\frac{2}{3}$

   C. $\frac{1}{3}$

   D. $\frac{1}{6}$

9. Daniel shuffles the cards and asks an audience member to choose and hold two cards. If the cards are chosen randomly, what is the chance that both will be marked with a square?

   A. 8 out of 14
   B. 3 out of 5
   C. 1 out of 3
   D. 1 out of 5

10. There are 15 colored chips in a bag. Eight are green, and seven are white. Five white chips are removed. What is the probability that the next chip selected will be green?

    A. 100%
    B. 80%
    C. 75%
    D. 25%

Answers and explanations begin on page 214.

DATA, STATISTICS, AND PROBABILITY

Combinations

Combinations with One Type of Item

Sometimes the GED® *Mathematical Reasoning Test* will ask you how many ways you can combine a set of items. Sometimes you may have only one type of item to combine, and sometimes you may have more than one type to combine. This difference will determine your problem-solving strategy.

Consider an example with *only one type of item:*

Example 1: Pablo is going shopping at a fruit stand that sells apples, bananas, grapes, and pears. Pablo will buy two different kinds of fruit. How many combinations of two kinds of fruit could Pablo buy?

The question is asking you to list possible groups of two out of the overall set of four. Notice that order doesn't matter—that is, *apples and bananas* is no different from *bananas and apples*. To solve this problem, you can make a list. Start with apples and list all of the **combinations** that include apples: AB, AG, AP. Then make a list of groups that start with bananas and include the remaining fruits: BG, BP. Don't include BA because that's the same as AB. Then make a list of groups that start with grapes and include only the remaining fruits: GP. There are no remaining groups that start with P. You may find it easier to make this list in columns, as follows:

AB

AG   BG

AP   BP   GP

There are **6** possible combinations.

You can also draw a quick table like the following. Include a column for each of the fruits, and let each row represent a possible combination. Place two *x*'s in each row to represent a combination of two fruits.

Apples	Bananas	Grapes	Pears
x	x		
x		x	
x			x
	x	x	
	x		x
		x	x

Notice that you could not draw any more rows with two *x*'s without duplicating some of the existing rows. Count the rows: there are **6** possible combinations of two fruits.

Key Ideas

- Combinations are used to select several things out of a larger group when the order doesn't matter.
- If you are asked to find how many ways to combine items from one group, use an organized list or table.
- If you are asked to find how many ways to combine one item from each of a number of different types of items, use a tree diagram or the fundamental counting principle.

ON THE GED® TEST

While you are taking the test on computer, you can use the provided marker and wipe-off board to make a tree diagram or other diagrams to help you visualize problems.

PRACTICE 8.1

A. Use counting, an organized list, or a table to solve the following problems.

1. As a supervisor, Rob is choosing four of his employees to work on a special project. The employees are Angela, Barbara, Colin, David, and Elizabeth. Of those five employees, how many teams of four are possible?

2. Jessica wants to take three books on vacation with her. She has five books to choose from. How many possible combinations of three books could she take on vacation?

3. Grant is cooking a homemade pizza, and he has the following toppings available: anchovies, ham, mushrooms, and sausage. He will choose three of those toppings. How many ways could Grant combine those toppings?

4. Five friends want to play a video game designed for two players. How many different combinations of two friends are possible, if the order of the friends does not matter?

B. Choose the <u>one best answer</u> to each question about combinations.

5. Celia is going to plant a small flower bed with four flowers. She can choose from begonias, fuchsias, hellebore, daisies, and salvia. How many combinations of four flowers are possible?

   A. 5
   B. 20
   C. 24
   D. 120

6. Regan owns a small business, and she wants to send three people from her business to an upcoming trade show. Regan plans to attend, and she will also choose two of her four employees to attend. How many combinations of employees could Regan choose to send to the trade show?

   A. 4
   B. 6
   C. 10
   D. 24

7. A book club, which has two women and three men, can send three of its members to a book signing. How many possible combinations of members could attend the book signing?

   A. 1
   B. 5
   C. 10
   D. 120

8. Given six people, how many combinations of three are possible if order does not matter?

   A. 20
   B. 120
   C. 180
   D. 720

9. The Sarkesian brothers own a hardware store. There are five items the owners might display in the window. Joe Sarkesian thinks that the window should have two items, but his brother Rick thinks the window should have three items. Counting both Joe's ideas and Rick's ideas for the window, how many possible combinations of items might go into the window display?

   A. 10
   B. 20
   C. 30
   D. 120

Answers and explanations begin on page 214.

Combinations with More Than One Type of Item

Sometimes you may be asked to count possible combinations with more than one type of item. Consider the following example:

Example 2: Sarah is deciding what to wear. She has three shirts, two pairs of pants, and two pairs of shoes. How many possible outfits does she have, if an outfit is one shirt, one pair of pants, and one pair of shoes?

This question differs from the question about Pablo on page 104. In that question, Pablo was choosing from one overall group of fruits. Here, Sarah is choosing one out of each of three groups—shirts, pants, and shoes. If you are given more than one type of item and must choose one of each type, you can use a tree diagram to figure out all the possible combinations. Study the following example:

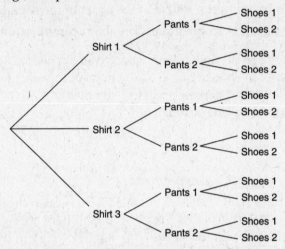

Each "branch" of the tree represents a possible combination. The number of branches on the right-hand side represents the possible number of combinations; in this case, there are **12** possible outfits.

However, you can solve the same type of problem (where you have more than one type of item and are choosing one of each type) using the **fundamental counting principle,** which works like this:

Start with shirts: for each shirt, Sarah has two pants options. That's $3 \times 2 = 6$. Additionally, for each of those six options, she has two options for shoes. That's $3 \times 2 \times 2 = \mathbf{12}$.

Use the fundamental counting principle to solve the following problem:

Example 3: Gordon is at a restaurant that serves a three-course meal: an appetizer, an entrée, and a dessert. There are three appetizers, six entrees, and four desserts to choose from. Gordon will order one of each. How many different meals could he order?

Multiply three appetizers by six entrees by four desserts: $3 \times 6 \times 4 = 72$. There are **72** possible ways Gordon could order his meal.

PRACTICE 8.2

A. Use a tree diagram or the fundamental counting principle to solve the following problems.

1. Frank is making a sandwich. His sandwich will have one type of bread, one type of meat, and one condiment. He has four types of bread: white, wheat, rye, and a Kaiser roll. Meats he can choose from are chicken, turkey, and roast beef. For condiments, Frank can choose mayonnaise, mustard, vinaigrette, or horseradish. How many ways can Frank make his sandwich?

2. Van Ahn attended a trivia contest and won three rounds. For the first round she won, she could choose one of three restaurant gift certificates. The prize for another round was one of two T-shirts. Winning the third round allowed her to choose one of four souvenir hats. How many possible combinations of prizes were available to Van Ahn?

3. Henry is wrapping a gift for his daughter. He will use one type of wrapping paper, one type of ribbon, and one bow. He has three different types of wrapping paper, three different types of ribbon, and three different bows. How many ways can Henry wrap the gift?

4. Julio is looking forward to a three-day weekend. On Friday, he will either go to the beach or attend a street festival. On Saturday, he plans to visit a museum, but he is trying to decide among three different museums. On Sunday, he will try one of four new restaurants. How many ways could Julio combine these weekend activities?

B. Choose the <u>one best answer</u> to each question about combinations. Determine whether you are being asked to find possible combinations from one type of item or from multiple types of items. You MAY use your calculator.

5. The Nu Mu Beta fraternity is deciding what secret passphrase it should require its members to say before being admitted to meetings. The first and third words of the passphrase will be the names of Greek letters. There are 24 letters in the Greek alphabet. The second word will be a number from one to nine. How many possible passphrases are there?

   A.   24
   B.   57
   C.   576
   D. 5,184

6. A video game designer is creating a new superhero, who will have three of five potential superpowers. How many combinations of superpowers could the new superhero have?

   A. 10
   B. 15
   C. 100
   D. 125

7. A chef will make a soup with five ingredients: one of four meats, one of four vegetables, one of four kinds of noodles, one of four kinds of broth, and one of four spices. How many possible combinations of ingredients could the chef put into the soup?

   A.   20
   B.   256
   C. 1,024
   D. 3,125

8. A doctor is deciding how to treat a given disease. The doctor will prescribe one medication, one dietary change, and one type of vitamin supplement. There are five medications, five dietary changes, and five types of vitamins the doctor might prescribe. How many combinations are possible?

   A.   125
   B.   625
   C. 1,250
   D. 3,125

Answers and explanations begin on page 214.

Permutations

On the *Mathematical Reasoning Test*, you may be asked how many possible permutations, or sequences, are possible given a group of items. Consider the following example:

Example 1: Eliza is planning her day off. She wants to visit the art museum, try the new coffee shop, call her mom, and take a walk, but not necessarily in that order. How many possible sequences of those four activities are there?

This question asks you for all possible permutations, or ways to sequence the items. Thus, *coffee-art-mom-walk* and *art-coffee-mom-walk* are two different possible outcomes. Consider how this problem differs from the combinations problems on pages 104–107. In those cases, order did not matter; in a permutations problem, order does matter.

To find how many ways you can sequence all the items in a list, multiply the possibilities like this. Start with how many things could go first: here, there are four possibilities for Eliza's first activity. Once she has done that first activity, three possibilities remain. After she has done a first and second activity, two possibilities remain, and then only one. So you simply multiply: $4 \times 3 \times 2 \times 1$. There are **24** possible permutations.

Some permutations questions may ask you to determine the possible orderings for only some of the items in a list. Consider this example:

Example 2: Ten runners are competing in a race. There are prizes for first, second, and third place. How many possible sequences of the top three prize winners are there?

Notice that you are not simply figuring out how many groups of three can be made out of the ten. Rather, you are figuring out how many sequences of three can be made out of the ten. That can sometimes be represented on the GED® Test with the notation $P(10, 3)$.

Now, multiplying $10 \times 9 \times 8 \times 7 \times 6 \times 5 \times 4 \times 3 \times 2 \times 1$ would give you all the possible permutations of all ten runners, so that approach will not work here. Instead, start with how many people could win first place: here, ten. Once someone has won first, there are nine possibilities for second place. Once someone has won first and someone else has won second, there are eight possibilities for third place. And then you stop multiplying: $10 \times 9 \times 8 = 720$. There are **720** possible ways that the runners could be arranged in the top three prize-winning slots. (Note that simply multiplying 10 by 3 will not work.)

Key Ideas

- Permutations are used to find the number of possible outcomes when the order does matter.
- Use the total number of people or items and the number of possible outcomes to find the number of permutations that are possible.

ON THE GED® TEST

When you are reading a question that suggests that you may want to find a combination or a permutation, ask yourself, "Am I finding a number of groups (combinations), or am I finding the number of possible sequences (permutations)?"

PRACTICE 9

A. Read the problems and decide whether you are being asked to find combinations or permutations. Then solve.

1. Noemi is trying to remember the password for her email. She knows that it has the following characters in it: M, Q, $, L, 7. But she can't remember the order they go in. How many possible sequences of those five characters are there?

2. Bilal is going to the museum. She wants to see the contemporary art exhibit, the Impressionists, the Greek vases, and a special Picasso exhibit but not necessarily in that order. How many sequences of those exhibits are possible?

3. Five students in a class have volunteered for a special project. Only three can actually help with the project. How many possible groupings of three out of the five are possible?

4. Tyrell is the curator at a gallery and is deciding how to arrange six paintings that will be displayed in a line along one wall. All six paintings will be included. How many possible sequences could Tyrell choose?

B. Choose the <u>one best answer</u> to each question about combinations or permutations. You MAY use your calculator.

5. Soraya has been given six tasks to do at work, but she has time to complete only four of them. She must decide in what order to do the tasks. How many possible orderings of four tasks are available to Soraya?

    A. 24
    B. 36
    C. 360
    D. 720

6. In a certain public garden, the gardener wanted to show the different visual effects that arranging flowers in different sequences can have. So he chose three kinds of flowers and planted flower beds showing each of the possible sequences of the three kinds. How many such flower beds did the gardener plant?

    A. 3
    B. 6
    C. 9
    D. 12

7. Ten people hope to become extras in a movie. The movie's casting director will choose four people to fill the following specific roles in the movie: Bystander #1, Bystander #2, Bystander #3, and Bystander #4. How many ways could those four roles be filled?

    A. 24
    B. 40
    C. 540
    D. 5,040

Questions 8 and 9 refer to the following information:

Clark and his daughter are at the amusement park, and Clark is offering his daughter a choice. They don't have time to ride all six rides at the amusement park, but they can ride three of them.

8. How many combinations of three rides could Clark's daughter choose?

    A. 18
    B. 20
    C. 120
    D. 720

9. Clark's daughter can also choose the order in which she wants to enjoy the rides. How many possible orderings of three out of the six rides are possible?

    A. 18
    B. 20
    C. 120
    D. 720

Answers and explanations begin on page 215.

DATA, STATISTICS, AND PROBABILITY PRACTICE QUESTIONS

Directions: You MAY use your calculator.

Questions 1 and 2 refer to the following graph.

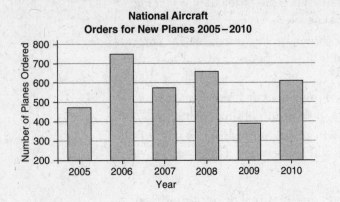

National Aircraft
Orders for New Planes 2005–2010

1. The mean number of aircraft orders for the six years shown on the graph is 573 planes. In which year was the number of orders closest to the mean?

   A. 2006
   B. 2007
   C. 2008
   D. 2009

2. By about what percent did orders at National Aircraft decrease from 2008 to 2009?

   A. 30%
   B. 40%
   C. 68%
   D. 75%

3. At a convention, Jim and his three friends each bought three raffle tickets. At the time of the drawing, 400 tickets had been sold. What is the probability that either Jim or one of his friends will win?

   A. $\frac{3}{100}$
   B. $\frac{1}{25}$
   C. $\frac{3}{50}$
   D. $\frac{9}{100}$

Questions 4 through 6 are based on the following table.

Southland Weather March 9			
Area	High Temp.	Low Temp.	Precipitation (in inches)
Downtown	65° F	53° F	0.45
Airport	62° F	50° F	0.63
Woodland Hills	68° F	50° F	1.34
East Village	56° F	48° F	3.53
Ventura	62° F	49° F	2.57
Highland Park	64° F	55° F	0.84

4. Based on the data in the table, what was the median low temperature for March 9?

   A. 62.8°
   B. 51.5°
   C. 50.8°
   D. 50°

5. What was the mean amount of precipitation (in inches) on March 9 for the areas listed in the table?

   A. 0.65
   B. 1.09
   C. 1.56
   D. 1.99

6. For which area on the table was there the greatest range, or difference, between the high and low temperatures?

   A. Ventura
   B. East Village
   C. Woodland Hills
   D. Downtown

Questions 7 and 8 refer to the graph.

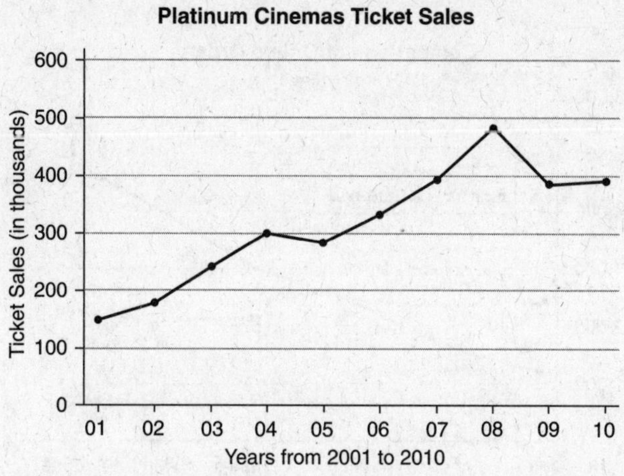

7. Platinum Cinemas opened its first theaters in 2001. The company's ticket sales increased steadily until what year, when there was a drop in sales?

   A. 2004
   B. 2005
   C. 2008
   D. 2009

8. Which year had the sharpest increase in ticket sales over the previous year?

   A. 2002
   B. 2006
   C. 2008
   D. 2009

9. At Nelson Stationers, the first 25 customers who visited the store on Monday morning received their choice of a gift. The table below shows how many customers chose each gift.

pen and pencil set	卌
calculator	卌 卌 ||
mouse pad	卌 |||

What percent of the customers chose a mouse pad?

A. 17%

B. 25%

C. 32%

D. $33\frac{1}{3}\%$

10. A standard deck of playing cards has 52 cards, with 13 cards each of hearts, diamonds, clubs, and spades. If a card is drawn randomly from the deck, what is the probability that it will be either hearts or diamonds?

    A. 1 in 2
    B. 1 in 4
    C. 1 in 8
    D. 1 in 16

11. Nita worked the following overtime hours over a six-week period.

    Week 1: 5 hours

    Week 2: $3\frac{1}{2}$ hours

    Week 3: 4 hours

    Week 4: 0 hours

    Week 5: $1\frac{1}{2}$ hours

    Week 6: 7 hours

    What is the mean number of overtime hours Nita worked each week?

    Write your answer on the line below.

    ____

12. A spinner has five equal sections, and they are numbered from 1 to 5. What is the probability of spinning a number greater than 3? (Express the answer as a fraction.)

    Write your answer on the line below.

    ____

Questions 13 through 15 refer to the following graph.

In a recent election, five candidates ran for the city council seat from District 11. The results of the race are shown in the graph below.

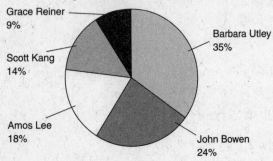

City Council Election Results

Grace Reiner 9%
Scott Kang 14%
Amos Lee 18%
John Bowen 24%
Barbara Utley 35%

13. The three city council candidates who received the fewest votes received what percent of the total vote?

    A. 23%
    B. 41%
    C. 56%
    D. 77%

14. Which two candidates combined received about $\frac{3}{5}$ of the votes cast?

    A. Reiner and Utley
    B. Kang and Utley
    C. Bowen and Utley
    D. Lee and Bowen

15. If 5100 votes were cast in the election, which of the following expressions could be used to find out how many votes Grace Reiner received?

    A. 5100×0.9
    B. $\frac{5100}{0.9}$
    C. $\frac{5100}{0.09}$
    D. 5100×0.09

Questions 16 through 18 refer to the following graph.

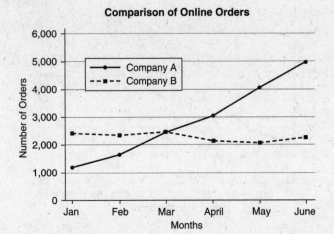

Comparison of Online Orders

16. In which month did Company A and Company B receive about the same number of online orders?

    A. February
    B. March
    C. April
    D. May

17. Based on the trends shown by the data, what would be the best prediction for the number of online orders in July for Company A?

    A. 7200
    B. 5900
    C. 5200
    D. 4900

18. About 18% of the online orders in April at Company A are returned for credit or exchange. How many orders at Company A were returned for credit or exchange in the month of April?

    A. 180
    B. 360
    C. 540
    D. 600

Questions 19 and 20 are based on the following information.

A basketball player's statistics for an eight-game series are shown in the table below.

Game	Shots Attempted	Shots Made
1	25	10
2	23	12
3	26	10
4	24	13
5	29	15
6	18	7
7	24	12
8	27	10

19. What was the median number of shots attempted by this player in the series?

    A. 24
    B. 24.5
    C. 25
    D. 26.5

20. What is the mode of the shots made by this player during the series?

    A. 12
    B. 11
    C. 10 and 12
    D. 10

21. A bag contains 24 marbles. Eight are red, six are blue, and ten are white. A marble is drawn from the bag and replaced. A second marble is chosen at random from the bag. What is the probability that the first marble is red and the second is white?

    A. $\frac{2}{5}$
    B. $\frac{5}{36}$
    C. $\frac{5}{48}$
    D. $\frac{1}{48}$

22. A company has 36 employees. For three months, the owner has kept track of the number of sick days used by her employees per month.

Month	Sick Days
Sept.	34
Oct.	31
Nov.	42

Which expression could be used to find the average number of sick days taken each month?

A. $\frac{34 + 31 + 42}{36}$

B. $\frac{34 + 31 + 42}{3}$

C. $\frac{34 + 31 + 42 + 36}{4}$

D. $(34 + 31 + 42) \times 3$

For questions 23 through 27, write your answers on the lines provided.

23. Andy rolls two standard six-sided dice. What is the probability of rolling two 1s? Express your answer as a fraction.

    _____

24. Kate drove 158 miles on Monday, 276 miles on Tuesday, 54 miles on Wednesday, 305 miles on Thursday, and 210 miles on Friday. In miles, what was the median distance she drove for the five days?

    _____

25. Angelique, a teacher, is making a reading list for her students. She wants to include one historical novel, one work of science fiction, one book of poetry, and one graphic novel. She has five of each type of book to choose from. How many possible combinations of books could she include in her reading list?

    _____

26. There are four children in Mr. Martin's class. Three of them will be selected to be hall monitors. How many combinations of hall monitors are possible?

    _____

27. A charity's board has ten members. One of the members will be elected president, then another will be elected treasurer, and then a third will be elected secretary. If no member can hold more than one position, how many ways can the members fill those positions?

_____

Questions 28 and 29 are based on the following information.

The frequency table below displays the reasons why patients visited a walk-in clinic during a certain week.

Reason	Number of Patients
Colds and Flu	۱۱۱۱۱ ۱۱۱۱۱ ۱۱۱۱۱ I
Cuts and Scrapes	۱۱۱۱۱ ۱۱۱۱۱ I I I
Sprained Muscles	۱۱۱۱۱ ۱۱۱۱۱ I I
Tetanus Shots	۱۱۱۱۱ I I
Severe Headaches	۱۱۱۱۱ ۱۱۱۱۱ I I

28. Write your answer on the line below. What percent of the patients represented in the table visited the walk-in clinic because of sprained muscles?

_____

29. In the week represented in the table, what was the ratio of the number of patients with colds or flu to the number of patients with severe headaches?

   A. 4:15
   B. 4:3
   C. 3:4
   D. 1:5

Questions 30 and 31 are based on the following information and graph.

A hundred people are participating in a medical study. As a first step, the researchers collected information about participants' weight. The graph below represents how many people fell into each weight category.

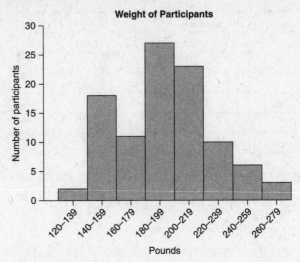

30. Which weight category displays the highest frequency?

   A. 120–139 lbs
   B. 180–199 lbs
   C. 200–219 lbs
   D. 260–279 lbs

31. Consider only the 100 individuals represented in the graph. Which one of the following groups contains the most people?

   A. Participants weighing 200 lbs or more
   B. Participants weighing less than 200 lbs
   C. Participants weighing 180–199 lbs
   D. Participants weighing less than 180 lbs

Questions 32 through 34 refer to the following information and table.

The owner of a taxi company measures the gas mileage of each of the cars in her fleet. The frequency table below shows her results.

Average miles per gallon	Number of cars
15	I I
20	HHI I I
25	HHI
30	HHI I
35	I

32. Which of the values (average miles per gallon) displays the highest frequency?

    A. 15 miles per gallon
    B. 20 miles per gallon
    C. 30 miles per gallon
    D. 35 miles per gallon

33. What is the ratio of taxis that get 35 miles per gallon on average to the number of taxis that get 15 miles per gallon on average?

    A. $\frac{1}{2}$

    B. $\frac{3}{2}$

    C. $\frac{4}{5}$

    D. $\frac{1}{10}$

34. The line plot below is based on the information in the table. Place additional points on the line to accurately represent the data.

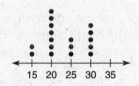

35. Ahmed works at the ticket window of a theater, and one night he decides to track when the patrons arrive for a 7:30 p.m. show. The table below represents his data.

Time period	Percent of patrons who arrive
5:30 to 5:59 p.m.	2%
6:00 to 6:29 p.m.	14%
6:30 to 6:59 p.m.	25%
7:00 to 7:29 p.m.	48%
7:30 to 8:00 p.m.	11%

Which one of the histograms below accurately represents Ahmed's data?

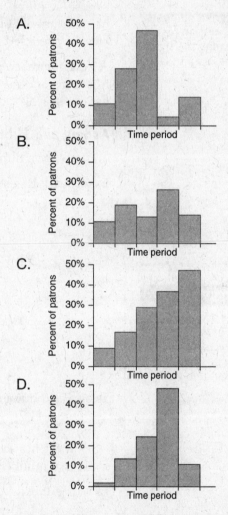

Answers and explanations begin on page 215.

The Number Line and Signed Numbers

Key Ideas

- If numbers have like signs, add and keep the same sign.
- If numbers have unlike signs, find the difference and use the sign from the larger number.
- To subtract signed numbers, change the operation to addition and change the sign of the number you are subtracting.

Understanding Signed Numbers

Signed numbers include zero, all positive numbers, and all negative numbers. Zero is neither positive nor negative. On a number line, the positive numbers are shown to the right of zero, and the negative numbers are shown to the left.

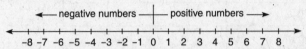

A positive number may be written with a plus (+) symbol. If a number has no symbol at all, we assume that it is positive. A negative number *must* be preceded by a minus (−) symbol.

A signed number provides two important facts. The sign tells the direction from zero, and the number tells you the distance from zero. For example, −5 lies five spaces to the left of zero, and +4 lies four spaces to the right of zero.

Adding and Subtracting Signed Numbers

You can use a number line to model the addition of signed numbers.

Examples: $1 + (-4) = -3$ Begin at +1; move 4 in a negative direction (left).

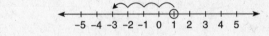

$-5 + 4 = -1$ Begin at −5; move 4 in a positive direction (right).

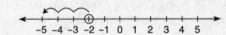

$-2 + (-3) = -5$ Begin at −2; move 3 in a negative direction (left).

To add without a number line, follow these steps:

- If numbers have like signs, add the numbers and keep the same sign.
- If the numbers have unlike signs, find the difference between the two numbers and use the sign of the larger number.

Example 1: Add $15 + (-25)$.

1. Since the numbers have unlike signs, subtract: $25 - 15 = 10$.

2. Use the sign from the larger number: $15 + (-25) = \mathbf{-10}$.

Subtraction is the opposite of addition. To rewrite a subtraction problem as an addition problem, change the operation symbol to addition and change the sign on the number you are subtracting. Then apply the rules for adding signed numbers.

Example 2: Subtract $3 - 8$.

1. Change the operation symbol and the sign of the number you are subtracting:

   $3 - 8$ becomes $3 + (-8)$.

2. Add: $3 + (-8) = -5$.

You can use the same rules to combine several signed numbers.

Example 3: $(-5) + 6 - 4 - (-2) = ?$

1. Rewrite each subtraction as addition: $(-5) + 6 + (-4) + 2$.

2. Add the positive terms: $6 + 2 = 8$. Add the negative terms: $-5 + (-4) = -9$.

3. Combine the results: $8 + -9 = -1$.

PRACTICE 1.1

A. Solve.

1. $8 + (-3)$
2. $50 - 5$
3. $11 - (-2)$
4. $-1 + 2$
5. $-4 - (-5)$
6. $8 - (-2)$
7. $6 - 9$
8. $2 + 11$

9. $(-7) - (-3)$
10. $(-4) + 6$
11. $-15 + (-7)$
12. $36 - 4$
13. $-60 - (-10)$
14. $-5 - 6$
15. $12 + 13$
16. $-55 + 20$

17. $7 + (-3) + (-5) - 10$
18. $66 + (-22) - 33$
19. $-14 - (-6) + 18$
20. $80 - (-15) - 20$
21. $6 - (-3) + (-5) + 8$
22. $-23 + (-11) - (-15) + 21$
23. $3 + 9 - 5 + 12 - 9 - 11$
24. $-7 - 20 - (-14)$

B. Choose the <u>one best answer</u> to each question.

<u>Question 25</u> refers to the following number line.

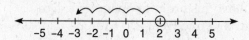

25. The number line above shows which of the following expressions?

   A. $2 + (-3)$
   B. $2 + (-5)$
   C. $-3 + 2$
   D. $-3 - (+2)$

26. At noon, the temperature in the high desert was 92°F. A scientist observed the following temperature changes over the course of the next two hours: +12°F, −5°F, +6°F, −3°F, and +13°F. What was the temperature, in degrees Fahrenheit at the end of the two-hour period?

   A. 95°F
   B. 103°F
   C. 115°F
   D. 131°F

Answers and explanations begin on page 216.

Multiplying and Dividing Signed Numbers

In algebra, multiplication is not shown using the times sign ($\times$) because the symbol could be easily mistaken for the variable x. Instead, multiplication is shown using a dot or by placing two numbers next to each other. To avoid confusion, one or both of the numbers may be enclosed in parentheses. For example, the expressions $-5 \cdot 6$ and $-5(6)$ and $(-5)(6)$ all mean "-5 times 6."

In algebra, division can be written with the $\div$ symbol, but it is usually shown with a line that means "divided by." The expression $\frac{20}{-5}$ means "20 divided by -5," as does $20/-5$.
When multiplying or dividing signed numbers, use the following rules:

- If the signs are the same, the answer is positive.
- If the signs are different, the answer is negative.

Example 1: Multiply $4(-25)$.

1. Multiply the numbers only: $4 \times 25 = 100$.

2. Determine the sign. Since the signs on the numbers are different, the answer is negative: $4(-25) = -\mathbf{100}$.

Example 2: Divide $\frac{-160}{-8}$.

1. Divide the numbers only: $160 \div 8 = 20$.
2. Determine the sign. Since the signs on the numbers are the same, the answer is positive:

$$\frac{-160}{-8} = \mathbf{20}.$$

A problem may contain more than two factors. Remember that each pair of negative factors will equal a positive product. Therefore, if there is an even number of negative terms, the product will be positive. If there is an odd number of negative terms, the product will be negative.

Example 3: $(-5)(6)(-1)(-2)(2) = ?$

1. Multiply: $5 \times 6 \times 1 \times 2 \times 2 = 120$.

2. There are three negative terms. Since 3 is an odd number, the product is negative: $-\mathbf{120}$.

When a problem contains more than one operation, follow this **order of operations**. Do multiplication and division operations first, working from left to right. Do addition and subtraction operations last, also working from left to right. If a problem contains division presented with a division bar, do any operations above and below the bar first and then divide.

Example 4: $(-4)(6) - \dfrac{3 + (-9)}{-2}$

1. Multiply: $-24 - \dfrac{3 + (-9)}{-2}$.

2. Do the operation above the fraction bar: $-24 - \dfrac{-6}{-2}$.

3. Divide: $-24 - (+3)$.

4. Subtract: $-24 - (+3) = -24 + (-3) = -\mathbf{27}$.

NOTE: *Notice how parentheses clarify meaning:* $4 - 5$ means "four minus five," but $4(-5)$ means "four times negative five."

PRACTICE 1.2

A. Solve. You MAY NOT use a calculator.

1. $(5)(4)$
2. $(7)(-3)$
3. $(-8)(6)$
4. $(-2)(-9)$
5. $(-10)(1)$

6. $9 \div 3$
7. $12 \div (-4)$
8. $-25 \div 5$
9. $(-18) \div (-9)$
10. $\dfrac{40}{-8}$

11. $(14)(-2)$
12. $(-75) \div 25$
13. $13 \div (-13)$
14. $(-5)(15)$
15. $\dfrac{18}{3}$

B. Solve. You MAY use a calculator.

16. $\dfrac{25(4)}{-5}$
17. $(-3)(-5)(2)(-10)$
18. $20 \div (-5) \div (-2)$
19. $\dfrac{6(5)}{(-3)(2)}$

20. $(-11)(2)(-5)(6)$
21. $(12)(-2) \div (-2)$
22. $(-4)(-6)(-5)$
23. $50 \div (2)(-5)$

24. $(-1)(2)(-3)(2)(-1)$
25. $\dfrac{(3)(-4)(2)(5)}{-6}$
26. $\dfrac{4(-4)}{-8(-2)}$
27. $(-5)(-2)(0)(-1)$

C. Choose the one best answer to each question.

28. Janice is creating a computer spreadsheet. A portion of her work is shown below.

	A	B	C
1	−3	4	7
2	2	−5	−8
3	−1	3	−2

Using the information from the spreadsheet, what is the value of the expression A1*C1*A3/(B3*A3)? (*Hint*: In a spreadsheet, the symbol * means multiplication.)

A. −21
B. −7
C. $\dfrac{-1}{7}$
D. 21

29. The product of 2 and 8 is divided by −8 . Which of the following expressions could be used to find the value of the statement?

A. $\dfrac{\frac{2}{8}}{-8}$
B. $2(8)(-8)$
C. $\dfrac{2(8)}{(-8)}$
D. $\dfrac{2(-8)}{8}$

30. Which of the following is a true statement about the value of the expression $(52)(-103)(-45)(-8)(3)$?

A. The result is a fraction.
B. The result is greater than 1.
C. The result is a negative number.
D. The result is a positive number.

Answers and explanations begin on page 216.

Powers and Roots

Key Ideas

- In the expression 2^3, the base is 2 and the exponent is 3.
- To raise a number to a certain power, write the base the number of times shown by the exponent and then multiply.
- To find a square root, think, "What number times itself equals this number?"

Powers are a special way to show repeated multiplication. For example, suppose you needed to multiply $5 \times 5 \times 5 \times 5$. This series of operations can be expressed as "five to the fourth power." In other words, the number 5 appears in the multiplication problem four times.

We can write the operations algebraically using **exponents**. In the expression $5 \times 5 \times 5 \times 5$ above, the number 5 is the base. The exponent, a small number written above and to the right of the **base**, tells how many times the base is repeated: $5 \times 5 \times 5 \times 5 = 5^4$.

To evaluate an expression, perform the multiplication indicated by the exponent.

Example 1: Find the value of 2^5.

Write the base the number of times indicated by the exponent and then multiply:

$$2^5 = 2 \times 2 \times 2 \times 2 \times 2 = \mathbf{32}.$$

You may encounter some special uses of exponents on the *Mathematical Reasoning Test*. An exponent can be any positive number, or it can be 0, 1, or a negative number. Memorize the situations described below.

1. A number raised to the first power equals itself: $8^1 = 8$.

2. A number other than zero raised to the power of zero equals 1: $6^0 = 1$.

3. A number raised to a negative exponent is equal to a fraction with a numerator of 1: $4^{-2} = \dfrac{1}{4^2} = \dfrac{1}{4 \times 4} = \dfrac{1}{16}$.

You can use a calculator to raise numbers to any power. Use the $\boxed{x^2}$ or $\boxed{\wedge}$ key.

Example 2: Find the square of 24.

Press: $24 \boxed{x^2}$ $\boxed{\text{enter}}$. The right side of the display reads 576.

The square of 24 is **576**.

Example 3: Find the value of 9^4.

Enter the base, press $\boxed{\wedge}$, and enter the exponent. Then press $\boxed{\text{enter}}$.

Press $9 \boxed{\wedge} 4 \boxed{\text{enter}}$. The right side of the display reads 6561.

Nine raised to the fourth power is **6561**.

NOTE: To raise a negative number to a power using the TI-30XS MultiView™ calculator, you must enter that number in parentheses: $\boxed{(}\boxed{(-)}4\boxed{)}$ $\boxed{x^2}$ $\boxed{\text{enter}}$.

To square a number, multiply the number by itself. For example, $6^2 = 6 \times 6 = 36$. In the expression $6 \times 6 = 36$, the number 36 is the square, and the number 6 is the **square root** of 36.

GED® TEST TIP

Make a list of common square roots by squaring the numbers from 1 to 15. Memorize them. You will need to know common square roots to solve geometry problems about area and right triangles.

The symbol for square root is $\sqrt{}$. To find a square root, think, "What number multiplied by itself is equal to the number in the bracket?"

Example 4: Find the value of $\sqrt{144}$.

You know that $12 \times 12 = 144$, so the square root of 144 is **12**.

Although $(-12) \times (-12)$ also equals 144, you will only be expected to find positive roots on the GED® Test.

You may have to approximate the value of a square root.

Example 5: What is the square root of 90?

You know that $9 \times 9 = 81$ and $10 \times 10 = 100$. Therefore, the square root of 90 is **between 9 and 10**.

You can also use your calculator to find a square root. On the TI-30SX MultiView™, you must first press the (2nd) key to access the square root function. The $\sqrt{}$ function is directly above the $\boxed{x^2}$ key. (Other calculators may not require the use of the (2nd) key.)

Example 6: Use your calculator to find $\sqrt{90}$ to the nearest tenth.

On the TI-30SX MultiView™, press (2nd) $\boxed{x^2}$ 90 (enter). The right side of the display reads $3\sqrt{10}$.

Press the toggle key, (◄►), to change the format of the answer into a decimal.

The right side of the display now reads 9.486832981.

Rounding to the tenths place, $\sqrt{90} \approx \mathbf{9.5}$.

PRACTICE 2

A. Solve each expression. You MAY NOT use a calculator.

1. 3^2
2. 4^1
3. $\sqrt{9}$

4. 25^0
5. $(-3)^2$
6. $\sqrt{49}$

7. 5^3
8. 4^{-2}
9. 2^4

10. $\sqrt{64}$
11. 10^{-3}
12. $\sqrt{121}$

B. Solve each expression below. You MAY use your calculator. Round your answer to the nearest tenth.

13. 3^8
14. $(-6)^4$
15. $\sqrt{150}$

16. 20^3
17. 1^{15}
18. $(-4)^{-2}$

19. $\sqrt{242}$
20. $(3.3)^2$
21. $\sqrt{57}$

22. $\sqrt{536}$
23. 112^0
24. $(-2)^8$

C. Choose the one best answer to each question.

25. The cube shown below measures 6 inches on each side. You can find the volume of the cube by multiplying length × width × height . Which of the following expressions represents the volume of the cube?

 A. 6^1
 B. 6^2
 C. 6^3
 D. 6^6

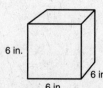

6 in.

6 in.

6 in.

26. Which of the following expressions has the least value?

 A. 3^{-3}
 B. 4^0
 C. 4^1
 D. 2^{-4}

Answers and explanations begin on page 216.

Scientific Notation

Scientific notation uses the powers of ten to express very small and very large numbers. In scientific notation, a decimal number (greater than or equal to 1 and less than 10) is multiplied by a power of ten.

Key Ideas

- In scientific notation, a number equal to or greater than 1 and less than 10 is multiplied by a power of ten.
- Very small numbers are expressed by multiplying by a negative power of ten.
- In scientific notation, the number with the greatest power of ten has the greatest value.

Look for patterns as you review these powers of ten.

$10^1 = 10$ $10^2 = 100$ $10^3 = 1,000$ $10^4 = 10,000$ and so on.

$10^{-1} = 0.1$ $10^{-2} = 0.01$ $10^{-3} = 0.001$ $10^{-4} = 0.0001$ and so on.

Did you find the patterns? In the row with positive exponents, the exponent is the same as the number of zeros in the number written in standard form. In the row with negative exponents, the exponent is the same as the number of decimal places in the number.

You can use these patterns to change scientific notation to standard form.

Example 1: Write 6.2×10^5 in standard form. 6.20000

Move the decimal point five places to the *right* (the same number as the exponent). Add zeros as needed.   **620,000**

Example 2: Write 3.82×10^{-3} in standard form.

Move the decimal point three places to the *left* (the same 0.00382
number as the exponent). Add zeros as needed.

Work backward to write large and small numbers in scientific notation.

Example 3: To reach Mars, the Viking 2 spacecraft traveled 440,000,000 miles. What is the distance traveled in scientific notation?

1. Move the decimal point to the left until there is 4.40000000
   only a single digit in the ones place.

2. Multiply by 10 raised to a power equal to 4.4×10^8
   the number of places you moved the decimal
   point.

Example 4: Scientists find that a kind of bacteria moves at a rate of 0.00016 kilometers per hour. Write the measurement in scientific notation.

1. Move the decimal place to the right until there is 0001.6
   a single digit in the ones place.

2. Multiply by 10 raised to a negative exponent equal 1.6×10^{-4}
   to the number of places you moved the decimal
   point.

You may be asked to compare numbers in scientific notation.

Example 5: Which is greater: 4.5×10^3 or 9.8×10^4?

You don't need to change the numbers to standard notation. Simply consider the powers of ten. Multiplying by 10^4, or 10,000, must have a greater result than multiplying by 10^3, which equals 1,000. In scientific notation, the number with the greater power of 10 has the greater value. Therefore, **9.8×10^4 is greater than 4.5×10^3.**

PRACTICE 3

A. Write each number in scientific notation.

1. 2300
2. 0.00042
3. 12,400,000

4. 14,320,000,000
5. 36,000,000
6. 0.0095

7. 0.00000058
8. 150,000,000,000
9. 0.000000009

B. Convert from scientific notation to standard notation.

10. 5.173×10^{-4}
11. 3.7×10^6

12. 4.8×10^8
13. 1.7×10^{-5}

14. 7.2×10^{-3}
15. 9.16×10^5

16. 8.591×10^7
17. 9.56×10^{-6}

C. Answer the following questions.

18. Many domestic satellites maintain an orbit approximately 23,500 miles above Earth. What is that distance, in miles, in scientific notation?

19. Modern technology measures very fast transactions in nanoseconds. One nanosecond equals 1.0×10^{-9} of a second. How many seconds is a nanosecond, in standard notation?

20. The average distance of Neptune from Earth is 2.67×10^9 miles. Write the distance, in miles, in standard notation.

21. Light in the vacuum of space travels at a speed of nearly 300 million meters per second. Write the speed, in meters, in scientific notation.

D. Choose the one best answer to each question.

Questions 22 and 23 refer to the following table.

Unit	U.S. Equivalent	Metric Equivalent
1 ton	2,000 lb	0.907 metric ton
1 acre	43,560 sq ft	4,047 square m

22. What is the number of square feet in an acre, written in scientific notation?
   A. 0.4356×10^6
   B. 4.356×10^4
   C. 4.356×10^3
   D. 43.56×10^3

23. A shipment of goods weighs 5 tons. Which of the following expressions could be used to express the weight in metric tons?
   A. $5 \times 0.907 \times 10^{-1}$
   B. $5 \times 9.07 \times 10^1$
   C. $5 \times 9.07 \times 10^{-2}$
   D. $5 \times 9.07 \times 10^{-1}$

Answers and explanations begin on page 216.

ALGEBRA BASICS, EXPRESSIONS, AND POLYNOMIALS

Order of Operations

Key Ideas

- To evaluate an expression correctly, you must follow the order of operations.
- If an expression uses more than one set of grouping symbols, start with the inside set and work to the outside.
- The division bar may be used as a grouping symbol.

When a mathematical expression contains more than one operation, its value may depend upon the order in which the operations are performed. To avoid confusion, mathematicians have agreed to perform operations in a certain order.

The Order of Operations
1. Parentheses or any other grouping symbols that enclose operations
2. Exponents and roots
3. Multiplication and division, working from left to right
4. Addition and subtraction, working from left to right

Study the following example to see how to apply the order of operations. Notice that parentheses are used in two places in the expression; however, only the first set of parentheses encloses an operation.

Example 1: Evaluate the expression $\dfrac{(5+3)^2}{4} + 3(-1)$.

1. Perform the addition operation in parentheses. $\qquad \dfrac{(8)^2}{4} + 3(-1)$

2. Raise 8 to the second power. $\qquad \dfrac{64}{4} + 3(-1)$

3. Divide, then multiply. $\qquad\qquad\qquad 16 + (-3)$

4. Add. $\qquad\qquad\qquad\qquad\qquad\qquad 13$

The value of the expression $\dfrac{(5+3)^2}{4} + 3(-1)$ is **13**.

In more complicated expressions, one set of grouping symbols may be nested within another set. To avoid confusion, you can also use brackets [ ] or braces { } to group operations. To evaluate an expression with more than one set of grouping symbols, work from the inside to the outside.

Example 2: Evaluate the expression $4[5(-4) + 3) + 2]$.

1. Perform the operation in the inner set of grouping $\qquad 4[5(-4+3)+2]$
   symbols: $(-4 + 3)$. $\qquad\qquad\qquad\qquad\qquad\qquad 4[5(-1)+2]$

2. Do the operations inside the brackets. Since multiplication $\quad 4[-5+2]$
   comes before addition in the order of operations, $\qquad\qquad 4[-3]$
   multiply 5 and -1 and then add 2.

3. Multiply 4 and -3. $\qquad\qquad\qquad\qquad\qquad\qquad\qquad -12$

The division bar is also a grouping symbol. Before you divide, perform any operations shown above and below the bar.

Example 3: Evaluate the expression $\dfrac{15+25}{2(5)}+6$.

1. Perform the operations above and below the fraction bar.

$$\dfrac{15+25}{2(5)}+6$$

$$\dfrac{40}{10}+6$$

2. Divide, then add.

$$4+6=\mathbf{10}$$

PRACTICE 4

A. Solve. You MAY NOT use a calculator.

1. $4(3)-2+(6+4\cdot2)$
2. $16\div(10-6)^2$
3. $5^2-(5-7)(2)$
4. $3(-3)+(7+4)$
5. $\dfrac{3^3}{5-2}-\dfrac{(4-2)^2}{2}$

6. $\dfrac{25}{(4+1)}\cdot3+(6-1)$
7. $2^3+(8-5)^2-3$
8. $(4-12)(-6)+(10-3)$
9. $30\div3(5-4)$
10. $15+(4)(3)-2^2$

11. $(4+2)^2+(7-2)^3$
12. $7^2\div(11-4)+(9+14)$
13. $2\left[(17-11)^2\cdot\dfrac{(15-5)}{2}\right]$
14. $(5^2+6-3)\div(16-3^2)$
15. $150-4\left[\dfrac{3+9}{4-1}\cdot(14-11)^2\right]$

B. Choose the one best answer to each question.

Question 16 refers to the following information.

Susan is in charge of planning Midvale Hospital's parent education classes. She uses the table below to determine the cost of each class to the hospital.

Midvale Hospital Parenting Workshops	
Type of Workshop	Cost per Participant
Childbirth Classes	$35 per couple
Infant Care	$30 per person
Teaching Your Child to Read	$60 per person

16. A local foundation has offered to pay 75% of the cost of infant care classes. The hospital will cover any remaining costs. There are 28 parents enrolled in the upcoming class. Which of the following expressions could be used to find the amount the hospital will pay?

A. $(75)(28)(30)$
B. $(28)(30)-(0.75)(30)$
C. $(1-0.75)(28)(30)$
D. $(1-0.75)(30)+28$

17. In the expression

$$5+2\left[7\left(\dfrac{10^2}{10}\right)+(6-2)(3)\right],$$

what is the last operation you should perform to find the value of the expression?

A. Subtract 2 from 6.
B. Add 5.
C. Multiply by 2.
D. Find the square of 10.

18. Find the value of the expression $22+6[(14-5)\div3(17-14)]$.

A. 2.73
B. 28
C. 76
D. 97

Answers and explanations begin on page 217.

Absolute Value

Key Ideas

- The magnitude of a number, without a sign, is called the absolute value.
- Absolute value is used to determine distance of a positive or negative number from zero.
- In the order of operations, absolute value is treated the same as a set of parentheses.

The **absolute value** of a number is its distance from zero on the number line. For example, the absolute value of 5 is 5, since 5 is five spaces away from zero on the number line. But the absolute value of -5 is also 5, since -5 is also five spaces away from zero on the number line. Because **distance** is always **positive**, the absolute value of any positive or negative number is always positive.

Absolute value is written as two straight lines around a number, like this: $|-5|$.

$$|-5| = 5 \qquad\qquad |5| = 5$$

Example 1: Which of the following is equal to $|-13|$?

   (1)   13

   (2) -13

The correct answer is **(1)**. Absolute value is always positive.

Treat the absolute value sign as you would treat parentheses in the order of operations. If numbers inside the absolute value sign are being added, subtracted, multiplied, or divided, then do that operation before you do anything else.

Example 2: Which of the following is equal to $-20\,|17-34|$?

   (1)   340

   (2) -340

The correct answer is **(2)**. First perform the subtraction within the absolute value sign. Because you first found the absolute value, change -17 to 17. Then multiply by -20, like this:

$$-20\,|17-34| = -20\,|-17| = -20\,(17) = -\textbf{340}.$$

We often think in terms of absolute value in real life, though we might not bother to call it that. For example, imagine that you have $314 in a checking account but you write a check for $400. You've overdrawn your account by $86. The bank will record your balance as –$86.00. But you'll think, "I'm $86 short." You'll just think of the absolute value, or **magnitude**, of the overdraft, without the negative sign.

Practice 5

A. Find the absolute values.

1. $|18|$

2. $|-107|$

3. $|423|$

4. $|95|$

5. $|-7026|$

6. $|-18|$

7. $|-5,708,432|$

8. $|-85.6|$

9. $|42|$

10. $|10.5|$

11. $|-163.24|$

12. $|-3.14|$

B. Use absolute value to find the solutions.

13. $5 + |-6|$

14. $-3|52|$

15. $3|-52|$

16. $12 \div |-4|$

17. $-|110 - 201|$

18. $-14 + |-28 \div 2|$

19. $706.2 - |-86.4 + 0.2|$

20. $49 \div (-|-7|)$

21. $-5|-4|$

22. $|-6| - |-7|$

23. $|17| \div |-8|$

24. $|-5.5| \times (-2)$

C. Choose the <u>one best answer</u> to each question.

25. The temperature in Northville at 9:00 p.m. was $-5°F$. By 5:00 a.m. the following morning, the temperature was $-15°F$. By how many degrees did the temperature change?

    A. -15 degrees
    B. -5 degrees
    C. 5 degrees
    D. 10 degrees

26. Bob has errands to run. He walks 5 blocks east from his apartment to the barber shop, then walks 6 blocks west to the grocery store, then walks another 2 blocks west to the post office, and finally walks back home. Assuming that Bob's apartment, the barber shop, the grocery store, and the post office are all located on the same street, how many blocks did Bob walk in completing his errands?

    A. 6
    B. 11
    C. 13
    D. 16

27. Milania has a score of -65 points, and Chris has a score of 55 points. By how many points is Milania losing to Chris?

    A. 55
    B. 65
    C. 120
    D. 150

28. Absolute error is the absolute value of the difference between an actual value and its measurement. A deli scale gives a measurement of 25 ounces for a cut of meat that actually weighs only 23.5 ounces. What is the absolute error, in ounces, of the deli scale in this instance?

    A. 1.5
    B. 23.5
    C. 25
    D. 48.5

Answers and explanations begin on page 217.

Algebraic Expressions

Writing Algebraic Expressions

An **algebraic expression** uses numbers, operations, and variables to show number relationships. **Variables** are letters (such as x and y) that represent unknown numbers. Each time a letter is used within the same expression, it represents the same number.

To solve algebra problems, you will need to be able to translate number relationships described in words into algebraic expressions. Study the following examples.

Algebraic Expressions in Words	In Symbols
the product of 5 and a number	$5X$
a number decreased by 12	$x - 12$
the sum of 3 and the square of a number	$3 + x^2$
6 less than the quotient of a number and 2	$\frac{x}{2} - 6$
one-half a number increased by 15	$\frac{1}{2}x + 15$
4 times the difference of -3 and a number	$4(-3 - x)$
a number less another number	$x - y$
10 less the square root of a number plus 3	$10 - \sqrt{x + 3}$

To do well on algebra questions on the GED® *Mathematical Reasoning Test*, you must be able to translate a common life situation into mathematical symbols. You will use this skill to write equations and functions, to apply formulas, and to solve word problems.

Example 1: Kyle processes sales for an online bookstore. The shipping and handling on an order is equal to 4% of the total cost of the order plus $0.95 per book. If c represents total cost and n represents the number of books in an order, which of the following expressions could be used to find the shipping and handling for an order?

   (1) $\frac{4}{100}nc + 0.95$

   (2) $(0.04 + 0.95)n + c$

   (3) $0.04c + 0.95n$

This kind of problem is called a **setup problem.** You need to recognize the correct way to find the shipping and handling based on the total cost and number of items. The relationship is described in the second sentence.

shipping and handling = 4% of total cost (c) plus $0.95 per book ($n$)

$$= \quad 0.04c \quad + \quad 0.95n$$

The correct answer is option **(3)**, **$0.04c + 0.95n$**.

Key Ideas

- Algebraic expressions show mathematical relationships using numbers, symbols, and variables.
- Variables are letters that take the place of unknown numbers.

GED® TEST TIP

To check whether the expression you have chosen is correct, substitute easy numbers into the expression and complete the operations. Then see if the result is reasonable for the situation.

PRACTICE 6.1

A. Write an algebraic expression for each description. Use the variables x and y.

1. a number decreased by 7

2. the product of 3 and the square of a number increased by that number

3. the product of 8 and a number less 10

4. the difference of −3 multiplied by a number and the product of 2 and another number

5. 5 less than the quotient of 10 and a number

6. the sum of −8 and the product of 7 and a number

7. the sum of 16 times a number and the number less another number times 3

8. a number squared plus the number raised to the fourth power

9. the sum of the square of a number and 4 divided by 7

10. 6 subtracted from the sum of 15 and the square root of a number

11. a number less the sum of another number and 13

12. the square of the sum of a number and 6

13. 17 less the sum of 2 times a number plus another number

14. a number increased by the quotient of 24 and the number

15. the difference of the product of 2 and a number and 15

16. 4 times the difference of two different numbers

17. 5 multiplied by the difference of a number squared and 3

18. the product of a number and the difference of 11 and the square root of 100

B. Choose the one best answer to each question.

19. A minor-league baseball team is giving a local charity the sum of $1500 and $0.50 for each ticket over 2000 sold for one game. Let x represent the number of tickets sold. If the team sells more than 2000 tickets, which of the following expressions could be used to find the amount of the donation?

    A. $1500 + \$0.50x$
    B. $1500 + \$0.50(2000 - x)$
    C. $1500 + \$0.50(x - 2000)$
    D. $1500(2000 - x)(\$0.50)$

20. The sum of 3 times a number and 4 times another number is divided by the sum of 2 and a third number. Which of the following expressions represents this series of operations?

    A. $(3x + 4y) \div (2 + z)$
    B. $3x + 4y \div (2 + z)$
    C. $3x + 4y \div 2 + z$
    D. $(3x + 4y) \div 2z$

Question 21 refers to the following information.

Appliance City employees earn an hourly wage plus commission. Wage options are shown below.

Option	Hourly Wage	Commission on Sales
A	$7.50	1%
B	$6.00	3%

21. Chandra is paid under Option B. If h represents the number of hours worked and s represents Chandra's total sales, which of the following expressions could be used to find her weekly pay?

    A. $6 + h + 0.03s$
    B. $6h + 0.03s$
    C. $6s + 0.03h$
    D. $0.03(h)(s)$

Answers and explanations begin on page 217.

Simplifying and Evaluating Expressions

Simplifying an expression means to perform all the operations you can within an expression. When working with variables, you must remember an important rule: you can add or subtract like terms only.

A **term** is a number, a variable, or the product or quotient of numbers and variables. A term cannot include a sum or a difference.

Examples: $5x$ $3y^2$ 13 x^3 $\dfrac{x}{2}$

Like terms have the same variable raised to the same power. For example, $3x^2$ and $5x^2$ are like terms. $8y$ and $4y$ are also like terms. However, $6x$ and $2x^2$ are not like terms because the variables are not raised to the same power.

To simplify an expression, combine like terms.

Example 2: Simplify $2x - 5 + 4x^2 - 8 + 6x$.

Combine like terms. It is customary to write the term with the greatest exponent first and to continue in descending order.

$$\begin{aligned} &2x - 5 + 4x^2 - 8 + 6x \\ &= (2x + 6x) + (-5 + -8) + 4x^2 \\ &= 8x + (-13) + 4x^2 \\ &= 4x^2 + 8x - 13 \end{aligned}$$

The **distributive property** allows you to remove grouping symbols to simplify expressions. We can state the distributive property using symbols.

$$a(b + c) = ab + ac \quad \text{and} \quad a(b - c) = ab - ac$$

In other words, each term inside the parentheses is multiplied by the term outside the parentheses, and the results are added or subtracted depending on the operation inside the parentheses. Example 3 applies the distributive property.

Example 3: Simplify $4x - 3(x + 9) + 15$.

1. Change subtracting to adding a negative number.
2. Use the distributive property. Multiply -3 by each term in the parentheses.
3. Combine like terms.
   (**NOTE:** $1x$ means x.)

$$\begin{aligned} &4x - 3(x + 9) + 15 \\ &= 4x + -3(x + 9) + 15 \\ &= 4x + (-3x) + (-3)(9) + 15 \\ &= 4x + (-3x) + (-27) + 15 \\ &= (4x + -3x) + (-27 + 15) \\ &= x - 12 \end{aligned}$$

Evaluating an expression means finding its value. To evaluate an expression, substitute a given number for each variable. Follow the order of operations.

Example 3: Find the value of the expression $\dfrac{3x + 2y}{4}$ when $x = 6$ and $y = 5$.

1. Replace the variables with the values given in the problem.

$$\frac{3x + 2y}{4} = \frac{3(6) + 2(5)}{4}$$

2. Perform the operations above the fraction bar. Then divide.

$$\frac{3(6) + 2(5)}{4} = \frac{18 + 10}{4} = \frac{28}{4} = 7$$

NOTE: To remove parentheses from an operation that follows a minus sign, imagine that the parentheses are preceded by 1. Then use the distributive property.

$$\begin{aligned} &-(2x + 3) \\ &= -1(2x + 3) \\ &= -1(2x) + (-1)(3) \\ &= -2x + (-3) \text{ or } -2x - 3 \end{aligned}$$

PRACTICE 6.2

A. Simplify.

1. $5 + x^2 - 3 + 3x$
2. $2y + 5 + 17y + 8$
3. $3x - 6(x - 9)$
4. $6x^3 + 4 + 2x^2(15) + x^2$
5. $4(y + 8) + 3(y - 6)$
6. $5 - (x - 3) + 4x$
7. $16x + 6(x - 2)$
8. $5y^2 + 4 - 3y^2 + 5 + y$
9. $-3(x + 3) - 2(x + 4)$
10. $5x - (x + 4) - 3$

B. Evaluate each expression as directed.

11. Find the value of $6(x + 2) + 7$ when $x = 2$.

12. Find the value of $3x^2 + 3(x + 4)$ when $x = 3$.

13. Find the value of $\frac{(x + y)^2}{2} - 10$ when $x = 2$ and $y = 4$.

14. Find the value of $y^2 + 16 - (y - 5)^2$ when $y = 3$.

15. Find the value of $8x + 9y - (2x + y)$ when $x = 4$ and $y = 6$.

16. Find the value of $x^2 + 3y - 4 + 2(x - z)$ when $x = 7$, $y = 5$, and $z = -3$.

17. Find the value of $(14 - x)^2 + 20\sqrt{x}$ when $x = 9$.

18. Find the value of $\frac{3(2x - y)}{3} + 6(y - 5)$ when $x = -2$ and $y = 3$.

19. Find the value of $x^2 - (x^3 + 3)$ when $x = -2$.

20. Find the value of $30x + 2 + 2y^2 - 3(x - 2)^2$ when $x = 1$ and $y = 4$.

C. Choose the one best answer to each question.

21. Which of the following expressions is equal to $3x^2 + 3(x - 3) + x + 10$?

   A. $x^2 + 9x + 1$
   B. $3x^2 + 4x + 19$
   C. $3x^2 - 2x + 19$
   D. $3x^2 + 4x + 1$

22. Given the expression $4x^2 - 3(y + 6)$, which of the following values for x and y will result in a value of -11?

   A. $x = 2, y = 3$
   B. $x = -2, y = 4$
   C. $x = -1, y = 2$
   D. $x = 1, y = 0$

Question 23 refers to the following information.

Temperature Conversion Formulas	
To convert Fahrenheit (F) to Celsius (C)	$C = \frac{5}{9}(F - 32)$
To convert Celsius (C) to Fahrenheit (F)	$F = \frac{9}{5}C + 32$

23. If the temperature is 68° Fahrenheit, what is the temperature in Celsius?

   A. 20°
   B. 36°
   C. 154.4°
   D. 180°

Answers and explanations begin on page 217.

ALGEBRA BASICS, EXPRESSIONS, AND POLYNOMIALS

Expressions and Calculator Skills

Key Ideas

- On the *Mathematical Reasoning Test*, you will use a scientific calculator that follows the order of operations.
- Use the *change sign* key to enter a negative number.
- Use the *grouping symbol* keys to change the order of operations.

When you take the GED® *Mathematical Reasoning Test*, you may use either a hand-held or an online version of a scientific calculator (TI-30XS MultiView™) to use on the second part of the test items. This calculator, like most scientific calculators, uses algebraic logic, which means that it follows the order of operations that you saw on page 124.

You need to practice using a scientific calculator with algebraic logic. You can find out whether your calculator uses algebraic logic by running this simple test.

Press: 4 ⊗ 3 x^2 (enter). (Your calculator may have an equal sign instead of an *enter* button.)

If the display reads **36**, your calculator uses algebraic logic.

If the display reads **144**, your calculator does not use algebraic logic. You should find another calculator to practice for the *Mathematical Reasoning Test*.

You can use a calculator to evaluate an expression that contains several operations.

Example 1: Find the value of the expression $2x^2 + 3x - 5$ when $x = -4$.

When you come to the variable x, enter -4 by pressing (−) 4. The (−) key is called the **change sign key**.

Press: 2 (((−) 4) x^2 + 3 × (−) 4 − 5 (enter).

The right side of the display reads 15.

The value of the expression is **15**.

Expressions sometimes contain grouping symbols to show a different order of operations. You can enter grouping symbols on a scientific calculator. On the TI-30XS MultiView™, the grouping symbols (and) are found above the 8 and 9, respectively. When you enter the left, or open, parenthesis, (, the calculator waits until you enter the right, or closing, parenthesis,), before it calculates what is inside the symbols.

Example 2: Find the value of the expression $2(x+4) + \frac{5x}{3}$ when $x = 6$.

Press: 2 × ((6 + 4)) + 5 × 6 ÷ 3 (enter).

The right side of the display reads **30**.

The value of the expression is **30**.

You can also use your calculator for only part of an expression.

Example 3: Find the value of the expression $\frac{3x+6}{2} + \sqrt{225}$ when $x = 4$.

Substitute 4 for x in the first part of the expression and calculate the results by hand or using your calculator: $\frac{3(4)+6}{2} = \frac{12+6}{2} = \frac{18}{2} = 9$.

Now use your calculator to find the square root of 225.

Press: 2nd x^2 225 (enter). The right side of the display reads 15.

Add the results of the two steps: $9 + 15 = 24$.

PRACTICE 7

A. Use a calculator as needed to find the value of the expressions as directed.

1. What is the value of $5x^2 - 3x + 5$ when $x = 2$?

2. Find the value of $\sqrt{7x} + 2x$ to the nearest tenth when $x = 5$.

3. If $x = -3$, what is the value of $7x^2 + 2x - 6$?

4. What is the value of $\frac{1}{2}x + 15$ when $x = 3$?

5. Find the value of $3(2x + 3 + y) - 14$ when $x = -2$ and $y = 9$.

6. If $y = -3$, what is the value of $4y^3 + 2(y^2 - 4)$?

7. What is the value of $2(x^2 + 6) + 3(x - 1)$ when $x = 5$?

8. If $x = 4$ and $y = -4$, what is the value of the expression $6x^2 + 3y^2 + 2$?

9. Find the value of $-2(x^3 + 3) + 16x + 2$ when $x = 2$.

10. If $x = 7$, what is the value of the expression $7 + 3(x - 2) - 2x^2$?

11. Find the value of $-(x + y) + 3(2z - y)$ if $x = -5$, $y = -7$, and $z = 4$.

12. What is the value of the expression $x^2 - 7(3 - y) + 4$ when $x = 5$ and $y = 4$?

13. If $x = -2$ and $y = 8$, what is the value of $x^2 + y - 6(y + 3)$?

14. What is the value of $\sqrt{760 - 4x^2}$ to the nearest tenth when $x = 6$?

15. If $x = 20$, what is the value of the expression $4(x + 7) - 3(x - 2)$?

16. Find the value of $\dfrac{x(25 + 2x - y)}{-z}$ when $x = -3$, $y = 4$, and $z = -1$.

17. What is the value of $5y^2 + 4x^2 - 6(x - y)$ when $x = 5$ and $y = -2$?

18. Find the value of $3x^2 \cdot \dfrac{2(x - 3y)}{6}$ when $x = 6$ and $y = 1$.

19. What is the value of the expression $(x^2 + 5)(x^2 - x + 2) - 3$ when $x = -4$?

20. Find the value of $(x + y)(x - y)(2x + y)$ when $x = 9$ and $y = 4$.

B. Choose the <u>one best answer</u> to each question.

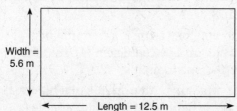

Width = 5.6 m

Length = 12.5 m

21. Jake has to buy enough fencing to enclose the rectangular garden shown above.

    The formula for finding the perimeter of (or distance around) a rectangle is $P = 2l + 2w$, where P = perimeter, l = length, and w = width. Using the values from the drawing, what is the perimeter in meters of the garden?

    A. 18.1
    B. 36.2
    C. 70
    D. 140

22. If $x = -5$ and $y = 2$, which of the following expressions has the greatest value?

    A. $x + y$
    B. $-x + y$
    C. xy
    D. $-2xy$

23. What is the value of the expression $2 \div x^{-4}$ when $x = 2$?

    A. 32
    B. 16
    C. 8
    D. -16

Answers and explanations begin on page 217.

Understand Polynomials

Key Ideas

- A polynomial is an expression with more than one term—any combination of coefficients, variables, exponents, and constants.
- Specific types of polynomials include monomials, binomials, and trinomials.

The GED® *Mathematical Reasoning Test* will expect you to understand polynomials. A **polynomial** is made up of terms, and since the prefix *poly-* means "many," a polynomial is a term in which many parts are being combined. Each term in a polynomial may be made up of a combination of coefficients, variables, exponents, and constants.

Coefficients include numbers such as 4, −25, or $\frac{1}{2}$ and will come before the variables. Coefficients can be negative, like −25. If there is no coefficient next to a variable, assume the coefficient is 1. In the expression $x + y + z$, the coefficient in front of each variable is equal to 1.

Variables are letters such as x and y in polynomial terms. In the polynomial $45a^2b$, the variables are a and b.

Exponents, or powers, are a way of showing repeated multiplication. This is also known as raising a number or variable to a power. Polynomials must be raised to whole number exponents. There are no negative or fractional powers in polynomials. In the polynomial $6x^3y^4$, the exponents are 3 and 4. The **degree** of a polynomial with only one variable is the largest exponent of that variable. For example, in the expression $4x^3 + 3x^2 - 5$, the degree is 3 (the largest exponent of x.)

A **constant** is a number on its own that will always remain the same. It is not next to a variable. A constant can be either positive or negative, depending on whether it is being added or subtracted. In the expression $4x^3 + 3x^2 + 5$, the constant is 5. No matter what value you substitute for x, 5 will always be just 5.

Polynomials are built out of all of the components above, and there are different types of polynomials, including monomials, binomials, and trinomials. These are important to know.

- A **monomial** is a polynomial with only one term. An example of a monomial is $4xy^2$. This term is made up of a coefficient (4), two variables (x and y), and an exponent (the power of 2).

- A **binomial** is a polynomial with two terms. An example of a binomial is $3x + 2$. The first term is made up of a coefficient (3) and a variable (x), and the second term consists of a constant (2).

- A **trinomial** is a polynomial with three terms. An example of a trinomial is $4x + 3y^2 - 4$. The first term is made up of a coefficient (4) and a variable (x). The second term is made up of a coefficient (3), a variable (y), and an exponent (the power of 2). The third term is made up of a constant, and this time it is a negative number (−4).

A few types of numbers are not categorized as polynomials and cannot be present in polynomial terms. These include the following:

- Division by a variable, such as $\frac{3}{x+3}$ or $\frac{1}{x}$
- Negative exponents, such as $4xy^{-2}$ (exponents can only be 0, 1, 2, etc.)
- Fractional exponents, such as $3a^{\frac{1}{2}}$
- Variables inside radicals, such as $\sqrt{x}$

In a polynomial term, however, you can divide by a constant or have numbers inside a radical. For example, $\frac{4x}{12}$ is allowed, as is $\sqrt{10}$.

PRACTICE 8

A. Identify whether each of the following is a monomial, binomial, or trinomial.

1. $25a$
2. $2xy^2z$
3. $x - 4$
4. $x^3 + y - 1$
5. $7y - 1$
6. $2x^4 + 3x + 4$
7. $\dfrac{x}{3}$
8. y^2
9. $g^2h^2i^2j^2$
10. $x^2 + x^2$
11. $x^2 + 14x + 3$
12. $x^2y + x^2 + y$
13. $g + h$
14. $\sqrt{49}$
15. $3x^2 - 5$

B. For each polynomial, identify the terms. Remember that a coefficient can be positive or negative.

16. $3x^4 - 2x^2 + 3$
17. $12a^2bc$
18. $3g - 4h$
19. $x^2 + y$
20. $-4a - 3b^2 + c$
21. 25
22. $x^2 + 3x - 7$
23. $\dfrac{3x}{8}$
24. $\sqrt{25}$
25. $\dfrac{x^2}{9}$
26. $49x^2y^2z^2$
27. $18y^2 - 4y^2 + 8$
28. $3h - 4$
29. $x^2 - x + y^2 - 2$
30. $ab + ab^2 + b^2 - 4$

C. Choose the <u>one best answer</u> to each question.

31. What is the sum of the exponents in the expression $4x^3 + 3x^2 + 5$?

    A. 3
    B. 5
    C. 12
    D. 17

32. What is the sum of the coefficients in the expression $a - 3b - c + 2d$?

    A. -3
    B. -1
    C. 2
    D. 3

Answers and explanations begin on page 218.

Simplify Polynomials

Combine Like Terms

When working with polynomials, you must work to combine like terms. **Like terms** have variables that are the same or are terms that have the same variable raised to the same power, or exponent. For example, $8x^3$ and $4x^3$ are like terms, and $5y$ and $3y$ are also like terms.

Unlike terms have variables that are different or have the same variable raised to different powers. For example, $3a$ and $5b$ are unlike terms. The terms $9x$ and $7x^2$ are also unlike terms because the variables are raised to different powers.

You can only combine like terms when simplifying polynomials. Unlike terms cannot be combined. For example, in the polynomial $7x^2 + 4x^3$, you cannot combine the terms because x is raised to different powers in each term. However, in the polynomial $7x^2 + 4x^2$, you can combine terms that all have the same variable and the same exponent: $7x^2 + 4x^2 = 11x^2$.

Example 1: Combine like terms in the polynomial $4y^3 + 2x^3 - 7y^3$.
1. First, identify and group the like terms. $\qquad$ $4y^3 - 7y^3 + 2x^3$

The two y^3 terms are alike; the x^3 term cannot be combined with them.

2. Combine the like terms. $\qquad\qquad\qquad\qquad$ $-3y^3 + 2x^3$

Simplify Polynomials

Some polynomials may contain both like and unlike terms. The following example shows how like and unlike terms are handled when you have to simplify a polynomial. Start by combining like terms from the exponent with the largest number, or degree, and proceed to the exponent with the smallest number.

Example 2: Simplify the polynomial $7x^4 - 13x^2 + x^4 + 2x^2 + 5x + 3 + x$.

1. Combine like terms with the largest degree, which is 4. Add:
   $7x^4 + x^4 = 8x^4$.
2. You now have $8x^4 - 13x^2 + 2x^2 + 5x + 3 + x$. Combine like terms from the exponent with the next largest degree, which is 2. Add:
   $-13x^2 + 2x^2 = -11x^2$.
3. You now have $8x^4 - 11x^2 + 5x + 3 + x$. Finally, combine like terms with the next largest degree, which is 1. Add: $5x + x = 6x$.
4. You now have $\mathbf{8x^4 - 11x^2 + 6x + 3}$.

This is as much as you can simplify this polynomial by combining like terms. The simplified polynomial has no more like terms and must remain as is.

Key Ideas

- Like terms can be combined; unlike terms cannot.
- Like terms are either numbers—positive or negative—or variables with the same degree of exponents.
- Polynomials with unlike terms cannot be simplified.

GED® TEST TIP

When working with polynomials, treat the minus sign before a coefficient or constant as an indicator of a negative number. This will help you to combine like terms using the rules of signed numbers that you learned on pages 116–117.

PRACTICE 9

A. For each pair of terms, indicate if they are like terms or unlike terms.

1. $4x^3, x^3$ _____ terms

2. $3x, x$ _____ terms

3. b, b^2 _____ terms

4. $-2x, 7y$ _____ terms

5. $-2x, 7x$ _____ terms

6. $4a, 4$ _____ terms

7. $g^2, g^2 hi$ _____ terms

8. $2x^2 y, 8x^2 y$ _____ terms

9. $-5m, -5m^2$ _____ terms

10. $x^2 y, xy^2$ _____ terms

11. $ab, 8ab$ _____ terms

12. $3y, 3y^2$ _____ terms

13. $14g, \frac{1}{3}g$ _____ terms

14. $12x^2, x^2$ _____ terms

15. a, ab^2 _____ terms

16. $15x^2, -x^2$ _____ terms

17. $10y, 11yz$ _____ terms

18. $x^2, \frac{x^2}{2}$ _____ terms

19. $g, -g^2$ _____ terms

20. $\frac{x}{8}, x^2$ _____ terms

B. Simplify each expression by combining like terms.

21. $3x^2 y + 4x^2 y$

22. $3b + b$

23. $a - 7a + 3$

24. $14ab + ab^2 + 2ab + 3$

25. $x^2 - 3x^2 + 7$

26. $ab + 2ab + ab$

27. $7g + 7gh + 7g + 7gh$

28. $g^2 + h^2 - 4g^2 h^2 + g^2 + h^2 - 4$

29. $9y + y - y^2 - y$

30. $x^2 - 8x^2 + y - 3$

31. $11y + 11y - 7$

32. $9x^2 y - 3x^2 y + 4y^2 - 21 + y^2 - 2$

33. $8x^2 - 4x + 7 + 4x^3 - x^2 + 7x - 2$

34. $-3x^2 + 6x - 2x^2 - 10x + 5$

35. $9x^2 - 3x^3 + x - 2x^2$

C. Choose the <u>one best answer</u> to each question.

36. What is the simplified form of the expression $3a^2 b + 4ab + 3a^2 b + 5ab$?

   A. $6a^3 b^2 + 8a^3 b^2$

   B. $6a^2 b + 9ab$

   C. $6a^2 b + 8ab$

   D. $15a^6 + b^4$

37. When simplified, how many terms are in the polynomial $j^2 + k^3 - 2j^3 + 5k^3 - 2j^2$?

   A. 2

   B. 3

   C. 4

   D. 5

Answers and explanations begin on page 218.

Add and Subtract Polynomials

Add Polynomials with One Variable

On the *Mathematical Reasoning Test*, you may be required to add polynomials that have one variable. You can add polynomials when they have like terms, including variables and exponents. When you see polynomials within parentheses linked by an addition sign, add them by combining the like terms across the polynomials.

Example 1: Add $(3x^2 + x + 4) + (2x^2 + 2x - 16)$.

1. To add these polynomials, simply combine like terms. Add: $3x^2 + 2x^2 = 5x^2$.
2. Add: $x + 2x = 3x$.
3. Add: $4 + (-16) = -12$.
4. Combine the results into one polynomial: $\mathbf{5x^2 + 3x - 12}$.

Sometimes, an expression needs to be simplified before you add and combine like terms.

Example 2: Add $(5x^2 + 8x - 4) + (2x^2 - 6x + 14x)$.

1. Simplify within the second parentheses. Add: $-6x + 14x = 8x$.
2. Combine like terms across the polynomials. Add: $5x^2 + 2x^2 = 7x^2$.
3. Use the simplified expression from step 1. Add: $8x + 8x = 16x$.
4. Combine the results into one polynomial: $\mathbf{7x^2 + 16x - 4}$.

Subtract Polynomials with One Variable

The only difference between adding and subtracting polynomials is the minus sign between the parentheses. You must distribute the negative sign across the second polynomial. To distribute the negative sign across the second polynomial, simply reverse the signs of each term. Then drop the parentheses and combine like terms across both polynomials.

Example 3: Subtract $(3x^2 + x + 4) - (7x^2 + 2x - 16)$.

1. Distribute the negative sign to everything in the second set of parentheses by reversing the sign of each term: $-7x^2 - 2x + 16$.
2. Drop the parentheses from the entire expression and combine like terms:
$3x^2 + x + 4 - 7x^2 - 2x + 16$

$-4x^2 + x + 4 - 2x + 16$
$-4x^2 - x + 4 + 16$
$-4x^2 - x + 20$

Note that subtracting a negative constant or coefficient is the same as adding a positive. In the next example, watch what happens to the negative coefficient inside the second set of parentheses when the sign is distributed.

Example 4: Subtract $(x^2 + 2x + 3) - (4x^2 - x + 6)$.

1. Distribute the negative sign to everything in the second set of brackets by reversing the sign of each term:
   $-4x^2 + x - 6$

2. Drop the brackets and combine like terms:
   $x^2 + 2x + 3 - 4x^2 + x - 6$
   $x^2 - 4x^2 + 2x + x + 3 - 6$
   $-3x^2 + 3x - 3$

PRACTICE 10.1

A. Add the following polynomials.

1. $(3x + 4) + (2x + 2)$
2. $(17y - y + 3) + (4y + 3y + 3)$
3. $(5x^2 - 3x - 4) + (3x^2 - 2x + 6)$
4. $(-a^2 + 2a) + (16a^2 + 6a)$
5. $(9x^2 - 3x - 2) + (2x^2 + 5x + 5)$

6. $(6a + 6) + (-5a - 5)$
7. $(-8g^2 + 7g + 6) + (8g^2 - 7g - 5)$
8. $(2x^2 + 5x) + (2x^2 + 4x + 7x - 9)$
9. $(13y + 4y + 4) + (7y - 7)$
10. $(-a^2 - a^2 - a - 4) + (-a^2 - a^2 - a - 5)$

B. Subtract the following polynomials.

11. $(3y - 4) - (2y - 2)$
12. $(x + 16) - (4x + 3)$
13. $(2a + 1) - (-a - 1)$
14. $(5x^2 + 2x + 4) - (2x^2 + x + 2)$
15. $(7y + 5y + 5) - (2y - 2)$
16. $(9x^2 + 4x + 5x + 4) - (7x^2 + 6x - 9)$

17. $(-g + g - 1) - (-g - g - 2)$
18. $(17a^2 - 4a - 4) - (16a^2 + 6a - 6)$
19. $(7b^2 + b - 8) - (7b^2 + b + 8)$
20. $(21x^2 + 3x^2 - 2x - 4 - 1) - $
    $(3x^2 + x^2 + x + 2x - 5 - 1)$

C. Choose the <u>one best answer</u> to each question.

21. What is the sum of the polynomials
    $(2xy + 3xy^2 - 4x^2y) + (5x^2y - 3xy^2 + 2xy)$?
    A. $x^2y + 4xy$
    B. $4xy + 3x + y$
    C. $7x - 2y$
    D. $7x^2y - 2xy$

22. Which of the following equals
    $(5x^2 - 2x + 1) - (3x^2 - 3x - 2)$?
    A. $x - 5x - 1$
    B. $2x^2 - x + 3$
    C. $2x^2 + x + 3$
    D. $2x^2 - 5x + 3$

Answers and explanations begin on page 218.

Simplifying Polynomials with More Than One Variable

Some polynomials contain terms with different variables—for example, the binomial $2x + 3y$ contains an x term and a y term. You add, subtract, and simplify polynomials with more than one variable just as you do polynomials with just a single variable. However, you have to be careful to add and subtract only like terms. Remember that in all polynomials, like terms have the *same variable* and the *same exponent*. For example, in the polynomial $x^2 + 2x + y^2 + 3x + 2y$, the only like terms are the two x^1 terms. You can combine the $2x$ and the $3x$, but you cannot combine x^2 with any other term, nor can you combine the y^2 or the $2y$ with any other term. The most simplified version of this polynomial is $x^2 + 5x + y^2 + 2y$.

A term that consists of two or more variables multiplied together cannot be combined with terms that contain only one of those variables. For example, you cannot combine $2xy + 7x$. However, you can combine $2xy + 7xy$ to get $9xy$.

Example 1: Simplify $6xy^4 - 20x^2 - 3 + xy^4 + 12x^2 - 30$.

Start by grouping the like terms together. Then add and subtract as appropriate.

$$6xy^4 - 20x^2 - 3 + xy^4 + 12x^2 - 30$$
$$= 6xy^4 + xy^4 - 20x^2 + 12x^2 - 3 - 30$$
$$= 7xy^4 - 8x^2 - 33$$

Adding Polynomials with More Than One Variable

Adding polynomials that contain more than one variable requires the same process as adding polynomials that have only one variable. Just remove the brackets and combine like terms across both polynomials. Remember that only like terms can be combined.

Example 2: Add $(3x^2 + 6x + 3xy) + (5x^2 - 6xy + 14y)$.

$$(3x^2 + 6x + 3xy) + (5x^2 - 6xy + 14y)$$
$$= 3x^2 + 5x^2 + 6x + 3xy - 6xy + 14y$$
$$= 8x^2 + 6x - 3xy + 14y$$

Subtracting Polynomials with More Than One Variable

Subtracting polynomials that contain more than one variable is exactly the same as subtracting polynomials that contain only a single variable. Remember to distribute the minus sign across the second polynomial when you remove the parentheses. Also remember that only like terms can be combined.

Example 3: Subtract $(3xy^2 + x + 2xy + 4) - (7xy^2 + 2xy - 16)$.

$$3xy^2 + x + 2xy + 4 - (7xy^2 + 2xy - 16)$$
$$= 3xy^2 + x + 2xy + 4 - 7xy^2 - 2xy + 16$$
$$= -4xy^2 + x + 20$$

Notice that there is no xy term in the final simplified expression because $2xy - 2xy = 0$.

PRACTICE 10.2

A. Simplify the following polynomials.

1. $a^2 + 2a + b^2 + 3a + 3b^2$

2. $x + 3xy + y + 16 - 5x - 4xy$

3. $yz^2 - z^2 + 5 + 3yz - 3z^2 + 4yz$

4. $ab - b + c + 17 + 6ab - 34$

5. $a^4 + c^2 + 3ac - 5a^4 - 2c^2 + 5$

6. $19xyz + x - y + 3xyz + 6 + y$

7. $ef + ef^2 - 10 + 6ef + f$

8. $p + pq - q - p + 3pq - 3 - q + 7$

B. Add the following polynomials.

9. $(ab + b - c + 6) + (3ab - b + c - 6)$

10. $(x^2 + xy - y - 3) + (-x^2 - xy + y + 3)$

11. $(p^6 + p^5 + pq - p^2) + (2p^6 - p^5 + 3pq - q^2)$

12. $(x + xy + 7) + (y - xy + 8)$

13. $(9a + bc + c^2) + (-9a - b + bc - c^2)$

14. $(4xyz + 4x - 4y) + (6xyz - 4x - 4y + 16)$

15. $(5a + 5b + 4c - 6) + (a - b - 4c + d + 6)$

16. $(pq - q + 15) + (6pq - 15)$

C. Subtract the following polynomials.

17. $(ab + a + b + 6) - (8ab + a - b - 6)$

18. $(xy + x + y) - (xy + x + y)$

19. $(p^2 + q^2 + 14) - (3p^2 - 4q^2 + 7)$

20. $(x^4 + yz + z^4) - (yz + z^5)$

21. $(bc^2 + bc + c - 7) - (2bc - c - 7)$

22. $(xy + xz - xyz) - (4xy + xyz)$

23. $(c^3d^7 + c^2 - d + 35) - (2c^2 - 3d + 35)$

24. $(ef^2g - fg + 16) - (ef^2 + fg + 8)$

D. Choose the one best answer to each question.

25. Which of the following equals
$(x + y + z) - (-2x + 2y + z)$?

A. $-x + 3y + 2z$

B. $-2x - y + 2z$

C. $3x - 2y + 2z$

D. $3x - y$

26. Which of the following equals
$(2g^2 + 3h - 5k) + (g^2 + 2h + 3k)$?

A. $g^2 + h - 8k$

B. $3g^2 + 5h - 2k$

C. $2g^2 + 6h^2 - 15k^2$

D. $2g^4 + 5h - 2k$

Answers and explanations begin on page 218.

Algebra Basics, Expressions, and Polynomials

Multiply Polynomials

Multiply a Monomial by a Monomial

To multiply two monomials, multiply each component separately. Start by multiplying the coefficients (or numbers). If there is no coefficient given, assume that the coefficient is 1 (for example, $xy = 1xy$). Then, multiply each variable separately by adding the exponents of like variables. Remember that a variable with no exponent is a variable raised to the first power (for example, $x = x^1$). So $x(x^3) = x^1(x^3) = x^4$.

Example 1: Multiply $(2ab)(4b)$.

$$2 \times 4 \times a \times b^1 \times b^1 = 8ab^2$$

Multiply a Monomial by a Binomial

To multiply a monomial by a binomial, multiply the monomial by the first term in the binomial, then multiply the monomial by the second term in the binomial. Finally, add the resulting terms.

Example 2: Multiply $-2z^2(z + 3yz)$.

1. Distribute the negative sign:

$$-2z^2(z + 3yz) = 2z^2(-z - 3yz).$$

2. Multiply the monomial by each term in the binomial:

$$2z^2(-z - 3yz) = [2 \times (-1) \times z^2 \times z^1] + [2 \times (-3) \times z^2 \times y^1z^1].$$

3. Add: $-2z^3 + (-6yz^3) = -2z^3 - 6yz^3$.

Multiply Two Binomials

To multiply two binomials, multiply the first terms, then the outer terms, then the inner terms, and, finally, the last terms. Add the results and combine like terms. You can remember this process by the acronym FOIL, which stands for *First, Outer, Inner, Last.*

Example 3: Multiply $(2g^2 + 9)(3g^2 - 4)$.

1. Multiply using FOIL:

$$(2g^2 + 9)(3g^2 - 4) = \overbrace{(2g^2)(3g^2)} + \overbrace{(2g^2)(-4)} + \overbrace{(9)(3g^2)} + \overbrace{(9)(-4)}.$$

2. Add: $6g^4 - 8g^2 + 27g^2 - 36$.

3. Combine like terms:

$$6g^4 - 8g^2 + 27g^2 - 36 = 6g^4 + 19g^2 - 36.$$

Key Ideas

- There are a number of ways to multiply polynomials.
- The basic concepts in all involve learning procedures for multiplying constants, variables, and exponents.
- A common method for multiplying binomials is called FOIL for short.

GED® TEST TIP

Always finish the FOIL method by combining like terms after you have multiplied.

PRACTICE 11

A. Multiply the monomials.

1. $(6x)(5x)$

2. $(2xy)(3y)$

3. $(7abc)(4bc)$

4. $(12y)(z)$

5. $(a)(9bc)$

6. $(5xyz)(2xy^2z^4)$

7. $(4ab)(bc^2)$

8. $(17f^2gh^3)(2fh^4)$

B. Multiply the binomials by the monomials.

9. $3z^2(6xy + 4z)$

10. $6x(7x - 6z)$

11. $-5ab(3b + 11c)$

12. $-3f^3(6h - 8fgh^2)$

13. $10z(7x^7 - 5z)$

14. $-z(-z - 6xy)$

15. $8b(9ab + 8a)$

16. $-9(-2x^4 + 3xy^2)$

C. Multiply the binomials by using FOIL. Remember to complete by combining like terms wherever possible.

17. $(x + 5)(x - 6)$

18. $(x + y)(x + y)$

19. $(z + 9)(z - 9)$

20. $(yz^2 + x)(yz^2 - 3x)$

21. $(3x + 3)(3x + 5)$

22. $(x + y)(x - y)$

23. $(y^2 - 6)(y^4 + 10)$

24. $(ab + 3)(ab - 4)$

D. Choose the one best answer to each question.

25. Which of the following expressions is equal to $(4a^3b^2)(3a^2c)$?

    A. $12a^5b^2c$
    B. $7a^5b^2c$
    C. $12a^6bc$
    D. $7a^6b^2c$

26. Martha has $2pc^2$ board games, and John has $6p^2c$ board games. Which of the following expressions represents the product of the number of board games that Martha and John have?

    A. $8p^3c^3$
    B. $8p^2c^2$
    C. $12p^2c^2$
    D. $12p^3c^3$

27. Which of the following expressions is equal to $(4ab + 2)(3ab - 7)$?

    A. $7a^2b^2 + 22ab + 5$
    B. $12a^2b^2 - 22ab - 14$
    C. $12a^2b^2 + 22ab + 14$
    D. $7a^2b^2 - 22ab - 5$

Answers and explanations begin on page 219.

Divide Polynomials

Key Ideas

- You can divide a polynomial by numbers, expressions, or other polynomials.
- The key to dividing a polynomial is to isolate a common factor that divides into the numerator and denominator.
- Common factors can be numbers, variables, or a combination of the two such as addition, subtraction, or multiplication expressions.

Divide Polynomials by a Number

The *Mathematical Reasoning Test* will sometimes ask you to simplify a polynomial that is written as a fraction. To simplify, divide the numerator and denominator by a common term. A common term can be the following:

- a number
- a variable with a number as a coefficient
- a more complicated expression

You may need to factor the common term out of the numerator or denominator before you can do the division.

Example 1: Simplify $\dfrac{3x + 6}{3}$.

$$\frac{3x + 6}{3} = \frac{3(x + 2)}{3} = \frac{\cancel{3}(x + 2)}{\cancel{3}} = x + 2$$

Divide Polynomials by an Expression

Dividing a polynomial by an expression is really no different from dividing by a number. You need a common term in the numerator and denominator, and you may have to factor out that common term (including any variables) before you can do the division.

Example 2: Simplify $\dfrac{25x^3 - 45x^2}{5x}$.

$$\frac{25x^3 - 45x^2}{5x} = \frac{5x(5x^2 - 9x)}{5x} = \frac{\cancel{5x}(5x^2 - 9x)}{\cancel{5x}} = 5x^2 - 9x$$

When the numerator has two added or subtracted expressions that both include the common term, it may be easier to split the polynomial into two separate fractions and simplify them separately. Doing it this way will help you keep straight exactly which terms you can cancel.

Example 3: Simplify $\dfrac{x(x + 7) - 3(x + 7)}{x + 7}$.

$$\frac{x(x + 7) - 3(x + 7)}{x + 7} = \frac{x(x + 7)}{x + 7} - \frac{3(x + 7)}{x + 7}$$

$$= \frac{x\cancel{(x + 7)}}{\cancel{x + 7}} - \frac{3\cancel{(x + 7)}}{\cancel{x + 7}} = x - 3$$

PRACTICE 12

A. To simplify, divide each polynomial by a number. (You may need to factor the numerator and/or denominator to find the common term.)

1. $\dfrac{2y + 30}{2}$

2. $\dfrac{7x + 21}{7}$

3. $\dfrac{4x + 20}{4}$

4. $\dfrac{3a + 3b}{3}$

5. $\dfrac{11x^2 + 22x}{11}$

6. $\dfrac{26x^2 + 39x + 13}{13}$

7. $\dfrac{5x + 10y}{5}$

8. $\dfrac{21a + 14b}{7}$

9. $\dfrac{48x + 32y}{32}$

10. $\dfrac{9a - 15b}{12}$

11. $\dfrac{6b + 24c}{18}$

12. $\dfrac{25a + 5b + 15c}{10}$

B. Divide each polynomial. Decide whether it is easier for you to divide the original numerator by the common term (as in Example 2) or whether to split the numerator first (as in Example 3).

13. $\dfrac{18x^2 + 6x}{3x}$

14. $\dfrac{10x^2 + 6x}{2x}$

15. $\dfrac{40y^2 + 10y}{5y}$

16. $\dfrac{42xy + 49x}{7x}$

17. $\dfrac{38xy + 38x}{19x}$

18. $\dfrac{3x + 18}{x + 6}$

19. $\dfrac{x(x + 4) - 6(x + 4)}{x + 4}$

20. $\dfrac{y(y + 3) + 7(y + 3)}{y + 3}$

21. $\dfrac{z(z + 2) - 5(z + 2)}{z + 2}$

22. $\dfrac{22x^2 + 66x}{11x}$

23. $\dfrac{x(y - 2) - 6(y - 2)}{y - 2}$

24. $\dfrac{a(b + 3) + 3(b + 3)}{b + 3}$

C. Choose the <u>one best answer</u> to each question.

25. Which of the following is equal to $\dfrac{21a + 14b}{7}$?
   A. $5a + 5b$
   B. $3a + 14b$
   C. $3a + 2b$
   D. $21a + 2b$

26. James has $27x$ apples, Rachel has $51y$ oranges, and Glen has $60z$ peaches. Which of the following expressions represents the average number of pieces of fruit that James, Rachel, and Glen have in their baskets?
   A. $9x + 51y + 60z$
   B. $46x + 46y + 46z$
   C. $9x + 17y + 60z$
   D. $9x + 17y + 20z$

27. Which of the following expressions is equal to $\dfrac{2z^2 - 12z + 2(z + 4) - 8}{2z}$?
   A. $z - 5$
   B. $z(z + 2) - 5$
   C. $z(z + 2) - 5(z + 2)$
   D. $z - 3$

Answers and explanations begin on page 219.

ALGEBRA BASICS, EXPRESSIONS, AND POLYNOMIALS PRACTICE QUESTIONS

1. Which of the following expressions is equal to $6 - 4(x + 3)$?

   A. $4x + 3$
   B. $4x - 9$
   C. $-4x + 9$
   D. $-4x - 6$

2. If Kris makes d dollars and Heidi makes 75 dollars less than 3 times Kris's wage, what does Heidi make in terms of d?

   A. $d + 75$
   B. $d - 225$
   C. $3d - 75$
   D. $3d - 225$

3. What is the product of 700 and 180,000 written in scientific notation?

   A. 12.6×10^9
   B. 1.26×10^8
   C. 1.26×10^9
   D. 1.26×10^{10}

4. If there are $4x$ identical schools in a region and each school has $3y$ classrooms each with $7x$ desks, how many desks are there in the region?

   A. $11x + 3y$
   B. $28x + 3y$
   C. $84xy^2$
   D. $84x^2 y$

5. Which of the following is equivalent to $x^2 - 25$?

   A. $x(x - 25)$
   B. $(x - 5)^2$
   C. $(x + 5)(x - 5)$
   D. $(x - 25)^2$

6. If Tom has $9x$ baseball cards, Adam has 13 more than Tom, and Dave has $2y$ baseball cards, together they would have how many cards?

   A. $9x + 2y + 13$
   B. $18xy + 13$
   C. $18xy + 2y$
   D. $18x + 2y + 13$

Questions 7 and 8 refer to the figure below.

The figure below is a multiplication box. Each place represents the horizontal number multiplied by the vertical number; for example, the 9 in the lower right corner equals 3 multiplied by 3.

	5	y	3
1	5		3
c	20	a	
3	b	d	9

7. Which of the following is equal to ab?

   A. $5y$
   B. $60y$
   C. $100y$
   D. $500y$

8. Which of the following is equal to $a - d$?

   A. b
   B. c
   C. x
   D. y

9. Multiply $7c^2(a^2 + 5b + 7c^2)$.

   A. $7a^2c^2 + 35bc^2 + 49c^4$
   B. $7(ac)^2 + 35(bc)^2 + 49c^4$
   C. $7a^2 + 35b + 49c^4$
   D. $a^2 + 5b + 14c^2$

10. A Little League pie sale fundraiser generated $900 in revenue. If there were $6x$ pies sold, how much did each pie cost?

    A. $10
    B. $15
    C. $\$\dfrac{x}{150}$
    D. $\$\dfrac{150}{x}$

11. Simplify the expression

    $$\frac{(a-4)^2\,(6b)}{2(3b)\,(a+4)\,(a-4)}.$$

    A. $\dfrac{a-4}{a+4}$
    B. $\dfrac{a+4}{a-4}$
    C. $\dfrac{a-2}{2}$
    D. 1

12. Emilie buys x ounces of chicken for each of her guests at a dinner party. There are $8y$ people coming, and chicken is $\$z$ a pound. How much will the total amount of chicken cost in dollars? (*Hint*: There are 16 ounces in one pound.)

    A. $8xyz$
    B. $16xyz$
    C. $\dfrac{xyz}{2}$
    D. $\dfrac{xyz}{8}$

13. What is the value of the expression $6(x - y) - 8x$ when $x = -2$ and $y = 5$?

    A. -58
    B. -26
    C. 2
    D. 34

14. Which of the following would be equal to $x^2 + 6z$ multiplied by $2y - 4z$ if $x = 2$, $y = 4$, and $z = 3$?

    A. -88
    B. -72
    C. 0
    D. 104

15. What is the value of the following expression?

    $$\frac{4^3 - [3(12 + 2^2)]}{6 + 5(4) - 15}$$

    Write your answer on the line below.

    _____

16. If every member of a team is paid $5p$ dollars for his or her participation, and Team Alpha has $6k$ members, Team Beta has $4p$ members, and Team Delta has $9h$ members, which of the following represents the total amount paid to the members of all three teams?

    A. $1080hkp$
    B. $1080hkp^2$
    C. $120p^2k + 45ph$
    D. $30kp + 20p^2 + 45hp$

17. Which of the following is equal to $7x - [(5y)2x - 9y + 8x]$?

A. $x - 9y + 10xy$
B. $-3x - 4y$
C. $-x + 9y - 10xy$
D. $15x - 9y + 10xy$

18. If Stephanie has $5c$ CDs for every DVD Alyshia has, and Jeff has $4d$ DVDs, which is 15 more than Alyshia has, how many CDs does Stephanie have?

A. $20cd - 75c$
B. $20cd + 15$
C. $80cd - 15$
D. $80cd - 75c$

19. Divide $\dfrac{56x^4 + 49x^3y^3 - 84x^3 - 7x^2}{7x^2}$.

A. $8x^2 + 7xy^3 - 12x - 1$
B. $8x^4 + 7x^3y^3 - 12x^3 - x^2$
C. $8x^4 + 7y^3 - 5x^3 - 1$
D. $49x^2 + 42xy^3 - 77x$

20. A charity with a yearly budget of $80d$ gets all of its money from either its yearly ball or from private donations. If the charity raised $64d$ from the silent auction at the ball and $4a$ from ticket sales at the ball, what will need to be raised in private donations to meet the budget?

A. $16d$
B. $16d - 4a$
C. $16d + 4a$
D. $144d - 4a$

21. Divide $\dfrac{x^4 + 4x^2y^4 - 8x - y^2}{2y^2}$.

A. $\dfrac{x^4}{2y^2} + 2x^2y^2 - \dfrac{4x}{y^2} - \dfrac{1}{2}$

B. $\dfrac{x^2}{2y} + \dfrac{2x^2y^2 - 4x}{y^2 - \dfrac{1}{2}}$

C. $\dfrac{2x^4y^2 + 8x^2y^2 - 16x}{y^2 + 2y^4}$

D. $\dfrac{x^4 - 4x}{2y^2 + 2x^2y^2 - \dfrac{1}{2}}$

22. If $12k$ privates, $8f$ lieutenants, and $6r$ captains are divided into $2r$ equal squads, which of the following would express the number of members of one squad?

A. $6k + 4f + 3r$
B. $\dfrac{6k + 4f}{r} + 3$
C. $12k + 8f + 4r$
D. $12k + 8f + 3r$

23. If $q = 2$ and $r = 4$, which of the following would equal $\dfrac{r^2 x^2 + q^3 x}{(q^2 x)}$?

A. $4x + 2$
B. $4x^2 + 2$
C. $16x^2 + 8x - 2$
D. $16x^2 + 21$

24. Simplify:

$$\dfrac{44x^6 + 55x^3y^4 + 88x^2 - 11y^2}{11x^2} - 6x^4 - 8$$

A. $4x^4 + 5xy^2 + 8x - 1$

B. $2x^4 + 5xy^3 - y^2 - 8$

C. $-2x^4 + 5xy^4 - \dfrac{y^2}{x^2}$

D. $10x^4 + 5y^4 - \dfrac{y^2}{x^2} - 8$

25. Simplify:

$(6x^2 + 5xy^2)(y) - (4xy - 9x)(4xy)$.

   A. $5xy^3 - 16x^2y^2 + 42x^2y$
   B. $5xy^3 \quad 16x^2y^2 \quad 30x^2y$
   C. $6x^2y - 11x^2y^2 - 36xy^2$
   D. $6x^2y + 5x^2y^2 - 36xy^2 + 16xy$

26. There are $4x$ workers, including managers, in an office. If the salaries of the 3 managers are not included, the average salary of each employee is $5x - 6$. What do the nonmanagerial employees earn in total?

   A. $20x^2 - 24x$
   B. $20x^2 - 24x - 3$
   C. $20x^2 - 9x + 18$
   D. $20x^2 - 39x + 18$

27. What is the value of $\dfrac{45xy + 63y^2}{9y}$ if $x = 6$ and $y = 3$?

   A. 12
   B. 51
   C. 108
   D. 153

28. Simplify

$$\frac{3x(x^2 + 3) - 2x(x^2 + 3) - (x^2 + 3)}{x^2 + 3}$$

   A. $x^3 - 1$
   B. $x^3 - 3x - 1$
   C. $3x - 1$
   D. $x - 1$

29. If the $3h$ people in one country and the $4k$ people in the neighboring country each consume $h - 17$ pounds of rice per year on average, how much rice would be consumed by both countries in one year?

   A. $4h + 4k - 17$
   B. $4h^2 + 4k - 68k$
   C. $12hk + h - 17$
   D. $3h^2 + 4hk - 51h - 68k$

30. Simplify:

$$\frac{4x^2(x + y) - 2(x + y)^2(x - y) - xy(x + y)}{x + y}$$

   A. $2x^2 + 2y^2 - xy$
   B. $4x^2 + xy - 2x - 2y$
   C. $4x^2 - xy - 2x - 2y$
   D. $3x^2 - 2xy^2 - xy$

Questions 31 and 32 refer to the figure below.

The figure below is a multiplication box. Each place represents the horizontal number multiplied by the vertical number; for example, the 20 in the lower right corner equals 5 multiplied by 4.

	a^2	ab	5
a			ab
c	$8b$		
4		40	20

31. Which of the following is equal to a?

   A. 2
   B. 4
   C. 5
   D. 10

32. Which of the following is equal to a^2c?

   A. 13
   B. 40
   C. 42
   D. 60

Answers and explanations begin on page 219.

Equations

Writing and Solving One-Step Equations

An **equation** is a mathematical statement that two expressions are equal.

Examples: $3 + 5 = 4 \times 2$ $10 - 1 = 3^2$ $5(3 + 4) = 35$

An equation can contain one or more variables. Solving an equation means finding a value for the variable that will make the equation true.

Examples: $4 + x = 11$ $3x = 24$ $x - 5 = -2$

$x = 7$ $x = 8$ $x = 3$

The basic strategy in solving an equation is to isolate the variable on one side of the equation. You can do this by performing **inverse**, or opposite, operations. However, you must always follow one basic rule: whatever you do to one side of the equation, you must also do to the other side.

Example 1: Solve $x - 23 = 45$.

On the left side of the equation, the number 23 is subtracted from x. The inverse of subtraction is addition. Add 23 to both sides of the equation.

$$x - 23 = 45$$
$$x - 23 + 23 = 45 + 23$$
$$x = 68$$

To check your work, replace the variable with your solution and simplify. When $x = 68$, the equation is true.

Check: $x - 23 = 45$
$68 - 23 = 45$
$45 = 45$

The following examples use the inverse operations of multiplication and division.

Example 2: Solve $\frac{x}{2} = 17$.

The variable x is divided by 2. Since multiplication is the inverse of division, you must multiply each side of the equation by 2.

$$\frac{x}{2} = 17$$
$$2\left(\frac{x}{2}\right) = 2(17)$$
$$x = 34$$

When $x = 34$, the equation is true.

Check: $\frac{34}{2} = 17$
$17 = 17$

Example 3: Solve $5x = 75$.

$5x = 75$

Since the variable x is multiplied by 5, divide both sides of the equation by 5.

$$\frac{5x}{5} = \frac{75}{5}$$
$$x = 15$$

When $x = 15$, the equation is true.

Check: $5(15) = 75$
$75 = 75$

PRACTICE 1.1

A. Solve for the variable in each equation.

1. $7x = 63$

2. $23 + m = 51$

3. $-13 = y - 12$

4. $\frac{x}{4} = -16$

5. $5a = 625$

6. $y - 17 = -30$

7. $x + 6 = 33$

8. $4c = 28$

9. $\frac{12}{x} = -3$

10. $26 = b + 33$

11. $93 = 3x$

12. $s + 16 = 8$

13. $36 = \frac{x}{3}$

14. $t + 14 = 53$

15. $\frac{x}{6} = 8$

16. $16y = -48$

17. $r - 35 = 75$

18. $24 = \frac{120}{x}$

19. $5y = -45$

20. $d + 45 = 20$

21. $16 = 4x$

22. $-4x = 24$

23. $19 = h - 7$

24. $\frac{x}{11} = 6$

25. $m + 24 = 14$

26. $5y = 45$

27. $14 - w = 42$

28. $18 = \frac{y}{4}$

B. Choose the <u>one best answer</u> to each question.

<u>Questions 29 and 30</u> refer to the following table.

April Time Sheet Summary
Hours Worked per Week

Week	1	2	3	4
Kayla Sax	36	40	40	
Erin Grady		24	28	38

29. Kayla and Erin worked a total of 77 hours during Week 1. Let x = Erin's hours for Week 1. Which of the following equations could be used to solve for Erin's hours during Week 1?
   A. $x - 36 = 77$
   B. $x + 77 = 36$
   C. $x + 36 = 77$
   D. $x - 77 = 36$

30. Erin worked twice as many hours as Kayla did during Week 4. Let y = Kayla's hours for Week 4. Which of the following equations could be used to solve for Kayla's hours during Week 4?

   A. $\frac{y}{2} = 38$
   B. $38y = 2$
   C. $2y = 38$
   D. $\frac{1}{2y} = 38$

31. The quotient of a number divided by 4 is 32. What is the number?
   A. 8
   B. 28
   C. 128
   D. 512

32. The solution $x = -5$ makes which of the following equations true?
   A. $14 - x = 9$
   B. $\frac{x}{5} = 1$
   C. $x + 3 = 8$
   D. $12x = -60$

33. Mike had $572.18 in his checking account. After writing a check, he had $434.68. Which of the following equations could be used to find the amount of the check (c)?
   A. $\$572.18 + c = \$434.68$
   B. $\$572.18 - c = \$434.68$
   C. $\$572.18c = \$434.68$
   D. $\dfrac{\$572.18}{c} = \$434.68$

Answers and explanations begin on page 220.

Solving Multi-Step Equations

Most equations require more than one operation in order to find a solution. Follow these basic steps:

- Simplify by combining like terms.

- Perform addition and subtraction steps.

- Perform multiplication and division steps.

Example 1: Solve $6x + 5 - 2x = 25$.

1. Combine like terms ($6x - 2x = 4x$).

2. Subtract 5 from both sides.

3. Divide both sides by 4.

4. Check by substituting the solution for x in the original equation.

$$6x + 5 - 2x = 25$$
$$4x + 5 = 25$$
$$4x + 5 - 5 = 25 - 5$$
$$4x = 20$$
$$\frac{4x}{4} = \frac{20}{4}$$
$$x = 5$$
$$6(5) + 5 - 2(5) = 25$$
$$30 + 5 - 10 = 25$$
$$25 = 25$$

In this example, the distributive property is used to simplify an expression. Notice that not every step is written out. As you gain experience, you can perform an operation on both sides of an equation mentally.

Example 2: Solve $-4(x - 6) = 2x$.

1. Use the distributive property to remove the grouping symbols.
2. Add $4x$ to each side.
3. Divide each side by 6.

4. Check.

$$-4(x - 6) = 2x$$
$$-4x + 24 = 2x$$
$$24 = 6x$$
$$4 = x$$

$$-4(4 - 6) = 2(4)$$
$$-4(-2) = 8$$
$$8 = 8$$

Some of the time you will be expected to write an equation from information given in the problem. The problem will describe two expressions that are equal. Write each expression in symbols and connect the expressions with the equal sign (=). In many problems, the word *is* indicates the = symbol.

Example 3: The product of a number and 6 is 44 more than twice the number. What is the number?

1. Write an equation. The word *is* represents the equal sign.
2. Subtract $2x$ from both sides.
3. Divide both sides by 4.

4. Check.

$$6x = 44 + 2x$$
$$4x = 44$$
$$x = \mathbf{11}$$

$$6(11) = 44 + 2(11)$$
$$66 = 44 + 22$$
$$66 = 66$$

The number described in the problem is **11**.

NOTE: Subtraction and division operations must be written in the order indicated by the words. "The difference between x and y" must be written $x - y$, <u>not</u> $y - x$. "The quotient of x and y" must be written $\frac{x}{y}$, <u>not</u> $\frac{y}{x}$.

PRACTICE 1.2

A. Solve for the variable in each equation.

1. $3x - 20 = 130$

2. $2y - 8 = -3y - 18$

3. $6m = 14m - 16$

4. $2x + 5 + 6x = -27$

5. $5y + 3(y + 2) = 54$

6. $17 - 4z + 2z = 13$

7. $6m - 4 = m + 11$

8. $35 = x + 7 + 6x$

9. $5p - 2 = 6p - 9$

10. $50 = 3(s + 16) - 2(s - 2)$

11. $\dfrac{5(2x - 10)}{2} + 14 = 19$

12. $3(3 + r) = 2r + 4$

13. $5y = 2y + 22 + y$

14. $38 = 5(2b - 3) + 3b + 1$

15. $-5 - x = 2x - (4x + 6)$

16. $\dfrac{3h}{2} = 30$

17. $4(3 + 2x) + 8 = 92$

18. $-5(3 - z) = z + 1$

19. $10 - 3b + 3 = -1 + (b + 2)$

20. $5n + 8 - n = 6(n - 1)$

B. Choose the <u>one best answer</u> to each question.

21. Three times a number increased by 9 is 15 less than six times the number. Let $x =$ the unknown number. Which of the following equations could be used to find the value of x?

    A. $3(9x) = 6(15x)$
    B. $3x(9) = 6x - 15x$
    C. $3x + 9 = 15 - 6x$
    D. $3x + 9 = 6x - 15$

22. Dave has 500 baseball cards, which is as many as Eric and Travis have combined. Eric has three times as many cards as Travis has.

Dave	Eric	Travis
500	3x	x

    From the information, you can write the equation $3x + x = 500$. How many cards does Eric have? (*Hint:* Solve for x. Then find how many cards Eric has.)

    A. 150
    B. 250
    C. 350
    D. 375

23. The difference of four times a number and 7 is 15 plus the quotient of the number and 3. Which of the following equations could be used to find the value of x?

    A. $4x - 7 = \frac{x}{3} + 15$
    B. $7 - 4x = \frac{x}{3} + 15$
    C. $7 - 4x = \frac{3}{x} + 15$
    D. $4x - 7 = \frac{3}{x} + 1$

24. Kim earned x dollars at his part-time job on Friday. His wife earned $12 more than twice Kim's pay $(2x + 12)$. Together, they earned $174. How much did Kim earn on Friday?
    (*Hint:* Use the equation $x + (2x + 12) = \$174$

    A. $54
    B. $87
    C. $108
    D. $120

Answers and explanations begin on page 220.

Equation Word Problems

Algebra problems describe how several numbers are related. One number is the unknown, which you will represent with a variable. Using the relationships described in the problem, you can write an equation and solve for the variable.

Example 1: There are twice as many women as men in a class on auto repair. If there are 24 students in the class, how many are women?

1. Express the numbers in the problem in terms of the same variable. Let x represent the number of men. Since there are twice as many women, let $2x$ represent the number of women.

2. Write and solve an equation. The total number of men and women is 24, so $x + 2x = 24$. Solve:
$$x + 2x = 24$$
$$3x = 24$$
$$x = 8$$

Since $x = 8$, $2x = 2(8) = 16$. There are 8 men and **16 women** in the class.

Consecutive numbers are numbers that follow in counting order. For example, 1, 2, and 3 are consecutive numbers. The numbers 2, 4, and 6 are consecutive even numbers, and 1, 3, and 5 are consecutive odd numbers.

Example 2: The sum of three consecutive numbers is 105. What is the greatest of the three numbers?

1. Let x represent the first number and $x + 1$ and $x + 2$ represent the other numbers.

2. Write an equation and solve:
$$x + (x+1) + (x+2) = 105$$
$$3x + 3 = 105$$
$$3x = 102$$
$$x = 34$$

3. Find the answer. The variable x represents the first number in the sequence, so the three numbers are 34, 35, and 36. The problem asks for the greatest number, which is **36**.

You may need to use the difference between numbers to write equations.

Example 3: The ticket prices for a play are $12 for adults and $8 for children. One evening, the box office sold 200 tickets. If the total box office receipts were $2240, how many adult tickets were sold?

1. Let x represent the number of adult tickets. Since 200 tickets were sold, the number of children's tickets sold can be written as $200 - x$.

2. Multiply each term by the cost for that type of ticket. Set the total equal to $2240, and solve for x.

$$12x + 8(200 - x) = 2240$$
$$12x + 1600 - 8x = 2240$$
$$4x + 1600 = 2240$$
$$4x = 640$$
$$x = 160$$

3. There were **160 adult tickets** sold.

PRACTICE 2

A. Solve.

1. Two houses are for sale on the same street. The second house has 1000 square feet less than twice the square feet of the first house. Together the houses have 4400 square feet. What is the square footage of the first house?

2. Julia has 24 coins in her pocket. The coins are either dimes or quarters. The total value of the coins is $4.50. How many coins are dimes? (*Hint:* The value of the dimes is $0.10x$, and the value of the quarters is $0.25(24 - x)$.)

3. The Bulldogs won twice as many games as they lost. If they played a total of 36 games, how many did they win? (There were no tied games.)

4. The sum of four consecutive even numbers is 212. What is the third number? (*Hint:* Let x = the first number, $x + 2$ = the the second number, $x + 4$ = the the third, and so on.)

5. A children's store is selling pants for $6 each and shirts for $4. Brenda bought 13 items and paid $62. How many shirts did she buy?

6. The sum of three consecutive numbers is 180. What is the least number in the series?

7. In a month Andrew spends twice as much on rent as he does on food for his family. Last month, he spent $1650 on rent and food. How much did he spend on rent?

8. George spends four times as much time helping customers as he does stocking shelves. Last week, he spent 35 hours on the two tasks. How many hours were spent helping customers?

B. Choose the <u>one best answer</u> to each question.

9. Sylvia scored 10 points better than Wiley on their science exam. Greg scored 6 points less than Wiley. Altogether, the students earned 226 points. How many points did Sylvia earn?

   A. 74
   B. 78
   C. 84
   D. 94

10. Two adults and four children paid $48 to get into the fair. A child's ticket is $6 less than an adult's ticket. What is the cost of an adult's ticket?

    A. $15
    B. $12
    C. $9
    D. $6

11. Jenny is four times as old as her niece Tina. In 12 years, Jenny will be only twice as old as Tina. The chart shows expressions for Tina and Jenny's ages now and in 12 years.

	Jenny's Age	Tina's Age
Now	$4x$	x
In 12 Years	$4x + 12$	$x + 12$

How old is Tina now?

   A. 4
   B. 6
   C. 8
   D. 12

Answers and explanations begin on page 221.

Inequalities

Key Ideas

- Use $<$, $>$, $\leq$, and $\geq$ to show the relationship between two unequal expressions.
- The symbol always points to the smaller expression.
- Use inverse operations to solve inequalities. Reverse the inequality sign if you multiply or divide by a negative number.

An **inequality** is a mathematical statement that connects two unequal expressions. The inequality symbols and their meanings are as follows:

$>$ greater than $\geq$ greater than or equal to

$<$ less than $\leq$ less than or equal to

An inequality is solved much as is an equation. Use inverse operations to isolate the variable.

Example 1: Solve for x in the inequality $3x + 2 < 8$.

1. Subtract 2 from both sides.
$$3x + 2 < 8$$
$$3x < 6$$
2. Divide both sides by 3.
$$x < 2$$

The solution $x < 2$ states that any number less than 2 makes the inequality true. Check by substituting 1 (a number less than 2) for x: $3(1) + 2 < 8$, which simplifies to $5 < 8$, a true statement.

There is one important difference between solving equalities and inequalities. Whenever you multiply or divide both sides of an inequality by a <u>negative</u> number, you must <u>reverse</u> the inequality symbol.

Example 2: Solve for n in the inequality $-2n - 5 \geq 3$.

1. Add 5 to both sides to remove -5 from the left side of the equation.
$$-2n - 5 + 5 \geq 3 + 5$$
$$-2n \geq 8$$
2. Divide both sides by -2 and *reverse the inequality symbol.*
$$\frac{-2n}{-2} \geq \frac{8}{-2}$$
$$n < -4$$

Check your work by substituting a number that is less than or equal to -4 into the <u>original</u> inequality. Here -5 is used for n. Since $5 \geq 3$ is a true statement, the answer is correct.

$$-2n - 5 \geq 3$$
$$-2(-5) - 5 \geq 3$$
$$5 \geq 3$$

GED® TEST TIP

Avoid the most common mistake with inequalities: reversing the symbol accidentally. Always check your work by substituting any number that fits the solution into the original inequality.

When an inequality contains a variable, there are usually several numbers that make the inequality true. For that reason, we often graph the solution. In the examples below, a closed dot means that the number is included in the solution set. An open dot means the number is not included.

Examples: $x < 2$

$x > -3$

$x \leq 1$

$x \geq -2$

A **compound inequality** combines two inequalities. To solve a compound inequality, separate the inequalities and solve both. Then combine the solutions.

Example 3: Solve $3x + 4 < 5x < 16 + x$.

1. Write two inequalities and solve each separately.

$$3x + 4 < 5x \qquad\qquad 5x < 16 + x$$
$$4 < 2x \qquad\qquad\quad 4x < 16$$
$$2 < x \qquad\qquad\quad\ x < 4$$

2. Write the result as a compound inequality. $\mathbf{2 < x < 4}$

In other words, any quantity that is greater than 2 *and* less than 4 will make the compound inequality true.

PRACTICE 3

A. Solve.

1. $3x - 7 > 5$

2. $13 < 2x - 1$

3. $4 + 2x \leq -2$

4. $\dfrac{4 + x}{5} \leq 8$

5. $2(x + 3) < 4$

6. $3 + 9x \geq 4(x + 7)$

7. $-4(x + 2) < 24$

8. $-2x + 9 < 1$

9. $\dfrac{x - 2}{3} > 2x + 11$

10. $6x < 5x + 2$

11. $x + 6 \leq 8x - 15$

12. $5x + 14 > 2 + 7x$

13. $13x - 7 > 25 - 3x$

14. $x - 6 < 2(x + 2)$

15. $-5 + 3x \geq 4(3x - 8)$

16. $36 > 4(x - 12)$

17. $6 \leq 3(x + 3)$

18. $\dfrac{4x}{3} > 8x - 20$

19. $x - 2 < \dfrac{2x + 6}{4}$

20. $x \geq 4x - 9$

21. $30 \geq 5(x + 4) \geq 10$

22. $-7x > -2(x + 15) < 10$

23. $3 < 5x - 27 < 53$

24. $22 \leq 6x - 2 \leq 4x + 16$

B. Choose the <u>one best answer</u> to each question.

25. The perimeter of a square can be found using the formula $P = 4s$, where s is one side of the square.

The perimeter of a square is less than or equal to 64 inches. Which of the following represents the possible measures of the side of the square in inches?

A. $s \leq 16$
B. $s \geq 16$
C. $s \geq 8$
D. $s \leq 64$

26. Three added to the product of −4 and a number (x) is less than 5 added to the product of −3 and the number. Which of the following is a graph of the solution set of x?

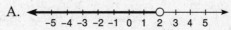

Answers and explanations begin on page 221.

Quadratic Equations

A **quadratic equation** contains a squared variable, for example, $x^2 - 3x = 4$. One way to solve quadratic equations is by factoring. This is the simplest method and the one you should use on the GED® *Mathematical Reasoning Test*. When you factor an expression, you find the terms that divide evenly into the expression.

Example 1: Factor the expression $15x^2 + 9x$.

Key Ideas

- A quadratic equation can have two solutions.
- Set the quadratic equation equal to 0 and factor.
- Find the values for x that will make each factor equal 0.

1. Look for a term that divides evenly into both $15x^2$ and $9x$. Both terms can be divided by $3x$.
   $$15x^2 \div 3x = 5x$$
   $$9x \div 3x = 3$$
2. Factor out $3x$. Write the terms as factors.
   $$15x^2 + 9x = 3x(5x + 3)$$

Study Example 2 to learn how to multiply factors with more than one term.

Example 2: Multiply $\overset{\text{(factor) (factor)}}{\underset{\text{four terms}}{(2x + 3)(x - 4)}}$.

1. Multiply each term in the first factor by each term in the second factor.
   $$2x \cdot x = 2x^2$$
   $$2x \cdot -4 = -8x$$
   $$3 \cdot x = 3x$$
   $$3 \cdot -4 = -12$$
2. Combine the results.
   $$2x^2 + (-8x) + 3x + (-12) =$$
   $$2x^2 - 5x - 12$$

This method of multiplying factors is called the FOIL method. The letters in FOIL stand for First, Outer, Inner, and Last. Use the word FOIL to make sure you have performed all the necessary operations.

You factor a quadratic equation to solve it. A quadratic equation may have two solutions. Find values that make the factors equal to 0. Since a number multiplied by 0 is 0, each of the values is a solution.

Example 3: Solve $x^2 - 3x = 4$.

GED® TEST TIP

Trial and error can help you factor quadratic equations. The more you practice, the better you will get at solving them.

1. Set the equation equal to 0 by subtracting 4 from both sides.
   $$x^2 - 3x = 4$$
   $$x^2 - 3x - 4 = 0$$

2. Factor by trial and error. Think: What factors of the last term, -4, when added, will equal -3, the number part of the middle term? $-4 \cdot 1 = -4$ and $-4 + 1 = -3$
   $$(x)(x) = 0$$
   $$(x + 1)(x - 4) = 0$$

3. If either one of the factors equals 0, then the product of the factors will be 0. Set each factor equal to 0 and solve for x.
   $$x + 1 = 0$$
   $$x = -1$$
   $$x - 4 = 0$$
   $$x = 4$$

The solutions to the quadratic equation are -1 and 4.

PRACTICE 4

A. Multiply.

1. $(x+4)(x+2)$
2. $(x-3)(x+5)$
3. $(x-1)(x+4)$
4. $(x-6)(x-3)$
5. $(x+8)(x-2)$

6. $(2x+1)(x-2)$
7. $(x-9)(x-5)$
8. $(x+1)(3x-2)$
9. $(x-2)(x+7)$
10. $(3x+8)(x+2)$

11. $(x-6)(x+5)$
12. $(x-10)(x-3)$
13. $(2x+1)(2x+2)$
14. $(x+9)(x-4)$
15. $(x-5)(x-5)$

B. Factor each expression.

16. x^2+4x+3
17. x^2+4x-5
18. $x^2+8x+12$
19. x^2-x-6
20. $x^2+5x-14$

21. x^2-x-12
22. $x^2+2x-35$
23. $x^2-12x+36$
24. x^2-6x-7
25. $x^2+4x-32$

26. $2x^2+5x-3$
27. $2x^2-8x-10$
28. $x^2+5x-50$
29. $4x^2+4x-3$
30. x^2+x-56

C. Choose the <u>one best answer</u> to each question.

31. What are two solutions for the equation $x^2-x=20$?

    A. −4 and 5
    B. 4 and −5
    C. −10 and 2
    D. −2 and 10

32. For which of the following equations is $x=-4$ a solution?

    A. $2x^2-8=0$
    B. $x^2-8x+64=0$
    C. $x^2-2x-15=0$
    D. $2x^2+2x-24=0$

33. What is the only positive solution for the equation $2x^2-7x-30=0$?

    A. 5
    B. 6
    C. 7
    D. 8

34. The area of a rectangle is found by multiplying the length by the width. In the rectangle below, the area of the rectangle is equal to the expression $2x^2-27x+70$.

    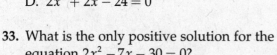

    ?

    2x − 7

    An expression equal to the length is shown on the diagram. Which of the following expressions is equal to the width of the rectangle?

    A. $x+10$
    B. $x-10$
    C. $2x+10$
    D. $2x-10$

    Answers and explanations begin on page 221.

EQUATIONS, INEQUALITIES, AND FUNCTIONS

Algebra Problem Solving

One strategy that can help you save time on the more complicated algebra problems is **guess-and-check.** Guess-and-check means selecting one of the answer choices and trying that value in the problem. If you guess correctly, you can move on to the next question. If not, guess again. Guess-and-check is a good strategy for problems involving quadratic equations and expressions.

Key Ideas

- Guess-and-check is a strategy for answering complicated multiple-choice problems.
- Choose an answer from the options and try the value in the problem. If it works, you have found the correct answer.

Example 1: Which of the following is a solution for the equation $2x^2 - 12 = 2x$?

    A.   4
    B.   3
    C.   0
    D. −1

To solve the problem, you would have to rewrite the equation so that the quadratic expression equals zero, factor the expression, and solve.

Instead, substitute each answer choice into the equation.

Option (A):
$$2x^2 - 12 = 2x$$
$$2(4)^2 - 12 = 2(4)$$
$$20 \neq 8$$

Option (B):
$$2x^2 - 12 = 2x$$
$$2(3)^2 - 12 = 2(3)$$
$$6 = 6$$

Option (B) 3 makes the equation true.

Guess-and-check can also save time when writing an equation seems difficult.

GED® TEST TIP

Use your judgment. Do not use guess-and-check if you can quickly see how to solve the problem. Trying each answer choice may take longer than simply solving the problem.

Example 2: Terry is ten years older than his brother Tomas. Twenty years ago, Terry was twice as old as Tomas. How old is Terry now?

    A. 25
    B. 30
    C. 40
    D. 45

Instead of writing an equation, try each age in the answer choices for Terry.

    A. If Terry is 25 now, Tomas is 15. Twenty years ago, Tomas would not have been born.
    B. If Terry is 30 now, Tomas is 20. Twenty years ago, Tomas would have been 0 years old, and Terry would have been 10.
    C. If Terry is 40 now, Tomas is 30. Twenty years ago, Tomas would have been 10, and Terry would have been 20, which is twice as old as 10.

Therefore, **option (C) 40** is correct.

PRACTICE 5

A. Use guess-and-check to solve the following problems.

1. A number divided by 2 is equal to 12 less than the original number. What is the number?

    A. 12
    B. 20
    C. 24
    D. 28

2. For a fund-raiser, Sandra raised three times as much money as Barbara, and Barbara raised $50 more than Matt. Together they raised $950. How much money did Barbara raise?

    A. $150
    B. $175
    C. $200
    D. $325

3. The three packages below weigh a total of 15 pounds.

    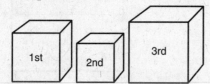

    The first package weighs twice as much as the second package. The third package weighs three times as much as the second package. How many pounds does the first package weigh?

    A. 2
    B. 4
    C. 5
    D. $6\frac{1}{2}$

4. Hannah scored a total of 170 points on two math tests. The score of the first test was 6 points lower than the score of the second test. How many points did Hannah score on the first test?

    A. 76
    B. 82
    C. 88
    D. 90

5. Nelson is twice as old as Maria. Six years ago, Nelson was five times as old as Maria. How old was Nelson six years ago?

    A. 5
    B. 10
    C. 15
    D. 20

6. Which of the following is a solution for the quadratic equation $2x^2 + x - 15 = 0$?

    A. −3
    B. −1
    C. 2
    D. 3

7. An amusement park sells adults' and children's passes. An adult's pass is $25, and a child's pass is $15. A group spent $440 on 20 passes. How many children's passes did the group purchase?

    A. 5
    B. 6
    C. 9
    D. 14

8. The rectangular garden below is twice as long as it is wide. If the total distance around the garden is 120 feet, what is the width of the garden in feet?

    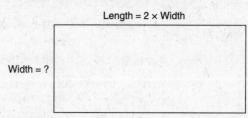

    A. 15
    B. 20
    C. 30
    D. 40

Answers and explanations begin on page 222.

The Coordinate Plane

Key Ideas

- A coordinate grid is formed by two intersecting axes, or number lines.
- The *x*-axis is horizontal, and the *y*-axis is vertical.
- The location of a point is shown by two numbers called an ordered pair: (*x*, *y*).

A **coordinate grid** is a way to locate points that lie in a **plane,** or flat surface. The grid is formed by two intersecting lines, an *x*-axis and a *y*-axis. The *x*-axis is actually a horizontal number line, and the *y*-axis is a vertical number line. The point at which the two axes intersect is called the **origin.**

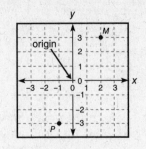

Each point on the grid can be named using two numbers called an **ordered pair.** The first number is the distance from the origin along the *x*-axis. The second number is the distance from the origin along the *y*-axis. The numbers are written in parentheses and are separated by a comma: (*x*, *y*).

Example 1: Write the ordered pairs for points *M* and *P*.

1. Point *M* lies 2 spaces to the right of the origin along the *x*-axis and 3 spaces above the origin along the *y*-axis. The coordinates are **(2, 3).**

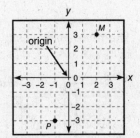

2. Point *P* lies 1 space to the left along the *x*-axis and 3 spaces down along the *y*-axis. The coordinates are **(−1, −3).**

To plot points on the grid, use the number lines located at the axes. Remember that right and up are the directions for positive numbers and left and down are the directions for negative numbers.

Example 2: Point *A* is located at (−2, 1), and point *B* is located at (3, −2). Plot these points on a coordinate grid.

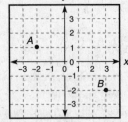

1. To plot point *A*, start at the origin. Count 2 spaces left along the *x*-axis. Count 1 space up along the *y*-axis.

2. To plot point *B*, start at the origin. Count 3 spaces right along the *x*-axis. Count 2 spaces down along the *y*-axis.

PRACTICE 6

A. Write the ordered pair for each point.

1. Point *A*
2. Point *B*
3. Point *C*
4. Point *D*
5. Point *E*
6. Point *F*
7. Point *G*
8. Point *H*

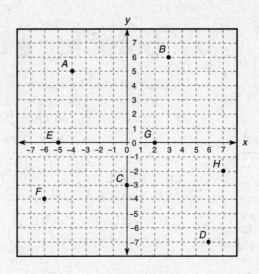

B. Plot the points on the coordinate grid.

9. Plot the following points:

   J at $(-3, -2)$
   K at $(4, 0)$
   L at $(1, -3)$
   M at $(-4, 2)$

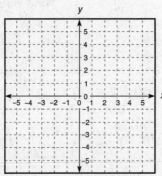

10. Plot the following points:

    N at $(0, -1)$
    O at $(-4, -4)$
    P at $(3, 1)$
    Q at $(-3, 0)$

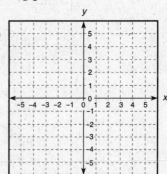

C. Choose the <u>one best answer</u> to each question.

11. On the coordinate grid below, a line passes through points *A* and *B*.

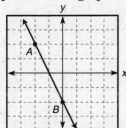

Which of the following ordered pairs also lies on the line?

A. $(1, 0)$
B. $(1, -1)$
C. $(0, -1)$
D. $(-1, 0)$

12. Two of the corners of a triangle are located at $(3, -3)$ and $(2, 3)$. What is the location of the third corner as shown in the diagram below?

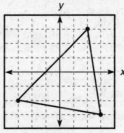

A. $(-3, -2)$
B. $(-3, 2)$
C. $(-2, -3)$
D. $(3, -2)$

Answers and explanations begin on page 222.

Graphing a Line

Using the coordinate system, we can graph equations. When an equation has only two variables, x and y, and neither is raised to a power, the graph of the equation will be a line. When the graph of an equation is a straight line, the equation is a **linear equation**.

To graph an equation, you need to solve for two points on the line.

Example 1: Graph the equation $y = 3x - 4$.

1. Choose any value for x and solve for y. Let $x = 1$.

$$y = 3(1) - 4$$
$$y = 3 - 4$$
$$y = -1$$

If $x = 1$, then $y = -1$. The ordered pair for the first point is $(1, -1)$.

2. Choose another value for x and solve for y. Let $x = 2$.

$$y = 3(2) - 4$$
$$y = 6 - 4$$
$$y = 2$$

If $x = 2$, then $y = 2$. The ordered pair for the second point is $(2, 2)$.

3. Plot the points on a coordinate grid and draw a line through them.

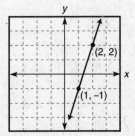

The line is the graph of all the possible solutions for the equation $y = 3x - 4$. Arrows at both ends of the line indicate that the line continues in both directions. From this, you can see that there is an infinite number of solutions to a linear equation.

Some linear equation problems don't require you to draw a graph.

Example 2: Point A lies at $(5, -6)$ on a coordinate grid. The graph of which of the following equations passes through point A?

(1) $y = -5x + 18$
(2) $y = -4x + 14$
(3) $y = -2x - 13$

Use the ordered pair given in the problem. Substitute the x-coordinate, 5, for x in each equation and solve for y. If $y = -6$, the value of the y-coordinate from the ordered pair, you have found the correct equation.

Option (2) is correct.

$$y = -4x + 14$$
$$y = -4(5) + 14$$
$$y = -20 + 14 = -6$$

Key Ideas

- A linear equation has two variables, x and y.
- When the solutions to a linear equation are graphed on a coordinate grid, the graph forms a line.
- To find a point on the line, substitute a value for x and solve for y.
- You must solve for at least two points in order to draw the line.

GED® TEST TIP

If a linear equation is not written with y on one side of the equation, use inverse operations to isolate y. Example: $2x + y = 15$. Subtract 2x from each side. $y = -2x + 15$.

A. Fill in the *y* column in each table and graph the equation.

1. $y = \frac{1}{2}x + 3$

If $x =$	then $y =$
−2	
0	
2	

2. $y + 3x = -1$

If $x =$	then $y =$
−1	
0	
1	

3. $-2 + y = -x$

If $x =$	then $y =$
1	
2	
3	

4. $y = 3 - 2x$

If $x =$	then $y =$
0	
1	
2	

B. Choose the <u>one best answer</u> to each question.

<u>Questions 5 and 6</u> refer to the following coordinate grid.

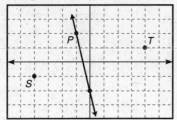

5. The graph of the equation $y = \frac{1}{4}x$ will pass through which of the following pairs of points?

   A. point *S* and (−1, 2)
   B. point *S* and (0, −2)
   C. point *T* and (0, 0)
   D. point *T* and (0, −2)

6. Line *P* is the graph of which of the following equations?

   A. $y = 4x + 1$
   B. $y = -4x - 1$
   C. $y = 4x + 2$
   D. $y = -4x - 2$

7. Point *C* is located at (−3, 5). A graph of which of the following equations would pass through point *C*?

   A. $3x + 2y = 5$
   B. $2x + 3y = 9$
   C. $4x - 2y = 8$
   D. $3x - 3y = 6$

Answers and explanations begin on page 222.

Equations, Inequalities, and Functions 165

EQUATIONS, INEQUALITIES, AND FUNCTIONS

Slope of a Line

Slope is the measurement of the steepness of a line. Imagine a road going up a hill. If the road must climb upward over a short forward distance, the road will be very steep. Slope measures the relationship between **rise** (how high the road must climb) and **run** (the distance the road goes forward).

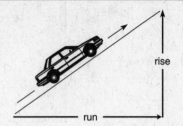

Key Ideas

- Slope is the ratio of rise to run.
- Moving from left to right, a line that goes upward has a positive slope, and a line that moves downward has a negative slope.
- You can find slope by counting spaces and writing a ratio or by using the slope formula.

On a coordinate grid, a line that moves upward from left to right has a **positive slope.** A line that moves downward from left to right has a **negative slope.** You can find the slope of a line on a coordinate grid by writing the ratio of rise to run.

Example 1: What is the slope of line P shown on the coordinate grid?

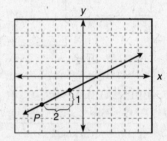

1. Find two points on line P. Count to find the rise and run. The line moves up 1 space for every 2 spaces it goes to the right.

2. Write the ratio: $\frac{\text{rise}}{\text{run}} = \frac{1}{2}$. The slope is $\frac{1}{2}$.

Example 2: What is the slope of line S shown on the coordinate grid?

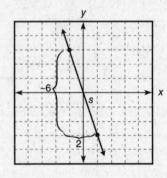

1. Find any two points on line S. The line moves down 6 spaces (a negative direction) and 2 spaces to the right.

2. Write the ratio: $\frac{\text{rise}}{\text{run}} = \frac{-6}{2} = -3$.

The slope of line S is -3.

You can also find slope using the slope formula on the GED® Formula Sheet. The formula will appear as follows:

slope of a line $(m) = \dfrac{y_2 - y_1}{x_2 - x_1}$, where (x_1, y_1) and (x_2, y_2) are two points on a line.

Example 3: A line passes through points at coordinates $(1, 4)$ and $(-5, 2)$. What is the slope of the line?

1. Choose one point to be (x_1, y_1). The other will be (x_2, y_2). It doesn't matter which you choose. For this example, $(x_1, y_1) = (1, 4)$ and $(x_2, y_2) = (-5, 2)$.

2. Substitute the values into the slope formula and solve:

$$\frac{y_2 - y_1}{x_2 - x_1} \qquad \frac{2-4}{-5-1} = \frac{-2}{-6} = \frac{1}{3} \qquad \text{The slope is } \frac{1}{3}.$$

Since the slope is positive, you know that the line rises from left to right. You also know that it goes up 1 space for every 3 spaces it moves to the right.

In working with slope, there are a few special circumstances that you should memorize. A horizontal line, just like a flat stretch of roadway, has a **slope of 0**. The slope of a vertical line is **undefined**; in other words, our definition of slope will not work for a line that has no run at all.

PRACTICE 8

A. Find the slope of each line.

1.
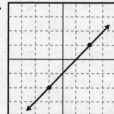

2.
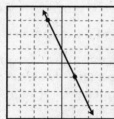

3.
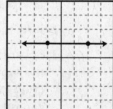

B. Use the slope formula to find the slope of a line that passes through the following pairs of points.

4. (3, 5) and (−1, 2)

5. (0, 2) and (4, 0)

6. (4, 2) and (2, 2)

7. (6, 1) and (0, 3)

8. (1, 4) and (−2, −2)

9. (4, −2) and (2, 4)

C. Choose the one best answer for each question.

<u>Question 10</u> refers to the following graph.

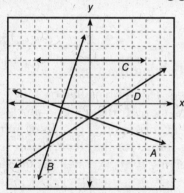

10. Which of the following lines shown on the graph has a slope of $-\frac{1}{3}$?

A. line *A*

B. line *B*

C. line *C*

D. line *D*

11. Line *N* passes through the following points: (0, 4), (1, 2), (2, 0), and (3, −2). What is the slope of line *N*?

A. −4

B. −2

C. 2

D. 4

12. Line *L* passes through point (1, 0) and has a slope of 3. Which of the following points also lies on line *L*?

A. (0, 3)

B. (1, 3)

C. (2, 3)

D. (2, 5)

Answers and explanations begin on page 223.

Slope and Equations

Key Ideas

- There are two ways to find an equation if you are given the slope of a line and a point.
- One method is the slope-intercept form.
- The other method is the point-slope form.

Use the Slope-Intercept Form to Find an Equation

Lesson 8 showed how to find the slope of a line and graph it. The examples in this lesson show how you can use the slope and a point on the line to find the equation of a line in two different forms. (You might also need to find the equation of a line from two points. In this case, you would calculate the slope first, then use the slope and one of the points to find the equation.)

The first of these forms is the **slope-intercept form:** $y = mx + b$. In this form of the equation, the variable m stands for the **slope** of the line. The variable b stands for the **y-intercept,** which is the y-value at the point where the line crosses the y-axis. The variables x and y are the **x-** and **y-coordinates** of any point on the line and are usually written as an ordered pair.

Follow these steps to find the equation of a line in the slope-intercept form.

1. Substitute the values that you are given for the slope (m) and the x- and y-coordinates (x, y) into the slope-intercept equation. Be careful not to mix up x and y.

2. Use inverse operations to isolate b.

3. Rewrite the equation in slope-intercept form, leaving x and y as variables and substituting values for m and b.

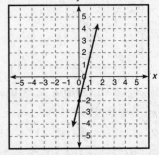

Example 1: Use the slope-intercept form to find the equation of a line that has the slope $m = 4$ and passes through the point $(-1, -6)$.

1. $-6 = (4) \times (-1) + b$
   $-6 = -4 + b$
2. $-2 = b$
3. $y = 4x - 2$

Use the Point-Slope Form to Find an Equation

The second important form that is used to describe a line on the *Mathematical Reasoning Test* is the **point-slope form:** $y - y_1 = m(x - x_1)$. In this form, (x_1, y_1) is an ordered pair that corresponds to a point on the line. As in the slope-intercept form, m stands for the slope. If you simplify an equation in point-slope form by solving for y, you will get the slope-intercept form of the equation.

Follow these steps to find the equation of a line in the point-slope form.

1. Call the point that you are given (x_1, y_1).

2. Put the x_1 and y_1 values into the point-slope equation.

3. Put the slope value in the point-slope equation for m.

Example 2: Use the point-slope form to find the equation of the line that passes through the point (4, 3) and has a slope of 2.

1. $(x_1, y_1) = (4, 3)$

2. $y - 3 = m(x - 4)$

3. $y - 3 = 2(x - 4)$

Notice that you can simplify the equation to find the slope-intercept form:

$$y - 3 = 2(x - 4)$$
$$y - 3 = 2x - 8$$
$$y = 2x - 5$$

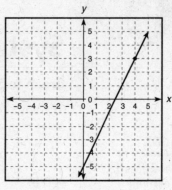

PRACTICE 9

A. Use the slope-intercept form, $y = mx + b$, to find the equation of the line that passes through the given point and has the given slope.

1. $(1, -2); m = -4$

2. $(-1, -4); m = 2$

3. $(-4, 2); m = -\frac{1}{3}$

B. Use the point-slope form, $y - y_1 = m(x - x_1)$, to find the equation of the line that passes through the given point and has the given slope.

4. $(2, 1); m = 3$

5. $(2, 0); m = -\frac{1}{3}$

6. $(1, -2); m = 1$

C. Find the equation of the line that passes through the given points. Write your answer in slope-intercept form.

7. $(-5, 3), (1, 1)$

8. $(-3, 0), (-2, 4)$

9. $(-3, -4), (7, 1)$

D. Choose the <u>one best answer</u> for each question.

10. Which of the following is an equation for the line that passes through $(-1, 0)$ and $(2, -3)$?

   A. $y = 3x + 3$
   B. $y = -3x + 9$
   C. $y = -x - 1$
   D. $y = x - 5$

11. Which of the following is an equation for the line that passes through $(-3, 4)$ and $(1, 4)$?

   A. $y = 0$
   B. $y = 4$
   C. $y = x + 3$
   D. $y = x + 7$

12. Which of the following equations describes the same line as $y - 2 = \frac{1}{2}(x - 6)$?

   A. $y = 3x + 2$
   B. $y = \frac{1}{2}x - 4$
   C. $y = -x + 12$
   D. $y = \frac{1}{2}x - 1$

Question 13 refers to the following graph.

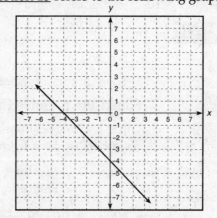

13. Which of the following equations correctly describes the line on the graph?

   A. $y = x - 4$
   B. $y = -x - 4$
   C. $y = x + 4$
   D. $y = -x + 4$

Answers and explanations start on page 223.

EQUATIONS, INEQUALITIES, AND FUNCTIONS

Systems of Linear Equations

Graph to Solve the System of Equations

The equations in Lessons 7 and 9 are **linear equations:** they have two variables, x and y, and represent straight lines in the coordinate plane. Two or more linear equations make up a **system of linear equations.** Solving a system of two equations means finding the values of both variables. The **solution** will give the x- and y-coordinates of the point at which the two lines intersect. You can express this solution as an ordered pair: (x, y).

One way to solve a system of equations is by graphing each equation using a **T-chart**—like those that you filled in for the Lesson 7 practice. Graphing a system of linear equations provides a picture of the intersection. Follow these steps to solve a system of equations by graphing.

1. Set up an x and y T-chart for each equation. Find two ordered pairs for each equation: use $x = 0$ and find y and then use $y = 0$ and find x.

2. Graph both lines, using the ordered pairs that you generated in step 1.

3. Find the point of intersection and express it in the form (x, y).

Example 1: Graph the equations $6x + 3y = 12$ and $5x + y = 7$ to find the solution.

1.

$6x + 3y = 12$

X	Y
0	4
2	0

$5x + y = 7$

X	Y
0	7
$\frac{7}{5}$	0

2.
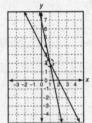

3. The point of intersection—that is, the solution—is **(1, 2)**.

Substitute to Solve the System of Equations

You can also use **substitution** to solve a system of linear equations. Follow these steps to solve a system of linear equations by substitution.

Example 2: Solve the equations $6x + 3y = 12$ and $5x + y = 7$ by substitution.

1. Solve the first equation so that y is expressed in terms of x.

$$6x + 3y = 12$$
$$3y = 12 - 6x$$
$$y = 4 - 2x$$

2. Substitute that value of y into the second equation and solve for x.

$$5x + (4 - 2x) = 7$$
$$3x + 4 = 7$$
$$3x = 3$$
$$x = 1$$

3. Substitute that value of x into the first equation and solve for y.

$$6(1) + 3y = 12$$
$$6 + 3y = 12$$
$$3y = 6$$
$$y = 2$$

The solution is **(1, 2)**.

PRACTICE 10

A. Find two pairs of coordinates for each equation by making a T-chart. Use the coordinates to graph the lines and find the solution.

1. $y = 3x - 15$
   $x + y = 13$

2. $4x + 2y = 10$
   $y = -5x - 4$

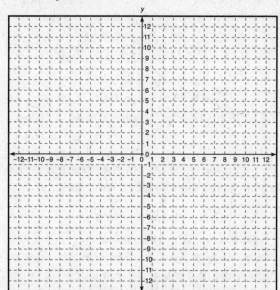 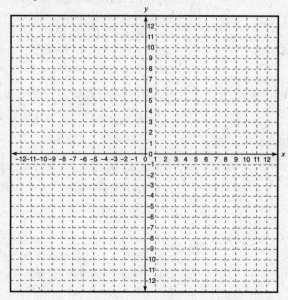

B. Find the solution for the two equations by substitution. Express as an ordered pair in the form (x, y).

3. $7x - y = 22$
   $4x + 2y = 10$

4. $x + y = 9$
   $2x - 3y = 8$

5. $y = 3x + 15$
   $5x - 2y = -26$

6. $10x - y = -1$
   $y = 12x$

C. Choose the <u>one best answer</u> for each question.

7. Where does the line with the equation $x - 2y = 4$ intersect with the line with the equation $6y + 5x = 4$?

   A. $(2, -1)$
   B. $(3, -2)$
   C. $(-2, 1)$
   D. $(-1, 2)$

8. Where does the line with the equation $y = x$ intersect with the line with the equation $y = -x$?

   A. $(1, -1)$
   B. $(-1, 1)$
   C. $(0, 0)$
   D. $(1, 0)$

9. Where does the line with the equation $y = -2$ intersect with the line with the equation $3y = 2x + 3$?

   A. $(-\frac{2}{9}, -2)$
   B. $(-\frac{1}{3}, -2)$
   C. $(-\frac{9}{2}, -2)$
   D. $(\frac{9}{2}, 2)$

10. Which of the following is the equation of a line that intersects $y = 4x + 2$?

   A. $2y = 8x + 2$
   B. $y = 4x - 2$
   C. $y = -4x + 2$
   D. $\frac{1}{2}y = 2x - 7$

Answers and explanations start on page 224.

EQUATIONS, INEQUALITIES, AND FUNCTIONS

Patterns and Functions

A **pattern** is a series of numbers or objects whose sequence is determined by a particular rule. You can figure out what rule has been used by studying the terms you are given. Think: What operation or sequence of operations will always result in the next term in the series? Once you know the rule, you can continue the pattern.

Example 1: Find the seventh term in the sequence: 1, 2, 4, 8, 16, . . .

1. Determine the rule. Each number in the sequence is two times the number before it.

2. Apply the rule. You have been given five terms and must find the seventh. Continue the pattern. The sixth term is $16 \times 2 = 32$, and the seventh term is $32 \times 2 = \textbf{64}$.

A **function** is a rule that shows how the terms in one sequence of numbers are related to the terms in another sequence. Each distinct number entered into the function produces a unique output. For example, a sidewalk vendor charges $1.50 for a slice of pizza. The chart below shows how much it would cost to buy one to six slices.

Number of Pizza Slices	1	2	3	4	5	6
Cost	$1.50	$3.00	$4.50	$6.00	$7.50	$9.00

Each number in the first row corresponds to a price in the second row. We could say that the amount a customer will pay is a function of (or depends upon) the number of slices the customer orders. This function could be written:

Cost = number of slices × $1.50, or $C = n(\$1.50)$.

If you know the function and a number in the first set of numbers, you can solve for its corresponding number in the second set.

Example 2: Using the function $y = 3x + 5$, what is the value of y when $x = -3$?

1. Substitute the given value of x. $y = 3(-3) + 5$
2. Solve for y. $y = -9 + 5$
     $y = \textbf{-4}$

Example 3: Using the function $n = 100 - 4(3 + m)$, what is the value of n when $m = 6$?

1. Substitute the given value of m. $n = 100 - 4(3 + 6)$
2. Solve for n. $n = 100 - 4(9)$
     $n = 100 - 36$
     $n = \textbf{64}$

Key Ideas

- A pattern is a sequence of numbers determined by a mathematical rule.
- A function is a rule that shows how one set of numbers is related to another set of numbers.
- To use a function, substitute values for variables and solve.

GED® TEST TIP

To figure out what rule has been used to form a pattern, begin by finding the difference between each term and the term that follows it in the sequence.

PRACTICE 11

A. Solve.

1. Which number should come next in the following pattern?

   $-12, -9, -6, -3,$ _____

2. What is the next number in the sequence?

   $21, 26, 31, 36,$ _____

3. In the function $y = 4x + 10$, if $x = -2$, what is the value of y?

4. In the function $y = 2x(4 + x) - 2$, if $x = 3$, what is the value of y?

5. Each term in the second row is determined by the function $y = 2x - 1$.

x	1	2	3	4	5	...	12
y	1	3	5	7	9	...	

   What number belongs in the shaded box?

6. In the function $y = \dfrac{x+3}{6} - 8$, if $x = 21$, what is the value of y?

7. What is the next term in the pattern below?

   1000, 500, 250, 125, 62.5, _____

8. What is the next number in the sequence?

   $3, -5, 7, -9, 11,$ _____

9. Each term in the second row is determined by the function $y = 3x + 5$.

x	-2	-1	0	1	2	...	9
y	-1	2	5	8	11	...	

   What number belongs in the shaded box?

10. In the function $y = (x - 7) + 12$, if $x = -10$, what is the value of y?

B. Choose the one best answer to each question.

Question 11 refers to the following drawing.

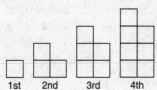

1st 2nd 3rd 4th

11. How many blocks would be needed to build the 25th construction in the sequence?

    A. 47
    B. 49
    C. 51
    D. 55

12. What is the sixth term in the sequence below?

    $-14, -8, -2, 4, \ldots$

    A. 10
    B. 14
    C. 16
    D. 22

13. The price per scarf is a function of the number of scarves purchased. The table shows the price per scarf for purchases of up to four scarves.

number (n) of scarves	1	2	3	4
cost (c) per scarf	$5.00	$4.75	$4.50	$4.25

    Which of the following functions was used to determine the prices shown in the table?

    A. $c = n(\$5.00 - \$0.25)$
    B. $c = \$5.00 - \$0.25(n - 1)$
    C. $c = \$5.00 - \$0.25n$
    D. $c = \$5.00n - \$0.25n$

14. Which of the following sequences of values of y could be created using the function
    $y = 4x - 3$?

    A. $1, 4, 7, 10, 13, \ldots$
    B. $1, 5, 9, 13, 17, \ldots$
    C. $1, 4, 8, 13, 19, \ldots$
    D. $1, -1, -3, -5, -7, \ldots$

Answers and explanations begin on page 224.

Function Applications

Key Ideas

- Functions are used to make many common work calculations.
- Functions can be used to make comparisons.
- To use a function, you must know the meaning of the variables. This information should be given in the text of the problem.

Functions are used in many business applications. For instance, they can be used to calculate profit, cost, employee wages, and taxes. On the *Mathematical Reasoning Test*, you will read about common work and life situations. The problems may contain or describe a function that you can use to solve the problem.

Example 1: Celino Advertising is finishing a series of print ads for a client. Finishing the project will cost $2000 per day for the first seven days and $3500 per day after seven days. The finishing costs can be found using the function $C = \$2000d + \$1500(d-7)$, where C = the cost of finishing the project and d = the number of days. If the project takes 12 days to complete, what will the project cost?

Use the function to solve the problem.

$$
\begin{aligned}
C &= \$2000d + \$1500(d-7) \\
&= \$2000(12) + \$1500(12-7) \\
&= \$24000 + \$1500(5) \\
&= \$24000 + \$7500 \\
&= \mathbf{\$31{,}500}
\end{aligned}
$$

You may be asked to use functions to make comparisons.

Example 2: Nita decides to join a health club. She gets brochures from two health clubs and compares the plans. Healthstars Fitness charges a one-time membership fee of $250 and $8 per month. Freedom Health Center charges $25 per month. At both health clubs, the price (P) Nita will pay is a function of the number of months (m) she attends the club. The functions are as follows:

Healthstars Fitness $\qquad P = \$250 + \$8m$

Freedom Health Center $\qquad P = \$25m$

Nita plans to move in 18 months. If she attends a health club until she moves, which one offers the better price?

1. Find the price at Healthstars Fitness:

$$
\begin{aligned}
P &= \$250 + \$8m \\
&= \$250 + \$8(18) \\
&= \$250 + \$144 \\
&= \$394
\end{aligned}
$$

2. Find the price at Freedom Health Center:

$$
\begin{aligned}
P &= \$25m \\
&= \$25(18) \\
&= \$450
\end{aligned}
$$

3. Compare the results. Even though Nita will have to pay a large amount up front, **Healthstars Fitness** offers the better price.

GED® TEST TIP

There is often more than one way to work a problem, even when a function is given. Solve using the function. If you see another way to solve the problem, use it to check your answer.

PRACTICE 12

A. Solve. You MAY use a calculator.

1. The Chimney Sweep charges $25 for a chimney inspection. If the customer purchases additional services, $15 of the inspection fee is deducted. Let s = the cost of any additional services. The total cost (C) of an inspection and services can be determined by the function $C = \$25 + (s - \$15)$ where s is not 0.

   a. Jan has her chimney inspected and purchases a smoke guard for $89. How much will she be charged?

   b. After an inspection, Ahmed decides to have a new damper installed for $255. How much will he pay?

2. Ricardo does a great deal of driving for his work. He generally estimates his driving time in hours (t) using the function $t = \frac{m}{60}$, where m = the number of miles.

   a. How many hours will it take Ricardo to drive 330 miles?

   b. How many hours will it take Ricardo to drive 255 miles?

3. A customer's phone charges are a function of the number of minutes of long-distance calls made. The graph shows a comparison of two plans available.

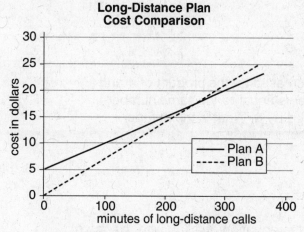

Long-Distance Plan Cost Comparison

   a. Michelle looks at her previous phone bills and finds that she makes about 350 minutes of long-distance calls per month. Which plan is better for her?

   b. Craig usually makes about 150 minutes of long-distance calls per month. Which plan is better for him?

B. Choose the one best answer to each question. You MAY use a calculator.

Questions 4 and 5 refer to the following information.

Alicia is considering three job opportunities. At all three jobs, weekly pay (P) is a function of the number of hours (h) worked during the week. The functions are shown below:

Job 1	$P = \$9.75h$
Job 2	$P = \$70 + \$8.40h$
Job 3	$P = \$380 \times \frac{h}{38}$

4. If Alicia works 30 hours in a week, how much more will she earn at Job 2 than at Job 1?

   A. $5.33
   B. $29.50
   C. $40.50
   D. $59.00

5. If Alicia works 40 hours per week, which of the following is a true statement?

   A. Alicia will earn the least at Job 3.
   B. Job 1 will pay more than Job 3.
   C. Job 3 will pay more than Job 2.
   D. Alicia will earn the most at Job 2.

6. A company is awarded a $95,000 job that will cost $5,400 per day in expenses. Profits (P) can be calculated using $P = \$95,000 - \$5,400d$, where d = days. What is the company's profit if the job takes 14 days to complete?

   A. $10,800
   B. $19,400
   C. $66,100
   D. $75,600

Answers and explanations begin on page 225.

EQUATIONS, INEQUALITIES, AND FUNCTIONS PRACTICE QUESTIONS

Directions: You MAY use your calculator.

1. Which of the following expressions is equal to $6 - 4(x + 3)$?

   A. $4x + 3$
   B. $4x - 9$
   C. $-4x - 3$
   D. $-4x - 6$

2. Three increased by the product of 4 and a number is equal to the same number decreased by 6. What is the number?

   A. -3
   B. -1
   C. 1
   D. 3

3. What is the equation of a line with a slope of -4 that passes through the point $(1, 2)$?

   A. $y = -4x + 2$
   B. $y = -4x + 6$
   C. $y = 4x + 1$
   D. $y = 4x + 6$

4. The ordered pair $(-2, -1)$ is a solution to which of the following equations?

   A. $-4x - y = 7$
   B. $4x + y = -7$
   C. $4x - y = -7$
   D. $-4x + y = -7$

5. For a two-week period, Jan earned $150 less than twice Tom's earnings. Together Jan and Tom earned $1380. How much did Tom earn?

   A. $720
   B. $660
   C. $510
   D. $360

Questions 6 and 7 refer to the following graph.

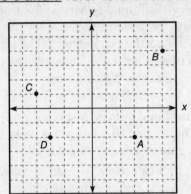

6. If the graph of the equation $y = -x - 5$ were drawn on the grid, which of the points would be on the line?

   A. A
   B. B
   C. C
   D. D

7. If a line were drawn through points B and C, what would be the slope of the line?

   A. -3
   B. $-\frac{1}{3}$
   C. $\frac{1}{3}$
   D. 3

8. Samuel is paid $350 per month plus a 10% commission on his total sales for the month. If he needs to earn at least $2100 per month, which of the following expressions represents the total sales (s) Samuel needs to achieve?

   A. $s \geq \$17,500$
   B. $s \leq \$17,500$
   C. $s \leq \$21,000$
   D. $s \geq \$21,000$

9. For its Checking Plus account, a bank charges $3.95 per month plus $0.10 for each check written after the first ten checks written that month. The function to find the total monthly fee (F) is $F = \$3.95 + \$0.10(n - 10)$, where $n =$ number of checks written.

Greg writes 24 checks in March. How much will he pay in fees for the month?

A. $6.35
B. $5.35
C. $2.40
D. $1.40

10. The sum of four consecutive odd numbers is 104. What is the largest number?

A. 23
B. 25
C. 27
D. 29

11. Which value for x makes the inequality $x > 400$ true?

A. 7^3
B. 4^4
C. 3^6
D. 6^3

12. Four less than the product of a number (x) and 5 is equal to 8 more than 2 added to 3 times the number. Which of these equations could be used to find the value of x?

A. $4 - 5x = 8 + 2 + 3x$
B. $5x - 4 = 8 + 2 + 3x$
C. $5x = 4 - 8 + 2 + 3x$
D. $5x - 4 = 8 + 2 + 3$

13. What is the slope of a line that passes through the points (2, 4) and (4, 6)?

A. -2
B. 1
C. 2
D. 4

14. What is the next number in the sequence?

1, 7, 14, 22, ...

A. 30
B. 31
C. 32
D. 33

15. What is the y-intercept of the line with a slope of 2 that passes through the point (1, 2)?

A. -2
B. $-\frac{1}{2}$
C. 0
D. $\frac{1}{2}$

16. The graphs of the equations $y = x + 3$ and $y = -2x - 3$ are drawn on a coordinate grid.

In the coordinate plane below, darken the circle corresponding to the point at which the two lines intersect.

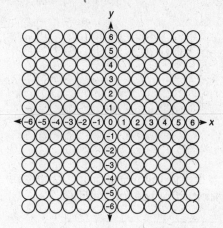

17. Which of the following shows the product of -7 and x decreased by the sum of 8 and y?

    A. $-7x - (8 + y)$
    B. $-7x - 8 + y$
    C. $(8 + y) - 7x$
    D. $(7 + x) - (8 + y)$

18. What are the possible solutions for the quadratic equation $x^2 - 5x = 24$?

    A. -8 and 3
    B. -6 and 4
    C. 8 and -3
    D. 4 and -6

19. Cynthia is 6 times as old as Rebecca. In 6 years, Cynthia will be only 3 times as old as Rebecca. How old is Rebecca now?

    A. 3
    B. 4
    C. 8
    D. 12

20. The graph of which equation will pass through points $(0, -3)$ and $(5, 7)$?

    A. $x = \frac{1}{2}x - 3$
    B. $y = 2x - 3$
    C. $y = 2x + 7$
    D. $y = -2x + 3$

21. Which of the following graphs represents the solution set of the inequality $-2(x - 6) > 8$?

    A. ![number line -5 to 5, open circle at -2]
       -5 -4 -3 -2 -1 0 1 2 3 4 5
    B. ![number line -5 to 5, open circle at 2]
       -5 -4 -3 -2 -1 0 1 2 3 4 5
    C. ![number line -5 to 5, open circle at -2]
       -5 -4 -3 -2 -1 0 1 2 3 4 5
    D. ![number line -5 to 5, open circle at 2]
       -5 -4 -3 -2 -1 0 1 2 3 4 5

Questions 22 and 23 refer to the following graph.

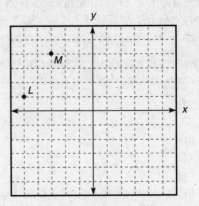

22. Which of the following ordered pairs shows the location of point L?

    A. $(-5, -1)$
    B. $(-5, 1)$
    C. $(-1, 5)$
    D. $(1, -5)$

23. What is the slope of the line that passes through points L and M?

    A. $\frac{-3}{2}$
    B. $\frac{-2}{3}$
    C. $\frac{2}{3}$
    D. $\frac{3}{2}$

24. Bob, Celia, Sam, and Daniel contributed money to buy their boss a retirement gift. Sam and Daniel each gave the same amount of money. Celia gave $12 more than Daniel. Bob gave half as much as Celia gave. If the four workers gave a total of $81, how much did Sam give?

    A. $9
    B. $15
    C. $18
    D. $21

25. What is the solution set of the inequality
$-7x - 4 \geq x - 28$

   A. $x \leq 3$
   B. $x \geq 3$
   C. $x \leq -3$
   D. $x \geq -4$

26. A line goes through the points (0, 2) and (1, 3). What is the equation of the line?

   A. $y = -\frac{1}{2}x + 3$
   B. $y = \frac{1}{2}x + 2$
   C. $y = x + 2$
   D. $y = x + 3$

27. In a recent election, Perez got 5512 more votes than $\frac{1}{3}$ of the leading candidate's votes. Together the two candidates received 18,072 votes. How many people voted for Perez?

   A. 6,024
   B. 8,652
   C. 9,420
   D. 12,560

28. What is the value of x in the equation $-4(x + 2) - 10 = 5x$?

   A. $x = -18$
   B. $x = -2$
   C. $x = 2$
   D. $x = 18$

29. Marcia counts the $5 bills and $10 bills in her cash register drawer. She counts a total of 35 bills with a total value of $240. If $x =$ the number of $5 bills in the drawer, which of the following equations could be used to find the number of $5 bills in the drawer?

   A. $\$5x + \$10x = 35$
   B. $\$5x + \$10x + 35 = \$240$
   C. $\$5(35 - x) + \$10x = \$240$
   D. $\$5x + \$10(35 - x) = \$240$

30. The sum of five consecutive numbers is 370. What is the fourth number in the sequence?

   A. 73
   B. 74
   C. 75
   D. 76

31. A baseball pitcher's earned run average (E) is a function of the number of earned runs (r) given up and innings pitched (i). The function is written $E = \dfrac{9r}{i}$. What is the earned run average of a pitcher who gives up 8 runs in 18 innings?

   Write your answer on the line below.

   _____

32. Point B is located halfway between $(-1, 5)$ and $(-1, -3)$. Name the location of point B.

   In the coordinate plane below, darken the circle corresponding to the location of point B.

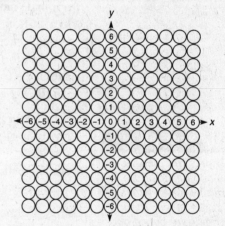

Answers and explanations begin on page 225.

GEOMETRY

Plane Figures

Key Ideas

- Plane figures are classified by the properties of their sides and angles.
- The sum of the interior angles of any four-sided plane figure is 360°.
- By using the properties of any four-sided plane figure and algebraic reasoning, you can find missing angle measures.

Four-Sided Plane Figures

A **plane figure** is a set of line segments, all lying on a single plane. To prepare for the GED® *Mathematical Reasoning Test*, learn the properties of each shape. You will need to identify the characteristics of different types of four-sided plane figures and draw conclusions about their angles and sides.

You are already familiar with rectangles and squares. A **rectangle** is a four-sided figure with four right angles. The opposite sides (sides across from each other) are the same length, and they are parallel.

Sides with the same markings are equal.

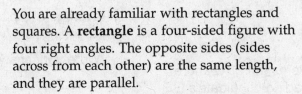
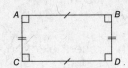

A **square** is actually a kind of rectangle. It, too, has four right angles with parallel opposite sides. However, a square has one additional property: its four sides are all the same length.

A **parallelogram** is a four-sided figure whose opposite sides are parallel and the same length. In addition, its opposite angles (the angles diagonally across from each other) are also equal in measure. A special parallelogram, called a **rhombus** (not shown), has four sides of equal length.

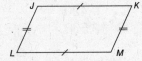

A **trapezoid** is a four-sided figure with exactly one pair of parallel sides. The definition of a trapezoid does not dictate the measure of the angles or the lengths of the sides.

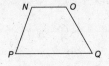

All four-sided plane figures have one important property in common. The sum of the measures of the interior angles is 360°. You can use this fact to find a missing angle measure.

Example: In figure *ABCD*, the opposite sides are parallel. What is the measure of ∠*A* ?

1. Identify the figure. The notation on the drawing tells you that the opposite sides are equal in measure. Since they are also parallel, the figure is a parallelogram.

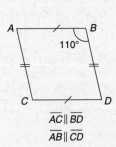

2. Find the measure of ∠*C*. The opposite angles of a parallelogram are equal in measure; therefore, $m\angle C = m\angle B$. Both ∠*B* and ∠*C* measure 110°.

3. Find the measure of $\angle A$. You know the measures of $\angle A$ $2x + 110° + 110° = 360°$
and $\angle D$ are equal and that the sum of all four angles $2x + 220° = 360°$
equals 360°. Let $x = m\angle A$. Therefore, $2x =$ the sum of $m\angle A$ $2x = 140°$
and $m\angle D$. Write an equation and solve. $x = 70°$

The measure of $\angle A$ is **70°**.

PRACTICE 1

A. List the names of four-sided plane figures introduced on page 180 that can exhibit the following properties. Write *None* if no four-sided plane figure has the given property.

1. four right angles
2. opposite sides are equal in length
3. exactly one pair of parallel sides
4. all angles are equal in measure
5. only three right angles

6. opposite angles are equal in measure
7. all four sides are equal in length
8. sum of interior angles is 360°
9. sides are all of different lengths
10. four equal angles and four equal sides

B. Choose the <u>one best answer</u> to each question.

<u>Questions 11 and 12</u> refer to the following figure.

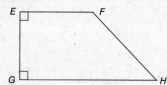

<u>Question 13</u> refers to the following figure.

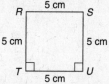

11. Angle F is 20° more than three times the measure of $\angle H$. What is the measure of $\angle F$?

A.   40°
B.   120°
C.   140°
D.   180°

12. In order for figure *EFGH* to be a trapezoid, which of the following must be a true statement?

A. *EF* is the same length as *FH*.
B. $EF \parallel GH$.
C. $m\angle F = m\angle H$.
D. $m\angle G = m\angle F$.

13. If the opposite sides in figure *RSUT* are parallel, what is the measure of $\angle R$?

A.   5°
B.   20°
C.   90°
D. 270°

14. A four-sided plane figure has sides measuring 10, 15, 10, and 15. The opposite angles are equal, but there are no right angles. What is the figure?

A. rhombus
B. rectangle
C. parallelogram
D. trapezoid

Answers and explanations begin on page 226.

GEOMETRY

Triangles

The Properties of Triangles

A **triangle** is a closed three-sided plane figure. From the definition, we can infer other properties. Since a triangle has three sides, it must also have three interior angles and three vertices.

A triangle is named by writing its vertices in any order. The triangle shown at right could be named $\triangle DEF$. Its sides are DE, EF, and DF.

Triangles can be classified by the lengths of their sides and by the measures of their angles. In the figures below, sides with the same number of marks are equal.

Classified by Side Lengths

equilateral triangle
All sides are equal in length. Note that the angles also are equal.

isosceles triangle
Exactly two sides are equal in length. Note that the two angles opposite these sides are equal.

scalene triangle
No sides are equal in length, and no angles are equal.

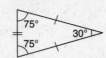

Classified by Angle Measures

right triangle
One angle measures 90°.

acute triangle
All angles measure less than 90°.

obtuse triangle
One angle is greater than 90°.

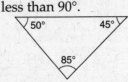
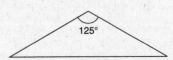

Each triangle can be classified in two ways.

Example 1: What kind of triangle is $\triangle PQR$?

1. Classify by its sides: Two sides have the same length, so $\triangle PQR$ is an isosceles triangle.

2. Classify by its angles: $\angle P$ is a right angle, so $\triangle PQR$ is a right triangle.

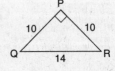

$\triangle PQR$ is a **right isosceles triangle**.

Key Ideas

- Triangles are named by their vertices.
- They are classified in two ways: by their side lengths and by their angle measures.
- The sum of the interior angles of any triangle is 180°.

GED® TEST TIP

Classify triangles by their properties, not by how they look. For example, the triangle in Example 1 may not immediately look like a right triangle because the right angle is at the top.

The sum of the measures of the interior angles of any triangle is 180°. We can use this fact to solve for a missing angle.

Example 2: In △ABC, ∠A measures 55° and ∠B measures 100°. What is the measure of ∠C?

Write an equation and solve.

$$55° + 100° + ∠C = 180°$$
$$155° + ∠C = 180°$$
$$∠C = 25°$$

The measure of ∠C is **25°**.

PRACTICE 2

A. Classify each triangle in two ways.

1.

2.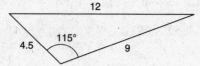

3.

B. Find the measure of the unknown angle in each triangle.

4.

5.

6.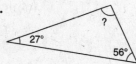

C. Choose the <u>one best answer</u> to each question.

<u>Questions 7 and 8</u> refer to the following figure.

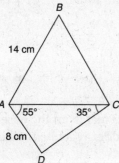

7. If ∠DAB measures 115° and ∠DCB measures 95°, what is the length of side AC in centimeters? (*Hint*: Use the facts in the problem to find *m*∠BAC and *m*∠BCA.)

    A. 6
    B. 8
    C. 14
    D. 22

8. What kind of triangle is △ACD?

    A. isosceles
    B. acute
    C. right
    D. obtuse

---

9. One angle in a scalene triangle measures 38°, and another angle measures 56°. What is the measure of the third angle?

    A. 38°
    B. 56°
    C. 86°
    D. 124°

Answers and explanations begin on page 226.

GEOMETRY

Pythagorean Relationship

As you know, a right triangle has one right angle. The side directly across from the right angle, called the **hypotenuse**, is the longest side of the right triangle. The remaining sides, the rays of the right angle, are the **legs** of the triangle.

Thousands of years ago, people found a special relationship, called the **Pythagorean relationship**, among the sides of a right triangle. You can use this relationship to find the measure of any side of a right triangle if the other two side measures are known.

Pythagorean relationship $a^2 + b^2 = c^2$; a and b are legs, and c is the hypotenuse of a right triangle

In other words, the square of the hypotenuse is equal to the sum of the squares of the two legs of the right triangle.

Example 1: What is the length of the hypotenuse of the right triangle shown in the diagram?

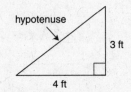

1. The lengths of the legs are 3 ft and 4 ft. Let one leg equal a and the other equal b.

2. Solve for c. Substitute the values.

3. When one side of an equation equals a squared variable, isolate the variable by finding the square root of both sides.

$$a^2 + b^2 = c^2$$
$$3^2 + 4^2 = c^2$$
$$9 + 16 = c^2$$
$$25 = c^2$$
$$\sqrt{25} = c$$
$$5 = c$$

The length of the hypotenuse is **5 feet**.

The Pythagorean relationship can also be used to solve for the length of a leg.

Example 2: If John places a 13-foot ladder 3 feet from the base of a wall, how far up the wall will the ladder reach to the nearest tenth of a foot?

The wall, ground, and ladder form a right triangle. The hypotenuse is 13 ft in length. One leg is 3 ft. You need to find the length of the other leg.

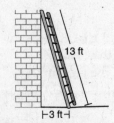

$$a^2 + b^2 = c^2$$
$$3^2 + b^2 = 13^2$$
$$9 + b^2 = 169$$
$$b^2 = 160$$
$$b = \sqrt{160}$$
$$b \approx 12.6$$

The ladder will extend **12.6 feet** up the wall.

NOTE: Most of the time, you will need to use your calculator for the final step when using the Pythagorean relationship. To find the square root of 160 on the TI-30XS MultiView™ calculator, press: (2nd) (x²) 160 (enter) (use ◄► to convert the result from a radical to a decimal format).

Key Ideas

- The hypotenuse is the longest side of a right triangle. It is found opposite the right angle.
- The sum of the squares of the legs of a right triangle equals the square of the hypotenuse.

GED® TEST TIP

Watch for right triangles with sides in a 3-4-5 or 5-12-13 ratio. These triangles often appear on math tests because the measures of the sides are all whole numbers.

Some right triangles display special proportions, which are worth memorizing.

- A right triangle whose angles are 45°, 45°, and 90° displays the following relationship:
leg : leg : hypotenuse $= x : x : x\sqrt{2}$.

- A right triangle whose angles are 30°, 60°, and 90° displays the following relationship:
leg : leg : hypotenuse $= x : x\sqrt{3} : 2x$.

PRACTICE 3

A. The lengths of two sides of a right triangle are given. Find the length of the remaining side to the nearest tenth unit. You MAY use a calculator.

1. leg *a*: 8 in.
   leg *b*: 8 in.
   hypotenuse *c*: ? in.

2. leg *a*: 9 yd
   leg *b*: 12 yd
   hypotenuse *c*: ? yd

3. leg *a*: 1.5 cm
   leg *b*: 2 cm
   hypotenuse *c*: ? cm

4. leg *a*: ? m
   leg *b*: 3 m
   hypotenuse *c*: 6 m

5. leg *a*: 6 mm
   leg *b*: ? mm
   hypotenuse *c*: 10 mm

6. leg *a*: ? ft
   leg *b*: 5 ft
   hypotenuse *c*: 18 ft

7. leg *a*: 7 cm
   leg *b*: 10 cm
   hypotenuse *c*: ? cm

8. leg *a*: 15 in.
   leg *b*: ? in.
   hypotenuse *c*: 30 in.

9. leg *a*: 4 km
   leg *b*: 5 km
   hypotenuse *c*: ? km

B. Choose the one best answer to each question.

10. On a coordinate plane, points *A*, *B*, and *C* can be connected to form a right triangle.

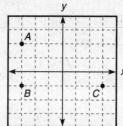

What is the distance from *A* to *C*, to the nearest tenth unit? (*Hint:* Count units to find the lengths of the sides and use the Pythagorean relationship to find the distance between the points.)

A. 5.2
B. 6.7
C. 8.4
D. 10.1

11. The two shorter sides of a right triangle measure 18 ft and 24 ft. What is the measure in feet of the third side?

A. 25
B. 28
C. 30
D. 42

12. Jan has built a rectangular frame out of wood to use for the bottom of a platform. He wants to add a diagonal brace as shown in the drawing below.

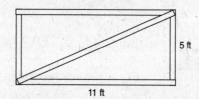

5 ft

11 ft

What will the length of the brace be, to the nearest tenth of a foot?

A. 16.0
B. 13.7
C. 12.8
D. 12.1

13. The hypotenuse of a right triangle measures 39 inches. If one leg measures 15 inches, what is the measure of the other leg, in inches?

A. 36
B. 24
C. 18
D. 12

Answers and explanations begin on page 227.

GEOMETRY

Perimeter and Area

Perimeter is the distance around a figure. To find perimeter, simply add the lengths of the sides. For common figures, you can apply a formula to find the perimeter. You need to memorize these formulas.

square	Perimeter = 4 × side	$P = 4s$
rectangle	Perimeter = 2 × length + 2 × width	$P = 2l + 2w$
triangle	Perimeter = side$_1$ + side$_2$ + side$_3$	$P = a + b + c$

Example 1: A rectangle is 16 inches long and 9 inches wide. What is the perimeter of the rectangle?

Use the formula: Perimeter = 2 × length + 2 × width
$$= 2 \times 16 + 2 \times 9$$
$$= 32 + 18$$
$$= \textbf{50 in.}$$

Area is the measure of the space inside a flat figure. Area is measured in square units. For example, if the sides of a figure are measured in inches, its area will be measured in square inches. The formulas for finding area are shown below.

square	Area = side^2	$A = s^2$
rectangle	Area = length × width	$A = lw$
parallelogram	Area = base × height	$A = bh$
triangle	Area = $\frac{1}{2}$ × base × height	$A = \frac{1}{2}bh$
trapezoid	Area = $\frac{1}{2}$ × height (base$_1$ + base$_2$)	$A = \frac{1}{2}h(b_1 + b_2)$

Three of the formulas mention two new measures: base and height. The **base** is one side of the figure. The **height** is the length from the vertex to the base, forming a right angle to the base.

Example 2: Find the area of figure *ABCD*.

1. Identify the figure. *ABCD* is a parallelogram.

2. Find the facts you need. To use the formula for finding the area of a parallelogram, you need to know the height and the length of the base. Ignore the length of side *BD*.

3. Use the formula Area = base × height.
   Area = 12 × 7
   $$= \textbf{84 sq cm or 84 cm}^2$$

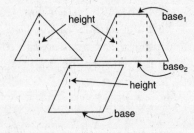

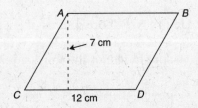

Key Ideas

- Perimeter is the distance around a figure.
- Area is the measure of the space inside a flat figure. It is measured in square units.
- When you are asked to calculate perimeter or area, start by identifying the measurements you need (such as length and width).

GED® TEST TIP

Several area formulas appear on the GED® formula sheet. You can check there if you don't remember a specific formula on test day. However, memorizing the most common ones (rectangle, triangle, and circle) will likely save you time as you're testing.

PRACTICE 4

A. Find the area and perimeter of each figure.

1.
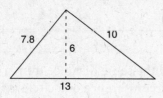

2.

3.

4.
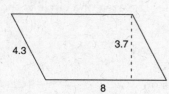

5.
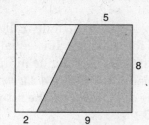

6.
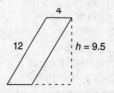

B. Choose the <u>one best answer</u> to each question.
<u>Question 7</u> refers to the following figure.

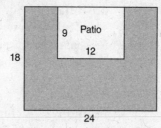

7. What is the area in square inches of the shaded portion of the rectangle?

   A. 38
   B. 40
   C. 56
   D. 88

   _____

8. The four sides of a retangle measure 9 feet, 6 feet, 9 feet, and 6 feet. What is the area of the retangle in square feet?

   A. 30
   B. 36
   C. 54
   D. 81

9. Martin is building a rectangular patio centered on one side of his yard. The rest of his yard, shown in the diagram, is planted in grass.

   If the measurements in the diagram are in feet, what is the square footage of the grass portion of Martin's yard?

   A. 108
   B. 162
   C. 324
   D. 432

10. A square measures 6 centimeters on one side. What is the perimeter of the square in centimeters?

    A. 12
    B. 24
    C. 36
    D. 216

Answers and explanations begin on page 227.

5

GEOMETRY

Circles

Circumference and Area

A **circle** is a closed set of points that are all the same distance from a single point, the center of the circle. The **circumference** of a circle is its perimeter, or the distance around the circle. The **area** of a circle is the space inside the circle.

- Pi, expressed as 3.14, is the ratio of the circumference of a circle to its diameter.
- To find circumference, multiply pi by the diameter (distance across) the circle.
- The radius is the distance from the center to the edge of the circle. To find area, multiply pi by the square of the radius.

To find perimeter and area of a circle, you need to know two other measures of a circle. The **diameter** is a line segment with endpoints on the circle that passes through the center of the circle. The **radius** is a line segment that connects the center of the circle to any point on the circle. As you can see from the diagram, the radius is one-half the diameter.

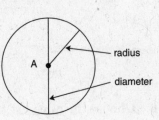

The formulas for circumference and area use a special quantity called **pi** (π). Pi is the ratio of the circumference to the diameter. It is equal to approximately 3.14. As far as we know, the digits for pi continue infinitely, so calculations with pi are always approximations. For the *Mathematical Reasoning Test*, you will use 3.14 as the value of pi. Below is the formula for finding the circumference of a circle.

$$\text{Circumference} = \pi \times \text{diameter, or } C = \pi d$$

Example 1: A china plate has a gold rim. If the plate's diameter is 10.5 inches, what is the distance around the rim to the nearest tenth of an inch?

Use the formula: $C = \pi d$

$= 3.14(10.5)$

$= 32.97$, which rounds to **33.0 inches**

Use this formula to find the area of a circle: Area $= \pi \times \text{radius}^2$, or $A = \pi r^2$.

Example 2: The circular surface of a satellite component must be covered with heat-resistant tiles. If the radius of the component is 4 meters, what is the area in square meters?

Use the formula: $A = \pi r^2$

$= 3.14(4^2)$

$= 3.14(16)$

$= $ **50.24 square meters**

In some situations, you may need to solve for either the diameter or radius. Remember, the diameter is twice the radius ($d = 2r$), and the radius is one-half the diameter: $r = \frac{1}{2}d$.

The areas for circumference and area of a circle appear on the GED® Formula Sheet. However, you may wish to memorize them in order to save time on test day.

Example 3: What is the circumference of circle B to the nearest tenth of a centimeter?

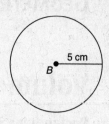

1. The radius of the circle is 5 cm. Therefore, the diameter is 2×5, or 10 cm.

2. Use the formula: $C = \pi d$
$$= 3.14(10)$$
$$= \mathbf{31.4\ cm}$$

PRACTICE 5

A. Find the circumference and area of each circle. Round answers to the nearest tenth.

1.

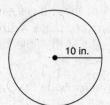

10 in.

2.

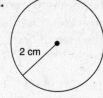

2 cm

3.

4 m

B. Choose the <u>one best answer</u> to each question.

<u>Questions 4 and 5</u> refer to the following drawing.

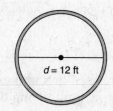

$d = 12$ ft

4. If workers lay a tile border around the edge of the fountain shown in the diagram, how many feet long will the border be to the nearest foot?

   A. 19
   B. 36
   C. 38
   D. 57

5. Which of the following expressions could be used to find the area of the bottom surface of the fountain?

   A. 3.14×6
   B. 3.14×6^2
   C. 3.14×12
   D. 3.14×12^2

6. The radius of a circle is 6.5 cm. What is the diameter of the circle in centimeters?

   A. 3.25
   B. 13.0
   C. 33.16625
   D. 132.665

7. On the target below, the 5- and 10-point bands are each 2 inches wide, and the inner circle has a diameter of 2 inches.

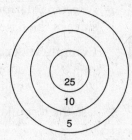

25

10

5

To the nearest inch, what is the outer circumference of the 10-point band?

   A. 6
   B. 13
   C. 19
   D. 113

Answers and explanations begin on page 227.

GEOMETRY

Volume

Rectangular Solids, Cubes, Cylinders, and Spheres

Volume, also called **capacity**, is the measure of space inside a three-dimensional object. You measure volume in cubic units. In other words, if the sides of an object are measured in inches, the volume is the number of cubes (one inch per side) you would need to fill the object.

Many common three-dimensional objects have at least two identical and parallel faces. Think of a cereal box or a soup can. Both objects have identical faces at the top and bottom of the container. Either of these faces can be called the base of the object. To find the volume of any container with identical bases, multiply the area of one base by the height of the object: Volume = area of base × height .

Another way to find the volume of an object is to use the formula that applies specifically to that object.

rectangular prism	Volume = base × height	$V = Bh$
cube	Volume = edge^3	$V = e^3$
cylinder	Volume = pi × radius^2 × height	$V = \pi r^2 h$
sphere	Volume = $\frac{4}{3}$ × pi × radius^3	$V = \frac{4}{3}\pi r^3$

In the examples below, formulas are used to find the answers, but the problems can also be solved by simply multiplying the area of the base by the height.

A **rectangular prism** has two identical rectangular bases. The remaining sides of the figure are also rectangles.

Example 1: A cardboard box has the dimensions shown in the diagram. What is the volume of the box in cubic feet?

Use the formula: $V = Bh$, where B is *length × width*
$= (4 \times 5)(3) =$ **60 cubic feet**

A **cube** is a rectangular prism with six identical faces. In a cube, each edge (where the sides meet) is the same length.

Example 2: A wood block measures 2 inches per edge. What is the volume of the block?

Use the formula: $V = e^3$
$= 2^3 =$ **8 cubic feet**

A **cylinder** has two circular bases. The bases are connected by a curved surface. Cans, barrels, and tanks are often in the shape of cylinders.

Key Ideas

- Volume is measured in cubic units that may be written using an exponent: 6 cubic inches or 6 in^3.
- Find volume by multiplying the area of one base by the height of the object.
- You can also use formulas to find volume.

GED® TEST TIP

Learn which area formula goes with which shape. Once you know the area formulas, you can change them to volume by putting an h at the end. Compare:
Area of circle: πr²
Volume of cylinder: πr²h

Example 3: A storage tank has a radius of 1.5 meters and a height of 3 meters. What is the volume of the tank to the nearest cubic meter?

Use the formula:
$$V = \pi r^2 h$$
$$= 3.14(1.5^2)(3) = 21.195 \text{ m}^3,$$
which rounds to **21 cubic meters**

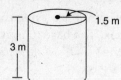

PRACTICE 6.1

A. Find the volume of each object to the nearest whole unit.

1.

3.

5.
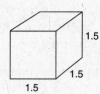

2.

4.
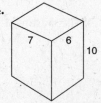

6.
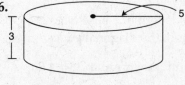

B. Choose the <u>one best answer</u> to each question.

<u>Question 7</u> refers to the following drawing.

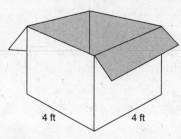

7. A rectangular box with a volume of 80 cubic feet has the length and width shown in the drawing. What is the height of the box?

   A. 5
   B. 10
   C. 16
   D. 20

---

8. A wooden crate measures 5 feet along each edge. What is the crate's volume in cubic feet?

   A. 15
   B. 25
   C. 125
   D. 150

<u>Question 9</u> refers to the following drawing.

9. Linda adds a water stabilizer to her children's swimming pool once a week. The instructions tell her to add one scoop of the product for every 20 cubic feet of water. About how many scoops should she add per week?

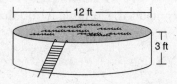

   A. 3
   B. 6
   C. 17
   D. 36

Answers and explanations begin on page 227.

Volume of Pyramids and Cones

A **pyramid** is a three-dimensional object with four triangle faces that connect to the same vertex. The base of a pyramid can be any closed figure, but the pyramids that you will see on the GED® *Mathematical Reasoning Test* will all have square bases.

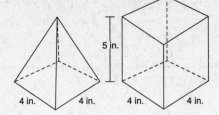

The rectangular prism and the pyramid shown here both have identical square bases and the same height. Compare the two figures. As you can see, the pyramid holds much less than the rectangular prism. In fact, it holds only one-third of the rectangular prism's volume.

The formula for finding the volume of a pyramid is as written below. Notice that B equals the area of the square base. The height of a pyramid is the perpendicular distance from the base to the vertex at the top.

square pyramid   Volume $= \frac{1}{3} \times$ base $\times$ height

Example 1: Find the volume of the pyramid shown below.

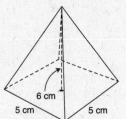

The length of a base edge is 5 cm. The height of the pyramid is 6 cm. Ignore the diagonal edges.

Apply the formula: $V = \frac{1}{3}Bh$

$$= \frac{1}{3}(5^2)(6)$$

$$= \frac{1}{3}(25)(6)$$

$$= \textbf{50 cm}^3$$

A **cone** is similar to a cylinder. Both have a circular base and a curved side. The curved side of a cone slants inward so that it meets at a point, or vertex. The volume of a cone is $\frac{1}{3}$ of the volume of a cylinder with the same size base and height.

On the GED® Formula Sheet, the formula for volume of a cone is based on the following relationship. Notice that the formula contains the formula for finding the area of a circle (πr^2).

cone   Volume $= \frac{1}{3} \times \pi \times$ radius$^2 \times$ height

Example 2: Find the volume of the cone shown below.

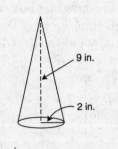

The radius of the base is 2 inches, and the height is 9 inches.

Apply the formula: $V = \frac{1}{3}\pi r^2 h$

$$= \frac{1}{3}(3.14)(2^2)(9)$$

$$= \frac{1}{3}(3.14)(4)(9)$$

$$= \textbf{37.68 in}^3$$

NOTE: In volume formulas for cones and square pyramids, the factor $\frac{1}{3}$ is shown first. Don't begin with this factor. Multiply the other factors first and then divide by 3, unless one of the numbers is easily divided by 3.

PRACTICE 6.2

A. Find the volume of each object to the nearest unit.

1.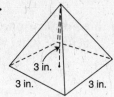

3 in.
3 in.   3 in.

3.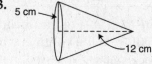

5 cm
12 cm

5.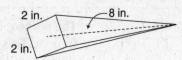

2 in.   8 in.
2 in.

2.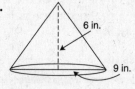

6 in.
9 in.

4.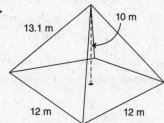

13.1 m   10 m
12 m   12 m

6.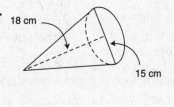

18 cm
15 cm

B. Choose the <u>one best answer</u> to each question.

7. Advertisers have designed this pyramid-shaped package to hold action figures.

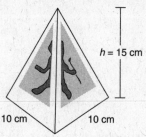

h = 15 cm
10 cm   10 cm

After testing the design, the manufacturer decides to increase both the length and width of the base by 4 cm. How many more cubic centimeters will the new package hold than the package shown above?

A. 480
B. 500
C. 980
D. 2940

8. The height of a cone is half the diameter of its base. If the cone's height is 4 inches, what is the cone's volume to the nearest cubic inch?

A. 21
B. 48
C. 67
D. 268

9. Which of the following is a true statement about the figures shown below?

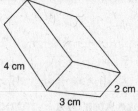

4 cm
3 cm   2 cm

Figure A

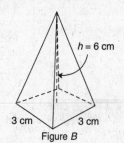

h = 6 cm
3 cm   3 cm

Figure B

A. The volume of A equals the volume of B.
B. The volume of B is greater than the volume of A.
C. Both A and B have a volume greater than 20 cubic centimeters.
D. The volume of B is less than the volume of A.

10. A cone's base is a circle with a radius of 8 inches. The cone's height is 15 inches. What is the cone's approximate volume in cubic inches?

A. 125
B. 250
C. 500
D. 1000

Answers and explanations begin on page 227.

GEOMETRY

Surface Area

The **surface area** is the total area of the outside **faces** of three-dimensional figures. This is different from the **volume**, which is the capacity of what a figure can hold. Surface area is expressed in square units.

Surface Area of a Square Prism

The surface area of a **square prism (cube)** is the sum of the areas of the six squares that form the prism. The area of one square is s^2. Since these sides are the same, find the area of one side and multiply by 6.

Example 1: Find the surface area of a cube with sides of 3 inches each.

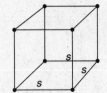

$SA = 6s^2$
$SA = 6(3 \text{ in})^2 = 6(9 \text{ in}^2) = 54 \text{ in}^2$

Surface Area of a Rectangular Prism

The surface area of a **rectangular prism** is the sum of the areas of the six rectangles that form the prism.

Example 2: Find the surface area of this box.

$SA = ph + 2B$
$SA = \text{perimeter} \times \text{height} + 2(\text{area of base})$
$SA = (5 \text{ m} + 6 \text{ m} + 5 \text{ m} + 6 \text{ m}) \times 7 \text{ m} + 2(6 \text{ m} \times 5 \text{ m})$
$SA = (22 \text{ m})7 \text{ m} + 2(30 \text{ m}^2) = 154 \text{ m}^2 + 60 \text{ m}^2 = \mathbf{214 \ m^2}$

Surface Area of a Pyramid

The surface area of a **pyramid** is $\frac{1}{2}$ the perimeter of the base (p) times the **slant height** (s) plus the area of the base (B). The slant height is the length of a line segment from the **apex** (top) to the **base**.

Example 3: What is the surface area of a pyramid with a slant height of 5 feet, a base with a perimeter of 14 feet, and a base with an area of 12 feet?

$SA = \frac{1}{2}ps + B$
$SA = \frac{1}{2} \text{perimeter} \times \text{slant height} + \text{base area}$
$SA = \frac{1}{2}(14 \text{ ft})(5 \text{ ft}) + 12 \text{ ft}^2$
$SA = \frac{1}{2}(70 \text{ ft}^2) + 12 \text{ ft}^2 = 35 \text{ ft}^2 + 12 \text{ ft}^2 = \mathbf{47 \ ft^2}$

Key Ideas

- The surface area is the area of the total surface of a three-dimensional object.
- To find the surface area of a cube, you need to multiply the area of one side by 6.
- To find the surface area of a rectangular prism and a pyramid, you need to use formulas to find several dimensions and combine them.

GED® TEST TIP

Memorize the process for finding the surface area of a cube. The formulas for surface areas of prisms and pyramids are listed on the online Formula Sheet on the GED® Mathematical Reasoning Test.

A. Find the surface area of each object in square units. Use the formulas on page 194.

1.

3.

5.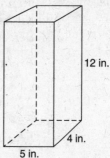

2.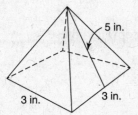

4.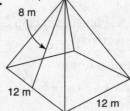

6.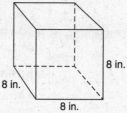

B. Choose the <u>one best answer</u> to each question. Use the formulas on page 194.

7. All the edges of a metal box are of equal length. If the surface area is 150 square inches, what is the length, in inches, of each edge of the box?

A. 5
B. 6
C. 25
D. 50

8. Which of the following is a true statement about the figures shown below? (Measurements indicated are all in the same units.)

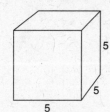 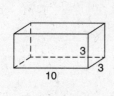

Figure A   Figure B

A. The surface area of Figure A is equal to the surface area of Figure B.
B. The surface area of Figure A is half of the surface area of Figure B.
C. The surface area of Figure A is greater than the surface area of Figure B.
D. The sum of the surface areas of both Figure A and Figure B is greater than 300.

9. If the dimensions of the box below are doubled, by how many square centimeters does the surface area increase?

A.   8
B.   54
C. 162
D. 216

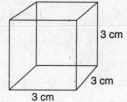

Answers and explanations begin on page 228.

Finding the surface areas of cylinders, cones, and spheres involves using some dimensions of circles.

Surface Area of a Cylinder

To find the surface area of a cylinder, multiply the circumference ($2\pi r$) by the **height** (h) and add the product to the area of the two ends of the cylinder, each of which is the area of a circle (πr^2).

Example 1: Find the surface area of a cylinder with a radius (r) of 4 inches and a height (h) of 3 inches.

$SA = 2\pi rh + 2\pi r^2$
$SA = (2 \times 3.14 \times 4 \times 3) + (2 \times 3.14 \times 4^2)$
$SA = (6.28 \times 12) + (6.28 \times 16) = 75.36 \text{ in}^2 + 100.48 \text{ in}^2$
$\quad = \textbf{175.84 in}^2$

You may find the on-screen calculator helpful to complete these calculations effectively.

Surface Area of a Cone

The surface area of a **cone** is found by combining the **lateral side surface** (πrs) with the area of its **base** (πr^2).

Example 2: Find the surface area of a cone with a radius of 2 feet and a slant height of 5 feet.

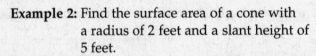

$SA = \pi rs + \pi r^2$
$SA = \text{lateral side surface with slant height} + \text{area of base}$
$SA = \pi(2)(5) + \pi(2^2)$
$SA = 10\pi \text{ ft}^2 + 4\pi \text{ ft}^2 = 14\pi \text{ ft}^2 = 14 \text{ ft}^2 \times 3.14 \cong \textbf{43.96 ft}^2$

Surface Area of a Sphere

The surface area of a **sphere** is four times the area of a circle with the same radius as the sphere.

Example 3: What is the surface area of this sphere with a radius of 10 feet?

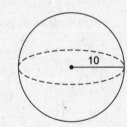

$SA = 4\pi r^2$
$SA \approx 4 \times 3.14 \times 10^2 \approx \textbf{1256 ft}^2$

PRACTICE 7.2

A. Find the surface area of each object in square units. Express your answer in terms of pi (for example, 36π). Use the formulas on page 196.

1.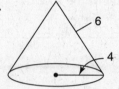

2.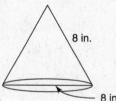

3.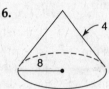

4.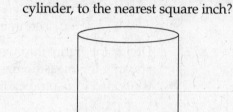

5.

6.

B. Choose the <u>one best answer</u> to each question. Use the formulas on page 196.

7. If the length of the diameter of a sphere is 8, how many square units is its surface area?

   A. 16π
   B. 64π
   C. 256π
   D. 512π

8. A cone, pictured below, has a slant height of 8 inches and a diameter of 8 inches. If the cone's slant height is doubled, and the diameter is halved, which of the following statements must be true?

   A. The new cone will have the same surface area as the original cone.
   B. The new cone will have a surface area exactly half of the surface area of the original cone.
   C. The new cone will have a surface area exactly double that of the surface area of the new cone.
   D. The new cone will have a surface area less than the surface area of the original cone.

9. In the cylinder below, the diameter of the circular base is equal to the height of the cylinder. What is the surface area of the cylinder, to the nearest square inch?

   A. 57
   B. 113
   C. 170
   D. 339

Answers and explanations begin on page 228.

GEOMETRY

Combined Figures

Key Ideas

- Combined figures are made from two or more regular figures.
- To find the perimeter of an combined figure, add the lengths of all the sides.
- To find area or volume of an combined figure, break the figure into parts and find the area or volume of each part; then combine the results.

Breaking Combined Figures into Parts

A combined figure puts together geometric figures to form a new shape. To find the perimeter of a combined figure, simply add the lengths of the sides. You may need to solve for one or more missing lengths.

Example 1: A family room has the dimensions shown in the diagram. All measures are in feet. What is the perimeter of the room?

1. Find the missing measures. Measurement x equals the combined lengths of the two opposite walls: $x = 8 + 4 = 12$ ft. You also know that $18 - 10 = y$, so $y = 8$ ft.

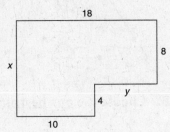

2. Add all distances to find the perimeter:
$12 + 18 + 8 + 8 + 4 + 10 = \textbf{60 ft.}$

To find the area or volume of a combined figure, break the figure into parts. Then apply the correct formula to each part.

Example 2: What is the area of the figure in square centimeters?

1. Divide the figure into two shapes and find any missing measurements. Here the figure is divided into a trapezoid and a rectangle.

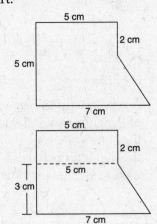

2. Calculate the area of each shape.
Rectangle: $A = lw$
$= 2(5) = 10 \text{ cm}^2$

Trapezoid: $A = \frac{1}{2}h(b_1 + b_2)$
$= \frac{1}{2}(3)(5 + 7) = 18 \text{ cm}^2$

3. Combine: $10 + 18 = \textbf{28 cm}^2$.

Example 3: Find the volume of the container shown below.

Break the figure into a cylinder and a cone and find the volume of each.

1. Cylinder: $V = \pi r^2 h$
$= (3.14)(1^2)(2) = 6.28 \text{ m}^3$
2. Cone: $V = \frac{1}{3}\pi r^2 h$
$= \frac{1}{3}(3.14)(1^2)(1.5) = 1.57 \text{ m}^3$

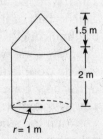

3. Combine: $6.28 + 1.57 = \textbf{7.85 m}^3$ or **7.85 cu m.**

PRACTICE 8

A. Find the perimeter and area of each figure.

1.

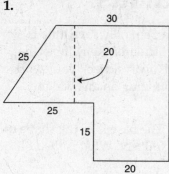

2.

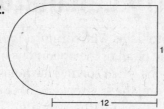

(*Hint:* Think of the figure as a rectangle and a half circle.)

3.

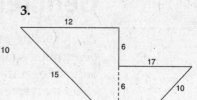

B. Find the volume of each figure to the nearest cubic unit.

4.

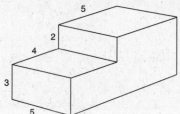

5.

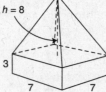

6.

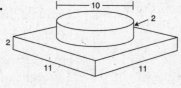

C. Choose the <u>one best answer</u> to each question.

7. A slab of concrete will have four concrete blocks in each corner as shown in the drawing below.

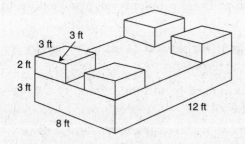

If each corner block has the same dimensions, what is the volume of the structure in cubic feet?

A. 72
B. 168
C. 288
D. 360

8. A candy package is in the shape of a cylinder with a cone on each end.

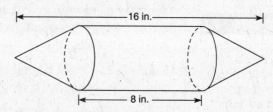

If the radius of the cylinder is 2 inches and the cones are identical, what is the capacity of the container to the nearest cubic inch?

A. 33
B. 100
C. 134
D. 201

Answers and explanations begin on page 228.

Geometry Calculator Skills

When solving problems with formulas, you can generally save time by performing some or all of the operations on a calculator. Remember the order of operations when solving formulas and always check your work, either by reentering the key sequence or by estimating an answer and comparing your answer to the estimate.

Example 1: A pyramid has a height of 81 feet. The base is in the shape of a square with each side measuring 40 feet. What is the volume in cubic feet of the pyramid?

Use the formula for the volume of a pyramid: $\frac{1}{3}Bh$. Begin by calculating the area of the base: 40×40, or 40^2. Multiply that by the height, 81. In the last step, dividing by 3 is the same as multiplying by $\frac{1}{3}$.

Evaluate the exponent.	40 $\boxed{x^2}$
Multiply by 81.	$\boxed{\times}$ 81
Divide by 3.	$\boxed{\div}$ 3 $\boxed{enter}$
The right side of the display	**43200**
shows the correct answer, **43,200**.	

To enter this formula using a fraction using one series of keystrokes on the TI-30XS MultiView™ calculator, enter the following: $\boxed{\frac{n}{d}}$ 1 $\boxed{\blacktriangledown}$ 3 $\boxed{\times}$ 40 $\boxed{x^2}$ $\boxed{\times}$ 81 $\boxed{enter}$.

The right side of the display shows 43200.

The volume of the pyramid is **43,200 square feet**.

You may need your calculator to find the exact answer to problems that involve the Pythagorean relationship. These problems can also be done in one series of keystrokes.

Example 2: A right triangle has legs 10 inches and 24 inches in length. What is the length of the hypotenuse?

Use the formula $a^2 + b^2 = c^2$. You will need to add the squares of the legs and then find the square root of the total.

Press: 10 $\boxed{x^2}$ $\boxed{+}$ 24 $\boxed{x^2}$ $\boxed{enter}$. The display will read 676. Then press $\boxed{2nd}$ $\boxed{x^2}$ 676 $\boxed{enter}$. The right side of the display shows **26**.

The hypotenuse is **26 inches** in length.

If you need to include the quantity pi (π) in a calculation, the TI-30XS MultiView™ calculator includes a *pi* key, located three keys below the *2nd* key on the left-hand side of the keypad.

Example 3: What is the area of a circle with radius 2.4 cm? Round your answer to the nearest tenth.

Use the formula Area $= \pi r^2$. Press $\boxed{\pi}$ $\boxed{\times}$ 2.4 $\boxed{x^2}$ and then press $\boxed{enter}$. The right side of the display reads 18.09557368.

Round that to find the answer: **18.1 cm²**.

Key Ideas

- When a problem involves many calculations, use the order of operations to decide which operation to do first.
- Check your work by estimating an answer or by quickly repeating the keystrokes to see if the result is the same.

GED® TEST TIP

Watch the calculator display while you are entering all of these keystrokes. If you make a mistake, use the delete *key to remove that mistake and then replace it with the correct number or function. Practice that with these examples.*

PRACTICE 9

A. Use your calculator to evaluate each formula.

1. Find the perimeter of a rectangle with a length of 16 inches and a width of 5 inches.
   Perimeter $= 2 \times$ length $+ 2 \times$ width

2. Find the area of a triangle with a base of 26 centimeters and a height of 15 centimeters.
   Area $= \frac{1}{2} \times$ base $\times$ height

3. What is the volume of a cube if the edge measures 3.5 feet? Round to the nearest cubic foot.
   Volume $=$ edge^3

4. What is the measure of the hypotenuse of a right triangle when the legs measure 13 cm and 9 cm? Round your answer to the nearest tenth.
   Pythagorean relationship: $a^2 + b^2 = c^2$

5. Find the circumference of a circle with a diameter of 12 inches. Round to the nearest tenth.
   Circumference $= \pi \times$ diameter

6. Find the volume of a cone with a radius of 12 cm and a height of 20 cm. Round to the nearest cm^3.
   Volume $= \frac{1}{3} \times \pi \times$ radius$^2 \times$ height

B. Choose the one best answer to each question. You MAY use your calculator.

Question 7 refers to the following drawing.

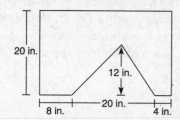

7. For a woodworking project, Paul cuts the shape shown above from plywood. What is the area in square inches of the piece? (*Hint:* Think of the shape as a triangle removed from a rectangle.)
   A. 400
   B. 480
   C. 520
   D. 640

8. To the nearest cubic meter, what is the volume of a cylinder with a radius of 1.5 meters and a height of 5 meters?
   A. 25
   B. 35
   C. 45
   D. 141

Questions 9 and 10 refer to the drawing.

All measurements are in centimeters.

9. How many cubic centimeters greater is the volume of Box A than the volume of Box B?
   A. 64
   B. 1,448
   C. 4,928
   D. 5,056

10. An advertiser plans to print advertisements on one side panel of each of the boxes (the shaded faces in the drawing). What is the total area, in square centimeters, that the advertiser will cover?
    A. 224
    B. 384
    C. 608
    D. 1448

Answers and explanations begin on page 228.

GEOMETRY PRACTICE QUESTIONS

1. What is the surface area, in square centimeters, of a cube with each edge length of 5 cm?

   A. 15
   B. 25
   C. 125
   D. 150

2. What is the surface area, in square centimeters, of a cylinder with a height of 10 cm and a radius of 6 cm?

   A. 136π
   B. 160π
   C. 192π
   D. 256π

3. What is the surface area, in square centimeters, of a cylinder that measures 8 cm tall with a diameter of 6 cm on its base?

   A. 48π
   B. 57π
   C. 66π
   D. 132π

4. A pyramid has a square base. If each edge of the pyramid is 4, what is the total surface area of the entire pyramid?

   A. $8\sqrt{3}$
   B. $8\sqrt{3} + 16$
   C. $16\sqrt{3} + 16$
   D. $64\sqrt{3}$

Question 5 refers to the following figure.

5. A toy factory paints all of its rubber balls with 2 coats of latex for durability. How many square centimeters of latex are needed to cover a rubber ball with a circumference of 16π cm?

   A. 64π
   B. 128π
   C. 256π
   D. 512π

6. The floor of a walk-in closet measures 7 feet by 4 feet. If the ceiling height is 8 feet, what is the volume in cubic feet of the closet?

   A. 28
   B. 56
   C. 112
   D. 224

Question 7 refers to the following figure.

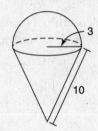

7. An ice cream cone has a spherical scoop of ice cream placed inside. Exactly one-half of the ice cream is visible above the rim of the cone. What is the surface area of the entire ice cream treat, in units squared?

   A. 24π
   B. 30π
   C. 48π
   D. 60π

8. The radius of Sphere A is 2, and the radius of Sphere B is 1. What is the ratio of the volume of Sphere A to that of Sphere B? (*Hint*: Use the formula for the volume of a sphere on page 190.)

   A. 1:2
   B. 4:1
   C. 8:1
   D. 8:3

9. A parallelogram has a base of 6 centimeters and a height of 10 centimeters. This parallelogram has the same area as a triangle with a height of 5 centimeters. What is the measure, in centimeters, of the base of the triangle?

   Write your answer in the box.

Question 10 refers to the following figure.

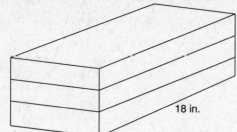

18 in.

10. Three identical rectangular boxes are stacked one on top of another. The total height of all three boxes is the same as the width of one box. The length of the boxes is 18 in., and the width is half the length. What is the combined volume, in cubic inches, of all three boxes?

   A. 1458
   B. 1800
   C. 2124
   D. 3136

11. Using a compass, Max hikes 300 yards due north of his campsite. From that point, he hikes 400 yards due east. If he were to hike directly to his campsite from this point, how many yards would he have to hike?

   A. 400
   B. 500
   C. 600
   D. 700

12. The rectangular base of a container is 9 inches long and 7 inches wide. By how many cubic inches will the volume of the container increase if you increase the length of the base by 2 inches?

   A. 84
   B. 126
   C. 168
   D. 216

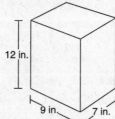

12 in.

9 in.   7 in.

13. In a right triangle, the hypotenuse measures 15 inches. If one leg of the triangle measures 6 inches, which of the following equations could be used to find the length of the other leg (x) in inches?

   A. $x = \sqrt{15 - 6}$
   B. $x = 15 - 6$
   C. $x^2 = 15^2 + 6^2$
   D. $x^2 = 15^2 - 6^2$

14. The length of a rectangle is three times its width. If the perimeter of the rectangle is 96 inches, what is its length in inches?

   A. 12
   B. 24
   C. 36
   D. 48

Question 15 refers to the following figure.

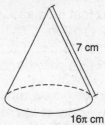

7 cm

16π cm

15. Sarah is making party hats for a birthday party. Each hat is in the shape of a cone and will have a circumference of 16π cm and a slant height of 7 cm. She will be making 20 hats. What is the total surface area, in square centimeters, of all 20 hats combined?

   A. 32π
   B. 56π
   C. 112π
   D. 1120π

Question 16 refers to the following figure.

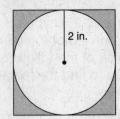

16. Use your calculator to make the following calculation. In the figure above, a square contains a circle such that each of the sides of the square is touching a point on the circle. What is the area, in square inches, of the shaded portion?

    A. 3.43
    B. 12.57
    C. 16.00
    D. 28.57

Questions 17 and 18 refer to the following.

A classroom is 40 feet long and 25 feet wide. The ceiling height is 12 feet. The school district plans to repaint the room and put in air-conditioning. The ceiling tile will not be painted.

17. What is the approximate total square footage of the four walls of the room? Ignore space taken up by windows and doors.

    A. 1200
    B. 1560
    C. 1920
    D. 4000

18. To choose an air-conditioning system, the school district must know the volume of the room. What is the volume in cubic feet?

    A. 1000
    B. 3120
    C. 12000
    D. 15625

Question 19 refers to the following figures.

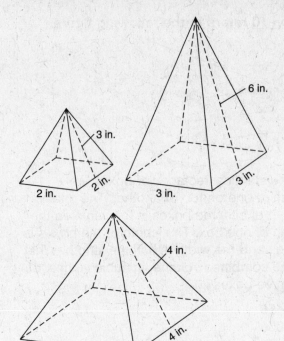

19. Laura is painting model pyramids for an art project. She needs one tube of paint for every 30 square inches of surface area. If Laura paints each pyramid and its base, approximately how many tubes of paint should she buy?

    A. 4
    B. 16
    C. 48
    D. 109

Answers and explanations begin on page 228.

2015 GED® Test Mathematics Formula Sheet

Area of a:

square	$A = s^2$
rectangle	$A = lw$
parallelogram	$A = bh$
triangle	$A = \frac{1}{2}bh$
trapezoid	$A = \frac{1}{2}h(b_1 + b_2)$
circle	$A = \pi r^2$

Perimeter of a:

square	$P = 4s$
rectangle	$P = 2l + 2w$
triangle	$P = s_1 + s_2 + s_3$
Circumference of a circle	$C = 2\pi r$ OR $C = \pi d$; $\pi \approx 3.14$

Surface area and volume of a:

rectangular/right prism	$SA = ph + 2B$	$V = Bh$
cylinder	$SA = 2\pi rh + 2\pi r^2$	$V = \pi r^2 h$
pyramid	$SA = \frac{1}{2}ps + B$	$V = \frac{1}{3}Bh$
cone	$SA = \pi rs + \pi r^2$	$V = \frac{1}{3}\pi r^2 h$
sphere	$SA = 4\pi r^2$	$V = \frac{4}{3}\pi r^3$

(p = perimeter of base with area B; $\pi \approx 3.14$)

Data

mean	mean is equal to the total of the values of a data set, divided by the number of elements in the data set
median	median is the middle value in an odd number of ordered values of a data set, or the mean of the two middle values in an even number of ordered values in a data set

Algebra

slope of a line	$m = \dfrac{y_2 - y_1}{x_2 - x_1}$
slope-intercept form of the equation of a line	$y = mx + b$
point-slope form of the equation of a line	$y - y_1 = m(x - x_1)$
standard form of a quadratic equation	$y = ax^2 + bx + c$
quadratic formula	$x = \dfrac{-b \pm \sqrt{b^2 - 4ac}}{2a}$
Pythagorean Theorem	$a^2 + b^2 = c^2$
simple interest	$I = Prt$ (I = interest, P = principal, r = rate, t = time)
distance formula	$d = rt$
total cost	total cost = (number of units) × (price per unit)

Provided by GED® Testing Service.

PRACTICE QUESTIONS ANSWERS AND EXPLANATIONS

Number Sense and Problem Solving

Lesson 1: Compare and Order Numbers

Practice 1, page 23

1. 4
2. 8
3. 9
4. 1
5. 6
6. 7
7. 3
8. 500
9. 80
10. 1100
11. 12,000
12. 2000
13. 100
14. 100
15. 341
16. 1145
17. 125,391
18. 18, 23, 39, 45
19. 89, 91, 109, 111
20. 909, 932, 1087, 1139
21. 1420, 1425, 1429, 1432
22. 11,098, 12,071, 12,131
23. 15,298, 15,309, 15,356
24. **C. 50, 48, 45, 40** Arrange the weights from heaviest to lightest.
25. **C. 1,500,000** The digit in the ten thousands column is less than 5, so round down.

Lesson 2: Whole Number Operations

Practice 2.1, page 25

1. 77
2. 100
3. 52
4. 36
5. 190
6. 4078
7. 43
8. 2117
9. 65
10. 114
11. 180
12. 293
13. 483
14. 456
15. 2419
16. 900
17. 11,308
18. 15,185
19. 131,197
20. 30,899
21. **B. 88** Calculate: $24 + 8 + 56 = 88$
22. **C. $13** Calculate: $20 - 7 = 13$

Practice 2.2, page 27

1. 484
2. 1000
3. 2736
4. 13
5. 105
6. 21
7. 1350
8. 2625
9. 3376
10. 28
11. 15
12. 6
13. 250
14. 44 r3
15. 300
16. 200 r4
17. 150
18. 67,068
19. 538
20. 384
21. 12,011 r8
22. **D. 96** Calculate: $16 \times 6 = 96$
23. **C. $75** Calculate: $15 \times 5 = 75$
24. **6** Calculate: $12 \div 2 = 6$

Lesson 3: GED® Test Calculator Skills

Practice 3.1, page 29

1. 153
2. 1187
3. 784
4. 24
5. 27,084
6. 14,442
7. 11,704
8. 54
9. 1580
10. **B. 26,179** Press (clear) 42920 ⊖ 16741 (enter).
11. **D. $19,900** Press (clear) 995 ⊗ 20 (enter).

Practice 3.2, page 31

1. 25
2. 18
3. 35
4. 136
5. 125
6. 5%
7. 2
8. 135
9. 5%
10. **C. $336** Press (clear) 1680 ⊗ 20 (2nd) (() (enter).
11. **A. 5%** Press (clear) 48 ⊕ 960 (2nd) ()) (enter). The right side of the screen will display 5%.

Lesson 4: Word Problems

Practice 4.1, page 33

1. **C. 10** No paint is needed for the floor, so ignore the 700 square feet. 3500 square feet of wall space ÷ 350 square feet per gallon = 10 gallons.
2. **D. 22** 11 children × 2 party favors per child = 22.
3. **A. 5** Calculate: $30 - 25 = 5$. The information that Sarah and Kate live 18 miles apart is not needed.
4. **90** Calculate: 450 gallons ÷ 5 gallons of *filtered* water use per day = 90 days.
5. **D. 90** The table states that it takes Joyce 30 minutes to give a pedicure. $3 \times 30 = 90$
6. **C. $25** Subtract the cost of the manicure & pedicure combination ($35) from the cost of a makeover ($60). $60 - 35 = 25$
7. **42** Calculate: $7 \times 6 = 42$
8. **$162** Calculate: $189 - 27 = 162$

Practice 4.2, page 35

1. **C. $103** Restaurant D ordered 2 cases of Boston lettuce and 3 cases of romaine lettuce in July. $(2 \times \$17) + (3 \times \$23) = \$103$.
2. **B. $18** Calculate: $4 + 4 + 2 + 2 + 1 = 13$ total cases, and delivery for the first 5 cases costs $2 each. $13 - 5 = 8$ cases remained after the first 5, so delivery for those 8 cases costs $1 each. $(5 \times \$2) + (8 \times \$1) = \$18$.
3. **B. Restaurant B** Calculate the totals for each restaurant:

Rest.	Asparagus	Tomatoes	Asparagus + Tomatoes
A	2 × $22	3 × $15	$44 + $45 = $89
B	4 × $22	1 × $15	$88 + $15 = $103
C	0 × $22	3 × $15	$0 + $45 = $45
D	1 × $22	4 × $15	$22 + $60 = $82

4. **C. 350** Calculate: $3 \times 150 = 450$ sheets will be used. Since the paper sells in packages of 400 sheets, 2 packages are needed, and $2 \times 400 = 800$. $800 - 450 = 350$ sheets left over.
5. **A. 9** Calculate: $19 \div 2 = 9$ r1, so the friends can make 9 whole batches using 2 cups of flour for each batch (and 1 cup will be left over).
6. **A. $1500** Calculate: $(6 \times \$750) - \$3000 = \$1500$.

Lesson 5: Distance and Cost

Practice 5, page 37

1. rate; $\frac{d}{t} = r$
2. distance; $d = rt$
3. time; $\frac{d}{r} = t$
4. price per unit; $\frac{c}{n} = r$
5. cost; $c = nr$
6. number of units; $\frac{c}{r} = n$
7. **$48** $c = nr$
   $4 \times \$12 = \$48$
8. **$36** $c = nr$
   $12 \times \$3 = \$36$
9. **$80** $\frac{c}{n} = r$
   $\frac{\$320}{4} = \$80$
10. **5** $\frac{c}{r} = n$
    $\frac{\$25}{\$5} = 5$
11. **$2** $\frac{c}{n} = r$
    $\frac{\$20}{\$10} = \$2$

12. **180 miles** $d = rt$
$60 \times 3 = 180$
13. **200 miles** $d = rt$
$50 \times 4 = 200$
14. **1 hour** $\frac{d}{r} = t$
$\frac{\$25}{\$25} = 1$
15. **90 miles per hour** $\frac{d}{t} = r$
$\frac{270}{3} = 90$
16. **3 hours** $\frac{d}{r} = t$
$\frac{75}{25} = 3$
17. **A. 32** $\frac{c}{r} = n$
$\frac{\$640}{\$20} = 32$
18. **D. 55** $\frac{d}{t} = r$
$\frac{275}{5} = 55$

Number Sense and Problem Solving Practice Questions, pages 38–41

1. **D. 96** Multiply: 12 servings × 8 ounces = 96
2. **B. $2092** Add to find the total: $839 + $527 + 726 = $2092
3. **A. 4** Divide the length of the sample board by the length of the brace you want: 12 foot board ÷ 2 feet per brace = 6 braces per board. Since you can get 6 braces from each board, divide the total number of braces you want by 6: 24 ÷ 6 = 4 boards.
4. **B. 21** Use the square root function on your calculator or multiply each answer option by itself to find 441.
5. **A. 30,589** Subtract to find the difference in mileage: 70,040 − 39,451 = 30,589
6. **C. $656** You can use your calculator. Multiply: $3280 × 20% = $656
7. **A. $5625** Multiply: $125 × 45 = $5625
8. **B. 420** Divide distance by time to find Lydia's speed per hour: 180 ÷ 3 = 60. Then multiply by the number of hours she drove on Tuesday: 60 × 7 = 420
9. **B. 8** Divide the distance by the speed to find the time: 480 ÷ 60 = 8 hours.
10. **B. 96** Divide the total cost by price per item to find the number of items: $1440 ÷ 15 = $96
11. **A. $200** Multiply the late fee by the number of times Richard has paid his bill late: $25 × 8 = $200

12. **D. $53** Calculate: 7 × $5 = $35 and 18 × $1 = $18. Add the two amounts: $35 + $18 = $53
13. **A. 5** Divide. 17,500 total miles ÷ 3,500 miles between oil changes = 5 oil changes.
14. **A. 134** Divide: 536 total children ÷ 4 months = 134 children per month
15. **198** Subtract to find the difference: 636 − 438 = 198
16. **$1072** Multiply: $268 per payment × 4 payments left = $1072
17. **C. 51, 48, 44, 40**
18. **C. 2,350,000** Since the digit to the right of the ten thousands place is less than 5, the digit in the ten thousands place remains the same.
19. **A. 83** Calculate: 18 + 23 + 42 = 83
20. **A. $6** Calculate: $20 − $14 = $6
21. **B. 60** Since the question says "about," you can use approximate, or rounded, figures. Round the amounts and add: 8 + 33 + 18 ≈ 10 + 30 + 20 = 60
22. **62** Divide distance by time to find the rate of speed: 248 ÷ 4 = 62
23. **C. 18** Calculate: 144 ÷ 8 = 18
24. **B. 30** Since the question says "about," you can use approximate figures. Round 299 to 300 and 9 to 10 and then divide: 300 ÷ 10 = 30
25. **C. 1200** Use rounded figures: 33 rounds to 30, and 41 pounds rounds to 40: 30 × 40 = 1200.
26. **C. $9** Find the total and divide by 4: $21 + $15 = $36, then $36 ÷ 4 = $9
27. **A. $12** Subtract the amount David paid from the total: $128 − $20 = $108. Then divide the remaining amount by the remaining number of people in the group: $108 ÷ 9 = $12.
28. **D. 260** 65 miles per hour × 4 hours = 260 miles.
29. **B. $18** Add the cost of a 1-topping pizza and $2 for each of the 2 additional toppings: $14 + $2 + $2 = $18
30. **C. 14** Multiply by 2 for each dollar: 2 × 7 = 14
31. **24** Calculate: $1800 ÷ $75 per month = 24 months
32. **14** Divide the maximum capacity by the number of pages per document: 630 ÷ 45 = 14

Decimals and Fractions

Lesson 1: Decimal Basics

Practice 1, page 43

1. 3.8	7. 0.45
2. 6	8. 0.08
3. 0.43	9. 4.68
4. 0.667	10. 1.85
5. 8.1	11. 1.029
6. 2.714	12. 0.14

13. 5.08, 5.6, 5.8, 5.802
14. 0.1136, 0.115, 0.12, 0.2
15. 4.52, 4.667, 4.8, 14.005
16. 0.8, 0.8023, 0.803, 0.823
17. **C. 0.6 g, 0.572 g, 0.0785 g** The correct answer lists the weights from greatest to least. Since none of the weights has a whole number part, compare the tenths places.
18. **D. 1.38** This is the only choice that is rounded to the hundredths place. Since the number in the thousandths place of 1.3815 is less than 5, round down.

Lesson 2: Decimal Operations

Practice 2.1, page 45

1. 7.996	13. 5.506
2. 10.508	14. 21.16
3. 12.26	15. 0.645
4. 5.85	16. 2.426
5. 7.426	17. 0.15
6. 2.11	18. 4.88
7. 18.094	19. 11.8
8. 5.117	20. 14.016
9. 21.32	21. 4.522
10. 0.895	22. 2.36
11. 3.84	23. 17.88
12. 2.35	24. 17.225

25. **A. 22.25** Add the times: 7.2 + 6.8 + 8.25 = 22.25 minutes. You do not need to use the 3-mile distance to solve the problem.
26. **C. 4.25** Add to find Claudia's total hours for the week: 8.5 + 9.25 + 8.75 + 10 + 7.75 = 44.25. Then subtract 40 to find the number of overtime hours: 44.25 − 40 = 4.25 hours.
27. **A. 1.8** Add the lengths cut from the pipe: 2.8 + 1.4 = 4.2. Then subtract from 6: 6 − 4.2 = 1.8 meters.
28. **C. $55.26** Add the amounts: $16.98 + $31.78 + $6.50 = $55.26

Practice 2.2, page 47

1. 2.65	12. 15,800
2. 12.8	13. 34.1

3. 0.496
4. 0.52
5. 3.6
6. 4.09
7. 8.75
8. 3.375
9. 9.6681
10. 24
11. 14.2
14. 2.36
15. 0.656
16. 2.64
17. 1.65
18. 4.275
19. 3.696
20. 1.002
21. 0.0072

22. D. 15.16 Multiply 3.79 liters by 4: $3.79 \times 4 = 15.16$ liters.

23. B. \$9.23 Multiply $\$0.45 \times 20.5$: $\$0.45 \times 20.5 = \$9.225$, which rounds to \$9.23.

24. C. 92.9 Divide to find the average daily miles: $278.7 \div 3 = 92.9$ miles.

25. C. \$0.26 There are 19 servings in a box of Toasted Oats. Divide: $\$4.94 \div 19 = \$0.26$.

26. B. 50.0 Find the weight in the table and multiply: $12.5 \times 4 = 50$ ounces.

Lesson 3: Fraction Basics

Practice 3, page 49

1. $\frac{3}{5}$
2. $\frac{2}{4}; \frac{1}{2}$
3. $\frac{2}{3}$
4. $\frac{7}{3}; 2\frac{1}{3}$
5. $\frac{7}{2}; 3\frac{1}{2}$
6. $\frac{15}{4}; 3\frac{3}{4}$
7. $5\frac{2}{3}$
8. $\frac{18}{5}$
9. 4
10. $\frac{47}{9}$
11. $4\frac{3}{4}$
12. $\frac{29}{12}$
13. $4\frac{7}{9}$

14. $\frac{7}{4}$
18. $8\frac{1}{4}$
16. $\frac{57}{10}$
17. $\frac{12}{16}$
18. $\frac{7}{21}$
19. $\frac{48}{60}$
20. $\frac{15}{40}$
21. $\frac{24}{100}$
22. $\frac{3}{4}$
23. $\frac{1}{6}$
24. $\frac{3}{5}$
25. $\frac{13}{15}$
26. $\frac{2}{3}$

27. A. $\frac{3}{4}$ Of those surveyed, $\frac{18}{24}$ went to at least one movie. Reduce the fraction to lowest terms: $\frac{18 \div 6}{24 \div 6} = \frac{3}{4}$.

28. C. $\frac{40}{100}$ Raise $\frac{2}{5}$ to an equivalent fraction with a denominator of 100 by multiplying both numbers by 20: $\frac{2 \times 20}{5 \times 20} = \frac{40}{100}$.

Lesson 4: Fraction Operations

Practice 4.1, page 51

1. $\frac{1}{2}$
2. 1
3. $\frac{1}{3}$
4. $\frac{1}{6}$
5. $\frac{11}{12}$
6. $1\frac{1}{8}$
7. $\frac{3}{10}$
8. $\frac{5}{18}$
9. $3\frac{13}{15}$
10. $1\frac{3}{4}$
11. $8\frac{1}{2}$
12. $11\frac{5}{8}$
13. $21\frac{7}{10}$

14. $7\frac{13}{18}$
15. $12\frac{5}{6}$
16. $2\frac{5}{8}$
17. $42\frac{5}{12}$
18. $22\frac{11}{20}$
19. $5\frac{1}{18}$
20. $11\frac{1}{8}$
21. $3\frac{23}{28}$
22. $1\frac{7}{24}$
23. $2\frac{3}{7}$
24. $8\frac{8}{9}$
25. $\frac{32}{35}$

26. B. $1\frac{3}{16}$ Add to find the total: $\frac{5}{16} + \frac{7}{8} = \frac{5}{16} + \frac{14}{16} = \frac{19}{16} = 1\frac{3}{16}$ inches.

27. C. $1\frac{5}{8}$ Subtract to find the difference in the lengths: $2\frac{7}{8} - 1\frac{1}{4} = 2\frac{7}{8} - 1\frac{2}{8} = 1\frac{5}{8}$ inches.

28. A. $14\frac{3}{8}$ Subtract the amount sold from the amount on the bolt: $23\frac{1}{4} - 8\frac{7}{8} = 23\frac{2}{8} - 8\frac{7}{8} = 22\frac{10}{8} - 8\frac{7}{8} = 14\frac{3}{8}$ yards.

29. C. $2\frac{11}{12}$ Add the amounts: $1\frac{2}{3} + \frac{1}{2} \cdot \frac{3}{4} = 1\frac{8}{12} + \frac{6}{12} + \frac{9}{12} = 1\frac{23}{12} = 2\frac{11}{12}$ cups.

Practice 4.2, page 53

1. $\frac{1}{6}$
2. $\frac{11}{12}$
3. 14
4. $18\frac{3}{4}$
5. $\frac{7}{8}$
6. $\frac{21}{32}$
7. $7\frac{14}{15}$
8. $41\frac{1}{4}$
9. $2\frac{1}{32}$

10. 14
11. $1\frac{4}{5}$
12. 48
13. $2\frac{2}{5}$
14. $2\frac{1}{4}$
15. 27
16. 8
17. $9\frac{1}{2}$
18. $\frac{3}{4}$

19. B. 75 Find $\frac{3}{16}$ of 400 by multiplying: $400 \times \frac{3}{16} = \frac{\overset{25}{400}}{1} \times \frac{3}{16} = \frac{75}{1} = 75$.

20. B. 7 Divide: $20 \div 2\frac{3}{4} = \frac{20}{1} \div \frac{11}{4} = \frac{20}{1} \times \frac{4}{11} = \frac{80}{11} = 7\frac{3}{11}$. Ignore the remainder since the problem asks how many shirts can be completed.

21. B. 33 You need to find how many $\frac{2}{3}$ hours there are in 22 hours. Divide: $22 \div \frac{2}{3} = \frac{22}{1} \div \frac{2}{3} = \frac{11}{1} \times \frac{3}{2} = \frac{33}{1}$.

22. C. $37\frac{7}{8}$ Multiply $12\frac{5}{8}$ inches by 3, the number of panels: $12\frac{5}{8} \times 3 = \frac{101}{8} \times \frac{3}{1} = \frac{303}{8} = 37\frac{7}{8}$.

Lesson 5: Fraction and Decimal Equivalencies

Practice 5, page 55

1. B. \$20.00 Instead of multiplying \$80 by 0.25, you can also find $\frac{1}{4}$ of \$80.

2. C. 480×0.3 Find $\frac{3}{10}$ of 480. "Of" in "of the workers" indicates multiplication, and the decimal equivalent of $\frac{3}{10}$ is 0.3.

3. B. $4\frac{2}{3}$ The decimal part of the calculator display equals the fraction $\frac{2}{3}$.

4. C. \$18.00 Multiply 12 by 1.5. The decimal $1.5 = 1\frac{1}{2}$. Convert that fraction to an improper fraction: $\frac{3}{2}$ Now multiply: $12 \times \frac{3}{2} = \frac{36}{2} = 18$.

5. B. $\frac{3}{4}$ Subtract: $1.875 - 1.125 = 0.75$, which equals $\frac{3}{4}$ inch.

6. C. 0.375 Instead of dividing 3 by 8, think: $3 \div 8$ means $\frac{3}{8}$, which equals 0.375.

Lesson 6: Decimals and Fractions on the Number Line

Practice 6, page 57

1. C. $\frac{2}{3}$ The number line is in increments of $\frac{1}{3}$, and the value you are asked to identify comes halfway between $\frac{1}{3}$ and 1.

2. D. 2.8 The number line is in increments of 0.2, and the value you are asked to identify comes halfway between 2.6 and 3.

3. C. 2 A minus B is $3\frac{1}{2} - 1\frac{1}{2} = 2$.

4. $\frac{2}{3}$ Angela gave 16 of 24 cookies to her neighbor: $\frac{16}{24} = \frac{2}{3}$.

5. **4.625** Each increment on this number line is 0.125 greater than the previous increment.

6. **9.33** Each increment on the number line is $0.3\overline{3}$ greater than the previous increment.

7. **$3\frac{1}{3}$** Each increment on the number line is $\frac{1}{3}$ greater than the previous increment.

8. **$11\frac{5}{6}$** Each increment on the number line is $\frac{1}{6}$ greater than the previous increment.

Lesson 7: Decimal and Fraction Calculator Skills

Practice 7, page 59

1. **7.379**

2. **$2\frac{1}{4}$** To work with mixed fractions on the TI-30XS MultiView™, use the $\boxed{2nd}$ function above the $\boxed{\frac{n}{d}}$ key: $\boxed{2nd}$ $\boxed{\frac{n}{d}}$ 3 ▶ 2 ▼ 3 ▶ $\boxed{-}$ $\boxed{2nd}$ $\boxed{\frac{n}{d}}$ 1 ▶ 5 ▼ 12 $\boxed{enter}$. The number $\frac{2}{4}$ will appear on the right-hand side of the display.

3. **$380.25**

4. **42**

5. **$84.44** Multiply: $\$95 \times \frac{8}{9} = 84.44\overline{4}$. Round to get \$84.44.

6. **$79.74** Divide: $\$956.88 \div 12 = \$79.74$.

7. **$1,475** Multiply: $\$118,000 \times 0.0125 = \$1,475$

8. **$4\frac{1}{4}$ cups** Add: $1\frac{1}{2} + 2\frac{3}{4} = 4\frac{1}{4}$.

9. **B. $6.67** Multiply the weight of the quilt by \$1.20: $5.56 \times \$1.20 = \$6.672$, which rounds to \$6.67.

10. **C. 24** You need to find $\frac{3}{8}$ of 64. Multiply. $64 \times \frac{3}{8} = 24$ acres.

Decimals and Fractions Practice Questions, pages 60–63

1. **C. $15\frac{3}{4}$** Subtract: $20\frac{1}{2} - 4\frac{3}{4} = 20\frac{2}{4} - 4\frac{3}{4} = 19\frac{6}{4} - 4\frac{3}{4} = 15\frac{3}{4}$

2. **B. $0.25** Divide the cost by the number of servings: $\$4.69 \div 19 \approx 0.247$, which rounds to \$0.25.

3. **C. $1386.20** To find the amount the 12-month plan will cost a customer, multiply \$98.85 by 12 and add \$200: $(\$98.85 \times 12) + \$200 = \$1386.20$.

4. **C. $30.12** Multiply using your calculator. Use 10.5 for $10\frac{1}{2}$: $\$2.869 \times 10.5 = \$30.1245$, which rounds to \$30.12.

5. **B. 2.85** Since the answer choices are decimals, use your calculator.

Use decimals instead of fractions: $1\frac{1}{2} = 1.5$, $4\frac{3}{4} = 4.75$, and $2\frac{3}{10} = 2.3$. To find the average, add the three weights and divide the total by 3: $\frac{.5 + 4.75 + 2.3}{3} = \frac{8.55}{3} = 2.85$

6. **C. $32\frac{1}{4}$** Divide: $\$258 \div \$8 = 32.25$, which equals $32\frac{1}{4}$.

7. **B. 57** Subtract $6\frac{1}{4}$ from $20\frac{1}{2}$ and divide the difference by $\frac{1}{4}$. To do the work quickly, use the fraction keys on your calculator or change the fractions to decimals: $20\frac{1}{2} - 6\frac{1}{4} = 14\frac{1}{4}$; $14\frac{1}{4} \div \frac{1}{4} = 57$.

8. **D. $90.00** Brand B costs \$0.09 more than Brand A, so the school will save \$0.09 on each marker. Multiply the savings by 1000: $\$0.09 \times 1000 = \$90.00$.

9. **B. $3\frac{1}{2}$** Add the times for the appointments: $\frac{3}{4} + \frac{3}{4} + 1\frac{1}{4} + \frac{3}{4} = 1\frac{10}{4} = 3\frac{2}{4} = 3\frac{1}{2}$

10. **C. 10** Divide $3\frac{1}{2}$ hours by the amount of time needed for a routine physical: $\frac{1}{2} \div \frac{1}{3} = \frac{7}{2} \div \frac{1}{3} = \frac{7}{2} \times \frac{3}{1} = \frac{21}{2} = 10\frac{1}{2}$ Therefore, Jennifer can complete 10 physicals. Ignore the fraction remainder.

11. **D. $\frac{11}{12}$** Write the fraction and reduce it to lowest terms. You can save time by using the fraction key on your calculator, which automatically reduces a fraction to lowest terms. Press 5500 $\boxed{\frac{n}{d}}$ ▼ 6000 $\boxed{enter}$. The right-hand side of the display will read $\frac{11}{12}$.

12. **C. $7.25** The first hour costs \$3.50, and there are $1\frac{1}{2}$ hours left. There are 3 half hours, or $1\frac{1}{2}$ hours, so you will pay $\$3.50 + (3 \times \$1.25) = \$7.25$.

13. **$\frac{2}{3}$** Write a fraction and reduce: $\frac{56}{84} = \frac{56 \div 28}{84 \div 28} = \frac{2}{3}$

14. **0.84** Subtract to compare: $3.97 - 3.13 = 0.84$

15. **B. $\frac{3}{10}$** Subtract: $250 - 175 = 75$. Thus, 75 out of 250, or $\frac{75}{250}$, have not been loaded. Reduce: $\frac{75 \div 25}{250 \div 25} = \frac{3}{10}$

16. **B. $\frac{5}{8}$** $A - B = \frac{7}{8} - \frac{1}{4}$. Find a common denominator and subtract: $\frac{7}{8} - \frac{2}{8} = \frac{5}{8}$.

17. **A. 285** To find $\frac{3}{4}$ of 380, multiply. Change $\frac{3}{4}$ to 0.75. Then $380 \times 0.75 = 285$.

18. **C. $\frac{5}{6}$** To find half of $1\frac{2}{3}$, either multiply by $\frac{1}{2}$ or divide by 2. Both results are the same: $1\frac{2}{3} \times \frac{1}{2} = \frac{5}{3} \times \frac{1}{2} = \frac{5}{6}$.

19. **D. core box, classic, bevel, cutter** You could change the fractions to decimals to solve the problem, but the quickest method is to rewrite the fractions with a common denominator of 32:
cutter: $\frac{9}{16} = \frac{18}{32}$;
core box: $\frac{5}{32}$;
classic: $\frac{3}{8} = \frac{12}{32}$;
bevel: $\frac{1}{2} = \frac{16}{32}$.
Then arrange the like fractions from least to greatest by their numerators.

20. **Points should be placed at $\frac{1}{8}$ and $\frac{1}{2}$.** The most Joe will eat will be $\frac{7}{8}$ of his pizza, so the minimum he'll have left over will be $\frac{1}{8}$ of it. The least Joe will eat will be $\frac{1}{2}$, so the maximum he'll have left over will be $\frac{1}{2}$ of the pizza.

21. **C. 8** Divide: $60 \div 7.5 = 8$ days.

22. **C. 150** You need to find $\frac{5}{8}$ of 240. Multiply: $240 \times \frac{5}{8} = \frac{\overset{30}{240}}{1} \times \frac{5}{\underset{}{8}} = \frac{150}{1} = 150$.

23. **A. $\frac{1}{2}$** Multiply: $\frac{2}{3} \times \frac{3}{4} = \frac{\overset{1}{2}}{\underset{1}{3}} \times \frac{\overset{1}{3}}{\underset{2}{4}} = \frac{1}{2}$.

24. **B. 56** Multiply: $140 \times \frac{2}{5} = \frac{\overset{28}{140}}{1} \times \frac{2}{\underset{}{5}} = \frac{56}{1} = 56$.

25. **C. 17.9** Maya travels five segments of the route. Add to find the total distance: $2.4 + 4.3 + 3.6 + 3.6 + 4.0 = 17.9$.

26. **D. 5** Add to find the total amount to be cut off: $3\frac{3}{4} + 3\frac{3}{4} = 6\frac{6}{4} = 7\frac{1}{2}$. Subtract from $12\frac{1}{2}$: $12\frac{1}{2} - 7\frac{1}{2} = 5$.

27. **B. $535.60** Multiply \$26.38 by 20 and add \$8 to the result: $\$26.38 \times 20 = \$527.60$. Then: $\$527.60 + \$8.00 = \$535.60$.

28. **80.** Divide: $60 \div 0.75 = 80$.

29. **$\frac{7}{12}$** Add the fractions and subtract the total from 1: $\frac{1}{6} + \frac{1}{4} = \frac{2}{12} + \frac{3}{12} = \frac{5}{12}$. Then: $1 - \frac{5}{12} = \frac{12}{12} - \frac{5}{12} = \frac{7}{12}$.

Ratio, Proportion, and Percent

Lesson 1: Ratio and Proportion

Practice 1.1, page 65

1. $\frac{24}{6} = \frac{4}{1}$

2. $\frac{\$250}{\$1500} = \frac{1}{6}$

3. $\frac{180}{15} = \frac{12}{1}$

4. $\frac{12}{30} = \frac{2}{5}$ Add 12 + 18 = 30 to find the total workers.

5. $\frac{336}{14} = \frac{24}{1}$

6. $\frac{\$1500}{\$2400} = \frac{5}{8}$

7. $\frac{20}{12} = \frac{5}{3}$ Subtract 32 − 20 = 12 to find the free throws missed.

8. $\frac{14}{24} = \frac{7}{12}$ Add 10 + 14 = 24 to find the total students.

9. $\frac{1440}{6} = \frac{240}{1}$

10. **A. 9:11** Write the ratio in fraction form and reduce: $\frac{180}{220} = \frac{9}{11}$.

11. **B. 3 to 10** Calculate: $\frac{180}{600} = \frac{3}{10}$.

12. **B. $\frac{1}{3}$** Subtract to find the voters who have made a decision: 600 − 150 = 450. Write the ratio and reduce: $\frac{150}{450} = \frac{1}{3}$.

13. **C. 1 to 2** Subtract to find the amount owed: $1200 − $400 = $800. Write the ratio and reduce: 400 to 800 = 1 to 2.

14. **D. 8:3** Subtract to find the number of losses: 77 − 56 = 21. Write the ratio and reduce: $\frac{56}{21} = \frac{8}{3}$.

Practice 1.2, page 67

1. 12
2. 45
3. 2.5 or $2\frac{1}{2}$
4. 60
5. $371
6. 96
7. 2.1 or $2\frac{1}{10}$
8. 72
9. 12.5 or $12\frac{1}{2}$
10. $8.94
11. 1.25 or $1\frac{1}{4}$
12. 37.5 or $37\frac{1}{2}$
13. 18
14. 32
15. $45.50
16. 28
17. **B. $1.23** Calculate: $\frac{4}{\$0.98} = \frac{5}{x}$ $0.98 × 5 ÷ 4 = $1.225, which rounds to $1.23.
18. **C. 96** Calculate: $\frac{5}{8} = \frac{60}{x}$; 8 × 60 ÷ 5 = 96.
19. **B. 23** Calculate: $\frac{414}{18} = \frac{x}{1}$; 414 × 1 ÷ 18 = 23.
20. **B. 345** Calculate: $\frac{2 \text{ cm}}{150 \text{ km}} = \frac{4.6 \text{ cm}}{x \text{ km}}$; 150 × 4.6 ÷ 2 = 345.
21. **A. $6\frac{2}{3}$** Write the proportions using fractions. The process is the same: $\frac{2\frac{1}{2}}{1\frac{1}{2}} = \frac{x}{4}$; $2\frac{1}{2} × 4 ÷ 1\frac{1}{2} = 6\frac{2}{3}$

22. **A. 155 × 7 ÷ 2.5** Set up the proportion and think about the order of operations you would need to solve for x: $\frac{155}{2.5} = \frac{x}{7}$; 155 × 7 ÷ 2.5 = x.

Lesson 2: Percents

Practice 2, page 69

1. base = $1000
   part = $200
   rate = 20%
2. base = 80
   part = 72
   rate = 90%
3. base = $13,700
   part = $2,740
   rate = 20%
4. base = $2000
   part = $500
   rate = 25%
5. base = 40
   part = 60
   rate = 150%
   60 is 150% *of* 40. The word *of* indicates that 40 is the base.
6. base = $38
   part = $3.23
   rate = 8.5%
7. base = $900
   part = $135
   rate = 15%
8. base = $10.70
   part = $1.07
   rate = 10%
9. base = 800
   part = 200
   rate = 25%
10. base = 12,500
    part = 5,000
    rate = 40%
11. **A. $\frac{9 \times 100}{122}$** Add the wins and losses to find the total games played: 9 + 3 = 12; then write the proportion: $\frac{9}{12} = \frac{x}{100}$. To solve the proportion, you need to find the expression that multiplies 9 and 100 and divides by 12. Only choice (A) does this.
12. **D. 50%** Bravo played 12 games (6 + 6 = 12). Then $\frac{6}{12} = \frac{x}{100}$ and 6 × 100 ÷ 12 = 50.
13. **C. $32** To find 25% of $128, solve the proportion: $\frac{x}{\$128} = \frac{25}{100}$; $128 × 25 ÷ 100 = $32. Since 25% = $\frac{1}{4}$, you can also find the answer by dividing $128 by 4.

Lesson 3: Using the Percent Formula

Practice 3.1, page 71

1. $5
2. 180
3. 140
4. 95%
5. 25%
6. 3%
7. 17
8. $60
9. 200%
10. 5%
11. 8%
12. $3.91
13. $6\frac{1}{2}$% or 6.5%
14. $364
15. 62.5% or $62\frac{1}{2}$%
16. 72
17. **C. 60%** Calculate: 72 ÷ 120 = 0.6 = 60%.

18. **B. $2,385** Calculate: $2,250 × 0.06 = $135, and $2,250 + $135 = $2,385.
19. **D. $6.90** Calculate: $46 × 0.15 = $6.90.
20. **D. 70%** Find what percent $45.50 is of $65 by dividing: $45.50 ÷ $65 = 0.7, which equals 70%.
21. **A. $\frac{\$3 \times 100}{\$50}$** You need to divide the part ($3) by the whole ($50) to find the rate; however, choice (D) states $3 ÷ $50, which equals 0.06. You still need to change 0.06 to a percent, which you can do by multiplying by 100. If you write a proportion to solve the problem, you will see that choice (A) is correct.

Practice 3.2, page 73

1. $175
2. 280
3. 6.4
4. $200
5. 30
6. $84
7. 200
8. 9
9. $13.50
10. 25%
11. $75
12. $9.30
13. 900
14. 90%
15. $780
16. $3120
17. 4000
18. 10%
19. **C. $1,230.00** Solve for the base: $\frac{\$369}{0.3} = \$1,230$.
20. **C. $1,200,000** Solve for the base. $\frac{\$72,000}{0.06} = \$1,200,000$.
21. **B. $\frac{160 \times 100}{5}$** Set up the problem as a proportion: $\frac{160}{x} = \frac{5}{100}$. To solve the proportion, you would multiply 160 × 100 and divide by 5. Only choice (B) carries out those operations.
22. **C. 720.** The base is 3600, the total number who received the application. The part is the unknown number who returned the application. Since 20% = 0.2, you can solve for the part by multiplying the base by the rate: 3600 × 0.2.

Lesson 4: Percent Calculator Skills

Practice 4, page 75

1. $59.80
2. $96
3. $15.12
4. 40
5. 3%
10. 79
11. 2.5% or $2\frac{1}{2}$%
12. 48
13. 78%
14. $16

6. 2080
7. 25%
8. 70
9. 25.2

15. 250
16. 14
17. 7%
18. 276

19. **C. $8.20** Chanel's order falls between $50.01 and $100. Find 5% of $84: press: 0.05 ⊗ 84 (enter). The right side of the display reads 4.2, or $4.20. Add $4: $4.20 + $4 = $8.20.

20. **A. $0.30** Find the shipping and handling for Jason's order: 8% of $110 = $8.80. Find the shipping and handling for Zola's order: 5% of $90 = $4.50, and $4.50 + $4.00 = $8.50. Then find the difference: $8.80 − $8.50 = $0.30.

21. **C. 88%** Press: 3190 ⊟ 3625 (2nd) ⟩ (enter). The right side of the display reads 0.88. You could also simply divide: 3190 ÷ 3625 = .88. Then mentally translate .88 into 88%.

22. **D. 15%** Divide strikeouts (63) by at bats (410): press: 63 ⊟ 410 (enter). The right side of the display reads 0.153658537, which rounds to 15%.

Lesson 5: Simple Interest

Practice 5, page 77

1. $360
2. $56
3. $420
4. $480

5. $1137.50
6. $1998. Note that 8 months = $\frac{2}{3}$ year.
7. $1700

8. **D. $1300 + ($1300 × 0.09 × 1.5)** Find the interest by multiplying the amount borrowed ($1300) by the interest expressed as a decimal (0.09) by the time period in years (1.5). To find the amount paid back, the amount borrowed must be added to the interest. Only choice (D) shows this series of operations.

9. **A. $2400** Multiply: $8000 × 0.06 × 5 = $2400.

10. **B. $1545** Find the amount of interest: for the time period, use $\frac{9}{12}$ months, which equals $\frac{3}{4}$, or 0.75; multiply: $1500 × 0.04 × 0.75 = $45. Add to find the amount paid back: $1500 + $45 = $1545.

11. **B. $144** Find the interest for each loan option: Option A: $2400 × 0.12 × 2.5 = $720; Option C: $2400 × 0.09 × 4 = $864. Subtract to find the difference: $864 − $720 = $144.

12. **D. $3640** Find the interest she will owe: $2800 × 0.1 × 3 = $840. Add to find the amount she will pay back: $2800 + $840 = $3640.

Lesson 6: Percent of Change

Practice 6, page 79

1. 50%
2. 38%
3. 200%
4. 45%
5. 20%

6. 32%
7. 21%
8. 86%
9. 420%
10. 34%

11. **B. 60%** Subtract: $448 − $280 = $168. Divide by the original weekly pay: $168 ÷ $280 = 0.6, which equals 60%.

12. **B. 25%** Subtract: $48 − $36 = $12. Divide by the original price: $12 ÷ $48 = 0.25, which equals 25%.

13. **C. 6%** Subtract: $636 − $600 = $36. Divide by the original rent: $36 ÷ $600 = 0.06, which equals 6%.

14. **C. 125%** The wholesale price of the model is $63, and the retail price is $141.75. Subtract: $141.75 − $63 = $78.75. Divide by the wholesale price: $78.75 ÷ $63 = 1.25, which equals 125%.

15. **B. 30%** The retail price of the model is $150.50, and the member's price is $105.35. Subtract: $150.50 − $105.35 = $45.15. Divide by the retail price: $45.15 ÷ 150.50 = 0.3, which equals 30%.

Ratio, Proportion, and Percent Practice Questions, pages 80–83

1. **C. 1:11** Subtract to find the dollars spent on other costs: $360,000 − $30,000 = $330,000. Write a ratio and reduce: $\frac{\$30,000}{\$330,000} = \frac{1}{11}$.

2. **A. $2 \times \frac{50}{5}$** Write a proportion: $\frac{5}{2} = \frac{50}{x}$. To solve it, multiply 2 × 50 and divide by 5. Only choice (A) performs these operations.

3. **B. $7.56** Find 35% of $5.60: $5.60 × 0.35 = $1.96; add: $1.96 + $5.60 = $7.56. Another way to get the answer is to find 135% of $5.60. $5.60 × 1.35 = $7.56.

4. **D. $20,000** The current worth of the car ($12,000) is part of the base. Solve for the base: $12,000 ÷ 0.6 = $20,000.

5. **C. 42** Solve the proportion: $\frac{7}{3} = \frac{x}{18}$; 7 × 18 ÷ 3 = 42.

6. **A. 6%** The commission is part of the base. Solve for the part: $954 ÷ $15,900 = 0.06 = 6%.

7. **B. 1:6** Add to find the total time spent on the project: $2 + 1\frac{1}{2} + 2 + 3\frac{1}{2} = 9$ hours. $1\frac{1}{2}$ hours = 1.5 hours. Write a ratio using decimals and reduce: $\frac{1.5}{9} = \frac{1}{6}$.

8. **B. 36%** Add to find the acres used for grains, vegetables, or fruits: 5,200 + 9,200 = 14,400. Solve for percent: 14,400 ÷ 40,400 = 0.36 = 36%.

9. **A. 35,600** Calculate the decrease in acres of dairy farmland: 22,000 × 20% = 4,400. Subtract that amount from the total acreage of farmland to determine how many acres of farmland will remain: 40,000 − 4,400 = 35,600.

10. **A. $\frac{3}{16}$** The total fat is 3 + 13 = 16 grams. Write the ratio of saturated fat (3 grams) to the total (16 grams). The ratio cannot be simplified.

11. **B. 10** Write a proportion and solve: $\frac{4}{5} = \frac{x}{12.5}$. Then 4 × 12.5 ÷ 5 = 10 inches.

12. **138** Write a proportion and solve: $\frac{4}{3} = \frac{184}{x}$. Then 3 × 184 ÷ 4 = 138 female patients.

13. **$900** If 20% is the amount of the discount, then the sale price must be 80% of the original price. The sale price is the part, and the original price is the base. Solve for the base: $720 ÷ 0.8 = $900.

14. **B. 40** If the ratio of wins to losses is 5:4, then the ratio of wins to games played is 5:9. Write a proportion and solve: $\frac{5}{9} = \frac{x}{72}$; 5 × 72 ÷ 9 = 40 games won.

15. **C. 192** Add to find the number that did not answer "no": 16% + 32% = 48%. Find 48% of 400: 400 × 0.48 = 192.

16. **C. 20%** To find the percent decrease, subtract the lower price from the higher price and divide the difference by the original price. In this case, the original price is $25, the higher price. To change the answer to a percent, you must move the decimal point two places to the right or multiply by 100.

17. **A. 121** When the rate is greater than 100%, the part will be greater than the base. Solve for the part: 55 × 2.2 = 121.

18. **D. 18%** There are 6 grams of fat in the roast beef sandwich, so there are 6 × 9 = 54 calories in the sandwich from fat.

The total number of calories in the sandwich is 300. Find what percent 54 is of 300: $54 \div 300 = 0.18 = 18\%$.

19. **D. $264** Write a proportion and solve: $\frac{\$8}{\$3} = \frac{\$704}{x}$; $\$3 \times \$704 \div \$8 = \$264$.

20. **C. 175** The 140 employees who have more than 12 days of sick leave are part of the whole workforce. You need to solve for the base: $140 \div 0.8 = 175$.

21. **D. 825** If the ratio of sold to unsold tickets is 11 to 1, then the ratio of sold to total tickets is 11 to 12. Write a proportion and solve: $\frac{11}{12} = \frac{x}{900}$; $11 \times 900 \div 12 = 825$.

22. **C. $2464** Use the formula for finding simple interest: $i = prt$: $\$2200 \times 0.08 \times 1.5 = \$264$. To find the amount in the account at the end of the time, add the interest to the original investment: $\$2200 + \$264 = \$2464$.

23. **B. $328** Once you find the discount by multiplying 0.2 by $410, you will need to subtract the discount from $410 to find the sale price.

24. **D. 330** After changing $2\frac{3}{4}$ to the decimal 2.75, write a proportion and solve: $\frac{0.5}{60} = \frac{2.75}{x}$; $60 \times 2.75 \div 0.5 = 330$.

25. **C. $\frac{(140-91)}{140} \times 100$** There were 140 customers on Sunday, and 91 made a purchase. Therefore, $140 - 91$ did not make a purchase. To find the percent rate, divide the difference by 140, the total number of customers on Sunday (the base). Then move the decimal point two places to the right or multiply by 100 to change the answer to a percent. Only choice (C) shows this sequence of operations.

26. **270** Write a proportion and solve: $\frac{9}{14} = \frac{x}{420}$.

27. **$\frac{3}{5}$** If Marcie spends 15 hours answering telephones, she spends $40 - 15$, or 25 hours doing other tasks. Write a ratio and reduce: $\frac{15}{25} = \frac{3}{5}$.

Data, Statistics, and Probability

Lesson 1: Tables and Pictographs

Practice 1, page 85

1. **9** Calculate: $22{,}707 \div 2523 = 9$
2. **6%** Calculate: $(139{,}510 - 130{,}748) \div 139{,}510 \approx 0.06$, or 6%.
3. **300** There are $6\frac{1}{2}$ symbols in the "North" row and $4\frac{1}{2}$ in the "South" row. Two more symbols translates to 300 more books.
4. **3000** Count the number of symbols, 20, and multiply by 150.
5. **D. Reads or pretends to read** If 100 children were surveyed in each year, then the number of children who recognized all letters increased from 11 to 17. To find the percent change, use the percent change formula:
$$\frac{\text{amount of change}}{\text{original value}} = \frac{17-11}{11} = \frac{6}{11},$$
or a roughly 55% increase. Performing similar calculators for all categories will reveal that "reads or pretends to read" showed the least percent increase:
$$\frac{67-66}{6} = \frac{1}{66} \approx 2\%.$$ Note that simply subtracting 66 from 67 does not give you the percent of change.
6. **C. 119** In 2010, 34% of 3-year-old children could write their own names. Find 34% of 350: $350 \times 0.34 = 119$.
7. **C. 375** There are $7\frac{1}{2}$ car symbols. Each symbol represents 50 cars. Multiply: $7\frac{1}{2} \times 50 = 375$
8. **A. 75** Compare the symbols for the two rows. There are $1\frac{1}{2}$ more symbols for 8 A.M. to noon than there are after 4:30 P.M. Multiply: $1\frac{1}{2} \times 50 = 75$

Lesson 2: Bar and Line Graphs

Practice 2.1, page 87

1. **50**
2. **about 15** Estimate 38 complaints in 2011 and 22 complaints in 2006. Subtract and round.
3. **20%** The number of complaints decreased by 5, from 25 to 20. This represents a $\frac{5}{25} = 20\%$ decrease.
4. **about $20 million** Estimate values from the graph and subtract.

Be sure to use the black bars that represent cost.

5. **Film A** Film A has the biggest difference in size between the bar representing box-office receipts and the bar representing cost.
6. **150%** Calculate: $\frac{60}{40} = \frac{3}{2} = 150\%$
7. **A. 40** There are approximately 110 T-shirts, more than 40 books, and a little fewer than 30 toys sold. Combined, about 70 books and toys were sold. Subtract 70 from 110, and you have about 40.
8. **D. $1000** There were about 50 games sold, so 25 sold for $16 and 25 sold for $24. Calculate: $(25 \times 16) + (25 \times 24) = 1000$.
9. **C. 14:3** Write a ratio and simplify: $\frac{70}{15} = \frac{14}{3}$
10. **D. September** Add the 2-day and 5-day permits for each month. Only September's permits equal 80.

Practice 2.2, page 89

1. **October** The point representing October is lower than the point representing the previous month, and the line leading to it slopes downward. This indicates a decrease.
2. **270** Estimate totals for the three months and add.
3. **from June to July** The number of visits increased more from August to September, but because the number in June was so low, the percentage increase from June to July is nearly 100%.
4. **$10** Estimate values and subtract.
5. **20%** The price increased from about $25 to about $30, an increase of $5. $\frac{5}{25} = 20\%$.
6. **$30** The price increased from about $18 to about $45. This increase is almost $30.
7. **A. 1930 to 1940** The price of goods decreased over two decades, 1920 to 1940. Note the downward movement of the line. Only the time period 1930 to 1940 is included among the answer options.
8. **D. $\frac{1}{5}$** The price of the same goods was about $20 in 1970 and $100 in 2000. Write a ratio and simplify: $\frac{\$20}{\$100} = \frac{1}{5}$

9. **B. 50** There were about 390 sales in Store 2 and 340 sales in Store 1 in the sixth week: 390 − 340 = 50.

10. **D. Week 5** The steepest line segment leads from week 4 to week 5, indicating the largest increase in sales from the previous week.

Lesson 3: Circle Graphs

Practice 3, page 91

1. **29%** Find those two categories on the circle graph and add.

2. $\frac{2}{25}$ $8\% = \frac{8}{100} = \frac{2}{25}$.

3. **$630** Use the total budget. $2250 \times 28\% = \$630$.

4. **$30.60** 17 cents of every dollar are spent on water heating: $\$180 \times 0.17 = \$30.60$.

5. **Heating and Air-Conditioning** The section labeled "Heating and Air-Conditioning" takes up more than half the circle.

6. **Cooking and Refrigeration** This section is 11 cents of every dollar, which is about 10%.

7. **A. 10** According to the graph, a records clerk spends 25%, or $\frac{1}{4}$, of his or her time preparing documents. Then 25% of 40 hours is 10 hours.

8. **D. 56%** If 44% of the time is spent on data entry, then 100% − 44%, which equals 56%, is spent on other tasks.

9. **B. 10%** Add: 3 cents plus 7 cents is 10 cents. Then 10 cents out of 100 cents is $\frac{10}{100}$, or 10%.

10. **C. $48** 40 cents out of every dollar, or 40%, is spent on public bonds. Then 40% of $120 is found by multiplying: $\$120 \times 0.4 = \$48$.

Lesson 4: Measures of Central Tendency

Practice 4.1, page 93

1. **57** Count the number of tally marks and add.

2. **6** Count the number of tally marks and subtract.

3. **1:2** Calculate: $\frac{15}{30} = \frac{1}{2}$.

4. **3:4** Calculate: $\frac{6}{8} = \frac{3}{4}$.

5. **46** Count the tally marks and add.

6. **14%** Count the total number of tally marks, then divide: $\frac{10}{70} \approx 0.14 = 14\%$.

7. **B. $\frac{4}{11}$** There are 16 tally marks next to the reason "wrong size." Add all the tally marks: 16 + 20 + 3 + 5 = 44. Write a ratio and reduce. $\frac{16}{44} = \frac{4}{11}$.

8. **C. 45%** Adding all the tally marks, you find that there were 44 clothing returns in all. Since there are 20 tally marks by "unwanted gift," $\frac{20}{44}$ or ≈ 45% of the total reasons given were "unwanted gift."

9. **D. 39%** Calculate: 35 applicants had a speed under 30 wpm, out of a total of 90 applicants, so $\frac{35}{90} \approx$ 39%.

10. **B. 1:2** To find those who could type above 45 wpm, add: 18 + 12 = 30. The number typing below 45 wpm is found by adding 35 + 25 = 60. Write a ratio and reduce: $\frac{30}{60} = \frac{1}{2}$.

Practice 4.2, page 95

1. mean: 80.14
   median: 80
   mode: 82
2. mean: $8487.17
   median: $8208.50
   mode: none
3. mean: $4.76
   median: $4.50
   mode: $4.50
4. mean: 309 miles
   median: 300 miles
   mode: none
5. mean: $101.83
   median: $101.81
   mode: none
6. mean: 86
   median: 88
   mode: 88
7. mean: 99.1°
   median: 99°
   mode: 98° and 100°
8. mean: 1.9 inches
   median: 1.8 inches
   mode: none
9. mean: 305
   median: 305
   mode: 305
10. mean: 38.8 hours
    median: 40 hours
    mode: 40 hours

11. **A. $117,100** Add the amounts in the column labeled "Asking Price" and divide by 6, the number of prices listed.

12. **C. $116,500** Arrange the selling prices in order: $124,800; $118,400; $116,500; $116,500; $109,000; $103,600. Since the number of items is even, there are two in the middle: $116,500 and $116,500. Since these are the same amount, the average of the two is also $116,500.

13. **A.** $\frac{790 + 1150 + 662 + 805}{4}$ To find the mean, add the numbers and divide by the number of items in the set. In this case, there are 4 numbers.

14. **C. $900** The median is the middle amount. Arrange the amounts in order and find the middle amount.

15. **B. 14** The mode is the number that occurs most often. Only 14 occurs more than once in the data.

Lesson 5: Line Plots

Practice 5, page 97

1. **C.** Look for a line plot that reflects that two zebras have 26 stripes, two have 28, two have 30, etc.

2. **B.** Look for a line plot that reflects three classes with 29 students, two classes with 32, etc.

3. Draw a dot for each person not already represented in the line plot. Your completed line plot should look like this:

4. **B. 3** Three people grew three vegetables—that's more people than grew any other specific number of vegetables.

Lesson 6: Histograms

Practice 6, page 99

1. **C.** Look for the histogram that begins with 30 and that has a second bar at 56, a third bar at 80, etc.

2. **D.** Look for the histogram that begins with 15 and that has a second bar at 22, a third bar at 35, etc.

3. **C. 36%** Estimate the percentages represented by the four bars that cover the time period of December 9 through January 5: 8%, 9%, 9%, and 10%. Add those estimates to find the approximate percentage of cases reported during that entire time period, resulting in 36%.

Lesson 7: Probability

Practice 7.1, page 101

1. $\frac{2}{5}$, 0.4, 40% Calculate: $\frac{20}{50} = \frac{2}{5}$

2. $\frac{3}{10}$, 0.3, 30% There were 12 non-blue spins out of 40 total spins: $\frac{12}{40} = \frac{3}{10} = 30\%$.

3. $\frac{1}{5}$, 0.2, 20% Calculate: $\frac{2}{2+4+4} = \frac{2}{10} = \frac{1}{5} = 20\%$

4. $\frac{1}{4}$, 0.25, 25% Calculate:
$\frac{60}{180+60} = \frac{60}{240} = \frac{1}{4} = 25\%$

5. $\frac{1}{3}$, 0.33, $33\frac{1}{3}$% Calculate: $\frac{2}{6} = \frac{1}{3}$

6. **C. 50%** There are 12 cards in the deck, and 6 are diamonds: $\frac{6}{12} = \frac{1}{2} = 50\%$

7. **A.** $\frac{3}{4}$ There are 3 clubs, so 9 are not clubs: $\frac{9}{12} = \frac{3}{4}$.

8. **D. 2 out of 5** Sixteen out of 40 trials resulted in tails: $\frac{16}{40} = \frac{2}{5}$.

9. **A. 3 out of 5** Twenty-four out of 40 trials resulted in heads: $\frac{24}{40} = \frac{3}{5}$.

Practice 7.2, page 103

1. $\frac{1}{36}$ The events are independent, so multiply: $\frac{1}{6} \times \frac{1}{6} = \frac{1}{36}$

2. $\frac{1}{4}$ Because the first card is replaced, the two choices are independent. The cards greater than 5 are 6, 7, 8, 9, 10. Multiply: $\frac{5}{10} \times \frac{5}{10} = \frac{1}{2} \times \frac{1}{2} = \frac{1}{4}$

3. $\frac{1}{8}$ Half of the sections are red, so there is a $\frac{1}{2}$ chance that the result will be red. Each spin is independent. Multiply: $\frac{1}{2} \times \frac{1}{2} \times \frac{1}{2} = \frac{1}{8}$

4. $\frac{9}{38}$ The marble is *not* replaced, so the probabilities are not the same. There is a $\frac{1}{2}$ chance the first marble is red. But once one red marble is removed, the odds of a second red become $\frac{9}{19}$. Multiply: $\frac{1}{2} \times \frac{9}{19} = \frac{9}{38}$.

5. $\frac{1}{16}$ Each flip is independent and has a $\frac{1}{2}$ chance of coming up heads: $\frac{1}{2} \times \frac{1}{2} \times \frac{1}{2} \times \frac{1}{2} = \frac{1}{16}$.

6. $\frac{1}{4}$ Half of the numbers on a standard die are odd: $\frac{1}{2} \times \frac{1}{2} = \frac{1}{4}$.

7. **A.** $\frac{1}{9}$ The probability of rolling a 5 is $\frac{1}{6}$. Of the six equal sections on the spinner, four are even numbers, so there is a $\frac{4}{6}$, or $\frac{2}{3}$, chance of spinning an even number. Multiply the probability of each outcome: $\frac{1}{6} \times \frac{2}{3} \times \frac{2}{18} = \frac{1}{9}$.

8. **D.** $\frac{1}{6}$ The only numbers that are on the spinner are 2, 3, and 4. There is only one 2 on the die, one 3 on the die, and one 4 on the die. So, no matter what number comes up on the spinner, there is a $\frac{1}{6}$ chance the die rolls that number.

9. **C. 1 out of 3** Of the 10 cards, 6 are marked with a square; therefore, there is a 6 in 10, or $\frac{3}{5}$, chance of getting a square on the first pick. Now there are only 9 cards left, and 5 are squares, so there is a a $\frac{5}{9}$ chance of getting a square on the second pick. Multiply: $\frac{3}{5} \times \frac{5}{9} = \frac{15}{45} = \frac{1}{3}$

10. **B. 80%** After the five white chips are removed from the bag, the bag contains 10 chips, with 8 green and 2 white. The probability of getting green is $\frac{8}{10}$, which equals 80%.

Lesson 8: Combinations

Practice 8.1, page 105

1. **5** Since Rob is choosing 4 team members, each possible team leaves out exactly 1 employee. There are 5 possible employees Rob could leave out, so there are 5 possible teams.

2. **10** Either an organized list or a table will work. To solve this problem using a list organized in columns, assign the books letters: A, B, C, D, and E. Count possible combinations:

A and B combinations	A and C combinations	A and D combinations	B and C combinations	B and D combinations	C and D combinations
ABC	ACD	ADE	BCD	BDE	CDE
ABD	ACE		BCE		
ABE					

3. **4** Use either a table or an organized list, as above.

4. **10** The problem does not give the names of the friends, so assign them letters: A, B, C, D, E. Then use a table or organized list, as above, to find possible combinations of two.

5. **A. 5** Use a table or an organized list.

6. **B. 6** Even though three people are going to the conference, you already know that one of them will be Regan. So the question is really asking how many combinations of two out of Regan's four employees could also go. Name the employees A, B, C, and D, and use a table or organized list.

7. **C. 10** The gender of the people sent to the signing is not relevant to answering this question, so you are being asked for possible combinations of 3 out of 5. Use a table or an organized list.

8. **A. 20** Assign letters to the six people (A, B, C, D, E, and F), and then use a table or organized list.

9. **B. 20** This question asks you to add the number of possible groups of 2 out of 5 to the number of possible groups of 3 out of 5. Perform each of those tasks separately, or realize that they will have the same solution because choosing 3 to be in the group is the same as choosing 2 to be out of the group. Then, add the possible combinations together.

Practice 8.2, page 107

1. **48** Use the fundamental counting principle:
4 (types of bread) × 3 (types of meat) × 4 (condiments) = 48.

2. **24** Use the fundamental counting principle: 3 (restaurant certificates) × 2 (T-shirts) × 4 (hats) = 24.

3. **27** Use the fundamental counting principle: 3 × 3 × 3 = 27.

4. **24** On Friday, Julio has 2 choices. On Saturday, he has 3. On Sunday, he has 4 choices. Use the fundamental counting principle: 2 × 3 × 4 = 24

5. **D. 5,184** There are three words in the passphrase: 24 choices for the first, 9 for the second, 24 for

the third. Use the fundamental counting principle: $24 \times 9 \times 24 = 5184$.

6. **A. 10.** You are asked for combinations from one set of items. Use either a table or an organized list. You can assign the superpowers letters A–E to make it easier to see how to combine them.

7. **C. 1,024** Use the fundamental counting principle: 4 (meats) × 4 (vegetables) × 4 (noodles) × 4 (broth) × 4 (spices) = 1024.

8. **A. 125** Use the fundamental counting principle: 5 (medications) × 5 (dietary changes) × 5 (vitamins) = 125.

Lesson 9: Permutations

Practice 9, page 109

1. **120** This is a permutations problem, because order matters. The question asks how many sequences of five items are possible. $5 \times 4 \times 3 \times 2 \times 1 = 120$.

2. **24** This question asks you how many sequences of four items are possible? $4 \times 3 \times 2 \times 1 = 24$

3. **10** This is a combinations problem: you are being asked how many groups of three are possible, given five students. Order does not matter. Use a table or an organized list; you may name the students A–E if that is easier.

4. **720** This is a permutations problem, because order matters. $6 \times 5 \times 4 \times 3 \times 2 \times 1 = 720$.

5. **C. 360** This is a permutations problem, in which you are counting possible sequences of four out of six tasks. $6 \times 5 \times 4 \times 3 = 360$.

6. **B. 6** This is a permutations problem: the question asks you how many possible sequences of three types of flowers are possible. $3 \times 2 \times 1 = 6$.

7. **D. 5,040** This is a permutations problem, because you are told that the role of Bystander #1 is different from the role of Bystander #4. (Notice the phrase "specific roles" in the question.) Thus, order matters. The question is asking how many sequences of four are possible given ten people. $10 \times 9 \times 8 \times 7 = 5040$.

8. **B. 20** This is a combinations problem asking how many groups of

three out of six are possible. Use a table or an organized list.

9. **C. 120** This is a permutations problem asking how many sequences of three out of six are possible. $6 \times 5 \times 4 = 120$.

Data, Statistics, and Probability Practice Questions, pages 110–115

1. **B. 2007** Only the bar for 2007 falls between 500 and 600 on the scale.

2. **B. 40%** Estimate the values for 1998 and 1999. Then find the percent of decrease. Estimate roughly 650 and 390 for 1998 and 1999. Subtract. 650 − 390 = 260. Divide by the original number. $260 \div 650 = 0.4 = 40\%$

3. **A. $\frac{3}{100}$** Jim and his friends bought a total of 12 tickets (4 people × 3 tickets). Then 12 out of 400 = $\frac{12}{400} = \frac{3}{100}$

4. **D. 50°** Arrange the low temperatures in order: 55°, 53°, 50°, 50°, 49°, and 48°. Find the middle of the list. Since there are two temperatures in the middle and both are 50°, the mean of the two must be 50°.

5. **C. 1.56** Add the six amounts, and divide by 6: 0.45 + 0.63 + 1.34 + 3.53 + 2.57 + 0.84 = 9.36, and 9.36 ÷ 6 = 1.56 inches. It makes sense to use your calculator on this question.

6. **C. Woodland Hills** Mentally subtract the low temperature from the high temperature for each area. The greatest difference is in Woodland Hills. 68° − 50° = 18°.

7. **B. 2005** Ticket sales increased each year from 2001 through 2004. The first year in which they declined was 2005.

8. **C. 2008** The line graph shows the steepest increase (line rising from left to right) from 2007 to 2008.

9. **C. 32%** Eight customers chose a mouse pad. 8 ÷ 25 = 0.32 = 32%

10. **A. 1 in 2** Of the 52 cards, 26 are either hearts or diamonds: $\frac{26}{52} = \frac{1}{2}$

11. **3.5 or $\frac{7}{2}$** Add the hours, and divide by 6, the number of weeks: 5 + 3.5 + 4 + 0 + 1.5 + 7 = 21 hours, and 21 hours ÷ 6 = 3.5 hours.

12. **$\frac{2}{5}$** Only the numbers 4 and 5 are greater than 3. The probability is 2 out of 5, $\frac{2}{5}$, or 0.4.

13. **B. 41%** The three candidates who received the smallest percentages of the vote also received the smallest number of votes. Add: 9% + 14% + 18% = 41%

14. **C. Bowen and Utley** Since $\frac{3}{5}$ = 60%, look for two candidates whose combined percent is close to 60%. Since 24% + 35% = 59%, the correct answer is choice (C).

15. **D. 5100 × 0.09** Grace Reiner received 9%, which equals 0.09. You know the percent and the base. Multiply to find the part.

16. **B. March** The lines for both companies cross in March.

17. **B. 5900** Company A's orders continue to climb at about the same rate. Imagine extending the solid line to the next month. The line would reach to almost 6000. Choice (A) is too high an increase.

18. **C. 540** The graph indicates that about 3000 orders were placed in April. Multiply: 3000 × 18% = 540.

19. **B. 24.5** Use only the Shots Attempted column. Put the numbers in order, and find the middle: 29, 27, 26, 25, 24, 24, 23, 18. The two in the middle are 25 and 24. Find the mean of those numbers: 25 + 24 = 49, and 49 ÷ 2 = 24.5.

20. **D. 10** Use the Shots Made column. The mode is the number that occurs most often. In this case the mode is 10, which occurs three times.

21. **B. $\frac{5}{36}$** The probability that a marble is red is $\frac{8}{24}$, or $\frac{1}{3}$. The chance that a marble is white is $\frac{10}{24}$, or $\frac{5}{12}$. Because the first marble is replaced, the two events are independent. Multiply: $\frac{1}{3} \times \frac{5}{12} = \frac{5}{36}$

22. **B. $\frac{34 + 31 + 42}{3}$** To find the mean, add the three numbers and divide by 3, the number of months in the list. There are 36 employees, but you don't need this number to solve the problem.

23. **$\frac{1}{36}$** The probability of rolling one "one" is $\frac{1}{6}$. Multiply to find the chance of rolling two ones: $\frac{1}{6} \times \frac{1}{6} = \frac{1}{36}$.

24. **210** Arrange the numbers in order, and find the middle number: 305, 276, 210, 158, 54.

25. **625** Use the fundamental counting principle: $5 \times 5 \times 5 \times 5 = 625$.

26. **4** This is a combinations problem; use a table or an organized list.

27. **720** This is a permutations question, because the board is not simply picking three members. Rather, those members will also be ordered in a specific way. Multiply:
10 options for president $\times$ 9 options for secretary $\times$ 8 options for treasurer = 720.

28. **20%** First find the total number of patients: 16 (colds and flu) + 13 (cuts and scrapes) + 12 (sprained muscles) + 7 (tetanus shots) + 12 (severe headaches) = 60. Now find what percent of 60 is represented by 12: $\frac{12}{60} \times 100 = 20\%$

29. **B. 4:3** The ratio of patients with colds or flu to the number of patients with severe headaches is 16:12, which simplifies to 4:3.

30. **B. 180–199 lbs** The bar corresponding to this weight range is the tallest bar on the graph.

31. **B. Participants weighing less than 200 lbs** Choices (C) and (D) are both subsets of choice (B), and so cannot be correct. Add the totals of the columns in the graph to reveal that the total for choice (B) is greater than that of choice (A).

32. **B. 20 miles per gallon** Seven cars got 20 miles per gallon on average, more than in any other line of the table.

33. **A. $\frac{1}{2}$** One car got 35 miles per gallon, and two got 15 miles per gallon.

34. Draw dots on the line plot so that it looks like the following:

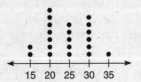

35. **D.**

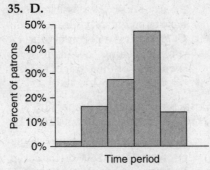

Only choice (D) reflects that 48% of visitors arrived during the fourth time period listed.

Algebra Basics, Expressions, and Polynomials

Lesson 1: The Number Line and Signed Numbers

Practice 1.1, page 117

1. 5	13. −50
2. 45	14. −11
3. 13	15. 25
4. 1	16. −35
5. 1	17. −11
6. 10	18. 11
7. −3	19. 10
8. 13	20. 75
9. −4	21. 12
10. 2	22. 2
11. −22	23. −1
12. 32	24. −13

25. **B. 2 + (−5)** The operation starts on + 2 and moves 5 units to the left (a negative direction).

26. **C. 115°** Begin with 92°. Then perform the following operations: $92° + 12° - 5° + 6° - 3° + 13° = 115°$

Practice 1.2, page 119

1. 20	15. 6
2. −21	16. −20
3. −48	17. −300
4. 18	18. 2
5. −10	19. −5
6. 3	20. 660
7. −3	21. 12
8. −5	22. −120
9. 2	23. −125
10. −5	24. −12
11. −28	25. 20
12. −3	26. −1
13. −1	27. 0
14. −75	

28. **B. −7** Substitute the numbers from the spreadsheet for the cells in the expression and solve. Note that A1 is column A, row 1; A3 is column A, row 3; and so on: $\frac{(-3)(7)(-1)}{(3)(-1)} = \frac{21}{-3} = -7$

29. **C. $\frac{2(8)}{(-8)}$** To find the product of two numbers, multiply: 2(8). Then divide by −8, as directed in the problem.

30. **C. The result is a negative number.** Do not do any calculations. Instead, examine the factors. Since there is an odd number of negative factors, the answer will be negative. This is the only possible option.

Lesson 2: Powers and Roots

Practice 2, page 121

1. 9	13. 6561
2. 4	14. 1296
3. 3	15. 12.2
4. 1	16. 8000
5. 9	17. 1
6. 7	18. $\frac{1}{16}$
7. 125	19. 15.6
8. $\frac{1}{16}$	20. 10.9
9. 16	21. 7.5
10. 8	22. 23.2
11. $\frac{1}{1000}$	23. 1
12. 11	24. 256

25. **C. 6^3** To find the volume, you would need to solve $6 \times 6 \times 6$, which can be written as 6^3.

26. **A. 3^{-3}** Examine the choices. Choices (A) and (D) will result in a fraction, a value less than 1. Choices (B) and (C) will each have a value of 1 or greater

Choice (A): $3^{-3} = \frac{1}{3^3} = \frac{1}{27}$

Choice (D): $2^{-4} = \frac{1}{2^4} = \frac{1}{16}$

Since $\frac{1}{27} < \frac{1}{16}$, choice (A) is correct.

Lesson 3: Scientific Notation

Practice 3, page 123

1. 2.3×10^3	12. 480,000,000
2. 4.2×10^{-4}	13. 0.000017
3. 1.24×10^7	14. 0.0072
4. 1.432×10^{10}	15. 916,000
5. 3.6×10^7	16. 85,910,000
6. 9.5×10^{-3}	17. 0.00000956
7. 5.8×10^{-7}	18. 2.35×10^4
8. 1.5×10^{11}	19. 0.000000001
9. 9×10^{-9}	20. 2,670,000,000
10. 0.0005173	21. 3×10^8
11. 3,700,000	

22. **B. 4.356×10^4** In scientific notation, the whole-number portion must be a digit from 1 to 9. Choice (B) is correct because the decimal place must be moved 4 places.

23. **D. $5 \times 9.07 \times 10^{-1}$** In scientific notation, a ton = 9.07×10^{-1} metric tons. Multiply this by 5 to find the equivalent weight of five tons.

Lesson 4: Order of Operations

Practice 4, page 125

1. 24
2. 1
3. 29
4. 2
5. 7
6. 20
7. 14
8. 55
9. 10
10. 23
11. 161
12. 30
13. 360
14. 4
15. 6

16. **C. $(1 - 0.75)(28)(30)$.** The total cost of the class can be found by multiplying 28 members by $30. Since the foundation pays 75%, or 0.75, the hospital will pay 100% − 75%, or (1 − 0.75). You must multiply the amount the class will cost by the percent that the hospital will pay. Only choice (C) performs these operations.

17. **B. Add 5** The operations in the brackets must be performed first. Once these are completed, multiply by 2 and then add 5. Notice that it is not necessary to find the value of the expression to answer the question.

18. **C. 76**
$$22 + 6[(14 - 5) \div 3(17 - 14)]$$
$$= 22 + 6[9 \div 3(3)]$$
$$= 22 + 6[3 \times 3]$$
$$= 22 + 6[9]$$
$$= 22 + 54 = 76$$

Lesson 5: Absolute Value

Practice 5, page 127

1. 18
2. 107
3. 423
4. 95
5. 7,026
6. 18
7. 5,708,432
8. 85.6
9. 42
10. 10.5
11. 163.24
12. 3.14
13. 11
14. −156
15. 156
16. 3
17. −91
18. 0
19. 620
20. −7
21. −20
22. −1
23. 2.125
24. −11

25. **D. 10 degrees** The change in temperature is the absolute value of the result of the new temperature minus the old temperature: $|(-5)-(-15)|=|10|$, or 10 degrees.

26. **D. 16** In order to find out how many blocks Bob walked in total, you also need to know how long the last leg of his journey (from the post office back to his apartment) was. To do this, you can think of movement east as having a positive value and movement west as having a negative value. So, on the first three legs of his journey Bob walked 5 + −6 + (−2), leaving him −3 blocks from his house. The last leg of his journey is 3 blocks, and you can simply add the absolute values of each part of the trip:
$|5| + |-6| + |-2| + |3| = 16$.

27. **C. 120** Add the absolute value of Milania's score to the absolute value of Chris's score:
$|-65|+|55|=65+55=120$

28. **A. 1.5** The question defines absolute error as the absolute value of the difference between the actual and approximate values: $23.5 - 25 = -1.5$, and $|-1.5| = 1.5$.

Lesson 6: Algebraic Expressions

Practice 6.1, page 129

1. $x - 7$
2. $3x^2 + x$
3. $8x - 10$
4. $-3x - 2y$
5. $\frac{10}{x} - 5$
6. $-8 + 7x$
7. $16x + x - 3y$
8. $x^2 + x^4$
9. $x^2 + \frac{4}{7}$
10. $15 + \sqrt{x}\ 6$
11. $x - (y + 13)$
12. $(x + 6)^2$
13. $17 - (2x + y)$
14. $x + \frac{24}{x}$
15. $2x - 15$
16. $4(x - y)$
17. $5(x^2 - 3)$
18. $x(11-\sqrt{100})$

19. **C. $1500 + 0.50(x - 2000)$** Let x represent the number of tickets sold. The expression $x - 2000$ is the number of tickets over 2000 sold. Multiply this expression by $0.50 to find the amount donated based on ticket sales. Then add $1500. Only choice (C) shows this sequence of operations.

20. **A. $(3x + 4y) \div (2 + z)$** The sum of 3 times a number and 4 times another number is represented by the expression $3x + 4y$. The sum of 2 and a third number is

represented by $2 + z$. The first expression is divided by the second. Parentheses are necessary to clarify the order of operations.

21. **B. $6h + 0.03s$** The correct sequence of operations shows the sum of 6 multiplied by the number of hours ($6h$) and 3% of the sales, or $0.03s$. Only choice (B) adds these two expressions.

Practice 6.2, page 131

1. $x^2 + 3x + 2$
2. $19y + 13$
3. $-3x + 54$
4. $6x^3 + 31x^2 + 4$
5. $7y + 14$
6. $3x + 8$
7. $22x - 12$
8. $2y^2 + y + 9$
9. $-5x - 17$
10. $4x - 7$
11. 31
12. 48
13. 8
14. 21
15. 72
16. 80
17. 85
18. −19
19. 9
20. 61

21. **D. $3x^2 + 4x + 1$** Simplify the expression:
$$3x^2 + 3(x - 3) + x + 10$$
$$= 3x^2 + 3x - 9 + x + 10$$
$$= 3x^2 + 4x + 1$$

22. **A. $x = 2, y = 3$** Substitute the values in the choices into the expression. Choice (A) equals −11.
$$4x^2 - 3(y + 6)$$
$$= 4(2^2) - 3(3 + 6)$$
$$= 4(4) - 3(9)$$
$$= 16 - 27$$
$$= -11.$$

23. **A. 20°** You need to convert a Fahrenheit temperature to Celsius.
$$C = \frac{5}{9}(F - 32)$$
$$C = \frac{5}{9}(68 - 32) = 20$$

Lesson 7: Expressions and Calculator Skills

Practice 7, page 133

1. 19
2. 15.9
3. 51
4. $16\frac{1}{2}$
5. 10
6. −98
7. 74
8. 146
9. 12
10. −76
11. 57
12. 36
13. −54
14. 24.8
15. 54
16. −45
17. 78
18. 108
19. 459
20. 1430

21. B. 36.2 Use the formula stated in the problem.
$$P = 2l + 2w$$
$$= 2(12.5) + 2(5.6)$$
$$= 25 + 11.2$$
$$= 36.2$$

22. D. $-2xy$ Try each expression, $x + y = -3$; $-x + y = 7$; $x - y = 3$; $xy = -10$; and $-2xy = 20$. The value of choice (D) is greatest.

23. A. 32 If $x = 2$, then $2 \div x^{-4} = 2 \div \frac{1}{2^4} = 2 \div \frac{1}{16} = 32$.

Lesson 8: Understand Polynomials

Practice 8, page 135

1. Monomial
2. Monomial
3. Binomial
4. Trinomial
5. Binomial
6. Trinomial
7. Monomial
8. Monomial
9. Monomial
10. Binomial
11. Trinomial
12. Trinomial
13. Binomial
14. Monomial
15. Binomial

16. First term: $3x^4$, second term: $-2x^2$, third term: 3
17. First term: $12a^2bc$
18. First term: $3g$, second term: $-4h$
19. First term: x^2 second term: y
20. First term: $-4a$, second term: $-3b^2$, third term: c
21. First term: 25
22. First term: x^2, second term: $3x$, third term: -7
23. First term: $\frac{3x}{8}$
24. First term: $\sqrt{25}$
25. First term: $\frac{x^2}{9}$
26. First term: $49x^2y^2z^2$
27. First term: $18y^2$, second term: $-4y^2$, third term: 8
28. First term: $3h$, second term: -4
29. First term: x^2, second term: $-x$ third term: y^2, fourth term: -2
30. First term: ab, second term: ab^2, third term: b^2, fourth term: -4
31. **B. 5** Two variables in the expression have exponents: x^3 and x^2. Add the values of the exponents: $3 + 2 = 5$
32. **B. -1** The coefficients in this expression are 1, -3, -1, and 2. Add those values:
$$1 + (-3) + (-1) + 2 = -1$$

Lesson 9: Simplify Polynomials

Practice 9, page 137

1. Like
2. Like
3. Unlike
4. Unlike
5. Like
6. Unlike
7. Unlike
8. Like
9. Unlike
10. Unlike
11. Like
12. Unlike
13. Like
14. Like
15. Unlike
16. Like
17. Unlike
18. Like
19. Unlike
20. Unlike

21. $7x^2y$
22. $4b$
23. $-6a + 3$
24. $ab^2 + 16ab + 3$
25. $-2x^2 + 7$
26. $4ab$
27. $14g + 14gh$
28. $-4g^2h^2 + 2g^2 + 2h^2 - 4$
29. $-y^2 + 9y$
30. $-7x^2 + y - 3$
31. $22y - 7$
32. $6x^2y + 5y^2 - 23$
33. $4x^3 + 7x^2 + 3x + 5$
34. $-5x^2 - 4x + 5$
35. $-3x^3 + 7x^2 + x$
36. **B. $6a^2b + 9ab$** Identify and group like terms. Then combine:
$$3a^2b + 4ab + 3a^2b + 5ab$$
$$= 3a^2b + 3a^2b + 4ab + 5ab$$
$$= 6a^2b + 9ab$$
37. **B. 3** Identify and group like terms. Then combine:
$$j^2 + k^3 - 2j^3 + 5k^3 - 2j^2$$
$$= j^2 - 2j^2 + k^3 + 5k^3 - 2j^3$$
$$= -j^2 + 6k^3 - 2j^3$$
The expression has three terms.

Lesson 10: Add and Subtract Polynomials

Practice 10.1, page 139

1. $5x + 6$
2. $23y + 6$
3. $8x^2 - 5x + 2$
4. $15a^2 + 8a$
5. $11x^2 + 2x + 3$
6. $a + 1$
7. 1
8. $4x^2 + 16x - 9$
9. $24y - 3$
10. $-4a^2 - 2a - 9$
11. $y - 2$
12. $-3x + 13$
13. $3a + 2$
14. $3x^2 + x + 2$
15. $10y + 7$

16. $2x^2 + 3x + 13$
17. $2g + 1$
18. $a^2 - 10a + 2$
19. -16
20. $20x^2 - 5x + 1$
21. **A. $x^2y + 4xy$** Identify, group, and combine like terms:
$$(2xy + 3xy^2 - 4x^2y) + (5x^2y - 3xy^2 + 2xy)$$
$$= 2xy + 2xy - 4x^2y + 5x^2y + 3xy^2 - 3xy^2$$
$$= 4xy + x^2y$$
22. **C. $2x^2 + x + 3$** Distribute the negative sign to everything in the second polynomial. Then group and combine like terms:
$$(5x^2 - 2x + 1) - (3x^2 - 3x - 2)$$
$$= 5x^2 - 2x + 1 - 3x^2 + 3x + 2$$
$$= 5x^2 - 3x^2 - 2x + 3x + 1 + 2$$
$$= 2x^2 + x + 3$$

Practice 10.2, page 141

1. $a^2 + 5a + 4b^2$
2. $-4x - xy + y + 16$
3. $yz^2 - 4z^2 + 7yz + 5$
4. $7ab - b + c - 17$
5. $-4a^4 - c^2 + 3ac + 5$
6. $22xyz + x + 6$
7. $7ef + ef^2 + f - 10$
8. $4pq - 2q + 4$
9. $4ab$
10. 0
11. $3p^6 + 4pq - p^2 - q^2$
12. $x + y + 15$
13. $2bc - b$
14. $10xyz - 8y + 16$
15. $6a + 4b + d$
16. $7pq - q$
17. $-7ab + 2b + 12$
18. 0
19. $-2p^2 + 5q^2 + 7$
20. $x^4 + z^4 - z^5$
21. $bc^2 - bc + 2c$
22. $-3xy + xz - 2xyz$
23. $c^3d^7 - c^2 + 2d$
24. $ef^2g - ef^2 - 2fg + 8$
25. **D. $3x - y$** Distribute the negative sign. Then identify, group, and combine like terms:
$$(x + y + z) - (-2x + 2y + z)$$
$$= x + y + z + 2x - 2y - z$$
$$= x + 2x + y - 2y + z - z$$
$$= 3x - y$$
26. **B. $3g^2 + 5h - 2k$** Identify, group, and combine like terms:

$$(2g^2 + 3h - 5k) + (g^2 + 2h + 3k)$$
$$= 2g^2 + g^2 + 3h + 2h - 5k + 3k$$
$$= 3g^2 + 5h - 2k$$

Lesson 11: Multiply Polynomials

Practice 11, page 143

1. $30x^2$
2. $6xy^2$
3. $28ub^2c^2$
4. $12yz$
5. $9abc$
6. $10x^2y^3z^5$
7. $4ab^2c^2$
8. $34f^3gh^7$
9. $18xyz^2 + 12z^3$
10. $42x^2 - 36xz$
11. $-15ab^2 - 55abc$
12. $-18f^3h + 24f^4gh^2$
13. $70x^7z - 50z^2$
14. $z^2 + 6xyz$
15. $72ab^2 + 64ab$
16. $18x^4 - 27xy^2$
17. $x^2 - x - 30$
18. $x^2 + 2xy + y^2$
19. $z^2 - 81$
20. $y^2z^4 - 2xyz^2 - 3x^2$
21. $9x^2 + 24x + 15$
22. $x^2 - y^2$
23. $y^6 - 6y^4 + 10y^2 - 60$
24. $a^2b^2 - ab - 12$
25. **A. $12a^5b^2c$** The coefficients of each term are 4 and 3, so the coefficient of their product is 12. The product of a^3 and a^2 is a^5. Only choice (A) contains both of these elements.
26. **D. $12p^3c^3$** You need the product of $2pc^2$ and $6p^2c$, which can be calculated as $(2pc^2)(6p^2c)$. The product of the coefficients 2 and 6 is 12, the product of p and p^2 is p^3, and the product of c and c^2 is c^3. Only choice (D) has all three of these elements.
27. **B. $12a^2b^2 - 22ab - 14$** Use FOIL: $(4ab \times 3ab) + (4ab \times [-7]) + (2 \times 3ab) + (2 \times [-7])$
   $= 12a^2b^2 - 28ab + 6ab - 14$
   $= 12a^2b^2 - 22ab - 14$

Lesson 12: Divide Polynomials

Practice 12, page 145

1. $y + 15$
2. $x + 3$
3. $x + 5$
4. $a + b$
5. $x^2 + 2x$
6. $2x^2 + 3x + 1$
7. $x + 2y$
8. $3a + 2b$
9. $\frac{3x}{2} + y$
10. $\frac{3a}{4} + \frac{5b}{4}$
11. $\frac{b + 4c}{3}$

---

12. $\frac{5a + b + 3c}{2}$
13. $6x + 2$
14. $5x + 3$
15. $8y + 2$
16. $6y + 7$
17. $2y + 2$
18. 3
19. $x - 6$
20. $y + 7$
21. $z - 5$
22. $2x + 6$
23. $x - 6$
24. $a + 3$
25. **C. $3a + 2b$** Break the fraction up into two separate fractions:
   $\frac{(21a + 14b)}{7} = \frac{21a}{7} + \frac{14b}{7}$
   Then divide each numerator by 7 to get $3a + 2b$.
26. **D. $9x + 17y + 20z$** The average of a set of terms is equal to the sum of terms divided by the number of terms in the set. In this case, that can be represented by the expression
   $\frac{(27x + 51y + 60z)}{3}$
   Break this up into three separate fractions:
   $\frac{27x}{3} + \frac{51y}{3} + \frac{60z}{3}$
   Then divide each numerator by 3 to get $9x + 17y + 20z$.
27. **A. $z - 5$** Distribute the 2 across the terms in the parentheses. Simplify the numerator. Then break the given expression into separate fractions:
   $\frac{2z^2 - 12z + 2(z + 4) - 8}{2z}$
   $= \frac{2z^2 - 12z + 2z + 8 - 8}{2z}$
   $= \frac{2z^2 - 10z}{2z}$
   $= \frac{2z^2}{2z} - \frac{10z}{2z}$
   $= z - 5$.

Algebra Basics, Expressions, and Polynomials Practice Questions, pages 146–149

1. **D. $-4x - 6$**
2. **C. $3d - 75$** Since Heidi makes 75 less than 3 times Kris's wage, multiply Kris's wage, d, by 3 and subtract 75 to get $3d - 75$.
3. **B. 1.26×10^8** Calculate: $700 \times 180,000 = 126,000,000$. Scientific notation reduces to a single digit in front of the decimal, and to do this requires moving up 8 digits, so it would be 1.26×10^8.

---

4. **D. $84x^2y$** Total desks = schools × rooms per school × desks per room. $4x \times 3y \times 7x = (4)(3)(7)(x)(x)(y) = 84x^2y$.
5. **C. $(x + 5)(x - 5)$** Multiply the monomials and polynomials in the answer choices until you find an answer choice that results in the expression in the question stem. For answer choice (C), use FOIL: $(x + 5)(x - 5) = x^2 - 5x + 5x - 25 = x^2 - 25$.
6. **D. $18x + 2y + 13$** Tom has $9x$, Adam $9x + 13$, and Dave $2y$: $9x + (9x + 13) + 2y = 18x + 2y + 13$.
7. **B. $60y$** The diagram shows multiplication problems done using a table, so the horizontal number times the vertical number will yield the value in the table. The table tells you that $a = yc$ and $b = 5 \times 3 = 15$. So $ab = 15yc$. Now look for a value for c. Since $20 = 5c$, c must equal 4, and you have $ab = (15)(4)y = 60y$. There is not enough information to deduce the value of y, but since y appears in all the answer choices, you do not need to try to find its value.
8. **D. y** The diagram shows multiplication problems done using a table, so the horizontal number times the vertical number will yield the value in the table. $d = 3y$ and $a = 4y$ so $a - d = 4y - 3y = y$.
9. **A. $7a^2c^2 + 35bc^2 + 49c^4$** Multiply each term by $7c^2$: $7c^2(a^2) + 7c^2(5b) + 7c^2(7c^2) = 7a^2c^2 + 35bc^2 + 49c^4$
10. **D. $\$\frac{150}{x}$** To figure out the individual pie cost, divide $900 by the number of pies, $6x$: $\frac{900}{6x} = \frac{150}{x}$.
11. **A. $\frac{a - 4}{a + 4}$** Cancel out $6b$ in the numerator and $2(3b)$ (which equals $6b$) in the denominator. Then, one $(a - 4)$ will cancel, leaving $\frac{a - 4}{a + 4}$.
12. **C. $\frac{xyz}{2}$** To find the total cost, multiply ounces per guest by the number of guests by the cost per ounce. Since $\$z$ is the cost per pound, the result needs to be divided by 16. $\frac{(x)(8y)(z)}{16} = xyz\left(\frac{8}{16}\right) = \frac{xyz}{2}$.
13. **B. -26** Substituting -2 for x and 5 for y leads to $6(-2 - 5) - 8(-2) = 6(-7) - (-16) = -42 + 16 = -26$.

14. A. −88 Substituting 2 for x, 4 for y, and 3 for z leads to a product of $[2^2 + 6(3)] \times [2(4) - 4(3)] = (4 + 18) \times (8 - 12) = 22 \times -4 = -88$.

15. $1\frac{5}{11}$ Calculate: $\frac{4^3 - [3(12 + 2^2)]}{6 + 5(4) - 15} =$

$\frac{64 - [3(12 + 4)]}{6 + 5(4) - 15} = \frac{64 - [3(16)]}{6 + 20 - 15} =$

$\frac{64 - 48}{6 + 20 - 15} = \frac{16}{11} = 1\frac{5}{11}$

16. D. $30kp + 20p^2 + 45hp$ Because $5p$ is paid to every member, each number of team members would be multiplied by $5p$, and the team totals would be added: $5p(6k) + 5p(4p) + 5p(9h) = 30kp + 20p^2 + 45hp$

17. C. $-x + 9y - 10xy$ Solve: $7x - [(5y)2x - 9y + 8x] = 7x - [10xy - 9y + 8x] = 7x - 10xy + 9y - 8x = -x - 10xy + 9y$.

18. A. $20cd - 75c$ Alyshia has $4d - 15$ DVDs. Multiply $5c$ by Alyshia's DVD total: $(4d - 15)$: $5c(4d - 15) = 5c(4d) - (5c)(15) = 20cd - 75c$

19. A. $8x^2 + 7xy^3 - 12x - 1$ Factor out $7x^2$: $\frac{56x^4 + 49x^3y^3 - 84x^3 - 7x^2}{7x^2}$

$= \frac{(7x^2)(8x^2 + 7xy^3 - 12x - 1)}{7x^2}$

$= 8x^2 + 7xy^3 - 12x - 1$

20. B. $16d - 4a$ The amount $80d$ is needed. Anything earned at the ball will be subtracted, and $64d$ and $4a$ were both earned: $80d - 64d - 4a = 16d - 4a$ left to raise.

21. A. $\frac{x^4}{2y^2} + 2x^2y^2 - \frac{4x}{y^2} - \frac{1}{2}$ Split the fraction: $\frac{x^4 + 4x^2y^4 - 8x - y^2}{2y^2}$

$= \frac{x^4}{2y^2} + \frac{4x^2y^4}{2y^2} - \frac{8x}{2y^2} - \frac{y^2}{2y^2}$

$= \frac{x^4}{2y^2} + 2x^2y^2 - \frac{4x}{y^2} - \frac{1}{2}$

22. B. $\frac{6k + 4f}{r} + 3$ The total of the three groups $(12k + 8f + 6r)$ should be divided by the number of squads, $2r$:

$\frac{2k + 8f + 6r}{2r} = \frac{12k}{2r} + \frac{8f}{2r} + \frac{6r}{2r}$

$= \frac{6k}{r} + \frac{4f}{r} + 3$

$= \frac{6k + 4f}{r} + 3$

23. A. $4x + 2$ Substitute 2 for q and 4 for r in the expression: $\frac{4^2x^2 + 2^3x}{2^2x} = \frac{16x^2 + 8x}{4x} = 4x + 2$.

24. C. $-2x^4 + 5xy^4 - \frac{y^2}{x^2}$ Split the fractions and then simplify by factoring out $11x^2$:

$\frac{11x^2(4x^4 + 5xy^4 + 8)}{11x^2} - \frac{11y^2}{11x^2} - 6x^4 - 8$

$= 4x^4 + 5xy^4 + 8 - \frac{y^2}{x^2} - 6x^4 - 8$

$= -2x^4 + 5xy^4 - \frac{y^2}{x^2}$

25. A. $5xy^3 - 16x^2y^2 + 42x^2y$ Distribute:

$(6x^2 + 5xy^2)(y) - (4xy - 9x)(4xy)$

$= 6x^2(y) + 5xy^2(y) - (4xy(4xy) - 9x(4xy))$

$= 6x^2y + 5xy^3 - (16x^2y^2 - 36x^2y)$

$= 42x^2y + 5xy^3 - 16x^2y^2$

26. D. $20x^2 - 39x + 18$ The question states that the average salary of the non-managerial employees is $(5x - 6)$. That means that

$5x - 6 = \frac{\text{Total of non} - \text{managers' salaries}}{\text{Number of non} - \text{managers}}$

The question also states that the number of non-managers in the office is $4x - 3$. So,

$5x - 6 = \frac{\text{Total of non} - \text{managers' salaries}}{4x - 3}$

Then $(5x - 6)(4x - 3) = total\ of\ non - managers' salaries = 20x^2 - 39x + 18$

27. B. 51 Factor before substituting. $\frac{5xy + 63y^2}{9y} = \frac{(9y)(5x + 7y)}{9y} = (5x + 7y)$

Substitute 6 for x and 3 for y: $5(6) + 7(3) = 30 + 21 = 51$.

28. D. $x - 1$ Split the fraction: $\frac{x(x^2 + 3) - 2x(x^2 + 3) - (x^2 + 3)}{x^2 + 3}$

$= \frac{3x(x^2 + 3)}{x^2 + 3} - \frac{2x(x^2 + 3)}{x^2 + 3} - \frac{x^2 + 3}{x^2 + 3}$

$= 3x - 2x - 1 = x - 1$.

29. D. $3h^2 + 4hk - 51h - 68k$ Add the populations of both countries $(3h + 4k)$ and multiply by the rice consumption: $(h - 17)$:

$(3h + 4k)(h - 17)$

$= (3h)(h) + (3h)(-17) + (4k)(h) + (4k)(-17)$

$= 3h^2 - 51h + 4hk - 68k$.

30. A. $2x^2 + 2y^2 - xy$ Split the fraction:

$\frac{4x^2(x+y)}{(x+y)} - \frac{2(x+y)^2(x-y)}{(x+y)} - \frac{xy(x+y)}{(x+y)}$

$= 4x^2 - 2(x + y)(x - y) - xy$

$= 4x^2 - 2(x^2 - y^2) - xy$

$= 2x^2 + 2y^2 - xy$

31. A. 2 The diagram shows multiplication problems done using a table, so the horizontal number times the vertical number will yield the value in the table. To figure out a, first look at the top right term. Since $5 \times a = ab$, $b = 5$. Another term with only a and b is the bottom middle, $4 \times ab = 40$. Substituting 5 for b shows that $20a = 40$, so $a = 2$.

32. B. 40 The table tells you that $a^2 \times c = 8b$. Use the table to find a value for b. Since the top right cell of the table shows that $5 \times a = ab$, b must equal 5, and $8b = 40$.

Equations, Inequalities, and Functions

Lesson 1: Equations

Practice 1.1, page 151

1. $x = 9$
2. $m = 28$
3. $y = -1$
4. $x = -64$
5. $a = 125$
6. $y = -13$
7. $x = 27$
8. $c = 7$
9. $x = -4$
10. $b = -7$
11. $x = 31$
12. $s = -8$
13. $x = 108$
14. $t = 39$
15. $x = 48$
16. $y = -3$
17. $r = 110$
18. $x = 5$
19. $y = -9$
20. $d = -25$
21. $x = 4$
22. $x = -6$
23. $h = 26$
24. $x = 66$
25. $m = -10$
26. $y = 9$
27. $w = -28$
28. $y = 72$

29. C. $x + 36 = 77$ Erin's hours (x) plus Kayla's hours (36) = 77 hours.

30. C. $2y = 38$ Erin worked twice as many hours as Kayla ($2y$), and Erin worked 38 hours, so $2y = 38$.

31. C. 128 A number (x) divided by 4 is 32. Solve for x: $\frac{x}{4} = 32$, $x = 128$.

32. D. $12x = -60$ Try -5 for x in each equation. Only choice (D) is true when -5 is substituted for x.

$12x = -60$

$12(-5) = -60$

$-60 = -60$

33. B. $\$572.18 - c = \$434.68$ When you subtract the check from the amount in the checking account, the result will be the current balance.

Practice 1.2, page 153

1. $x = 50$
2. $y = -2$
3. $m = 2$
4. $x = -4$
5. $y = 6$
6. $z = 2$
7. $m = 3$
8. $x = 4$
9. $p = 7$
10. $s = -2$
11. $x = 6$
12. $r = -5$
13. $y = 11$
14. $b = 4$
15. $x = -1$
16. $h = 20$
17. $x = 9$
18. $z = 4$
19. $b = 3$
20. $n = 7$

21. D. $3x + 9 = 6x - 15$ "Three times a number" is $3x$ and "increased by 9" means to add 9. "Six times the number" is $6x$, and "15 less" means to subtract 15. The word "is" shows that the two expressions should be connected by the = symbol.

22. **D. 375** Solve:
$$3x + x = 500$$
$$4x = 500$$
$$x = 125$$
The variable x is the number of cards that Travis has. Eric has $3x$, or 3×125, which equals 375.

23. **A.** $4x - 7 = \frac{x}{3} + 15$ Remember that differences and quotients must be written in the order stated in the problem. The difference of four times a number and 7 is $4x - 7$. The quotient of the number and 3 plus 15 is $\frac{x}{3} + 15$.

24. **A. $54** Solve:
$$x + (2x + 12) = \$174$$
$$3x + 12 = \$174$$
$$3x = \$162$$
$$x = \$54$$

Lesson 2: Equation Word Problems

Practice 2, page 155

1. **1800 sq. ft.** Let the square footage of the first house be h, and the second house's square footage will then be $(2h - 1000)$. Then write an equation that combines both houses. The equation is $h + (2h - 1000) = 4400$. Solve for h.

2. **10 dimes** Let x equal the number of dimes in Julia's pocket. The equation is $0.10x + 0.25(24 - x) = 4.50$.

3. **24 games** Let w represent the number of wins, and then the number of losses will be half of w. Write an equation:
$$w + \frac{1}{2}w = 36$$
$$1\frac{1}{2}w = 36$$
$$\frac{3}{2}w = 36$$
$$3w = 72$$
$$w = 24$$
Alternatively, you could solve the equation by calculating the number of losses. Let l = losses. Wins will be twice that much. Then the equation would read $l + 2l = 36$. Once you find l, remember to multiply it by two to find the number of wins.

4. **54** The equation is $x + (x + 2) + (x + 4) + (x + 6) = 4x + 12 = 212$. Solve for $x + 4$, the third number.

5. **8 shirts** Let s represent the number of shirts Brenda bought, and then the number of pants she

bought will be equal to $13 - s$. Then, write an equation using the dollar amount she spent: $\$6(13 - s) + \$4s = \$62$. Solve for s.

6. **59** Let x equal the smallest of the three consecutive numbers. Then: $x + (x + 1) + (x + 2) = 180$. Solve for x.

7. **$1100** Andrew spends twice as much on rent, which means he spends half as much as his rent on food. The equation is $r + \frac{1}{2}r = \$1650$. Solve for r.

8. **28 hours** Let h represent the time he spends helping customers, and then stocking shelves will be one-fourth of h. Write an equation:
$$h + \frac{1}{4}h = 35$$
$$1\frac{1}{4}h = 35$$
$$\frac{5}{4}h = 35$$
$$5h = 140$$
$$h = 28$$

9. **C. 84** Let w = Wiley's points, $w + 10$ = Sylvia's points, and $w - 6$ = Greg's points. Write and solve an equation:
$$w + w + 10 + w - 6 = 226$$
$$3w + 4 = 226$$
$$3w = 222$$
$$w = 74$$
Wiley scored 74 points, so Sylvia scored $74 + 10 = 84$ points.

10. **B. $12** Let a = the price of an adult's ticket and $a - \$6$ = the price of a child's ticket. The question states that the cost of 2 adults' tickets and 4 children's tickets is $48. Write and solve an equation:
$$2a + 4(a - 6) = 48$$
$$2a + 4a - 24 = 48$$
$$6a - 24 = 48$$
$$6a = 72$$
$$a = 12$$

11. **B. 6** You know that in 12 years, Jenny will be twice as old as Tina. Therefore, if you multiply Tina's age in 12 years by 2, it will equal Jenny's age in 12 years. Write and solve an equation:
$$4x + 12 = 2(x + 12)$$
$$4x + 12 = 2x + 24$$
$$2x = 12$$
$$x = 6$$

Lesson 3: Inequalities

Practice 3, page 157

1. $x > 4$
2. $x > 7$
3. $x \le -3$
4. $x \le 36$
5. $x < -1$
6. $x \ge 5$
7. $x > -8$
8. $x > 4$
9. $x < -7$
10. $x < 2$
11. $x \ge 3$
12. $x < 6$
13. $x \ge 2$
14. $x > -10$
15. $x \le 3$
16. $x < 21$
17. $x \ge -1$
18. $x < 3$
19. $x < 7$
20. $x \le 3$
21. $-2 \le x \le 2$
22. $-20 < x < 6$
23. $6 < x < 16$
24. $4 \le x \le 9$

25. **A.** $s \le 16$ The perimeter must be less than or equal to 64, so solve the inequality: $4s \le 64$, which leads to $s \le 16$.

26. **D.**

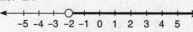

Solve the inequality:
$$-4x + 3 < -3x + 5$$
$$-x < 2$$
$$x > -2$$
To graph the solution $x > -2$, place an open circle at -2, because -2 is not included in the solution. Then, extend the line to the right to include all values greater than -2.

Lesson 4: Quadratic Equations

Practice 4, page 159

1. $x^2 + 6x + 8$
2. $x^2 + 2x - 15$
3. $x^2 + 3x - 4$
4. $x^2 - 9x + 18$
5. $x^2 + 6x - 16$
6. $2x^2 - 3x - 2$
7. $x^2 - 14x + 45$
8. $3x^2 + x - 2$
9. $x^2 + 5x - 14$
10. $3x^2 + 14x + 16$
11. $x^2 - x - 30$
12. $x^2 - 13x + 30$
13. $4x^2 + 6x + 2$
14. $x^2 + 5x - 36$
15. $x^2 - 10x + 25$

For questions 16–30, the order of the factors does not matter: $(2x - 1)(x + 3) = (x + 3)(2x - 1)$

16. $(x + 1)(x + 3)$
17. $(x - 1)(x + 5)$
18. $(x + 2)(x + 6)$
19. $(x - 3)(x + 2)$
20. $(x - 2)(x + 7)$
21. $(x - 4)(x + 3)$
22. $(x - 5)(x + 7)$
23. $(x - 6)(x - 6)$
24. $(x - 7)(x + 1)$
25. $(x - 4)(x + 8)$
26. $(2x - 1)(x + 3)$
27. $(2x - 10)(x + 1)$ or $(2x + 2)(x - 5)$ or $(2)(x - 5)(x + 1)$
28. $(x - 5)(x + 10)$
29. $(2x - 1)(2x + 3)$
30. $(x - 7)(x + 8)$

31. **A. –4 and 5** Get 0 on one side of the equation: $x^2 - x - 20 = 0$. Then, factor: $(x + 4)(x - 5) = 0$. Determine which values of x will make each factor equal to 0. The solutions 5 and –4 will make the equation true.

32. **D. $2x^2 + 2x - 24 = 0$** Substitute –4 for x in the answer choices. Only choice (D) works.
$2(-4)^2 + 2(-4) - 24$
$= 2(16) + (-8) - 24$
$= 32 - 32 = 0$

33. **B. 6** Substitute the answer choices for x in the equation. Only choice (B) makes the equation true: $2(6)^2 - 7(6) - 30 = 2(36) - 42 - 30 = 72 - 72 = 0$. You can also factor the original equation: $(x - 6)(2x + 5)$, so $x = 6$ or $x = -\frac{5}{2}$.

34. **B. $x - 10$** You know that length × width = area. You need to factor the expression $2x^2 - 27x + 70$, and you know that one of the factors is the length, $(2x - 7)$. So $2x^2 - 27x + 70 = (2x - 7)(x - 10)$. The width is $(x - 10)$.

Lesson 5: Algebra Problem Solving

Practice 5, page 161

1. **C. 24** Take each answer choice and divide it by 2. Then, check to see if the resulting number is 12 less than the answer choice. For example, choice (A): 12: 12 ÷ 2 = 6. And 6 is not 12 less than 12. Thus, choice (A) is incorrect. Only choice (C) works: 24 ÷ 2 = 24 – 12.

2. **C. $200** Try each number. Choice (A) says Brenda raised $150. If she did, Sandra would have raised $450, and Matt would have raised $100. Also, the three of them together would have raised $150 + $450 + $100 ≠ $950. Since those numbers don't total to $950, choice (A) must be incorrect. Only choice (C) works: $200 + $600 + $150 = $950.

3. **C. 5** The answer choices represent possible weights for the first package. Try choice (A): if the first package weighs 2, the second package would weigh 1, and the third package would weigh 3. Add them together to see if they total 15: 2 + 1 + 3 ≠ 15. So choice (A) is incorrect. Only choice (C) works: 5 + 2.5 + 7.5 = 15.

4. **B. 82** The answer choices represent possible scores for the first test. If choice (A) 76 is Hannah's score on the first test, then her score on the second test would be 82, and 76 + 82 ≠ 170. Only choice (B) works: 82 + 88 = 170.

5. **B. 10** The answer choices represent how old Nelson might have been six years ago. If choice (A) were correct, then Nelson would have been 5 six years ago, and he would be 11 now. Also, six years ago Maria would have been 1 year old, and today she would be 7. Now, the question is, is Nelson's current age twice Maria's age? 11 ≠ 2 × 7. So choice (A) is incorrect. Choice (B) does work: if Nelson was 10 six years ago, then Maria would have been 2. Today Nelson would be 16 and Maria would be 8, and 16 is two times 8.

6. **A. –3** To solve by guessing, plug each answer choice into the equation. Try choice (A):
$2(-3)^2 + (-3) - 15 = 0$.
$2(9) - 18 = 0$.
$18 - 18 = 0$.

7. **B. 6** If the group purchased 5 children's passes, as choice (A) suggests, then they would have purchased 15 adults' passes. Multiply each amount by the cost of that type of ticket, to see if the total equals $440: (5 × $15) + (15 × $25) = $450. Thus, choice (A) is incorrect. Choice (B) works: (6 × $15) + (14 × $25) = $440.

8. **B. 20** The answer choices represent possible values for the width. If choice (A) were correct, then the width would be 15 and the length would be 30. Add to find out whether choice (A) would give the value of 120 for the perimeter: 15 + 15 + 30 + 30 = 90. Thus, choice (A) is incorrect. Choice (B) works: 20 + 20 + 40 + 40 = 120.

Lesson 6: The Coordinate Plane

Practice 6, page 163

1. (–4, 5)
2. (3, 6)
3. (0, –3)
4. (6, –7)
5. (–5, 0)
6. (–6, –4)
7. (2, 0)
8. (7, –2)

9.

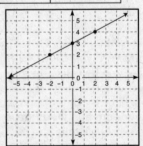

10.

11. **D. (–1, 0)** Plot each point in the answer choices. Only choice (D) lies on the line that passes through points A and B.

12. **A. (–3, –2)** Find the two points discussed in the problem. Then locate the third corner of the triangle, and find the coordinates of the corner. The missing corner is 3 spaces to the left of the origin and 2 spaces down: (–3, –2).

Lesson 7: Graphing a Line

Practice 7, page 165

1.

If $x =$	Then $y =$
–2	2
0	3
2	4

2.

If $x =$	then $y =$
−1	**2**
0	**−1**
1	**−4**

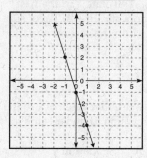

3.

If $x =$	then $y =$
1	**1**
2	**0**
3	**−1**

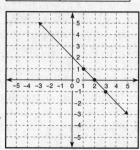

4.

If $x =$	then $y =$
0	**3**
1	**1**
2	**−1**

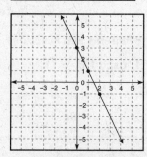

5. **C. point T and (0, 0)** Try the coordinates for points S and T in the equation. Both lie on the graph of the equation. Check the remaining points in the answer choices. Only (0,0) will make the equation $y = \frac{1}{4}x$ true.

6. **D. $y = -4x - 2$** Choose two points on line P. The easiest points to work with are the ones

represented by dots: (−1,2) and (0,−2). Try one of those points in the equations. If the point works in the equation, try the other point as well. (You must try both because any number of lines may pass through a single point. To establish that the equation represents line P, it must fit both points.) Both points work only in choice (D): $y = -4x - 2$.

7. **B. $2x + 3y = 9$** Try the coordinates (−3, 5) in each equation. Only choice (B) is true.
$$2x + 3y = 9$$
$$2(-3) + 3(5) = 9$$
$$-6 + 15 = 9$$
$$9 = 9$$

Lesson 8: Slope of a Line

Practice 8, page 167

1. 1
2. −2
3. 0
4. $\frac{3}{4}$
5. $-\frac{1}{2}$
6. 0
7. $-\frac{1}{3}$
8. 2
9. −3

10. **A. line A** Of the answer choices, only line A has a negative slope, so it must be the correct answer. Line A moves down 1 space each time it goes 3 spaces to the right, a ratio of −1 to 3 or $-\frac{1}{3}$.

11. **B. −2** You have more information than you need. Choose any two points and use the slope formula to solve for the slope. For example, if you choose points (0, 4) and (1, 2), your calculations would be: $\frac{2-4}{1-0} = -\frac{2}{1} = -2$.

12. **C. (2, 3)** The best way to solve the problem is probably to make a quick sketch. Because the line has a slope of 3, start at point (1, 0) and count 3 spaces up and 1 space to the right. You are now at point (2, 3), which is choice (C). You can check your work using the slope formula.

Lesson 9: Slope and Equations

Practice 9, page 169

1. $y = -4x + 2$
$x = 1; y = -2; m = -4$
$-2 = -4(1) + b$
$b = 2$

2. $y = 2x - 2$
$x = -1; y = -4; m = 2$
$-4 = 2(-1) + b$
$b = -2$

3. $y = -\frac{1}{3}x + \frac{2}{3}$
$x = -4; y = 2; m = -\frac{1}{3}$
$2 = -\frac{1}{3}(-4) + b$
$b = \frac{2}{3}$

4. $y - 1 = 3(x - 2)$
$x_1 = 2; y_1 = 1; m = 3$

5. $y = -\frac{1}{3}(x - 2)$
$x_1 = 2; y_1 = 0; m = -\frac{1}{3}$

6. $y + 2 = x - 1$
$x_1 = 1; y_1 = -2; m = 1$

7. $y = -\frac{1}{3}x + \frac{4}{3}$
First, find the slope:
$$m = \frac{3-1}{-5-1} = -\frac{1}{3}$$
Choose either ordered pair to substitute for x and y:
$m = -\frac{1}{3}; x = 1; y = 1$
Follow the steps to find the equation of a line in the slope-intercept form.
$1 = -\frac{1}{3}(1) + b$
$b = \frac{4}{3}$

8. $y = 4x + 12$
$n = \frac{4-0}{-2-(-3)} = 4$
$0 = 4(-3) + b$
$b = 12$

9. $y = \frac{1}{2}x - \frac{5}{2}$
$$m = \frac{1-(-4)}{7-(-3)} = \frac{1}{2}$$
$1 = \frac{1}{2}(7) + b$
$b = -\frac{5}{2}$

10. **C. $y = -x - 1$** Plug both points into the slope formula.
$m = \frac{-3-0}{2-(-1)} = -1$.
Then, use m and one of the points to solve for b.
$0 = -1(-1) + b$
$b = -1$

11. **B. $y = 4$** Plug both points into the slope formula. $m = \frac{4-4}{1-(-3)} = 0$. Then, use m and one of the points to solve for b.
$4 = -3(0) + b$
$b = 4$
Because this line has a slope of zero, there is no x term in the equation. Rather, y is always equal to 4, no matter what the value of x is.

12. **D. $y = \frac{1}{2}x - 1$** To answer this question, simplify the equation in the question to find an

answer that matches:
$$y - 2 = \frac{1}{2}(x - 6)$$
$$y - 2 = \frac{1}{2}x - 3$$
$$y = \frac{1}{2}x - 1$$

13. **B.** $y = -x - 4$ Because the line on the graph slopes down from left to right, its slope is negative, so you can eliminate choices (A) and (C) immediately. Then note that the line crosses the y-axis at $(0, -4)$, so the y-intercept is -4. Therefore, the correct choice is (B).

Lesson 10: Systems of Linear Equations

Practice 10, page 171

1. **(7, 6)**

   $y = 3x - 15$

x	y
0	−15
5	0

   $x + y = 13$

x	y
0	13
13	0

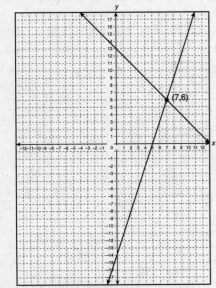

2. **(−3, 11)**

   $4x + 2y = 10$

x	y
0	5
$\frac{5}{2}$	0

   $y = -5x - 4$

x	y
0	−4
$-\frac{4}{5}$	0

3. **(3, −1)**

   Isolate y:
   $$-y = -7x + 22$$
   $$y = 7x - 22$$
   Substitute:
   $$4x + 2(7x - 22) = 10$$
   $$4x + 14x - 44 = 10$$
   $$18x = 54$$
   $$x = 3$$
   Substitute back:
   $$y = 7(3) - 22$$
   $$y = -1$$

4. **(7, 2)**

   Isolate y:
   $$y = 9 - x$$
   Substitute:
   $$2x - 3(9 - x) = 8$$
   $$2x - 27 + 3x = 8$$
   $$5x = 35$$
   $$x = 7$$
   Substitute back:
   $$y = 9 - 7$$
   $$y = 2$$

5. **(−4, 3)**

   y is already isolated.
   $$y = 3x + 15$$
   Substitute:
   $$5x - 2(3x + 15) = -26$$
   $$5x - 6x - 30 = -26$$
   $$-x = 4$$
   $$x = -4$$
   Substitute back:
   $$y = 3(-4) + 15$$
   $$y = 3$$

6. **$(\frac{1}{2}, 6)$**

   y is already isolated.
   $$y = 12x$$
   Substitute:
   $$10x - (12x) = -1$$

$$-2x = -1$$
$$x = \frac{1}{2}$$
Substitute back:
$$y = 12\left(\frac{1}{2}\right)$$
$$y = 6$$

7. **A. (2, −1)** Isolate x in the first equation. $x = 2y + 4$. Then, substitute into the second equation to find a value for y.
   $$6y + 5(2y + 4) = 4$$
   $$16y + 20 = 4$$
   $$y = -1$$
   Finally, use that value of y in the first equation to find a value for x.
   $$x = 2(-1) + 4 = 2$$

8. **C. (0,0)** The equation $y = x$ represents a line whose x-coordinate is always equal to the y-coordinate. The equation $y = -x$ represents a line whose y-coordinate is always equal to the negative of the x-coordinate. Neither line has a b term in its equation, so both lines have a y-intercept of zero, meaning that they both cross the y-axis at (0,0).

9. **C. $\left(-\frac{9}{2}, -2\right)$** Since the only possible y-value for the line $y = -2$ is −2, simply substitute that value for y in the equation $3y = 2x + 3$ to find the intersection:
   $$3(-2) = 2x + 3$$
   $$-9 = 2x$$
   $$x = -\frac{9}{2}$$

10. **C.** $y = -4x + 2$ Two different lines cannot intersect if they are parallel. Lines are parallel if they have the same slope. Only choice (C) does not have a slope of 4, so this is the correct choice.

Lesson 11: Patterns and Functions

Practice 11, page 173

1. 0
2. 41
3. 2
4. 40
5. 23
6. −4
7. 31.25
8. −13
9. 32
10. −5

11. **B. 49** To highlight the pattern, it might be useful to make a table or list:

1st	2nd	3rd	4th
1 block	3 blocks	5 blocks	7 blocks

   The number of blocks in each construction equals $2n - 1$, where n is the number in the sequence. The 25th construction would require $2(25) - 1 = 49$ blocks.

12. **C. 16** Each term is 6 greater than the term before it. The next (that is, the fifth) term in the sequence is 10, and the sixth term is 16.

13. **B. $c = \$5.00 - \$0.25\ (n - 1)$** The original price per scarf (\$5) is reduced by 25 cents starting with the second scarf.

14. **B. 1, 5, 9, 13, 17 . . .** Try the numbers 1, 2, and 3 for x in the function. This will result in the first three terms of the pattern: 1, 5, and 9. Only choice (B) contains these three terms.

Lesson 12: Function Applications

Practice 12, page 175

1. a. \$99
   b. \$265
2. a. 5.5 hours
   b. 4.25 hours
3. a. Plan A
   b. Plan B
4. **B. \$29.50** Use the functions for the two jobs, substituting 30 hours for h:
   Job 1: $P = \$9.75h = \$9.75(30) = \$292.50$
   Job 2: $P = \$70 + \$8.40h = \$70 + \$8.40(30) = \$70 + \$252 = \$322$
   Subtract: $\$322 - \$292.50 = \$29.50$
5. **D. Alicia will earn the most at Job 2.** Use the functions to find Alicia's wages at all three jobs based on 40 hours:
   Job 1: $P = \$9.75h = \$9.75(40) = \$390$
   Job 2: $P = \$70 + \$8.40h = \$70 + \$8.40(40) = \$70 + \$336 = \$406$
   Job 3: $\$380 \times \frac{h}{38} = \$380 \times \frac{40}{38} = \$10 \times 40 = \$400$
   Compare the three results. Alicia will earn the most at Job 2.
6. **B. \$19,400** Use the function to calculate the profit:
   $P = \$95,000 - \$5,400d$
   $P = \$95,000 - \$5,400(14)$
   $P = \$95,000 - \$75,600$
   $P = \$19,400$

Equations, Inequalities, and Functions Practice Questions, pages 176–179

1. **D. $-4x - 6$** Use the order of operations: $6 - 4\ (x + 3) = 6 - 4x - 12 = -4x - 6$

2. **A. -3**
   $3 + 4x = x - 6$
   $3x = -9$
   $x = -3$
3. **B. $y = -4x + 6$** Choices (A) and (B) are the only two choices with the correct slope. Plug in $x = 1$ and $y = 2$ into both equations; only choice (B) works.
4. **C. $4x - y = -7$** Try $x = -2$ and $y = -1$ in each equation. Only choice (C) is true: $4(-2) - (-1) = -8 + 1 = -7$
5. **C. \$510** Let $t =$ Tom's earnings and $2t - \$150 =$ Jan's earnings.
   $2t - \$150 + t = \$1380$
   $3t - \$150 = \$1380$
   $3t = \$1530$
   $t = \$510$
6. **D. D** The coordinates of D are $(-3, -2)$, which make the equation $y = -x - 5$ true.
   $y = -x - 5$
   $-2 = -(-3) - 5$
   $-2 = 3 - 5$
   $-2 = -2$
7. **C. $\frac{1}{3}$** Count the rise and run from C to B. The line moves up 3 spaces as it moves 9 to the right: $\frac{3}{9} = \frac{1}{3}$.
8. **A. $s \geq \$17,500$** Samuel's earnings can be represented by the expression $\$350 + 0.1s$, where s represents total sales. Since Samuel needs to earn at least \$2,100, this expression must be greater than or equal to \$2,100. Solve:
   $\$350 + 0.1s \geq \$2,100$
   $0.1s \geq \$1,750$
   $s \geq \$17,500$
9. **B. \$5.35** Substitute 24 for n and solve:
   $F = \$3.95 + \$0.10(24 - 10)$
   $F = \$3.95 + \$0.10(14)$
   $F = \$3.95 + \$1.40$
   $F = \$5.35$
10. **D. 29** Let $x =$ the first number. The remaining numbers are $x + 2$, $x + 4$, and $x + 6$. Solve:
    $x + (x + 2) + (x + 4) + (x + 6) = 104$
    $4x + 12 = 104$
    $4x = 92$
    $x = 23$
    The numbers are 23, 25, 27, and 29. The problem asks for the largest of these numbers.
11. **C. 3^6** Calculate: $3 \times 3 \times 3 \times 3 \times 3 \times 3 = 729$. The other expressions are less than 400. You could also use estimation to help with this problem. For

example, to evaluate choice (A), remember that $7 \times 7 = 49$. Then, since 49 is almost 50, round up to make the calculation easier: $7 \times 50 = 350$. So $7^3 < 350$, and it is definitely less than 400.

12. **B. $5x - 4 = 8 + 2 + 3x$** Translate each part of the problem to numbers and symbols and then connect the parts with the = symbol.

13. **B. 1** To find the slope of a line that crosses two points, find the difference between the y-coordinates and then divide by the difference in the x-coordinates: $\frac{6 - 4}{4 - 2} = \frac{2}{2} = 1$.

14. **B. 31** From 1 to 7, there is a difference of 6. From 7 to 14, there is a difference of 7. From 14 to 22, there is a difference of 8. To find the next term, add 9 to 22: $22 + 9 = 31$.

15. **C. 0** To find the y-intercept of a line when given the slope and a point, plug the x- and y-coordinates and the slope into the point-slope form, $y = mx + b$. This results in $2 = 2(1) + b$. Solve for b.

16. **(−2, 1)**

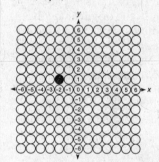

Create tables for each linear equation to find values of y when substituting values for x:

$y = x + 3$

x	y
0	3
−3	0

$y = -2x - 3$

x	y
0	−3
$-\frac{3}{2}$	0

Graph the two lines. They intersect at point (−2,1).

17. **A. $-7x - (8 + y)$** The word *product* indicates multiplication, and the word *sum* indicates addition. Choice (B) means that y is added, rather than subtracted, from the product (due to order of operations), so it is incorrect.

18. **C. 8 and –3** Either solve by factoring or by trying each option in the equation. The correct factorization is as follows:
$x^2 - 5x - 24 = 0$
$(x - 8)(x + 3) = 0$
$x = 8$ or $x = -3$

19. **B. 4** Cynthia's age right now is six times Rebecca's, or $6r$. Thus, in six years, Cynthia will be $6r + 6$ years old, and Rebecca will be $r + 6$ years old. Write an equation and solve for r:
$6r + 6 = 3(r + 6)$

20. **B. $y = 2x - 3$** Try the given points in the equations in the answer options. Only choice (B) works with both points.

21. **B.**
$-2(x - 6) > 8$
$-2x + 12 > 8$
$-2x > -4$
$x < 2$

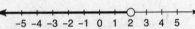

Remember to reverse the inequality symbol when you divide both sides by a negative number.

22. **B. (–5, 1)** Point L is 5 spaces to the left of the origin along the x-axis and 1 space above the origin along the y-axis.

23. **D. $\frac{3}{2}$** The coordinates of point L are (–5, 1), and the coordinates of point M are (–3, 4). Find the slope by finding the difference of the y-coordinates, and divide by the difference of the x-coordinates: $\frac{1-4}{-5-(-3)} = \frac{-3}{-2} = \frac{3}{2}$.

24. **C. $18** Let s = Sam's gift. Then:
Daniel's gift = s.
Celia's gift = $s + 12$ (since Sam and Daniel gave the same amount).
Bob's gift = $0.5(s + 12)$ (that is, one-half of Celia's gift).
Add those four quantities together and set the sum total to $81:
$s + s + (s + 12) + .5(s + 12) = 81$
$3.5s + 18 = 81$
$3.5s = 63$
$s = 18$

25. **A. $x \leq 3$** Remember to reverse the inequality sign when dividing by a negative number:
$-7x - 4 \geq x - 28$
$-8x \geq -24$
$x \leq 3$

26. **C. $y = x + 2$** Start by finding the slope: $\frac{3-2}{1-0} = 1$. Now you know

that the equation will be $y = x + b$, and you can eliminate choices (A) and (B). And in this case, no calculations are required to find the y-intercept, because one of the points given in the question is (0, 2)—the point where the line crosses the y-axis.

27. **B. 8,652** Let x = votes for the leading candidate and p = votes for Perez. Write an equation:
$p = \frac{1}{3}x + 5,512$.
Additionally, you can say that $p + x = 18,072$, or $p = 18,072 - x$
Substitute for p:
$18,072 - x = \frac{1}{3}x + 5,512$
$12,560 = \frac{4}{3}x$
$x = 9420$
That number represents the number of votes the opposing candidate received. Now, substitute that value back into the simpler of the two original equations:
$p + 9,420 = 18,072$
$p = 8,652$

28. **B. $x = -2$** Simplify:
$-4(x + 2) - 10 = 5x$
$-4x - 8 - 10 = 5x$
$-4x - 18 = 5x$
$-18 = 9x$
$-2 = x$

29. **D. $5x + $10(35 - x) = 240** The total value of the $5 bills is $5x. Since there are 35 bills, the number of $10 bills must be $35 - x$. The value of the $10 bills is $10(35 - x). The sum of the value of the $5 bills plus the value of the $10 bills is $240.

30. **C. 75** Let x = the first number in the sequence. Then write an equation:
$x + (x + 1) + (x + 2) + (x + 3) + (x + 4) = 370$
$5x + 10 = 370$
$x = 72$
The first number in the sequence is 72. That means the fourth number (which equals $x + 3$) is 75.

31. **4** Substitute and solve: $E = \frac{9(8)}{18} = 4$.

32. **(–1, 1)** The given points lie in a vertical line. Since the distance between the points is 8 spaces, the midpoint is (–1, 1), which is 4 spaces from either point.

Geometry

Lesson 1: Plane Figures

Practice 1, page 181

1. rectangle, square
2. parallelogram, rectangle, square, rhombus
3. trapezoid
4. rectangle, square
5. none
6. rectangle, square, parallelogram, rhombus
7. square, rhombus
8. rectangle, square, parallelogram, rhombus, trapezoid
9. trapezoid
10. square
11. **C. 140°** Let h = the measure of $\angle H$. Then $3h + 20° = m\angle F$. The sum of the angles of a quadrilateral is 360°, so $3h + 20° + h + 90° + 90° = 360°$
Solve the equation:
$4h + 200° = 360°$, so $4h = 160°$, $h = 40°$, and $3h + 20° = 140°$.
12. **B. $EF \parallel GH$** In other words, line EF is parallel to line GH. A trapezoid is a quadrilateral with exactly one pair of parallel sides.
13. **C. 90°** If the opposite sides of a figure are parallel and all four sides are equal, then the figure is either a square or rhombus. Since $\angle T$ is a right angle, the figure is square. Therefore, all the angles measure 90°.
14. **C. parallelogram** This quadrilateral has opposite sides that are equal and opposite angles that are equal. It has no right angles, and the two sets of sides are different lengths. The quadrilateral must be a parallelogram.

Lesson 2: Triangles

Practice 2, page 183

1. equilateral, acute
2. scalene, obtuse
3. isosceles, acute
4. 64°
5. 45°
6. 97°
7. **C. 14** Solve for $\angle BAC$: $m\angle BAC + 55° = 115°$, so $m\angle BAC = 60°$. Solve for $\angle BCA$: $\angle BCA + 35° = 95°$, so $\angle BCA = 60°$. If two of the angles of $\triangle ABC$ each measure 60°, the third angle also measures 60°. The triangle is equilateral,

and all the sides of ABC are equal to side AB.

8. **C. right** $55° + 35° + m\angle D = 180°$. Solve for the missing angle: $m\angle D = 90°$. Therefore, the triangle is a right triangle.

9. **C. 86°** The angles of a triangle add up to $180°$. $38° + 56° = 94°$, so the third angle can be found by subtracting $94°$ from $180°$: $180° - 94° = 86°$.

Lesson 3: Pythagorean Relationship

Practice 3, page 185

1. $c = 11.3$ in
2. $c = 15$ yd
3. $c = 2.5$ cm
4. $a = 5.2$ m
5. $b = 8$ mm
6. $a = 17.3$ ft
7. $c = 12.2$ cm
8. $b = 26.0$ in
9. $c = 6.4$ km

10. **B. 6.7** The distance from A to C is 3 units, and the distance from B to C is 6 units.
$$c^2 = a^2 + b^2$$
$$c^2 = 3^2 + 6^2$$
$$c^2 = 9 + 36$$
$$c^2 = 45$$
$$c = \sqrt{45} \approx 6.7$$

11. **C. 30** The shorter sides are the legs. Solve for the hypotenuse:
$$c^2 = a^2 + b^2$$
$$c^2 = 18^2 + 24^2$$
$$c^2 = 324 + 576$$
$$c^2 = 900$$
$$c = \sqrt{900} = 30$$

12. **D. 12.1** The brace divides the rectangle into two right triangles with the brace as the hypotenuse of each. Solve for the hypotenuse of one of the triangles:
$$c^2 = a^2 + b^2$$
$$c^2 = 5^2 + 11^2$$
$$c^2 = 25 + 121$$
$$c^2 = 146$$
$$c = \sqrt{146} \approx 12.08$$, which rounds to 12.1.

13. **A. 36** Calculate:
$$c^2 = a^2 + b^2$$
$$39^2 = 15^2 + b^2$$
$$1{,}521 = 225 + b^2$$
$$1{,}296 = b^2$$
$$b = \sqrt{1{,}296} = 36$$

Lesson 4: Perimeter and Area

Practice 4, page 187

1. area: 39 sq units
   perimeter: 30.8 units
2. area: 16 sq units
   perimeter: 16 units

3. area: 640 sq units
   perimeter: 104 units
4. area: 29.6 sq units
   perimeter: 24.6 units
5. area: 616 sq units
   perimeter: 109 units
6. area: 38 sq units
   perimeter: 32 units

7. **C. 56** The shaded portion is a trapezoid: $\frac{1}{2} \times (5 + 9) \times 8 = 56$.

8. **C. 54** The area of a rectangle is its base times its height. $9 \times 6 = 54$.

9. **C. 324** Subtract the area of the patio from the area of the entire yard. Both are rectangles, so multiply length and width to find the area:
$(24 \times 18) - (12 \times 9) = 324$.

10. **B. 24** Add all four sides:
$6 + 6 + 6 + 6 = 24$ centimeters.

Lesson 5: Circles

Practice 5, page 189

1. $C = 62.8$ in; $A = 314.2$ in^2
2. $C = 12.6$ cm; $A = 12.6$ cm^2
3. $C = 25.1$ m; $A = 50.2$ m^2
4. **C. 38** Use the formula $C = \pi d$, where $d = 12$. $12 \times 3.14 = 37.7$

5. **B. 3.14×6^2** The formula for the area of a circle is $A = \pi r^2$. The radius of a circle is half of the diameter. Half of 12 is 6. Substitute 6 for r and 3.14 for π. $A = 3.14 \times 6^2$.

6. **B. 13.0** The diameter of a circle is twice the radius. $6.5 \times 2 = 13$.

7. **C. 19** Find the circumference of the 10-point band. First find the diameter, which passes through the 10-point band, the inner circle, and the 10-point band a second time on its way from one edge of the circle to the other. Add the width of the 10-point band twice and the diameter of the inner circle: $2 + 2 + 2 = 6$ inches. Now you can use the formula for circumference: $6 \times 3.14 = 18.84$, which rounds to 19 inches.

Lesson 6: Volume

Practice 6.1, page 191

1. 160 cubic units
2. 27 cubic units
3. 141 cubic units
4. 420 cubic units
5. 3 cubic units

6. 236 cubic units

7. **A. 5.** $V = lwh$ You know that the length and width of the box both equal 4 and that the volume equals 80. Solve the equation:
$$80 = 4 \times 4 \times h$$
$$80 = 16h$$
$$5 = h$$

8. **C. 125** If each edge measures 5 feet, then the figure is a cube. $5^3 = 125$.

9. **C. 17** First, you must find the volume of the pool. The radius of the pool is 6 and the height is 3.
$$V = \pi r^2 h$$
$$\approx 3.14 \times 6^2 \times 3$$
$$\approx 3.14 \times 36 \times 3$$
$$\approx 339.12$$
Therefore, the volume is about 339. Solve the proportion $\frac{1}{20} = \frac{x}{339}$, where x equals the number of scoops Linda must add: $20x = 339$; $x = 16.95$, about 17.

Practice 6.2, page 193

1. 9 in^3
2. 127 in^3
3. 314 cm^3
4. 480 m^3
5. 11 in^3
6. 1060 cm^3

7. **A. 480** First, find the volume of the original package. Substitute the numbers given into the volume equation: $V = \frac{1}{3} \times 10^2 \times 15 = 500$. Then find the volume of the new package. Add 4 to the length and width of the base to get 14. Substitute into the volume equation again and solve: $V = \frac{1}{3} \times 14^2 \times 15 = 980$. Find the difference of the two volumes: $980 - 500 = 480$.

8. **C. 67** You know that the height of the cone is half of the diameter of the base. Since the radius of the base is also half of the diameter, the radius must equal the height. Therefore, the radius is 4. Now solve the equation: $V = \frac{1}{3} \times \pi \times 4^2 \times 4 \approx 67$

9. **D. The volume of B is less than the volume of A.** First, find the volumes of the two figures. Figure A is a rectangular solid. Use the formula $V = lwh = 4 \times 3 \times 2 = 24$. Figure B is a pyramid. Use the formula $V = \frac{1}{3}Bh = \frac{1}{3} \times 3^2 \times 6 = 18$. Now compare the

two volumes. Since 24 > 18, choice (D) must be the answer.

10. **D. 1,000** Use the formula $V = \frac{1}{3}\pi r^2 h = \frac{1}{3} \times \pi \times 8^2 \times 15 \approx 1,005$, which is about 1,000.

Lesson 7: Surface Area

Practice 7.1, page 195

1. 108
2. 39
3. 24
4. 336
5. 256
6. 384
7. **A. 5** If all the edges are the same length, then the box must be a cube, and each square face has the same area. There are 6 faces. Divide 150 by 6 to get an area of 25 for each face. Then $25 \div 5 = 5$, so each side has a length of 5 in.
8. **C. The surface area of Figure A is greater than the surface area of Figure B.** Calculate both surface areas. Figure A: $25 \times 6 = 150$. Figure B: $(30 \times 4) + (9 \times 2) = 138$. Therefore, Figure A's surface area is greater than Figure B's.
9. **C. 162** The original box has a side length of 3 centimeters, so the surface area is 54 square centimeters. When the dimensions are doubled, the new box has a side length of 6 centimeters, so the surface area is 216 square centimeters. The difference in surface areas is 216 cm – 54 cm, which is 162 square centimeters.

Practice 7.2, page 197

1. 168π 4. 378π
2. 40π 5. 400π
3. 36π 6. 96π

7. **B. 64π** The formula for the surface area of a sphere uses the radius, and the radius is half the diameter, so $8 \div 2 = 4 = r$. Now use the formula for the surface area of a sphere: $SA = 4\pi r^2 = 4 \times \pi \times 4^2 = 64\pi$.
8. **D. The new cone will have a surface area less than the surface area of the original cone.** The original cone has a radius of 4, so its surface area is $\pi(4)(8) + \pi(4^2) = 32\pi + 16\pi = 48\pi$. The new cone will have a slant height of 16, a diameter of 4 and a radius of 2, so its surface area is: $\pi(2)$

$(16) + \pi(2^2) = 32\pi + 4\pi = 36\pi$, which is less than 48π.

9. **C. 170** The surface area of the cylinder is $\pi(6)(6) + 2\pi(3^2) = 36\pi + 18\pi = 54\pi = 54(3.14) \approx 170$ square inches.

Lesson 8: Combined Figures

Practice 8, page 199

1. $P = 150$ units
   $A = 1050$ sq units
2. $P = 49.7$ units
   $A = 159.3$ sq units
3. $P = 72$ units
   $A = 168$ sq units
4. $V = 185$ cubic units
5. $V = 278$ cubic units
6. $V = 399$ cubic units
7. **D. 360** Find the volume of the main rectangular slab: $V = lwh$, so $V = 3 \times 8 \times 12 = 288$ cubic feet. Find the volume of one of the blocks: $V = lwh$, so $V = 3 \times 3 \times 2 = 18$ cu ft. Multiply by 4, the number of blocks: $18 \times 4 = 72$ cu ft. Finally, add the main slab to the blocks: $288 + 72 = 360$ cu ft.
8. **C. 134** The radius of both the cones and the cylinder is 2. The height of one cone is 4 inches. Find the volume of one cone: $V = \frac{1}{3}\pi r^2 h = \frac{1}{3} \times 3.14 \times 2^2 \times 4 \approx 16.7$ cu in. Multiply by 2 to find the volume of both cones: $16.7 \times 2 = 33.4$ cu in. Find the volume of the cylinder: $V = \pi r^2 h \approx 3.14 \times 2^2 \times 8 \approx 100.48$ cu in. Add to find the total volume: $33.4 + 100.48 = 133.88$ cu in, which rounds to 134 cu in.

Lesson 9: Geometry Calculator Skills

Practice 9, page 201

1. 42 in   4. 15.8 cm
2. 195 cm²   5. 37.7 in
3. 43 ft³   6. 3016 cm³

7. **C. 520** Use the formulas for finding the area of a rectangle and the area of a triangle, and subtract the area of the cut-out triangle from the area of the rectangle. On the TI-30XS MultiView™ calculator, enter the following: 32 ⊗ 20 ⊖ 20 ⊗ 12 ⊗ .5 (enter). The right side of the display will read **520**. You can enter the entire calcula-

tion in this fashion because the TI-30XS™ understands the algebraic order of operations. If you press enter after each of those operations, your answer will be incorrect.

8. **B. 35** Use the formula for finding the volume of a cylinder. Press: (π) ⊗ 1.5 (x²) ⊗ 5 (enter). The right side of the display will read **35.34291735**, which rounds to 35 meters.
9. **D. 5,056** Use the formula for finding the volume of a rectangular solid. Subtract the volume of Box B from the volume of Box A. Press: 26 ⊗ 12 ⊗ 32 ⊖ 22 ⊗ 8 ⊗ 28 (enter). The right side of the display will read **5056**.
10. **C. 608** Use the formula for finding the area of a rectangle. Combine the areas of the two faces. Press: 32 ⊗ 12 ⊕ 28 ⊗ 8 (enter). The right side of the display will read **608**.

Geometry Practice Questions, pages 202–204

1. **D. 150** If the edge length is 5 cm, then each square surface has an area of 25 cm². There are 6 faces, so multiply by 6 to get 150 cm².
2. **C. 192π** Substitute the values given in the question into the formula for the surface area of a cylinder:
   $SA = 2\pi rh + 2\pi r^2$
   $SA = 2\pi(6)(10) + 2\pi(6^2)$
   $SA = 120\pi + 72\pi = 192\pi$
3. **C. 66π** The surface area of a cylinder is calculated with the formula $SA = 2\pi rh + 2\pi r^2 = (2 \times \pi \times 3 \times 8) + (2 \times \pi \times 9) = 48\pi + 18\pi = 66\pi$.
4. **C. 16√3 + 16** The surface area of a pyramid with a four-sided base is $SA = \frac{1}{2}ps + B$, where p is the perimeter of the base, s is the slant height of a face of the pyramid, and B is the area of the base. The pyramid described in this problem has a square base with sides of length 4, so both the perimeter (p) and the area of its base (B) are 16. Each face of the pyramid is an equilateral triangle, the height of which represents the slant height (s) of the pyramid. Divide one of the equilateral triangles into two 30:60:90 triangles and use

the side length ratio $x: x\sqrt{3} : 2x$ to determine the slant height of the pyramid. Since the base of one of these 30:60:90 triangles is 2 (half the length of a side of the pyramid's base) and the hypotenuse is 4 (the length of a side of the equilateral triangles making up the faces of the pyramid), the height of each 30:60:90 triangle (and, therefore, of each equilateral triangle face of the pyramid) is $2\sqrt{3}$. That is the slant height (s) of the pyramid as well. Now, plug in all of the relevant measures and solve: $\frac{1}{2}ps + B = \frac{1}{2} \times (16 \times 2\sqrt{3}) + 16 = 16\sqrt{3} + 16$.

5. **D. 512π** The circumference is 16π so the diameter is 16, and the radius is 8. The surface area is $4\pi r^2 = 256\pi$. The paint covers the ball twice, so multiply by 2 to get 512π.

6. **D. 224** A closet is in the shape of a rectangular solid. To find the volume, multiply: $V = lwh = 7 \times 4 \times 8 = 224$ cubic feet.

7. **C. 48π** The cone has a surface area of $\pi rs = \pi \times 3 \times 10 = 30\pi$ (don't include the base of the cone). A sphere with radius 3 has a surface area of $4\pi r^2 = 4 \times \pi \times 3^2 = 36\pi$. The surface area of the ice cream is half of that, or 18π. Add to get $30\pi + 18\pi = 48\pi$.

8. **C. 8:1** The formula for the volume of a sphere is $V = \frac{4}{3}\pi r^3$. Find the volumes of both spheres and simplify the ratio between those volumes. Or think about it this way: the ratio of the volume of Sphere A to that of Sphere B would be as follows. $(\frac{4}{3}\pi \times 2^3)$ to $(\frac{4}{3}\pi \times 1^3)$ Find the value of the exponents: $(\frac{4}{3}\pi \times 8)$ to $(\frac{4}{3}\pi \times 1)$ You know that you can simplify a ratio by dividing both sides of the ratio by a number. Here, divide both sides by $\frac{4}{3}\pi$ to get: 8 to 1.

9. **24** The parallelogram has an area of 60 square cm. The area of the triangle is $\frac{1}{2}bh = \frac{1}{2}b \times 5 = 2.5b$, so $60 = 2.5b$ and $b = 24$.

10. **A. 1458** The height of all three boxes is 9 in, the length is 18 in, and the width is 9 in. The total volume is $18 \times 9 \times 9 = 1458$.

11. **B. 500** Since Max hikes directly east after hiking directly due north, he has made a 90° turn. The distances hiked therefore form a right triangle. The legs are 300 and 400 yards. To solve for the hypotenuse, use the Pythagorean relationship:
$$a^2 + b^2 = c^2$$
$$300^2 + 400^2 = c^2$$
$$90{,}000 + 160{,}000 = c^2$$
$$250{,}000 = c^2$$
$$500 = c$$
A quicker solution would be to notice that the distances form a large triangle with sides in the 3:4:5 ratio. Then it is easy to see that the hypotenuse of a triangle with legs of 300 and 400 yards is 500 yards.

12. **C. 168** The volume of the container as drawn in the diagram is $V = lwh = 9$ in $\times$ 7 in $\times$ 12 in $= 756$ in^3. If you increase the length by 2 inches, the volume is 11 in $\times$ 7 in $\times$ 12 in $= 924$ in^3. Find the difference: 924 in^3 – 756 in^3 = 168 in^3. You can solve the problem more easily by multiplying the added length by the width and height: $2(7)(12) = 168$.

13. **D. $x^2 = 15^2 - 6^2$** Use the Pythagorean relationship. If $a^2 + b^2 = c^2$ and c is the hypotenuse, then $b^2 = c^2 - a^2$ and $x^2 = 15^2 - 6^2$.

14. **C. 36** Use the formula for finding the perimeter of a rectangle. Let $3w$ = length.
$P = 2l + 2w$
$96 = 2(3w) + 2w$
$96 = 8w$
$w = 12$
So the width is 12 inches, and the length is $3 \times 12 = 36$ inches.

15. **D. 1120π** The circumference is 16π, so $r = 8$ cm. A cone-shaped party hat does not have a base, so $SA = \pi rs = 56\pi$. Multiply by 20 to get 1120π.

16. **A. 3.43** To find the area of the shaded region, subtract the area of the circle from the area of the square. One side of the square is equivalent to the diameter of the circle. The radius is 2, so the diameter—and each side of the square—is 4. So $A = 4^2 - \pi \times 2^2 \approx 3.43$.

17. **B. 1,560** You may find it helpful to draw a sketch of the room. Two walls measure 40 by 12 feet. Two measure 25 by 12 feet. Find the total area: $2 \times 40 \times 12 + 2 \times 25 \times 12 = 960 + 600 = 1{,}560$.

18. **C. 12,000** Use the formula $V = lwh$. Multiply: $40 \times 25 \times 12 = 12{,}000$.

19. **A. 4** Begin by finding the total surface area of all three pyramids. The formula for the surface area of a pyramid is $SA = \frac{1}{2}ps + B$. For each pyramid, plug in the values and calculate:
Top left pyramid:
$SA = \frac{1}{2}(2 + 2 + 2 + 2)(3) + (2 \times 2)$
$= 16$
Top right pyramid:
$SA = \frac{1}{2}(3 + 3 + 3 + 3)(6) + (3 \times 3)$
$= 45$
Bottom pyramid:
$SA = \frac{1}{2}(4 + 4 + 4 + 4)(4) + (4 \times 4)$
$= 48$
Thus, the total surface area for all three pyramids is:

$16 + 45 + 48 = 109$

The problem states that Laura needs one tube of paint for each 30 square inches. Thus, she needs $109 \div 30 \approx 3.6$. In order to finish her project, she should buy four tubes of paint.

Practice Test

1. To practice for the actual GED® Mathematical Reasoning Test, you can take the following practice test. When you do, follow the same time limits you will face on the actual test.
   - **Mathematical Reasoning, 46 Questions, 1 Hour, 55 Minutes**
     - First Section—no calculator allowed
     - Second Section—calculator allowed

   Just as on the actual tests, you will work with a variety of formats:
   - For the **multiple-choice questions**, you may fill in the circles next to the correct answers in this book, or you can write your answers on a separate piece of paper.
   - For **other formats**, directions will indicate where you can write in boxes, on lines, or place a dot on a specific place on a graphic.
2. **You may use your calculator** beginning on page 234.
3. **Check** your answers using the *Practice Test Answers and Explanations* that begin on page 246, and fill in the *Practice Test Evaluation Chart* on page 249. This chart will allow you to see which study areas may still need work.
4. **Confirm** your readiness to take the actual GED® Mathematical Reasoning Test.

MATHEMATICAL REASONING FORMULA SHEET

You may use formulas from this sheet to answer questions on the test.

Area of a:

square	$A = s^2$
rectangle	$A = lw$
parallelogram	$A = bh$
triangle	$A = \frac{1}{2}bh$
trapezoid	$A = \frac{1}{2}h(b_1 + b_2)$
circle	$A = \pi r^2$

Perimeter of a:

square	$P = 4s$
rectangle	$P = 2l + 2w$
triangle	$P = s_1 + s_2 + s_3$
Circumference of a circle	$C = 2\pi r$ OR $C = \pi d$; $\pi \approx 3.14$

Surface area and volume of a:

rectangular/right prism	$SA = ph + 2B$	$V = Bh$
cylinder	$SA = 2\pi rh + 2\pi r^2$	$V = \pi r^2 h$
pyramid	$SA = \frac{1}{2}ps + B$	$V = \frac{1}{3}Bh$
cone	$SA = \pi rs + \pi r^2$	$V = \frac{1}{3}\pi r^2 h$
sphere	$SA = 4\pi r^2$	$V = \frac{4}{3}\pi r^3$

(p = perimeter of base with area B; $\pi \approx 3.14$)

Data

mean	mean is equal to the total of the values of a data set, divided by the number of elements in the data set
median	median is the middle value in an odd number of ordered values of a data set, or the mean of the two middle values in an even number of ordered values in a data set

Algebra

slope of a line	$m = \dfrac{y_2 - y_1}{x_2 - x_1}$
slope-intercept form of the equation of a line	$y = mx + b$
point-slope form of the equation of a line	$y - y_1 = m(x - x_1)$
standard form of a quadratic equation	$y = ax^2 + bx + c$
quadratic formula	$x = \dfrac{-b \pm \sqrt{b^2 - 4ac}}{2a}$
Pythagorean Theorem	$a^2 + b^2 = c^2$
simple interest	$I = Prt$ (I = interest, P = principal, r = rate, t = time)
distance formula	$d = rt$
total cost	total cost = (number of units) × (price per unit)

Directions: Use 20 or fewer minutes to answer the following 5 questions. You may fill in the circles next to the correct answers or write your answers in boxes. Refer to the formula sheet on page 232 as needed. YOU MAY NOT USE YOUR CALCULATOR ON THIS SECTION.

1. Mike borrowed $400 from his brother for six months. He agreed to pay simple interest at the annual rate of 5%. Including interest and principal, how much will Mike have paid his brother at the end of the six months?

   ○ A. $10
   ○ B. $120
   ○ C. $410
   ○ D. $500

2. What is the value of the expression $3(2x - y) + (3 + x)^2$ when $x = 4$ and $y = 5$?

   ○ A. 49
   ○ B. 58
   ○ C. 61
   ○ D. 82

3. Which of the following is equal to the expression below?

   $(3x + 2y)(5x - 6y)$

   ○ A. $8x - 4y$
   ○ B. $15x^2 - 12y^2$
   ○ C. $15x^2 + 10xy - 12y^2$
   ○ D. $15x^2 - 8xy - 12y^2$

4. John needs to replace the boards on a 22-foot section of his fence. He plans to place the boards as shown below.

   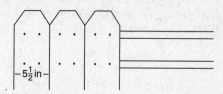

   If the boards are $5\frac{1}{2}$ inches wide, how many boards should he buy to cover the distance?

   ○ A. 4
   ○ B. 12
   ○ C. 48
   ○ D. 121

5. What is the value of this expression?

   $$-3 \times 5^2 + 2(4 - 18) + 3^3$$

   Write your answer in the box below.

Directions: Use a maximum of 1 hour and 35 minutes to answer 42 questions. You may fill in the circles next to the correct answers or write your answers in boxes. Refer to the formula sheet on page 232 as needed. YOU MAY USE YOUR CALCULATOR ON THIS SECTION.

6. A storage shelf has room for only two containers on the bottom shelf. The heaviest boxes should be placed on the bottom. Which two boxes should be placed on the bottom shelf? Write the letters of the boxes in the spaces below.

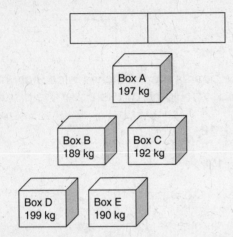

7. Brad's average golf score after six rounds was 81. For the first five rounds his scores were 78, 86, 82, 81, and 82. What was his score on the sixth round?

   Write your answer in the box below.

8. A kayaker spends 2 hours paddling up a stream from point A to point B, quickly turns her kayak around, and immediately heads back downstream. It takes her only 1 hour to float back down the stream from point B to point A. If points A and B are 6 miles apart, what was the kayaker's average rate of speed in miles per hour?

   ○ A. 12 mph
   ○ B. 6 mph
   ○ C. 4 mph
   ○ D. 2 mph

9. In quadrilateral *ABCD*, side *AB* is parallel to side *CD*. Sides *AD* and *BC* are not parallel. What is the area of the figure to the nearest square centimeter?

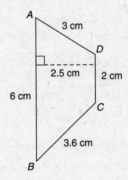

   Write your answer in the box below.

10. Simplify the following expression:

$2x^2 - 2xy + 4xy$

- ○ A. $x(x + y)$
- ○ B. $x(x - y)$
- ○ C. $2x(x - y)$
- ○ D. $2x(x + y)$

11. A scientist measures the outside temperature at noon each day over a 3-day period.

Day	Temperature at noon (°F)
Saturday	−1
Sunday	2
Monday	−4

What was the average temperature on these three days? Place an X on the number line below to represent your answer.

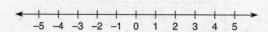

12. What is the value of 4^7?

Write your answer in the box below.

13.

	A	B	C
1	−2	−4	1
2	8	4	3
3	5	2	−1

In the computer spreadsheet above, $-[A1 - (C2 - A3) + C2 * B1]$ is equal to which of the following? (*Hint: on a spreadsheet,* * *means multiplication*)

- ○ A. −22
- ○ B. −12
- ○ C. 12
- ○ D. 22

14. Simplify the expression:
$(6x^4 + 7x + 5x^3) - (4x^4 - 2x^3 + 3x)$

  ○ A. $10x^4 + 7x^3 + 18x$
  ○ B. $2x^4 + 7x^3 + 4x$
  ○ C. $2x^4 + 7x^3 + 18x$
  ○ D. $10x^4 + 3x^3 + 12x$

15. The perimeter of the trapezoid below is 50. What is its area?

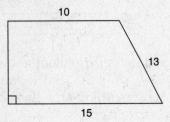

  ○ A. 12
  ○ B. 60
  ○ C. 120
  ○ D. 150

16. Risa wants to order business cards. A printing company determines the cost (C) to the customer using the following function, where $b =$ the number of boxes of cards and $n =$ the number of ink colors.

$$C = \$25.60b + \$14.00b(n - 1)$$

If Risa orders 4 boxes of cards printed in 3 colors, how much will the cards cost?

  ○ A. $214.40
  ○ B. $168.00
  ○ C. $144.40
  ○ D. $102.40

17. The graph of the equation $y = -\frac{3}{4}x + 1$ is a line that passes through points C and D on the coordinate plane. Which of the following points also lies on the graph of the equation?

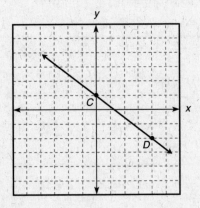

  ○ A. (3, 1)
  ○ B. (8, −5)
  ○ C. (5, 3)
  ○ D. (10, 6)

18. Which of the following equations correctly describes the line on the graph?

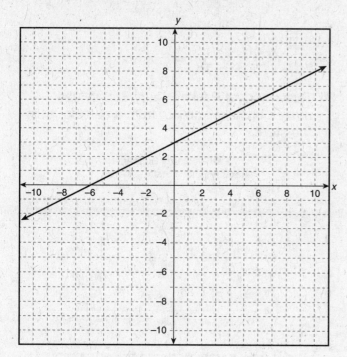

○ A. $y = -\frac{1}{2}x - 6$

○ B. $y = 2x + 3$

○ C. $y = \frac{1}{2}x - 6$

○ D. $y = \frac{1}{2}x + 3$

19. What is the 6th term in the sequence below?

1, 3, 7, 15, 31, ___ , 127

○ A. 62
○ B. 63
○ C. 68
○ D. 77

20. Evening tickets to a play are $24.50 each. Tickets for the afternoon show are $19 each. Janice wants to buy 6 tickets. Arrange terms from the options below to construct the expression Janice would use to determine how much less she would spend if she chooses an afternoon show instead of an evening show. (You do not need to use all of the terms offered as options. Use any term only once.)

+		$19

(		÷

)		$24.50

6		$\frac{1}{2}$

−

21. In a certain state, the legislature has 100 seats. In 2010, Party X held 54 seats. In the 2012 election, the party gained two seats. If, in the 2014 election, Party X loses 6 seats, but gains 2 seats in the 2016 election, what will the absolute change in the number of seats held by Party X from 2010 to 2016 be?

Write your answer in the box below.

22. What is the surface area of the cylinder below?

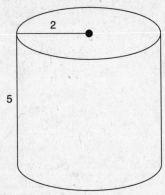

- A. 20π
- B. 28π
- C. 32π
- D. 50π

23. $\dfrac{2x^2 - 6x - 36}{2x - 12} =$
- A. $x - 6$
- B. $x - 3$
- C. $x + 3$
- D. $x^2 + 3x + 18$

24. Customers of Paul's Beauty Supply can make purchases online, from a catalog, or in the store.

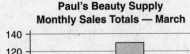

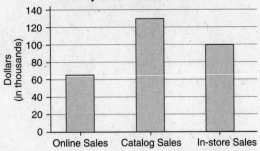

About how much more did the company make from catalog sales than from online sales in March?

- A. $35,000
- B. $65,000
- C. $130,000
- D. $195,000

25. Which of the following is a graph of the inequality $-2 \leq x < 4$?

A.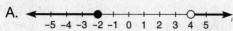
-5 -4 -3 -2 -1 0 1 2 3 4 5

B. ◄——————○——————————●——►
-5 -4 -3 -2 -1 0 1 2 3 4 5

C. ◄——————●———————————●——►
-5 -4 -3 -2 -1 0 1 2 3 4 5

D. ◄——————●———————————○——►
-5 -4 -3 -2 -1 0 1 2 3 4 5

26. At what point does the line with the equation $y = 2x + 3$ intersect with the line with the equation $y = -\frac{1}{2}x - 7$?

○ A. $(-4, -5)$
○ B. $(0, -7)$
○ C. $(0, 3)$
○ D. $(2, 7)$

27. A pole is supported by a cable as shown. The cable is attached to the ground 9 feet from the base of the pole, and it is attached to the pole 12 feet above the ground.

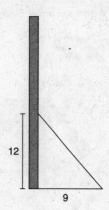

Which of the following expressions could be used to find the length of the cable?

○ A. $9^2 + 12^2$
○ B. $12^2 - 9^2$
○ C. $\sqrt{9^2 + 12^2}$
○ D. $\sqrt{12^2 - 9^2}$

28. Meg is an interior designer who is looking to place two chairs against an accent wall. She has four different chairs from which to choose, each a different color: yellow, red, green, and blue. How many different combinations of chairs can Meg use in her design?

Write your answer in the box below.

29. The Whitmans are trying to pay off their credit card debt, so they developed the following budget based on their monthly take-home pay.

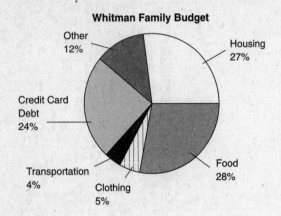

Whitman Family Budget

Other 12%
Housing 27%
Credit Card Debt 24%
Transportation 4%
Clothing 5%
Food 28%

If the Whitmans' monthly take-home pay is $2500, about how much do they plan to pay each month on their credit card debt?

○ A. $600
○ B. $450
○ C. $300
○ D. $240

30. A market sells all varieties of pasta at a rate of 4 boxes for $5.00. Jennifer needs 3 boxes of ziti and 3 boxes of spaghetti. At this rate, how much will she spend for the pasta?

Write your answer in the box below.

31. Inge has been finding spiders in her apartment. In order to help her landlord understand the problem, she has kept track of how many spiders she found each week over an eight-week period. This is her record:

Week	Number of spiders found
1st	3
2nd	4
3rd	6
4th	5
5th	4
6th	4
7th	7
8th	2

The line plot below is based on the table Inge created, above. However, it is incomplete. Place additional dots on the line plot until it accurately reflects Inge's records over the eight week period.

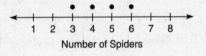

1 2 3 4 5 6 7 8
Number of Spiders

32. If the area of circle O is 36π, what is its diameter?

   ○ A. 6
   ○ B. 6π
   ○ C. 12
   ○ D. 18

33. In 2011, Karen's base salary was $52,500, and she earned an end-of-year bonus of $6250. In 2012, her base salary was raised to $56,300 and her end-of-year bonus was $4100. What was the percent increase or decrease in her overall earnings from 2011 to 2012?

Write your answer in the box below. Round your answer to the nearest tenth of a percent.

```
┌──────────────────────────────┐
│                              │
└──────────────────────────────┘
```

34. Imtaez works as a server in a restaurant. On a certain night, he collected $157 in tips and paid y dollars to the food runner who helped him. The amount Imtaez had remaining after paying the runner was equal to ($101 + y$).

Arrange terms from the options below to construct the equation you would use to determine how much Imtaez paid to the food runner. (You may not need to use all of the terms offered as options. Use any term only once.)

```
┌──────┬──────┬──────┬──────┬──────┐
│      │      │      │      │      │
└──────┴──────┴──────┴──────┴──────┘
```

$=$	$+ y$
$101	$157
x	$\div$
$-y$	y^2

35. Place a dot on the coordinate plane below to represent the solution to the following system of equations:

$y = x + 4$

$2y + 4x = 44$

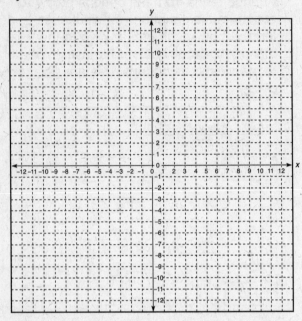

36. A bag contains 12 red, 3 blue, 6 green, and 4 yellow marbles. If a marble is drawn from the bag at random, what is the probability that the marble will be either blue or yellow?

- ○ A. 7%
- ○ B. 12%
- ○ C. 25%
- ○ D. 28%

37. The right cone shown below has a base with a radius of 6.4 cm.

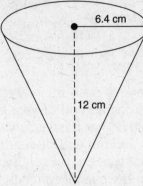

To the nearest cubic centimeter, what is the volume of the cone? (Use 3.14 for π.)

- ○ A. 40
- ○ B. 81
- ○ C. 129
- ○ D. 514

38. Ten artists have entered an art show. There are three prizes to be awarded in the art show: first prize, second prize, and third prize. How many possible ways could those prizes be awarded among the ten artists?

Write your answer in the box below.

39. Archie has made a huge pot of chili. He cannot eat it all himself, so he is going to share some with his neighbors and family. Archie will give 1/4 of the chili to his parents. He will give 1/8 of it to his neighbor Cecilia. He will give another 1/8 of it to his neighbor Chang. How much of the chili will Archie have left over? Place a dot on the number line below to reflect the correct answer.

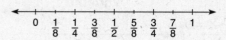

40. At the end of baseball season, 5% of the children enrolled in a local youth baseball program will be chosen to play in the state tournament. If 12 children will be chosen to play in the tournament, how many children are enrolled in the program?

○ A.   60
○ B. 120
○ C. 240
○ D. 600

41. Fabio has his own computer repair business. He uses the following guidelines to estimate how long a project will take.

Install operating system: 1 hour
Replace motherboard: $1\frac{1}{2}$ hours
Reimage hard drive: 2 hours
Upgrade memory: 20 minutes
Install new hard drive: 45 minutes
Install sound card: 30 minutes
Install video card: 30 minutes

Fabio needs to install a new hard drive and an operating system for a customer. If Fabio charges $65 per hour, what will he charge the customer for his time?

○ A. $94.25
○ B. $105.00
○ C. $113.75
○ D. $146.25

42. There are approximately 1,335,000,000 cubic kilometers of water in Earth's oceans. Which of the following expresses that number in scientific notation?

○ A. $1.335 \times 100 \times 100$
○ B. 1.335×10^3
○ C. 1.335×10^6
○ D. 1.335×10^9

43. What is the slope of the line shown below?

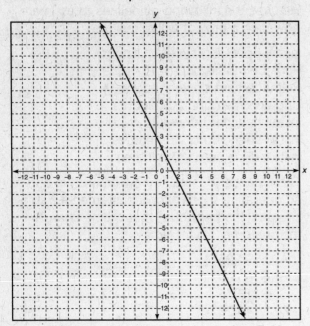

Write your answer in the box below.

[ ]

44. One number is 12 more than 3 times another number. The sum of the two numbers is −20. What are the numbers?

○ A. 8 and 12
○ B. 8 and −12
○ C. −2 and −18
○ D. −8 and −12

45. Which of the following pairs of numbers is a solution to the equation $3x^2 - 54 = -21x$?

○ A. −6 and 3
○ B. −2 and 9
○ C. −3 and 6
○ D. −9 and 2

46. Match the solutions to the equations.

Equation	Value of the variable
$x - 2 = 9$	
$\frac{a}{10} = 5$	
$3y = -21$	
$14 + m = 6$	

50
−8
−7
11

Answers and explanations begin on page 246.

STOP

Congratulations! You have completed the GED® Mathematical Reasoning Practice Test.

Reminder: your next step is to check your answers with the
Practice Test Answers and Explanations and fill in the evaluation
chart that follows those explanations.

PRACTICE TEST ANSWERS AND EXPLANATIONS

Pages 231–244

1. **C. $410** Use the formula Simple interest = principal × rate × time. Note that time is expressed in terms of a year, so 6 months = $\frac{1}{2}$ year: $I = \$400 \times 0.05 \times \frac{1}{2}$ which equals $10. This is the interest, so Mike will pay back the interest plus the $400 principal for a total of $410.

2. **B. 58** Plug in the values given for x and y and then follow the order of operations:
$3[2(4) - 5] + (3 + 4)^2 = 3(8 - 5) + 7^2 = 3(3) + 49 = 9 + 49 = 58$

3. **D. $15x^2 - 8xy - 12y^2$** Use FOIL to distribute the terms in the expression:
$(3x)(5x) + (3x)(-6y) + (2y)(5x) + (2y)(-6y) = 15x^2 - 18xy + 10xy - 12y^2 = 15x^2 - 8xy - 12y^2$

4. **C. 48** First, convert the length of the section of fence into inches: 22×12 in $= 264$. That number represents how many inches John must cover with new boards. Divide that number by the width of each board to find out how many boards will be required: $\frac{264}{5.5} = 48$.

5. **–76** Following the order of operations, first simplify anything in parentheses:
$(4 - 18)$ becomes -14
Next, simplify any terms with exponents:
$5^2 = 25$ and $3^3 = 27$
Now you have:
$-3 \times 25 + 2(-14) + 27$.
Next, do multiplication and division in the order in which they appear:
$-3 \times 25 = -75$ and $2(-14) = -28$
Last, add and subtract in the order in which they appear:
$-75 + (-28) + 27 = -76$

6. **Box A and Box D** All boxes share the same first digit in their weight. By comparing the second digit, you can eliminate Box B. Comparing the third digit of the remaining choices, you find Box A and Box D are the heaviest and should be placed on the bottom shelf.

7. **77** Brad's average golf score would be found like this:
$\frac{sum\ of\ scores}{number\ of\ scores} = average\ score$

Plug the information you are given in the question into the formula and solve for the unknown:
$\frac{78 + 86 + 82 + 81 + 82 + x}{6} = 81$
$78 + 86 + 82 + 81 + 82 + x = 486$
$409 + x = 486$
$x = 77$

8. **C. 4 mph** The kayaker traveled for a total of 12 miles: 6 miles upstream and 6 miles downstream. This took her 3 hours (2 hours upstream + 1 hour downstream). Divide the distance by the time to find her average rate of speed per hour: $\frac{12\ miles}{3\ hours} = 4$ miles per hour.

9. **10** Because sides AB and CD are parallel, the figure is a trapezoid. Use the formula for the area of a trapezoid: $A = \frac{1}{2}h(b_1 + b_2)$ and plug in the values given:
$A = \frac{1}{2}(2.5)(2 + 6)$
$A = \frac{1}{2}(2.5)(8)$
$A = 10$

10. **D. $2x(x + y)$** To begin adding the polynomials together, factor out any like terms: $2x(x - y + 2y)$. Then combine any like terms together: $2x(x + y)$

11.

Find the average of the three temperatures:
$\frac{-1 + 2 + (-4)}{3} = \frac{-3}{3} = -1$.

12. **16,384** Calculate: $4^7 = 4 \times 4 \times 4 \times 4 \times 4 \times 4 \times 4 = 16{,}384$. On the TI-30SX MultiView™, press 4 ⊗ 7 [enter]. The right side of the display reads 16,384.

13. **C. 12** Substitute appropriate values from the spreadsheet, then multiply, add, and subtract carefully, using order of operations:
$-[-2 - (3 - 5) + 3 \times (-4)] =$
$-[-2 - (-2) + (-12)] =$
$-[-2 + 2 - 12] =$
$-[-12] = 12$

14. **B. $2x^4 + 7x^3 + 4x$** Combine like terms from the exponent with the largest degree, which is 4: $6x^4 - 4x^4 = 2x^4$. Combine like terms from the exponent with the next largest degree, which is 3: $5x^3 + 2x^3 = 7x^3$. Finally, combine the terms from the exponent with the smallest degree: $7x - 3x$

$= 4x$. The simplified polynomial is $2x^4 + 7x^3 + 4x$.

15. **D. 150** The perimeter of the trapezoid is given as 50. Since the three sides shown add up to 38, the remaining side must be 12. The missing side is the height, so use the height and the two bases in the formula for the area of a trapezoid, as found on the formula sheet:
$\frac{1}{2} \times 12(10 + 15) = 150$

16. **A. $214.40** Substitute 4 for b and 3 for n into the function. Then solve the equation:
$C = \$25.60(4) + \$14(4)(3 - 1)$
$= \$102.40 + \$112.00$
$= \$214.40$

17. **B. (8, –5)** Substitute the x and y values from each ordered pair into the equation. Only choice (B) makes the equation true:
$y = -\frac{3}{4}x + 1$
$-5 = -\frac{3}{4}(8) + 1$
$-5 = -6 + 1$
$-5 = -5$

18. **D. $y = \frac{1}{2}x + 3$** You can use the point-slope form to figure out the slope of the line first. Use $(-6, 0)$ and $(0, 3)$ as two points:
$0 - 3 = m(-6 - 0)$
$-3 = m(-6)$
$-3 = -6m$
$m = \frac{-3}{-6} = \frac{1}{2}$
Now you have the slope of the line, use either of the points to plug into the equation for a line, $y = mx + b$. Using $(0, 3)$,
$3 = \frac{1}{2}(0) + b$
$3 = 0 + b$
$b = 3$
The equation of the line is $y = \frac{1}{2}x + 3$.

19. **B. 63** The pattern is that the next number is 1 more than double the previous number. To find the 6th term, use the 5th term, in this case 31. $31 \times 2 + 1 = 63$.

20. | 6 | (| $24.50 | – | $19 |) |

To determine how much Janice will save, she needs to determine the price difference between one evening and one afternoon ticket ($24.50 – $19) and then multiply that number by 6, the total number of tickets she intends to purchase. Thus, the equation that will supply her total savings is 6($24.50 – $19).

21. 2 Absolute change refers to the difference, either positive or negative, between two numbers. Over the three elections listed, party x gained 2 seats, lost 6 seats, and then regained 2 seats. That's a net loss of 2.

22. B. 28π Use the radius of 2 and the height of 5 in the formula for the surface area of a cylinder, which can be found on the formula sheet. $2\pi(2 \times 5) + 2\pi(2^2) = 20\pi + 8\pi = 28\pi$

23. C. $x + 3$ Every term in the expression is divisible by two, so begin by simplifying: $\frac{2x^2-6x-36}{2x-12} = \frac{x^2-3x-18}{x-6}$. Next, factor the numerator of the fraction and cancel: $\frac{x^2-3x-18}{x-6} = \frac{(x-6)(x+3)}{x-6} = x+3$

24. B. $65,000 About $130,000 was made from catalog sales. About $65,000 was made from online sales. Subtract $65,000 from $130,000.

25. D. The ≤ symbol indicates "greater than or equal to," which is indicated with a filled-in dot. The symbol < indicates "less than" (but not equal to), which is indicated with an open dot.

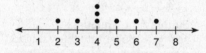

26. A. (–4, –5) Solve by graphing or by substitution. The point of intersection will be where the lines cross each other. The lines intersect at the point (–4, –5). To solve by substitution, use the first equation to substitute the value of y in the second equation:
$2x + 3 = -\frac{1}{2}x - 7$
$2\frac{1}{2}x = -10$
$x = \frac{-10}{2\frac{1}{2}} = -4$
Now use that value of x to find the value of y using the first equation:
$y = 2(-4) + 3 = -5$
The solution of the equation set is (–4, –5).

27. C. $\sqrt{9^2 + 12^2}$ The cable forms the hypotenuse of a triangle with side lengths of 9 feet and 12 feet. Use the Pythagorean theorem

$(9^2 + [12]^2 = c^2)$ to determine the length of the hypotenuse c: $c = \sqrt{9^2 + 12^2}$.

28. 6 This question is simply asking for the number of possible combinations of two differently colored chairs, so the order of the chairs does not matter. To determine the number of different pairs of chairs that could be selected for the design, draw a table to illustrate the possibilities. There are six possible ways that two different chairs could be chosen for Meg's design.

Yellow	Red	Green	Blue
X	X		
X		X	
X			X
	X	X	
	X		X
		X	X

29. A. $600 Find 24% of $2500. $2500 × 0.24 = $600 You could estimate this answer by thinking 24% is roughly $\frac{1}{4}$, and choice (A) is closest to one-fourth of the Whitman's budget.

30. $7.50 Six boxes of pasta will be purchased: 3 of ziti and 3 of spaghetti. Set up the proportion $\frac{4}{5} = \frac{6}{x}$ where x is the price of 6 boxes of pasta. Cross-multiply and divide to solve for x: 5 × 6 = 30 and 30 ÷ 4 = 7.5

31. Place four additional dots on the line plot to represent the data. Count this question as correct only if you placed all of the dots properly.

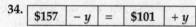

32. C. 12 The formula for the area of a circle is $A = \pi r^2$ where r refers to the radius of the circle. The diameter of a circle (a straight line segment that goes from one edge of the circle to the other and passes through the center of the circle) is $2r$, or two times the length of the radius. The circle shown in this problem has an area of 36π. Plug that into the

area formula and find the length of the circle's radius:
$36\pi = \pi r^2$
$\frac{36\pi}{\pi} = \frac{\pi r^2}{\pi}$
$36 = r^2$
$\sqrt{36} = \sqrt{r^2}$
$6 = r$
Now that you know the radius has a length of 6, multiply that length by 2 to get the diameter: $6 \times 2 = 12$
The diameter of the circle has a length of 12.

33. 2.8% To calculate the percent increase or decrease from Karen's 2011 earnings to her 2012 earnings, first find exactly how much she earned in each year. In 2011, she earned $52,500 + $6,250, which equals $58,750. In 2012, she earned $56,300 + $4,100, which equals $60,400. To calculate the percent change from 2011 to 2012, use the percent change formula: $\frac{amount\ of\ change}{original\ value}$
In this case, that gives you $\frac{60,400 - 58,750}{58,750} = \frac{1,650}{58,750}$ which equals .028, or 2.8%.

34.

$157	– y	=	$101	+ y

Imtaez had $101 + y remaining after paying y to the runner. The equation would be $157 – y = $101 + y.

35. Place a dot on the graph as shown:

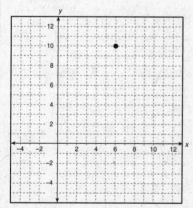

You can solve either by graphing the lines or by substitution. To solve by substitution, use the first equation to substitute the value of y in the second equation:

$$2(x + 4) + 4x = 44$$
$$2x + 8 + 4x = 44$$
$$6x + 8 = 44$$
$$6x = 36$$
$$x = 6$$

Now use that value of x to find the value of y using the first equation:

$$y = 6 + 4$$
$$y = 10$$

36. **D. 28%** Probability is the ratio of the number of favorable outcomes to the number of possible outcomes. Add up the numbers of marbles to find out how many marbles are in the bag. $12 + 3 + 6 + 4 = 25$. Therefore, 25 is the number of possible outcomes. 7 marbles are either blue or yellow. 7 is the number of favorable outcomes. $\frac{7}{25} \times \frac{4}{4} = \frac{28}{100}$, or 28%.

37. **D. 514** To find the volume of a cone, use the formula from the formula sheet: $V = \frac{1}{3}\pi r^2 h$. Plug in values from the question stem and the approximate value of pi:

$$V = \frac{1}{3}\pi(6.4)^2(12)$$
$$V = \frac{1}{3}(3.14)(40.96)(12) \approx 514.$$

38. **720** This question asks how many orderings, or permutations, of three out of ten are possible. Multiply: $10 \times 9 \times 8 = 720$.

39. Place a dot on the number line as shown below:

Archie is giving away half his chili: $\frac{1}{4} + \frac{1}{8} + \frac{1}{8} = \frac{1}{2}$. So he will have one half left over.

40. **C. 240** Use the percent formula, $\% = \frac{\text{part}}{\text{whole}} \times 100\%$. We are given the part and the percent, and are solving for the whole.

$$5\% = \frac{12}{x} \times 100\%$$
$$x = \frac{12 \times 100}{5\%}$$
$$x = 12 \times 20 = 240$$

41. **C. $113.75** It takes Fabio 45 minutes, or $\frac{3}{4}$ of an hour to install a hard drive. It takes him exactly one hour to install an operating system. It will take him $1\frac{3}{4}$ hours to complete the job. Since he charges $65 per hour, multiply $1\frac{3}{4}$ by $65 to find the total charge:

$$1\frac{3}{4} \times \$65 = \$113.75$$

42. **D. 1.335×10^9** You move the decimal point 9 places to the left to get 1.335. Multiply this by 10^9 to get the scientific notation 1.335×10^9.

43. **−2** To find slope, calculate $\frac{\text{rise}}{\text{run}}$. In this case, the line moves up two units for each unit it moves to the left. Thus, the slope is negative: $\frac{2}{-1} = -2$

44. **D. −8 and −12** To solve this system of linear equations, first write two equations with the information given. Call the numbers x and y. The first sentence tells you that $x = 12 + 3y$, and the second sentence tells you that $x + y = -20$. Rewrite the second equation so that x is isolated on one side of the equals sign: $x = -20 - y$. Now that each equation is written in terms of x, set the two expressions for x equal to each other: $12 + 3y = -20 - y$.

Simplify this equation: $4y = -32$, so $y = -8$. Substitute this value for y back into the second equation: $x + -8 = -20$, so x must equal −12.

45. **D. −9 and 2** To find the solutions to this quadratic equation, start by setting it equal to 0. The equation then becomes $3x^2 + 21x - 54 = 0$. Then, divide each term by 3 to make the equation $x^2 + 7x - 18 = 0$. Now that the x^2 term has a coefficient of 1, factor the equation into two terms: $(x + 9)(x - 2)$. So $x + 9 = 0$, and $x - 2 = 0$. $x = -9$ and $x = 2$. The correct answer is D.

46. Match the solutions to the equations:

Equation	Value of the variable	Explanation
$x - 2 = 9$	11	$x - 2 + 2 = 9 + 2$ $x = 11$
$\frac{a}{10} = 5$	50	$\frac{a}{10} \times 10 = 5 \times 10$ $a = 50$
$3y = -21$	−7	$3y = -21$ $y = -\frac{21}{3} = -7$
$14 + m = 6$	−8	$14 + m - 14 = 6 - 14$ $m = -8$

PRACTICE TEST EVALUATION CHART

Circle the numbers of the questions that you answered correctly and then total them in the last column of each row.

Content Area	Question Numbers	Number Correct/Total
Number Sense and Problem Solving Pages 22–41	6, 8	___/2
Decimals and Fractions Pages 42–63	4, 39, 41	___/3
Ratio, Proportion, and Percent Pages 64–83	1, 30, 33, 40	___/4
Data, Statistics, and Probability Pages 84–115	7, 24, 28, 29, 31, 36, 38	___/7
Algebra Basics, Expressions, and Polynomials Pages 116-149	2, 3, 5, 10, 11, 12, 13, 14, 20, 21, 23, 42	___/12
Equations, Inequalities, and Functions Pages 150–179	16, 17, 18, 19, 25, 26, 34, 35, 43, 44, 45, 46	___/12
Geometry Pages 180–204	9, 15, 22, 27, 32, 37	___/6
TOTAL		___/46

If you do not have time to review all the material in this book, you may want to review the sections that need the most work. You can use your total above (___/46) to figure out your percentage correct for the entire *Mathematical Reasoning* test. Divide the numerator by the denominator and multiply by 100.

GED® MATHEMATICAL REASONING RESOURCES

Formula Sheet

Area of a:

square	$A = s^2$
rectangle	$A = lw$
parallelogram	$A = bh$
triangle	$A = \frac{1}{2}bh$
trapezoid	$A = \frac{1}{2}h(b_1 + b_2)$
circle	$A = \pi r^2$

Perimeter of a:

square	$P = 4s$
rectangle	$P = 2l + 2w$
triangle	$P = s_1 + s_2 + s_3$
Circumference of a circle	$C = 2\pi r$ OR $C = \pi d$; $\pi \approx 3.14$

Surface area and volume of a:

rectangular/right prism	$SA = ph + 2B$	$V = Bh$
cylinder	$SA = 2\pi rh + 2\pi r^2$	$V = \pi r^2 h$
pyramid	$SA = \frac{1}{2}ps + B$	$V = \frac{1}{3}Bh$
cone	$SA = \pi rs + \pi r^2$	$V = \frac{1}{3}\pi r^2 h$
sphere	$SA = 4\pi r^2$	$V = \frac{4}{3}\pi r^3$

(p = perimeter of base with area B; $\pi \approx 3.14$)

Data

mean	mean is equal to the total of the values of a data set, divided by the number of elements in the data set
median	median is the middle value in an odd number of ordered values of a data set, or the mean of the two middle values in an even number of ordered values in a data set

Algebra

slope of a line	$m = \dfrac{y_2 - y_1}{x_2 - x_1}$
slope-intercept form of the equation of a line	$y = mx + b$
point-slope form of the equation of a line	$y - y_1 = m(x - x_1)$
standard form of a quadratic equation	$y = ax^2 + bx + c$
quadratic formula	$x = \dfrac{-b \pm \sqrt{b^2 - 4ac}}{2a}$
Pythagorean Theorem	$a^2 + b^2 = c^2$
simple interest	$I = Prt$ (I = interest, P = principal, r = rate, t = time)
distance formula	$d = rt$
total cost	total cost = (number of units) × (price per unit)

Provided by GED® Testing Service.

TI-30XS Calculator Reference Sheet

An on-screen calculator reference sheet, similar to what appears on these two pages, will be available to you on Test Day. However, you should understand how to use the calculator before you take the GED® Test.

To perform basic arithmetic, enter numbers and operation symbols using the standard order of operations.

Example:    −25

To calculate with percentages, enter the number, then

Example: 224

To perform calculations with scientific notation, use the key.

Example: 630000000

To perform calculations with fractions, use the key. The answer will automatically be formatted in reduced form.

Example: $\dfrac{2}{21}$

To perform calculations with mixed numbers, use

As with fractions, the answer will automatically be formatted in reduced form.

Example: 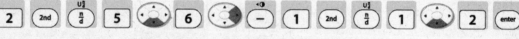 $\dfrac{34}{3}$

To perform calculations with powers and roots, you will use the following keys:

$\boxed{\sqrt{}\ x^2}$ $\boxed{\wedge}$ $\boxed{\text{2nd}}$ $\boxed{\sqrt{}\ x^2}$ $\boxed{\text{2nd}}$ $\boxed{\wedge}$

Example: $\boxed{1}\ \boxed{.}\ \boxed{2}\ \boxed{x^2}\ \boxed{\text{enter}}$ **1.44**

Example: $\boxed{7}\ \boxed{\wedge}\ \boxed{4}\ \boxed{\text{enter}}$ **2401**

Example: $\boxed{\text{2nd}}\ \boxed{x^2}\ \boxed{5}\ \boxed{2}\ \boxed{9}\ \boxed{\text{enter}}$ **23**

Example: $\boxed{3}\ \boxed{\text{2nd}}\ \boxed{\wedge}\ \boxed{1}\ \boxed{7}\ \boxed{2}\ \boxed{8}\ \boxed{\text{enter}}$ **12**

The answer toggle key $\boxed{\leftrightarrow}$ can be used to toggle the display result between fraction and decimal answers, exact square root and decimal, and exact pi and decimal.

Example: $\boxed{\frac{n}{d}}\ \boxed{9}\ \boxed{\odot}\ \boxed{1}\ \boxed{0}\ \boxed{\text{enter}}\ \boxed{\leftrightarrow}$ **0.9**

Æ SYMBOL TOOL EXPLANATION

Starting in 2014, test-takers will take the GED® Test on the computer. On the computer-based test, some fill-in-the-blank questions require you to insert mathematical symbols.

You can access the "Symbol Selector" by clicking on this icon when it appears on the computer screen:

Æ Symbol

Choose the symbol you want, and click on Insert at the bottom of the screen. When you are done, close the screen.

Æ Symbol												
$\sqcap$	f	$\geq$	$\leq$	$\neq$	^{2}	^{3}	$\mid$	$\times$	$\div$	$\pm$	∞	$\sqrt{}$
$+$	$-$	$($	$)$	$>$	$<$	$=$						

Below are the meanings of the symbols. Learn the meanings before you take the test because only the symbols will be available to you.

▣ "pi" symbol π

f "function" symbol

$\geq$ greater than or equal to

$\leq$ less than or equal to

$\neq$ not equal to

^{2} 2 exponent ("squared")

^{3} 3 exponent ("cubed")

$\mid$ "absolute" value

$\times$ multiplication sign

$\div$ division sign

$\pm$ "positive-or-negative" sign

∞ "infinity" symbol

$\sqrt{}$ "square root" symbol

$+$ plus sign or "positive" symbol

$-$ minus sign or "negative" symbol

$($ open (or left) parenthesis

$)$ close (or right) parenthesis

$>$ "greater than" symbol

$<$ "less than" symbol

$=$ "equals" sign

INDEX

A

Absolute value, 126
Acute triangles, 182
Addition
  decimal numbers, 44
  fractions, 50
  on calculator, 28, 58, 251
  order of operations, 118, 124
  polynomials, 138, 140
  signed numbers, 116
  whole numbers, 24
  word problems, 32
Algebra. *See also* Variables
  absolute value, 126
  coordinate planes, 162–170
  distributive property, 130
  equations, 150–155
  expressions, 124–125, 128, 130, 160
  FOIL, 142, 158
  functions, 172, 174
  inequalities, 156–157
  on calculator, 132
  operation signs, 118
  order of operations, 118, 124–125, 126, 132
  patterns, 172
  polynomials, 134–144
  power, 120, 122–123, 130, 134, 252
  problem solving, 160
  quadratic equations, 158, 160
  scientific notation, 122–123, 251
  setup problems, 128
  signed numbers, 116–118. *See also* Signed
    numbers
Algebra. *See also* Variables
  checking answers, 128, 132, 174
Amount paid back, 76
Answers. *See also* Checking answers
  "extra" information, 32
  fraction vs. decimal, 54, 100
  in scientific notation, 122
  partial solution, 34
  ratio order, 64
  reducing fractions, 50
Apex, 194
Approximation
  for checking answers, 23, 45
  pi (π) calculations, 188, 252
  square roots, 120
Area
  formula sheet, 205, 250
  plane figures, 185, 188, 198, 200
  surface area, 194–196

Arithmetic average, 94
Averages, 94

B

Bar graphs, 86
Bars on computer screen
  Symbol Selector, 17, 18, 21, 253
Base of exponent, 120
Base of figure, 186, 190, 192
Base of percent, 68–74
Binomials, 134

C

Calculator
  2nd key, 20, 30–31, 58–59, 74,
    121
  algebraic expressions, 132
  decimals, 58, 252
  description of, 251–252
  exponents, 120, 253
  fractions, 58–59, 251
  geometry, 200
  grouping symbols, 124, 132
  mean, 94
  percents, 31, 74, 251
  practice with, 20, 28, 74, 132, 251
  proportions, 66
  Pythagorean relationships,
    184, 200
  reference sheet, 251–252
  roots, 30, 121, 184, 252
  scientific notation, 251
  signed numbers, 116, 132
  square roots, 30, 120, 184
  test for algebraic logic, 132
Canceling fractions, 52
Central tendency, 92–94
Change
  line graphs, 88. *See also* line graphs
  percent of change, 78, 89
Charts. *See* Graphic information; Tables
Checking answers
  algebraic expressions, 128, 132
  approximation for, 24, 44
  equations, 150
  functions, 174
  inequalities, 156
  percents, 70
  word problems, 32, 36
  working backward, 78

Intervals in grouped data, 92
Inverse operations
   inequalities, 156
   linear equations, 164
   one-step equations, 150
   slope-intercept equation, 168
Inverting fractions, 52
Isosceles triangles, 182

L

Labels
   graphs, 86, 88, 90
   ratios vs. fractions, 64
   tables, 84
Legs of triangle, 184
Less than sign, 22, 156, 253
Like fractions, 50
Like terms, 130, 136, 140
Linear equations
   as line graphs, 164, 170
   from slope, 168–169
   systems of, 170
Line graphs
   linear equations, 164, 170
   slope, 166–169
Line plots, 96
Lists
   combination visualization, 104

M

Mathematical Reasoning. *See also* Algebra;
   Calculator; Geometry; One (1); Symbols in
   math; Variables; Zero (0)
   checking answers, 24, 32, 36, 44, 70, 79
   combinations, 104, 106
   computer-based format, 18, 18–21
   data, 84–85, 86, 92, 96
   data central tendency, 92–94
   decimals, 42–47, 54–56, 57. *See also*
      Decimals
   formula sheet, 205, 250. *See also* Formulas
   fractions, 48–56, 58–59. *See also* Fractions
   graphic information, 84–90, 96, 99
   number sense, 22–27
   order of operations, 118, 124–125,
      126, 132
   partial solutions, 34
   percents, 68–78. *See also* Percents
   permutations, 108
   probability, 100–106
   problem solving, 28–36

proportions, 66, 68
ratios, 64, 66, 92, 100
remainders, 55
score needed to pass, 17
wipe-off board, 17, 21, 144
Mathematical Reasoning. *See also* Algebra;
   Calculator; Geometry; One (1); Symbols in
   math; Variables; Zero (0)
   graphic information, 104, 106
Mean, 94
Measures of central tendency, 92–94
Median, 94
Memorization
   cube surface area, 194
   exponents, 120
   formulas, 76
   fraction-decimal equivalents, 54–55
   multiplication tables, 27
   plane figures, 185, 188
   square roots, 120
   symbols of math, 21
Mixed numbers
   definition, 48
   improper fractions and, 49, 50, 52,
      58–59
   on calculator, 58–59, 251
   on number line, 56
   ratios, 64
Mode, 94
Monomials, 134
Multiple-choice questions
   algebra, 150, 160
   fraction vs. decimal answer, 54
   Mathematical Reasoning, 17
   pretests, 1
Multiplication
   decimal numbers, 46
   factors, 158
   fractions, 52
   fundamental counting principle, 106
   on calculator, 29, 58, 251
   order of operations, 118, 124
   permutations, 108
   polynomials, 142
   powers, 120
   probability, 102
   proportion cross products, 66
   raising fractions, 49
   scientific notation, 122–123
   signed numbers, 118
   symbols for, 118, 253
   whole numbers, 26
   word problems, 32

Q

Quadratic equations, 158, 160, 205, 250
Questions. *See also* Extended Responses;
    Multiple-choice questions
  drag-and-drop, 19
  drop-down, 18
  fill-in-the-blank, 17, 18
  hot-spot, 19
  Symbol Selector toolbar, 17, 21, 253
Quotient, 26

R

Radius, 188–189
Raising fractions, 49–50
Range of data, 97
Rate problems
  amount paid back, 76
  cost, 36
  distance and time, 37
  percents, 68, 70, 74
  per in word problems, 66
  proportions, 66
  simple interest, 76
Ratios, 64, 66, 92, 100
Rectangles, 180, 186
Rectangular prisms
  surface area, 194, 205, 250
  volume, 190, 192, 205, 250
Reducing fractions, 49–50, 52
Reference sheet for calculator,
    251–252
Remainders, 55
Resources for GED. *See also* Natural
    resources
Rhombuses, 180
Right angles, 180, 184–185
Right triangles, 182, 184–185
Roots
  calculating, 121
  on calculator, 121, 252
  order of operations, 124
  symbol for, 121, 253
Rounding numbers, 22, 24, 42

S

Scalene triangles, 182
Scientific notation, 122–123, 251
Scores needed to pass
  Mathematical Reasoning, 17

Setup problems, 128
Short-Answer questions
    pretest, 1
Signed numbers
  absolute value, 126
  addition, 116
  coordinate planes, 162
  division, 118
  exponents as, 120, 122
  inequalities, 156
  multiplication, 118
  on calculator, 116, 132
  polynomials, 136, 138
  subtraction, 116–117
  Symbol Selector toolbar, 253
Simple interest, 76, 205, 250
Simple probability, 100
Simplifying
  expressions, 130
  polynomials, 136, 140, 144
Slope
  equations and, 168–169
  formula, 166–167, 205, 250
Spheres
  surface area, 196, 205, 250
  volume, 190, 205, 250
Square prisms, 190, 194
Square roots
  approximating, 121
  memorization of, 120
  on calculator, 30, 121, 184
  Symbol Selector toolbar, 253
Squares, 180, 186
Statistics
  data central tendency, 92–94
Structure of text. *See* Organizational structure;
    Text structures
Subtraction
  decimal numbers, 44
  fractions, 50
  on calculator, 29, 58, 251
  order of operations, 118, 124
  percent of change, 78
  polynomials, 138–139, 140
  signed numbers, 116–117
  whole numbers, 24–25
  word problems, 32
Summarizing
  data central tendency, 92–94
Surface area, 194–196, 205, 250
Symbol Selector toolbar, 17, 21, 253
Symbols in graphics, 84

Symbols in math
    absolute value, 126
    algebraic expressions, 128
    angles, 180–181
    bar for repeating, 54
    division, 36, 118, 253
    inequalities, 22, 156
    multiplication, 36, 118, 253
    percent symbol, 68, 70
    permutations, 108
    pi (π), 188, 252, 253
    signed numbers, 116
    square root, 121
    Symbol Selector toolbar, 17, 21, 253

T

Tables
    combination visualization, 104
    labeled data, 84
    on test, 84
    T-charts, 170
Test formats. *See* Computer-based test format;
    Paper-based test format
Theoretical probability, 100
Three-dimensional figures
    surface area, 194–196, 205, 250
    volume, 190–192, 198, 205, 250
Time management
    Mathematical Reasoning, 17
Time problems
    distance and rate, 37
    line graphs, 88
    simple interest, 76
Trapezoids, 180, 186, 205, 250
Tree diagrams, 104, 106
Triangles, 182–185, 185, 200
Trinomials, 134

U

Unlike terms, 136

V

Variables
    algebraic expressions, 128
    coefficients, 134

equations, 150
formulas, 36, 76
inequalities, 156–157
polynomials, 134
simplifying expressions, 130
word problems, 154–155
Visualization
    combinations, 104
    fractions, 48
    percents, 70
    sketching for, 156
Volume
    capacity formulas, 190–192, 199, 205, 250

W

Wipe-off board
    frequency tables, 92
    Mathematical Reasoning, 17, 21, 144
    sketching for visualization, 156
Word problems
    equations, 152, 154–155
    five-step process, 32, 34
    of as base of percent, 68
    per meaning, 36, 66
    translating to math, 128, 152
Workers. *See* Labor

X

x-axis, 162

Y

y-axis, 162
y-intercept, 168

Z

Zero (0)
    as placeholder, 26, 44, 46
    as signed number, 116
    decimal numbers, 42
    exponents, 120
    horizontal line slope, 167
    probability, 100
    quadratic equations, 158, 160
    scientific notation, 122